PSYCHOLOGICAL EMERGENCIES &

CRISIS INTERVENTION

A COMPREHENSIVE GUIDE FOR EMERGENCY PERSONNEL

Brent Q. Hafen & Kathryn J. Frandsen

BRADY
PRENTICE HALL
Upper Saddle River, NJ 07458

Printed in the United States of America

10 9 8 7

ISBN 0-13-736406-7

Prentice-Hall International (UK) Limited, London
Prentice-Hall of Australia Pty. Limited, Sydney
Prentice-Hall Canada Inc., Toronto
Prentice-Hall Hispanoamericana, S.A., Mexico
Prentice-Hall of India Private Limited, New Delhi
Prentice-Hall of Japan, Inc., Tokyo
Pearson Education Asia Pte. Ltd., Singapore
Editoria Prentice-Hall do Brasil, Ltda., Rio De Janeiro

Contents

Understanding Crisis 1
Psychiatric Emergencies 37
Suicide 70
Death and Dying 112
Rape and Sexual Assault 143
Child Abuse 185
Violence 220
Drug and Alcohol Emergencies 256
Psychological Aspects of Disaster 295
Burnout and Emergency Personnel 322
Understanding and Coping with Stress 351
Index 415

Understanding Crisis

Crisis.
The word brings to mind all kinds of terrifying situations. You think of the armed robber pressing the cold metal of a pistol against the forehead of his hostage as police negotiators shout desperate instructions through bullhorns.

You think of the crowd of frightened tenants huddled together on the sidewalk as the crumbling building is devoured by flames—and as a fireman teeters at the end of an extension ladder to reach a mother and child stretching from a fifty-floor window.

You think of the deeply disturbed mother who methodically murders each of her four children before turning the gun on herself.

You see the haunted expressions of brown-skinned children crouched at the edge of a dusty road near the carnage of a crumpled school bus, the pounding metal of the freight train silenced in the morning air.

Most of all, you think of the anguished. The psychotic. The insane. The desperately dangerous. The "crazies." Because, after all, those are the ones who experience crisis. Right?

Wrong!

If there is one general rule that applies to crisis, it is this: **most people in crisis are normal**.

Most people in crisis are even capable of helping themselves.

And, if they're given a little help, most people in crisis are capable of turning the crisis situation into an opportunity for growth.

What it means is this: every person who lives probably will experience a crisis. Some people will experience many of them. What it also means is that most emergencies involve "normal" people who have suddenly been thrown into a crisis-provoking situation. What it also means is that most people in crisis are people like you—not severely mentally disturbed people.

That's a critical key in learning to deal with crisis.

The desperate voice on the other end of the phone, the frantic man threatening his wife with a hunting knife, the woman who inches along the ledge and threatens to jump were probably acting "normal" a few short hours earlier. They were probably productive, functioning members of society. With a little help, they will probably resume their productive roles again—in a shorter time than you might think possible. They can even emerge from the fray as better, stronger people.

Most important, they probably feel much like you do. Think about the simple act of losing your keys. Most of the time, it's an irritation. Nothing more serious. But if you lose your keys under certain circumstances, you may experience an emotional crisis.

How?

Greg lost the keys to his apartment. But it was a particularly bad day for Greg, and it came at the end of a particularly bad week. Greg worked as legal counsel for an embattled federal agency, and government investigators had spent the week interrogating members of the executive team—including Greg—about possible misuse of government funds. Midmorning, when Greg first noticed that his keys were missing, he called his sister—she had a spare set of keys to his apartment. She and her roommates had just left for a weekend trip to New York. Later that day, the agency director was dismissed in a flurry of allegations, and Greg learned that she had not signed the necessary papers for his pay raise. As he dashed out of the building to meet his carpool, it was raining— so he dodged into a nearby building to wait where he could keep dry. The members of the carpool didn't see him, and he couldn't see them—so they left without him.

There stood Greg: almost an hour from home, his job security threatened, his promised raise demolished. The rain poured outside, and he had no way home. Suddenly the fact that he had no keys became unbearable.

Greg had reached his breaking point.

The Breaking Point

Every person has a breaking point. **Every person.** You have one, just as does the hysterical woman in the shoestore or the man who starts to cry uncontrollably on the bus. But human beings are complex, and each one is unique—so your breaking point is different than your partner's or your child's or your friend's.

But it's important to remember that **any** person can reach the breaking point. It can happen to you, just as it has happened to the person you are trying to help.

That's the key. A person in crisis is probably **not** mentally ill. She is probably **not** diseased. She is probably **not** crazy. She is probably a person just like you—a person who has reached her own breaking point. And you can help her bounce back.

The Delicate Balance

Most of the time, people live in a steady state—a balance between emotions and thoughts. Most of the time, a person fluctuates narrowly around the baseline state of equilibrium. When a person's own balancing system fails and his equilibrium is disrupted, crisis can occur.

The potential for crisis depends on how completely the state of equilibrium—the delicate balance—has been upset. When equilibrium shifts rapidly, the person experiences a **problem.** If the problem is not resolved quickly, she enters a state of **stress**. Stress usually causes enough tension that she works to resolve her problem and, in the process, reestablish her equilibrium; but if that doesn't happen within a reasonable amount of time, **crisis** occurs.

What, then, is crisis?

Crisis is a serious interruption in equilibrium. It is a state of emotional turmoil, a state in which emotions overcome thoughts. It is a state in which the delicate balance breaks down under stress, a state in which emotional pressure simply becomes too great for the individual to cope with. **Crisis—that state of disruption, of imbalance—can happen to anyone at any time in life.**

A crisis state is relatively infrequent for most people because of "coping mechanisms"—self-regulating mechanisms we use to avoid, reduce, or control pain. Most of us become expert at using coping mechanisms to deal with stress, and by so doing we are able to reestablish and maintain a state of equilibrium.

Sometimes, though, coping mechanisms don't work, seriously jeopardizing equilibrium. There are several reasons why coping mechanisms sometimes fail:

The problem is too great. Most of us, under usual circumstances, can cope with life's little problems—short-term illness, a dented fender, a flooded basement. But sometimes we encounter problems that are simply too great to deal with—the death of a spouse, the breakup of a marriage, financial collapse. Somehow the strength we muster to cope with a dented fender doesn't quite do when a spouse dies from a heart attack.

The problem has special significance that makes it overwhelming. A woman who normally demonstrates great emotional strength and equilibrium completely crumbles when she learns that her husband has cancer. Why? As a child she watched her own father suffer for four painful years from cancer, dying an inch at a time. She simply feels she can't face that agony again.

The problem occurs at a time of special vulnerability. A man may have already taxed his coping mechanisms in dealing with a separate problem: he's managed to maintain his state of equilibrium through the ordeal of his daughter's drug problem, and now the news that he faces major surgery overwhelms him. A series of problem may occur within a short period of time, as they did to Greg—he lost his keys, learned that he didn't get a raise, found out his job stability was in jeopardy, and missed his carpool, all within eight or nine hours. Or the problem may occur when a person's normal coping mechanisms are blocked for one reason or another.

The problem is a new one, so appropriate coping mechanisms haven't been developed. A woman whose family has always enjoyed financial security may not be able to deal with the situation she encounters in her early marriage: each meager paycheck is doled out with exactness, and there is nothing to spare. When she sets her sights on a suit she wants, she is surprised by the fact that she can't simply write out a check and buy it.

A man who has never had to deal with the death of a loved one may have problems coping with the death of his child. A man and woman who have never been exposed to the pain of divorce may have particular problems coping with the breakup of their own marriage.

The usual network of social support fails. Under normal circumstances, each of has a network of social support—family members, friends, and loved ones who help provide the strength that enables us to cope. A person who suddenly finds herself alone—abandoned by friends or family members in a time of stress—may find it extremely difficult to cope. She feels alone, frightened, forgotten, and deserted.

Characteristics of Crisis

Simply put, a crisis is a special kind of predicament that has two major characteristics: **size** and **urgency**. Almost always, it's a pivotal point—a turning point in life that can leave a person defeated or strengthened.

Four general characteristics mark most crisis situations:

1. The crisis is sudden. The breakdown in equilibrium is an isolated incident, not a usual pattern of life—it is unforeseen and unexpected.
2. Normal coping methods have failed. The person tries, but he is unsuccessful. He may be exhausted, drained of energy—and this problem represents the so-called "last straw." He is unable to draw on his intellect, his emotional resources, his self-motivation, his internal strengths, his hope, or even outside support.
3. The crisis is short in duration. A true crisis rarely lasts longer than six weeks; most are resolved within thirty-six hours. Why? People simply can't remain in a crisis state for very long—it's unbearable. A person in crisis will do **something** (even to the point of taking his own life if he is desperate enough) to end the pain and suffering.
4. Crisis may result in dangerous, unacceptable, or self-destructive behavior. Crisis brings with it feelings of panic and defeat; if these are not resolved, a person may become homicidal or suicidal.

Along with these four characteristics, there are two general classifications of crisis: **predictable** and **unpredictable**.

Predictable Crises

Some crises can be "predicted"—they are part of the natural order of life, and they result from normal and expected life experiences. People have a drive to grow, and they undergo transition as they progress from one stage of life to another.

But any change (even positive change) can be stressful or threatening.

Entering adolescence is certainly predictable, but it can be a time of stress and uncertainty that can breed crisis. So can the experiences associated with middle age or old age. Other life changes—getting married, getting pregnant, advancing through school, getting a job, retiring—can be anticipated but can usher in a crisis.

Unpredictable Crises

These are the sudden, completely unexpected situations that can snap a life in two. A woman is raped; a bank president who sleeps in on a Sunday morning is shot by two young robbers who think he might have cash at home. The residents of a small Midwestern town find themselves devastated by a tornado. A mother and her two small children are critically injured in a car accident. An executive is fired suddenly and unexpectedly. A professor who goes to the doctor for a routine checkup faces unexpected surgery. A woman comes in from raking the leaves to find her husband dead from cerebral hemorrhage. A woman faced with the breakup of her marriage commits suicide. suicide.

The Stages of Crisis

Regardless of its cause, the crisis is marked by several distinct stages. The initial stages are usually brief, rarely lasting more than an hour or two. Later stages may last longer, with resolution and the resumption of normal activities sometimes requiring several months.

Impact

Impact is the occurrence of the stressful event—it is the final blow that destroys equilibrium. It is the rape, the sudden death, the automobile accident. It usually occurs swiftly, but its effects are like the ripple effect of the pebble dropped into the pond.

During the impact stage, the victim feels dazed and shocked; he may become disoriented or distracted. Many victims feel charged with energy. The body prepares for the traditional "fight-or-flight" response—adrenalin is pumped into the bloodstream, eyesight and hearing become keen, and muscles tense up. All of the victim's energies are concentrated on the present and on the upsetting event.[1]

Crisis

Within a few minutes to a few hours after impact, the crisis occurs. Simply stated, it is the victim's reaction to the stressful or hazardous event. The victim, in a sense, "recoils" from the stressful event, almost as if to protect himself from further hurt or upset.

The range of emotions during the crisis can go all the way from rage and hostility to uncertainty and detachment. Detachment is an important part of the crisis reaction. At first, the victim is preoccupied with the past—he concentrates on the stressful event, mulling it over and over. (If only he had left half an hour earlier and missed the storm—there would have been no accident! If only she had heeded the warnings of friends about the dangers of jogging alone! If only he had settled for a less expensive car instead of borrowing all this money!) Only when detachment occurs can he face the future and begin to solve the problem.

Resolution

As the crisis period wanes, the period of resolution—adjustment—begins. During this stage, the victim regains control of herself; she begins to think clearly, explore alternatives, make plans, set goals, and carry out what she has planned.

During resolution, the victim looks toward the future with hope and energy. Remember that a crisis can leave a person better and stronger! Crisis generally motivates people to make changes in their lives—and a person who is going through a crisis is usually highly suggestible to change. A man whose crop was destroyed when his farmland was inundated by flooding from a broken dam decided to turn a hobby into a livelihood: he began making and repairing guns as an independent businessman. He had always had a fine reputation for the work he had done as a hobby, and now people throughout the state placed special orders for his custom work.

Reconstruction

Once resolution is complete—a stage that requires several weeks to several months, depending on the person—the victim resumes his normal activities or style of living. While a few scars may linger, most of the signs and effects of the crisis are over and forgotten.

Problems Associated With Helping

On the surface, it's easy to see why helping a victim of crisis is difficult. A person in crisis may be withdrawn; it may be difficult to talk to him. He may be disoriented or confused, and you might have a hard time getting information from him. In cases of severe crisis, the person might be hostile, argumentative, aggressive, or combative—and you as rescuer might be in clear danger.

In addition to these obvious problems, though, a number of other problems make it difficult to help:

—The management of crisis is one of the most frequently neglected areas in the training of emergency services personnel. Without specific training, it can be terrifying to approach a crisis situation—and you can make errors while trying to intervene.

—Even when training is present, it tends to be inadequate and nonuniform. The lack of clear-cut guidelines throughout the industry to confusion and reluctance to take aggressive action.

—The person with whom you are dealing is not in a state of rational, coherent thought. **He is at the height of crisis.** He is probably experiencing incredible stress. His normal coping ability is gone. He won't be reacting to you like he would if you ran into him on a sunny day in the grocery store.

—The person may consider you to be an intruder. A person in crisis may feel as though her entire world is crumbling around her; she may be paranoid or feel threatened. She probably won't be thinking clearly—and she may panic at your arrival. She may try to attack you, or she may become abusive. Remember: **don't take those threats or attacks personally.**

—Real problems can be associated with assessment. It is often difficult to determine whether a victim is experiencing an emotional crisis or a physical disability (such as dementia, drug overdose, alcoholism, or delirium). And when a family is involved, it is often extremely difficult to determine exactly **who** is experiencing the crisis.

—As an emergency worker, you usually have little (if any) background information about the person. And once you've intervened, it can be extremely difficult to get sound information. A person who is embroiled in a crisis isn't likely to sit down and give you credible background; friends or family members are likely to be upset, too. You go into a situation having to assume a great deal.

—You are going into an unknown situation (there is almost always an element of the unknown in a crisis), so you are faced with overcoming your own feelings of fear and apprehension.

—You can't concentrate your treatment on the person in crisis: **every crisis involves at least one other person who is impacted by that crisis.** As a rescuer, you face the task of identifying those people who need help, determining what kind of help is needed, and offering it.

—There is a lack of twenty-four-hour professionals to which you can turn for help. If it's 2 a.m. and you're trying to coax a suicidal man out of a locked bathroom, you're probably on your own—local psychiatrists and social workers have probably been in bed for hours.

—Finally, one of the greatest problems lies in the fact that psychological crisis is still virtually an unknown in many ways. Psychological crisis can be every bit as horrific as physical crisis, but it's often not recognized as such. When you arrive at the scene of an automobile accident, for example, you are likely to rush to the aid of a victim of physical injury; you splint fractures and bandage wounds. But you are likely to pay minimal attention to the uninjured victim who is undergoing tremendous emotional trauma—she may be ignored or, at best, soothed in a superficial and passing way.

Recognizing A Person in Crisis[2]

Human beings are complex. As a result, each crisis situation has unique characteristics.

Think about what that means to you as an emergency worker. You've probably learned to count on many "checklists" in your assessment work: you have a checklist that helps you determine whether a victim might be having a heart attack, might have sustained a skull fracture, or might have overdosed on drugs. You learn to look for specific signs: If a victim has a head injury, you look for drainage of cerebrospinal fluid from the ears or nose, bluish discoloration around the ear, unevenly dilated pupils, loss of consciousness, and vomiting.

It's impossible to develop that kind of "checklist" to assess psychological crisis. The variables are simply too numerous. It **is** possible to examine generalized signs or common reactions. Consider some of the following as you try to determine whether an individual is experiencing a crisis:

—The person might have lost some or all contact with reality. She might have trouble distinguishing between what is really happening and what she imagines to be happening. This is different from a simple distortion of perception: She might be imagining smells, sights, sounds, people, or elements that clearly do not exist.

—The person probably isn't acting the way he usually does. If he's normally talkative and aggressive, he may become quiet and passive. His habits may change. To make this kind of determination, you'll have to rely on reports from friends and family members if you don't know the person yourself.

—When you talk to the person, you may feel as though you're talking to a brick wall. The person is preoccupied—he doesn't have the ability to listen to you and concentrate on what you're saying. In serious situations, he may be completely unresponsive.

—The person is unable to work at her maximum or usual level. She may be unable to concentrate on her work because she is so involved with her crisis. Her productivity may go down, or she may be completely unable to perform her usual tasks.

—The person may seem withdrawn. He is there physically but is somewhere else emotionally and mentally.

—The person shows signs of trying to avoid a **sensory overload**. What it means is this: She is so concerned about her crisis that she can't deal with anything else right now. It's as though she is "shutting out" the rest of the world. She has to use all her mental energy to think of how she will get out of the crisis situation, so she doesn't listen. She looks at you without really **seeing** you. In severe situations, she may not even remember where she is.

—The person may exhibit an extraordinary amount of unwarranted fear. A man may be terrified of driving up to a gasoline pump, for example, or may suddenly become frightened of walking two flights of stairs down to the storage area in the office building. A woman may become extremely afraid of the people living next door without apparent cause. The person in crisis may even be afraid of you as a rescuer.

—The person may also exhibit an extraordinary amount of anger, usually at an inappropriate source. These outbursts are usually brief but are often destructive. You may encounter a woman recovering from knee surgery who is pounding holes through the bathroom door with her crutch. A man in crisis over an impending job change may thrash at his child with a garden hose. Keep in mind that such anger can be directed toward you. In severe cases, you should approach with caution and with a companion.

—While a certain degree of tension is normal a person in crisis may experience an extreme amount of anxiety.[3] He may be unable to focus his attention on one thing; he may be preoccupied by a sense of impending doom, or feelings of dread. He may fear that he is losing control. He may even fear that he is "going crazy."

People who are extremely anxious may exhibit certain physical symptoms, such as chest or abdominal pain, excessive sweating, rapid heatbeat, or headache. They may suffer from excessive frequent urination, diarrhea, nausea, or vomiting. They may develop a rash. They may even experience menstrual irregularities or a loss of sexual drive.

—The person may seem confused. During crisis, the memory may be altered and perceptions distorted, resulting in a maze of events that don't seem to fit together. Ironically, the ability to come through a crisis easily depends on the ability to make decisions and solve problems—but the state of mind experienced during a crisis may alter the person's ability to do just that.

Remember: the person in crisis **is usually not mentally ill.** Confusion, distorted perception, and altered memory are the

usual patterns of thinking for the person who is mentally ill; they are temporary disturbances for the person who is experiencing a crisis.

—The person may seem unusually depressed. Because she is overwhelmed by the crisis, she may feel helpless or hopeless; in some cases, she may be burdened by feelings of guilt or unworthiness. Depression covers an entire range of severity. In mild depression, the person may simply seem sad or tend to cry; in severe depression, he may attempt suicide.

—During a crisis, the person may become impulsive or take foolish risks. A woman may career recklessly through rush-hour traffic on a busy freeway, disregarding her own safety. A may attack his boss in the elevator. A teenager may impulsively slash her wrists with a kitchen knife.

—Some people in crisis become overly dependent on others. they become terrified of being alone; they become demanding and possessive of others, especially family members.

—Many people in crisis reject offers of help. They are feeling weak, helpless, and hopeless; to admit to needing help simply confirms their feelings of weakness and worthlessness.

Each specific crisis situation—such as attempted suicide, death of a loved one, or divorce—has its own set of telltale signs or common denominators; these will be discussed in individual sections as appropriate. Regardless of the cause of the crisis, though, there are some common feelings that earmark the imbalanced equilibrium: extreme anxiety, fear, anger, guilt, embarrassment, helplessness, confusion, memory loss, inability to concentrate, and inability to perform usual tasks.

You might also watch for **five behavioral clues**. While they are not always present, they can be indicators that you can add to an overall set of signs:

1. The person doesn't seem able to use available help. A man whose wife is hospitalized with a serious illness rejects friends' offers to care for the young children, bring in hot meals, and so on.

2. The person can't manage his own feelings. He feels as though he is losing control and gives in to episodes of depression, anger, or hostility.

3. The person may develop suicidal or homicidal tendencies. In this crisis, you must take aggressive action to protect the individual and those around him.

4. The person may be involved in drug and/or alcohol abuse. In some cases, a person who was formerly not involved may have turned to drugs or alcohol in an attempt to resolve feelings of anxiety, panic, or fear.

5. The person may be having problems with the law.

Emotional Reactions to Crisis

The emotional reactions to crisis progress through certain stages—and they are very much like the stages associated with the grief that follows the death of a loved one.

Why?

Because inherent in every crisis is a loss. In dealing with the crisis itself, the person must also deal with the loss. A woman who is raped loses her sense of security and peace of mind, as well as her sense of virtue and privacy. Those are important losses with which she must deal in addition to the physical and emotional trauma of the rape itself.

What makes this unusually difficult is the condition of the crisis victim: his defenses have already been weakened. He is under stress, and his equilibrium has been disturbed; his usual coping mechanisms aren't working. That's why he's in a crisis to begin with—so he doesn't have much on reserve with which to battle.

There are six stages of emotional reaction to crisis:[4]

Emotional shock. The person may either be hysterical or stunned; he may even be combative. He may panic—and may in the process demonstrate irrational fear. A hysterical person may be nauseated or may vomit; he may seem hyperactive, crying or screaming loudly, wringing his hands, breathing rapidly, and speaking rapidly and at a high pitch. He may seem agitated and out of control.

On the other hand, a person who is in a state of stunned shock may wander around aimlessly, staring into space, or may lapse into complete inactivity. She may experience nausea, vomiting, cold or clammy skin, excessive sweating, low blood pressure, a rapid and thready pulse, pale skin, and dull eyes.

People in a state of shock tend to act irrationally. A man who has been saved from a burning apartment building may try to dash through flames to retrieve his cat's favorite feeding dish. Emotional shock can also be dangerous—the victim may interfere with efforts of police, firefighters, or other emergency rescuers.

Denial. During the denial stage, the person is attempting to protect himself. He can't let too much happen too quickly—so he denies that the crisis is happening. A woman whose child has been abducted convinces herself that he is simply playing at a friend's house and that he will be discovered soon. She simply won't allow herself to admit that he is gone. A man who is suffering a heart attack convinces himself that his pain is due to indigestion, not heart problems—he can't face losing his health and his vitality that way.

Anger. Everyone feels angry occasionally. And once the victim passes through the denial stage and admits that the crisis has occurred, it is a normal and understandable emotion.

Unfortunately, a person who is experiencing crisis may direct his anger in inappropriate ways. A woman whose sixteen-year-old daughter was killed in an accident on a snow-packed road while using the car without permission probably won't be angry at her daughter. Instead, she will be angry at the highway department for not clearing the road. She will be angry at the ambulance staff for not doing more at the scene. She will be angry at the doctors in the emergency room for not saving her daughter.

Remember that it is common for people in this stage of crisis to direct their anger at people who are trying to help. **Never** take that anger personally; it is born of frustration and an inability to cope and is not really directed at you. Let the person hurl all the verbal abuse in the world at you, but don't let him strike you.

Remorse. In this stage, the person is overwhelmed by guilt and sorrow. Even when events were clearly out of his control, he chastises himself and places the burden for the problem on himself. The father of the sixteen-year-old girl who was killed in the accident blames himself. *If only I had agreed to drive her to the movies. If only I had taken the car myself . . . it wouldn't have been there. If only I had hidden the keys. If only I had insisted that she join the rest of the family for dinner.*

During this stage, the victim may twist events out of proportion and may create scenarios that are clearly irrational or impossible.

Grief. Once the victim begins to grieve, he enters the first real stage of healing. Just as with traditional grief associated with death and dying, the grieving associated with crisis is an essential step. The grieving process must be completed before the person can go on to overcome the crisis.

Reconciliation. Finally, the victim passes through the crisis and emerges *at least* at the level of functioning he enjoyed before the crisis. In many cases, especially when the victim has been helped through the crisis, he may emerge stronger and better able to cope with life's frustrations. During reconciliation, the victim resumes his normal life-style and is no longer preoccupied by the crisis.

Goals of Crisis Intervention

Crisis intervention is unlike traditional methods of treatment for emotional problems. A crisis is ordinarily a brief disturbance in equilibrium—and, because of that, treating the crisis involves intensive effort over a short period of time. **Crisis intervention** is earmarked by narrow goals of short duration.

In a nutshell, crisis intervention is aimed at helping a person regain equilibrium—return to normal functioning—by providing emotional support during a time of emotional vulnerability. In crisis intervention, unlike traditional emotional therapy, the emphasis in on what's happening **now**, not on what has happened in the past.

The goals of crisis intervention can be summed up in four main statements:

The goal of crisis intervention is to protect the victim from additional stress. In some cases, that includes literally protecting the victim from harm (as in suicide).

The goal of crisis intervention is to give the victim a sense of hope. As mentioned, a person suffering through a crisis is likely to feel helpless and hopeless. In the initial stages of crisis, he may fear that things will never get better—that he will suffer this agonizing pain and confusion forever. You need to help him realize that things **will** get better. By instilling him with a sense of hope, you give him a reason to work through the crisis.

The goal of crisis intervention is to help the victim mobilize his resources. External resources are pretty easy to identify. A woman whose husband undergoes sudden surgery can turn to friends, family members, and coworkers for support. A man who is crippled by severe depression can be referred to a competent counselor for help. A family whose home burns to the ground can be directed to various community organizations or church-sponsored groups who can help with temporary shelter, food, and clothing.

But the other resources—**internal resources**—might be a little more difficult for the victim to cling to. The victim probably feels defeated, confused, hopeless, and worthless. You need to help him remember that he is strong, intelligent, resourceful, and creative. He can draw from within himself to work through this crisis, because he has what it takes!

The goal of crisis intervention is to leave the person at least as well as he was before the crisis occurred. Often you will find that the person is actually better off than before the crisis. She has learned new coping mechanisms; she has learned ways to cope and adjust when her old methods let her down. Her level of functioning is improved. The result? She is less vulnerable—and is less likely to have future crises.

On the other hand, a person who does not receive help in dealing with a crisis may turn to destructive or self-defeating behavior in an attempt to cope with the crisis. Watch for the following danger signs:[5]

—The person seems to be living in a fantasy world, where he has difficulty separating fact from fiction. Sometimes the fantasy will merge with reality; at other times, it may replace reality altogether.

—The person won't ask for help. When help is offered, she refuses it. Even when help is thrust upon her, she seems unable to utilize it for her own benefit.

—The person uses extreme withdrawal, retreat, avoidance, or denial to try to escape from the pain of the crisis. This is a normal stage of crisis, but it should be short-lived. A person who continues to deny the crisis or retreat from it emotionally cannot work through it and recover.

—The person turns to drugs, alcohol, or overeating as a way of coping with the crisis. When the senses are dulled, as with powerful drugs, he no longer has to worry about what's happening.

—The person seems to be consumed with rage. Again, it's normal to be angry, but that anger should not escalate into full-scale rage and hostility. Watch out for the person who is striking out uncontrollably at people who are relatively weak or powerless—he may be using those people as scapegoats on which he can ventilate his rage.

—The person can't seem to accomplish his work during the time he should be working, and he can't seem to rest during the time when he should be resting. He is habitually fatigued by the stress of the crisis, and his usual cycles are severely disrupted.

—The person continues to act on impulse after the stage of emotional shock has passed. A woman whose financial situation begins to collapse quits her job, leaves most of her belongings behind (without caring what happens to them), loads a few things in her car, and moves across the country to a town she's never visited. When she arrives, she has no place to stay, no means of support, and no familiar faces. The move itself may not have been destructive if it had been carefully planned and executed instead of done on impulse.

—The person may become despondent and hopeless and may, simply, give up. This person has lost the desire to work through the crisis; she has lost the desire to get "better." In severe cases, the person loses the desire to live. At that point, suicide becomes a real possibility.

—The person becomes extremely dependent on others, almost to the point of losing the ability to function as an independent person. There is a real difference between mobilizing resources—turning to friends and family members for support—and surrendering independence. On the one hand, the individual is saying, *I am capable of getting through this crisis, but for now, I need a little help and understanding.* On the other hand, the person is begging, *I have been defeated by this overwhelming situation. I will never be the same. Please take care of me forever.*

—The person comes across as "a rock" in the midst of crisis. He is denying or suppressing his emotions, and they are likely to be expressed later in inappropriate ways. Sixteen-year-old Clark was driving the car when it overturned, killing his mother and niece and critically injuring his other niece. Other family members who gathered at the hospital wept openly, wrung their hands, and clearly shared the agony of the situation. Clark, on the other hand, sat quietly against the wall reading a magazine. Even during the funeral he seemed detached and controlled. He readily accepted the reality of the deaths but didn't seem affected by the situation. Two months later Clark set his mother's home on fire just before realtors were ready to close on the sale.

In cases where you see a red flag, step up your efforts at crisis intervention. These danger signals are your first clue that the person isn't dealing well with the crisis. Give extra care and consideration to help get the healing process started.

Preventing Crisis[6]

Obviously, you can't prevent or even predict many of the things that will cause a crisis. But you **can** sometimes prevent a person from lapsing into an emotional crisis in response if you know a little bit about who is at risk and what you can do.

Several factors can help you identify whether a person is crisis-prone:

—You know that a disturbing or hazardous event will probably occur. The death of a close family member is highly probably; a natural disaster, such as a tidal wave or tornado, is much less probable. In some cases, you can predict with accuracy that a disturbing event will occur—a woman's husband is in the final stages of terminal cancer, a couple's child has developed deadly leukemia, two hikers determined to scale a sheer cliff don't return by sundown.

—You know that certain individuals will be exposed to the disturbing event. When a man dies of cancer, his wife and children will be directly impacted; so will his parents, his brothers and sisters, and his friends. Depending on the situation, his coworkers may even be upset to the extent of developing a crisis.

—You know that one of the individuals who is exposed to the disturbing event is especially vulnerable. As a rule, an adult has better coping mechanisms than a child. Something in a person's background may make him more vulnerable to a particular crisis. A person who is under a great deal of stress or who has had a series of difficult events spaced closely together may have reached a breaking point. A person who is ill may have a difficult time coping.

To prevent a hazardous or disturbing event from blossoming into a crisis, try some of the following:

—Modify or eliminate the hazardous situation. This isn't always possible, but you'd be surprised at what can be done with a little foresight. If a six-year-old girl must be hospitalized to have her tonsils removed and is terrified at the prospect of being separated from her parents, arrange to let her mother sleep in the room with her at the hospital.

—Reduce the person's exposure to the hazardous or disturbing situation. A woman who is contemplating a difficult course of study in graduate school might be screened and advised about the difficulty of the proposed course; she might then be helped to choose a less rigorous course or one better suited to her talents and innate abilities. A woman contemplating foreign service with the state department might be informed of the risks associated with assignment to certain areas and might be given the chance to choose more politically stable areas in which to work.

—Prepare the person by helping to increase his coping skills. A man who faces the birth of his first child can be appropriately helped by encouraging him to take a childbirth class, giving him good literature about childrearing, and exposing him to children. (The same kind of preparation can occur for other predictable life events, such as marriage and retirement.)

Every crisis situation is unique, because every person is individual—and every person will react differently to a disturbing event. Many variables—including state of health, recent occurrences, stress levels, coping ability, and availability of support from friends or family members—affect how a person will react to a disturbing event. Many people will sail through with little or no problem. Occasionally, a person will be overwhelmed. His coping mechanisms that have always worked before will fail. He will enter a state of emotional crisis.

Remember one thing: **he is "normal."** This is **a temporary** state of being for him. In his place, **you** might react in much the same way. He is simply out of balance right now, and—with your help—he can regain that balance.

The information that follows will give you clues about how to deal with specific situations. Regardless of the situation, bear in mind the very individual, human drama that is unfolding—and bear in mind your ability to make a significant difference in the outcome.

Effecting Change in Crisis

The goal of psychological first aid—crisis intervention—is to quickly help the person begin again to function normally on his own. Your role is to help ("How can I assist this person?")—not to analyze ("Why did this happen?"). An important factor in psychological first aid is **urgency**. A person in crisis feels out of control, anxious, tense, and panicked—a delay in help could upset the person to the point of self-destruction.

In general, you must present a sharp contrast to the person's panic. Approach him in a controlled, warm, reassuring way; if the person's emotional crisis is too intense for you to handle, send for professional help, but never abandon him.

Don't overreact to whatever the person says or does. Reassure him that his need for help is legitimate and normal—not shameful or abnormal.

Try to **do** something. In many cases, listening is helpful, but then follow up with action. After listening to a young man's story about the fire that destroyed his apartment and its contents, help him find new housing and clothing.

Never make false assurances, but extend hope and confidence. Don't promise the person that everything will work out; instead, make a sincere offer of help.

In addition to these suggestions, here are ten more specific ideas that will help you assist someone in crisis:[7]

1. **Act quickly.** As mentioned above, a person experiencing a crisis may become so overwhelmed that he may become self-destructive if he does not receive help immediately. Most crises are short-lived, and even long-term ones work themselves out in about six weeks. But your quick help can make the crisis less severe and can help protect the person from hurting himself.

   Help the person understand the crisis; many people have no idea that the crisis they are experiencing is even related to any event. Help the person form the link between his feelings of despair and an actual event that occurred in his immediate past. Show that you understand the person's feelings by asking him questions: "You appear to be a little nervous. Is something bothering you?" Acknowledge the person's feelings—"I can understand why you would be angry"—and encourage him to express his feelings of guilt, fear, anger, and anxiety. As he talks, give him feedback; ask him to clarify things you don't understand ("Why did it bother you when Chris asked for the car?").

   Once the person is expressing himself well, help him explore the alternatives for dealing with the crisis—help him remember what he has done in the past in similar situations. As you talk about attempts at solving the crisis, ask, "What else could you have done in this situation?"

   Lead the person to his support system—he may not have considered talking to his mother, his bishop, his best friend. You might offer to call someone. Or you could offer to drive him somewhere or arrange for someone to stay with his children if necessary.

2. **Control the environment.** A person in crisis will perceive his environment as one of chaos—something he can't possibly manage. Take immediate steps to make the environment less threatening and more calm. Move the person to a quiet area, away from noise and onlookers; by this simple step you can often reduce the problem to one that is within the person's scope.

   If the person doesn't seem to know you, identify yourself

immediately ("I'm your neighbor, Alice; I live in the yellow house on the corner, and I want to help you now"). Identify the problem, and let the person know that you understand and are there to help. Unless the person has been seriously injured physically, wait to call an ambulance to drive the person to the hospital—rushing him off to a hospital will only confirm his fears that something is terribly wrong. Talk to him wherever you find him—in his living room, in the grocery store parking lot, in his backyard—and ask other relatives or friends to leave for a few minutes while you talk to the person alone. (Too many people will intimidate the person, and he will feel compelled to maintain control rather than letting his feelings out; one-on-one discussion at this point is most beneficial.)

3. **Assess the person.** Look at the situation carefully; assess what the person is telling you as it compares to the situation. Remember—it is the person's perception that triggers crisis. You may think that a man is reacting beyond rationality after some neighborhood children plucked the heads off his roses; what you may not see immediately is that the man learned that morning of his wife's terminal cancer.

   Assess the person's general alertness and ability to communicate by asking him questions that force him to respond. As you talk to him, try to identify the cause of the crisis by asking open-ended questions that call for answers from the person ("What's happened to make you so upset?" "Why are you away from home?" "Have you recently lost someone?" "Is there a reason you need help right now?"). Watch the person's posture, body movements, eye glances, and mannerisms. Note whether the person is disheveled, intoxicated, distracted, forgetful, abnormally depressed or euphoric, or worried.

4. **Set a limited goal.** Part of resolving a crisis lies in the fact that the person can once again achieve some balance in his life. As a first step, help the person achieve a limited goal; make it something that will challenge but not overwhelm

him. A person who is suffering a crisis after the death of a spouse may achieve a goal of collecting keepsakes and storing them in a safe place for his children to cherish in the future.

5. **Foster hope and expectations.** People in crisis help hopeless, and one of the best ways to help restore hope is to clearly express expectations of the victim. Plan with the person in crisis; help him set goals. This kind of exercise helps restore the person's self-esteem.

6. **Assess the person's support system.** Find out what kinds of external resources the person has (school, church, friends, family members) and whether he is using them. Find out how he has reacted in the past when presented with a stressful environment; will past solutions work again? To utilize supports, the person must be able to think relatively clearly, have control of some of his emotions, recognize that there are significant people who can help him , and want to help himself regain control.

7. **Plan for the future.** When you set goals with the person assign each a time frame; place limits on the achievement of each goal so that the individual clearly understands that certain things must be accomplished within a certain amount of time. Aim these goals toward the future, helping the person move forward.

8. **Promote a good self-image.** As discussed earlier, guilt and feelings of incapacity can lead to a poor self-image among those who are suffering a crisis. To promote a better self-image, treat the person with courtesy and respect. Show interest in the areas of the person's life that are not involved with the problem. Make sure that others are kind and treat the individual with respect, and let the person do as much for himself as possible.

9. **Encourage self-reliance.** A crisis can cause a person to revert to an earlier time in life that was less threatening, with the result that a competent, independent person can

become unable to do things for himself. Find things that the person can successfully accomplish, and urge him to do everything possible.

10. **Listen actively.** To listen actively, you need to use three ears: two to hear the verbal message, and one to sense the underlying feelings. As you listen to the person, question him occasionally by rewording what he is saying to demonstrate that you are interested and that you understand. You can't just sit back and passively listen— you need to question, repeat, and lend support as the person attempts to express his emotions.

As you listen, don't try to solve the person's problems for him—it is critical that he do that himself. Help him express even painful emotions, such as guilt, hatred, or fear; sometimes simply coming to terms with such feelings can help an individual place them in proper perspective and regain some control. Let the person cry or shout if necessary.

Help the person gain an understanding of the connection between a hazardous event and the current crisis—much of the person's panic could be a result of confusion. Help the person confront the reality of the situation, and tell him that he need not accept the burden of change all at once—he can work at it gradually, as he is able.

Encourage the individual to assume regular chores, and discourage the use of medication (medication can block the person's ability to adapt and solve the problem). As you listen, be prepared to list alternatives that the person may not have considered.

Crisis Intervention Skills[8],[9]

The most important crisis intervention tools are verbal and nonverbal communication skills. Careful use of these skills will help the individual reduce emotional overreaction, make sense out of what is happening to him, and find short-term solutions to the problem.

Guideline 1: Provide a Reality Basis

When you contact an individual in crisis, clearly **identify yourself and your position**. Tell the person or group who you are and what you are trying to do. This is a common-sense issue but it is often forgotten or taken for granted. Your uniform is not enough. The person in crisis is often too disoriented or frightened to take the time to read or ask who you are. Identifying yourself and your role will help the individual, family, and friends know not only who you are, but what they can expect from you. It is even good to reassure someone who is well acquainted with you that you are willing and in a position to help. Be sure to **use the individual's name** as you talk to him.

Anticipate the concerns of the individual, family, and friends. The more you can predict and clarify what the person in crisis is experiencing or might experience, the more the pressure on him is reduced, and the quicker that person will be able to handle the experience and regain control. Persons in crisis tend to experience exaggerated reactions of anxiety when people, places, or events are unfamiliar. The fewer unknowns and surprises, the better.

Give supportive but truthful information. Let the individual know what you expect of him and what he may expect of you. A number of common areas of concern that cause tension and anxiety can be anticipated and explained. Honestly and specifically tell the people involved the amount of physical or psychological danger the individual is in. The individual and his family or friends are often imagining the worst. Silence or evasion on your part often confirms that expectation.

Inform those present about reasons for questions, investigation, or treatment being conducted and the outcomes. Common questions you might hear are, "What am I going to do?", "Why did they take him to the hospital?", "Will it hurt?", "Why are the police here?"

Explain any emotional or physical reactions the person might have as a result of stress or intervention. For example: "When you have been under that must stress it is not unusual to have a headache or feel nauseated." Or "We are taking your blood pressure now to see how your body is reacting to the stress you've been under."

Explain the presence of legal authorities such as police. Reassure the individual of the confidentiality of his remarks and the situation. If the person requests action that you feel would be harmful or inappropriate, explain why you feel that way. Explain unusual equipment or procedures including strange sights, sounds, and smells.

Be calm and self-assured. A person in crisis is often very frightened at losing self-control. Your behavior should indicate that you have confidence in the person's ability to maintain control. Indeed, one of the main purposes of your interview is to help the individual reestablish some mastery of himself. If you manifest anxiety or panic, you will only increase the individual's conviction that the situation is overwhelming.

Persons in crisis are very suggestible. If you are nervous, the individual will be more so. The calmer you are, the better able you will be to intervene actively in those areas where the person is unable to manage for himself. Use gentle strength in your verbal statements. Your ability to be firm and direct in reassuring the individual results in trust-building and increased confidence in you as a caring and competent provider of help. Honest and sincere reassurance is communicated by such phrases as "I am sure that," "I know," "I'm convinced," and "I understand."

Be nonjudgmental. Maintain a nonjudgmental attitude. Accept an individual's right to have his own feelings, and do not blame or criticize him for feeling as he does. Your approval or disapproval of the individual as a person, or of the actions he took that resulted in his being in the present circumstances will not help him through the crisis. You may offer information, but do not judge. Being nonjudgmental involves an awareness of your own feelings and attitudes toward the individual.

One common reaction among health professionals is a feeling of irritation at a person who does not appear to be particularly upset or ill. This is especially true of emergency personnel, who are psychologically geared to deal with life-threatening and catastrophic events and who often regard apparently minor complaints as a burdensome annoyance. However, you must recall that when a person calls for help, he does so because something is worrying him. It may be an injury, a pain, a disturbing feeling, or a bodily function which the individual perceives as somehow disordered. It is not your function to pass judgment on the validity of the complaint. While it is much more dramatic to rescue a victim of mutiple trauma than to reassure the person with a minor cold, both individuals by virtue of a stated or implicit request for help have indicated that they are in some way distressed and are looking to you for assistance. Your role is to be supportive and nonjudgmental, rendering whatever care is needed under the circumstances.

Being nonjudgmental also means that you do not take sides in a conflict within a group. It is important to maintain objectivity and assume that both parties in a conflict contribute to the situation rather than try to fix the blame on one responsible "scapegoat."

Guideline 2: Provide Appropriate Verbal and Nonverbal Support

Maintain a relaxed body posture. Sit down near the individual. If you are stiff or far away, you may appear afraid, uninterested, put off. Never tower over him.

Touch the person if it seems appropriate. Physical contact is an important element of nonverbal support. Holding an individual's hand, grasping a shoulder, or even holding the person in your arms is sometimes the most effective treatment you can provide. In some instances, however (for example, with a hostile, suspicious, or psychotic person), touching should sometimes be avoided.

Stay with the individual at all times, especially if suicidal risk is present. Once you have responded to the emergency, the individual's well-being becomes your responsibility.

Throughout the interview, provide support and reassurance through actions that communicate an interest in the individual. Reassurance should never be unrealistic or foster unreasonable expectations (e.g., "You have nothing whatsoever to worry about"). Rather, you should seek to identify the patient's strengths and reinforce them (e.g., "Despite all the troubles you have had, you seem to have done a very good job").

Be interested in the individual's story, but not oversympathetic. If you overwhelm him with pity, he will be convinced that his situation is indeed hopeless. Treat him as though you expect him to improve.

Encourage communication with gestures or noncommittal words, such as a nod of the head or a phrase like "Go on" or "I see." This technique may also be used to return to a topic on which you would like an individual to elaborate. For example, the person may have made passing reference to suicidal thoughts and then moved on to another subject. When he finishes, you might say, "You say you have had thoughts of suicide?" This suggests to the person that you are interested in what he has been saying and would like to learn more.

Guideline 3: Listen and Respond

Careful listening is a prerequisite for being able to respond in a helpful manner. It is necessary for establishing and maintaining effective communication. An individual does not know that you understand what he is saying unless you show him you do. One of the most effective ways of showing this understanding is to reflect back to him (summarize) the feelings you heard him talk about or the feelings you guess he is experiencing because of what he says and does. Reflecting what you have heard also gives you a chance to make sure you have heard the individual accurately.

There are real skills involved in listening and responding effectively in facilitating crisis resolution. Some basic communication skills designed for one-to-one interaction include:

—**Attending.** Demonstration of concern for and interest in an individual by eye contact, body posture, and accurate verbal following.

—**Paraphrasing.** A statement that mirrors an individual's statement in exact or similar wording.

—**Reflection of feeling.** The essence of an individual's feelings, either stated or implied, as expressed by the helper.

—**Summarizing.** A brief review of the main points discussed to insure continuity in a focused direction.

—**Probing.** A response that directs an individual's attention inward to help both parties examine the individual's situation in greater depth.

—**Helper self-disclosure.** The helper's sharing of his personal feelings, attitudes, opinions, and experiences for the benefit of the individual.

—**Interpreting.** Presenting the individual with alternative ways of looking at his situation.

—**Confrontation.** A statement or question intended to point out contradictions in an individual's behavior and statements or to induce the individual to face an issue that the helper feels the individual is avoiding.

Attending can be classified as a listening skill; the remaining seven can be classified as response, or feedback, and as such, provide evidence of the quality of the listening and processing that precede the feedback.

Paraphrasing, reflection of feeling, and summarizing are primarily the feedback skills that demonstrate to an individual that the helper is paying attention to what is being expressed verbally and nonverbally. The helper can also use these skills to help the individual recognize and clarify his own understanding of what he says and the feelings related to these messages. The helper applies the other four skills—probing, helper self-disclosure, interpreting, and confrontation—to promote a mutual identification and understanding of the individual's problems and ways to deal with those problems.

The communication skills mentioned above constitute only a partial listing of skills that facilitate communication. Other dimensions of processing include the helper's technical knowledge about particular crises, specific treatment techniques (behavior shaping, modeling, goal setting, assertiveness training, relaxation training), various theories of psychological development and human behavior, self-awareness of feelings, values, and attitudes, and past personal and professional experiences.

Guideline 4: Ask Clear, Simple Questions

Communication is simplified or hampered by the type of questions the helper asks the individual. After obtaining basic, identifying information about an individual (name, age, address, etc.), an interview should be open-ended. That is, you should try not to direct the patient, but rather let him tell his own story in his own fashion.

It may be necessary to ask specific questions, but these too should be as nondirective as possible. Avoid questions that can be answered with a yes or no. "How" and "what" questions are preferred. As you let the individual tell his story in his own way, don't attempt to direct the conversation, and allow him to ventilate his feelings as they surface.

Ask clear, simple questions. Just as your responses should be clear, direct, and honest, so should your questions be understandable and focused. The person in crisis is overloaded. Too many confusing questions can increase the stress.

Ask questions one at a time. Keep them simple and wait for a reply. For example: "Do you remember when you started to feel this pain?" The individual answers. "And do you remember exactly where you felt it then?" The individual answers.

Compare this approach with the difficulty, from the individual's perspective, of: "Do you remember when you started to feel the pain, exactly where it was, and how long it lasted?"

Close-ended questions are those that can be answered "yes," "no," or multiple-choice style. These questions are useful when you want to gather very specific information. However, they can be limiting by being so narrow as to close off further comments or information. Open-ended questions are those that require a statement or information that cannot be provided by a "yes," "no," or multiple-choice answer. For example:

Closed: Are you in pain?
Open: You tensed up just now. Why was that?
Closed: Are you allergic to any medication?
Open: What can we do to make you more comfortable?
Closed: Has this happened before, or is this the first time?
Open: When did you take the drug?
Closed: Can you think of any other information that would help us?
Open: How do you think he got so frightened?

Although questioning should be open-ended, persons in crisis need direction. Some individuals find it difficult to deal with the unstructured situation of nondirective questioning. This is particularly true of adolescents, severely depressed persons, and confused or disorganized individuals. In such instances, where open-ended questions are met with uncomprehending silence, adapt your techniques to the situation and take a more directive approach.

Taking a definite plan of action gives the individual the feeling that something is being done to help, which in turn relieves anxiety. Do not confront an individual with decisions (such as "Do you want to go to the hospital?") But rather state what you think is the best course of action.

Other Hints to Improve Communication

Tolerate repetition. The person in crisis may ask the same question many times, or may ask you to repeat diagnostic or treatment information. Keep doing this. If there is something you want the individual to do, you might ask him to repeat the instructions to you to make sure that he understands. If you have instructions that should be remembered for more than a few moments, you can also write those down and have the individual read and say them aloud.

Communicate to the individual—not through others. Take care not to talk about a person to a third party where the person can see or hear you, unless you have already communicated that same information directly to the person.

Take time. Be prepared to spend time with the individual in crisis. You cannot be in a hurry. Take the time to talk with and learn what it is that is bothering him. These individuals require patient, concerned attention.

Don't be afraid of silences. Even though they may sometimes seem intolerably long, maintain an attentive and relaxed attitude. It is especially important to be silent when an individual must stop speaking because he is overwhelmed by emotion. Avoid the temptation to forestall expressions of emotion, such as crying, by saying something. The expression of feelings is often therapeutic, and it is likely that the individual will be better able to express himself after intense emotion has been released. Furthermore, your silence gives the person the opportunity to get control of himself in his own way.

Reinforce progess. Keep the individual informed of the positive steps he has made, even if they are very small steps. Your "that's good" or "fine" makes a big difference to the person who is struggling to regain control. However, don't be patronizing.

REFERENCES

1. This and some of the following information is from Ralph G. Hirschowitz, "Crisis Theory: A Formulation," *Psychiatric Annals* 3:12, p. 38.

2. Some of the following information was taken from Lee Ann Hoff, *People in Crisis: Understanding and Helping* (Menlo Park, Calif.: Addison-Wesley Publishing Company, Medical/Nursing Division, 1978), pp. 34-40; and Paul Welter, *How to Help a Friend* (Wheaton, Ill.: Tyndale House Publishers, Inc., 1984), pp. 67-68.

3. Hoff, pp. 34-35.

   Jeffrey T. Mitchell and H.L.P. Resnik, *Emergency Response to Crisis* (Bowie, Md.: Robert J. Brady Company, 1981), pp. 6-10.

4. Jeffrey T. Mitchell and H.L.P. Resnik, *Emergency Response to Crisis* (Bowie, Md.: Robert J. Brady Company, 1981), pp. 6-10.

5. Hirschowitz, p. 43.

6. Adapted from Hoff, pp. 27-28 and 48-50.

7. Brent Q. Hafen and Brenda Peterson, *The Crisis Intervention Handbook* (Englewood Cliffs, N.J.: Prentice Hall, Spectrum Division, 1982).

8. *EMT-Advanced*, DOT HS 501207, National Highway Traffic Safety Administration.

9. John B. Schultz, *Emergency Technician Booklet*, National Institute on Drug Abuse.

Psychiatric Emergencies

Dealing with a psychiatric emergency can be difficult and frightening. Occasionally, you may be faced with a chronic psychiatric patient who is legitimately disturbed; in those cases, your primary task is to keep the victim from hurting himself and/or others while you transport him to a facility where he can get help.

More often, you will be faced with healthy, balanced people who have reached a breaking point. They are experiencing the emergency that occurs when a hazardous or stressful situation taxes them beyond their ability to cope.

Think about the mother who creeps quietly into her baby's room during naptime and finds the infant dead of Sudden Infant Death Syndrome. Consider the woman who sustained only minor injuries in the accident that killed her husband. Put yourself in the place of the young family who watched the flames devour everything they had worked for.

Physical injury is almost always apparent. The care you render, too, is tangible: if you see a compound fracture, you splint it. Psychiatric emergencies are often not so noticeable—and the care you give may not have immediate and obvious effects. But psychiatric emergencies are every bit as crucial and horrific as physical emergencies—and they require just as immediate treatment.

Remember this: **every victim of every emergency has the potential for developing a psychiatric emergency, or crisis.** No one is immune. At the scene of an automobile accident, don't overlook anyone—not even the child who sits calmly on the back seat, seemingly unharmed.

Once you understand the way that people respond under stress, you can begin to anticipate their reactions. With that understanding and anticipation, you are equipped to handle psychiatric emergencies.

The Principles of Psychiatric Emergency Care

Guiding the efforts of rescuers in psychiatric emergencies are principles—and once you understand the principles, you can better prepare yourself to help victims of emotional crisis.

Remember the following:

Emotional injury is every bit as real (and as serious) as physical injury. Unfortunately, it can't be seen as easily, so it is not as readily accepted. You would never expect a person to go skiing the week after he broke his neck, but you might expect a man who loses his wife to go about his normal business the following week.

Any person who is involved in a disaster or who is injured will experience some emotional disturbance. Sometimes the reaction to injury is mild—for example, a person merely resents the inconvenience of doctor visits or a hospital stay. At other times, the reaction is extreme. Even an injury that appears to be mild may bring on a deep emotional crisis: a seemingly mild foot injury may ruin the career of a marathon runner, bringing on a full-blown crisis.

Every person has a breaking point. No two people are alike, and every person has limitations. Look at your own capabilities. You may well be able to cope nicely with a situation that would be extremely difficult for your father, your partner, your child, or your best friend. On the other hand, your best friend may be able to deal well with a situation that would severely tax your coping abilities.

Every person's feelings are valid to him. No matter how irrational, silly, unrealistic, or melodramatic a person's feelings seem to you, to him they are real and valid. You can look at a closet door and know that demons do not lurk behind it, but a victim of a psychiatric emergency may be convinced they do. For him, at that particular time, those demons are real. To understand him well enough to help him, you must accept that notion.

Every person has a right to his feelings. You've heard the phrase, "You have no right to be upset! You have so many things to be thankful for!" How wrong that is. A person who is depressed or angry or confused has a **right** to feel that way, no matter how you assess the situation. Your job is not to question the victim's right to feel depressed—it is to help the victim mobilize her resources so that she can overcome her depression.

No one chooses to be disturbed. A person who has been trapped in a crisis does not **want** to be there. He does not **want** to be unhappy, angry, panicked, confused, hostile, or helpless. But those feelings are real, and he needs help to turn things around. (Remember that when he refuses help, he may not know how to accept it!)

Every person has more psychological strength than he appears to have. People are amazingly resilient. Even under stress and in very difficult situations, people have reservoirs of emotional strength that can be tapped. Remember that as you approach a person who seems completely out of control, under it all, there is probably a hint of strength left—enough to help him get going again.

Your job is to keep the person from hurting more and to help him return to normal as quickly as possible. You often can't stop the situation that has led to the crisis. But you **can** run interception—you can offer help that will prevent more hurt. You can help the victim mobilize his resources, explore his options, set new goals, and come out a winner.

Emotional Responses to Physical Illness and Injury

Although each person will react to illness or injury based largely on coping mechanisms he has already developed, most reactions follow common patterns. Victims usually become aware of painful or unpleasant sensations—and sometimes of decreased energy and strength—when they become ill. The common response to that awareness is anxiety. Some victims will attempt to deny or minimize the signs and symptoms at that point, while others will become irritable or angry.

Once a victim perceives himself as injured, the following reactions may occur:

—**Realistic fears.** The victim may fear pain, disability, death, or financial problems. Such fears are normal and reasonable.

—**General anxiety.** Feelings of loss of control are common. Victims may feel helpless, knowing that they are completely dependent on someone else (often a stranger) whose knowledge of medical care and ability they cannot easily evaluate. A victim whose self-esteem depends on being active, independent, and aggressive is particularly prone to anxiety in such a situation.

—**Depression.** Depression is a natural response by some victims to the loss of some bodily functions as well as to feelings of loss of control over their destiny.

—**Regression.** The victim may return to earlier or more primitive modes of behavior. His behavior may appear to be childlike; such a reaction is natural and normal, because ill or injured people, like children, must depend on others for their survival.

—**Denial.** Many victims try to deny or ignore the seriousness of their injury or illness because it causes them anxiety. Denial is often seen as a tendency to dismiss all signs and symptoms with words like "only" or "a little." When a victim uses this mechanism, you may need to find out more from a family member or friend who can give an accurate history.

—Displacement of anger. Victims often respond to discomfort or limitations of activity by becoming resentful and suspicious of those around them. They may vent this anger on you by becoming impatient, irritable, or extremely demanding. It is critical that you realize that the victim's anger stems from fear and discomfort and is not really directed at you.

—Confusion. Illness or injury can cause disorientation, especially among the elderly. Such confusion is increased by the presence of unfamiliar people and equipment. In these cases, explain who you are, what you plan to do, and what will be involved in each procedure.

In addition to the common pattern of reactions, victims will experience something else: many people are uncomfortable about being examined by a stranger. Some people consider a physical assessment to be a humiliating invasion of privacy. If you think a victim might be experiencing these feelings, try to establish a relationship with the victim before you conduct the physical assessment. Always remember that an unclothed person is probably embarrassed and ashamed, and make sure that the victim is properly draped or shielded from the stares of curious bystanders. Conduct the examination in an efficient, businesslike way, and keep talking to the victim throughout the procedure.

Responses of Family, Friends, and Bystanders

People who are at the scene with the victim may show many of the same responses. Family members may be anxious, panicky, or angry—and anger often stems from guilt. To cope with their own anxiety, they may demand immediate action or pressure you to move the victim to the hospital before you can make proper assessment or take the time to properly stabilize the victim. Remember that this is a reaction to stress.

Responses of Emergency Helpers

Your own reaction during a psychiatric emergency might startle you. You might be irritated by the victim's demands, anxious by the scope of the injuries, defensive about implications that you are not capable of handling the situation, and grieved in response to tragedy. You might also feel irritated at the victim who does not appear to be particularly ill. Try not to judge whether the person's ills are real or imagined—give calm, confident support.

The Signs and Symptoms of Psychiatric Emergencies

The range of **physical and emotional responses** during a psychiatric emergency covers a broad spectrum, from mild nausea and a feeling of sadness to frenzied hallucinations and severe depression.

Signs, symptoms, and reactions will vary, depending on the victim and the situation. Some of the more common include:[1]

—The victim will do things that are dangerous to himself or others. He may seem oblivious to "punishment" and to physical pain and may repeatedly hurt himself in a variety of ways.

—The victim begins behaving in ways that are radically different from the way he usually acts. A man who has been aggressive and competitive suddenly becomes passive and withdrawn. A woman who has been quiet and shy suddenly becomes talkative and animated. A college student who has thrown her all into her studies suddenly becomes distracted, stops studying, and stops attending class.

Obviously, you'll have to rely on friends and family members to provide you with these details, since you won't know the victim's background. But be aware that this is a common reaction—so don't forget to ask.

—The victim may be extremely frightened, even to a point of panic. You may not be able to readily tell exactly **what** he is frightened of, but his behavior should clearly indicate that he is afraid. Watch for nausea and vomiting, low blood pressure, slow heartbeat, limp muscles, and a facial expression of terror. A victim who is afraid should be monitored closely—he might try to escape or run away.

—The victim may experience memory loss. She might not be able to tell you her name, her address, her phone number, or any details about the crisis. Memory loss is a serious sign and calls for immediate asistance.

—The victim may seem extremely preoccupied. In essence, the difficulty of coping with the situation overwhelms him; he can concentrate on little or nothing else. He doen't listen to people who are talking to him, doesn't pay attention to road signs or traffic signals, and loses track of what day it is.

—The victim may complain of body ailments or diseases that are clearly not possible. At first, the victim of a crisis may complain of problems that very well **could** be possible, such as generalized aches and pains; while he insists on frequent visits to the doctor, the physician can find no explanation for the problems. As the crisis worsens, the person starts to complain about ailments that are not possible: his heart has stopped, his stomach has become detached, his brain is dissolving. While these are clearly not possible, **to him they are real.** They are so real that he may become panic-stricken, believing he will die. If you try to convince him that his ailments are imaginary, he will either think you are stupid or that you are his enemy.

—The victim may believe that people are plotting against

him. There is a big difference between this reaction and a nonemergency reaction. A person who isn't undergoing a psychiatric emergency may think, *Bill is really out to get me. I guess he's jealous of my success on the last conference. He really seems determined to run me down in front of everyone else.* This kind of a person may accurately perceive that one or two people are "out to get him." Contrast this with the person who is going through a crisis. He may think, *Everyone is plotting against me. Everyone wants to hurt me. I'm not safe anymore; if I go outside, someone will kill me.*

A person who is suffering this kind of reaction can become suspicious, hostile, secluded, and uncooperative. He may also be dangerous: if he is honestly convinced that he is about to be hurt or murdered, he may suddenly lash out in a violent attack as an attempt to protect himself.

You need to use extra caution with this person. Explain carefully and clearly who you are, state repeatedly that you are not going to hurt him.

—The victim may be confused. The problem may be mild, such as temporary forgetfulness, or it may be severe—the confusion becomes so intense that the person is disabled. Most of the time, the confusion results from preoccupation with the crisis and with desperate mental energy spent on trying to resolve it.

—The person talks to himself loudly and persistently in front of other people.

—The person may exhibit intense, brief, and inappropriate anger, almost like an explosion. In cases of psychiatric emergency, the anger is often misplaced and directed at inappropriate people or things; it is almost always out of proportion for the situation. A long line and congested crowd at the subway stop would irritate most people, but a person in crisis may lunge through the crowd and attack a person near the front of the line.

—The person may lose touch with reality. He may hallucinate: he may hear voices, smell strange odors, taste peculiar tastes, or see visions. Any of the five senses may be involved. The victim may freely tell you about these: a voice has told him to climb to the top of the press tower at the football stadium. He has seen God, or an angel. He can smell smoke.

—The victim may have delusions of grandeur: he believes he is all-powerful, all-knowing. He's not just trying to convince other people—**he sincerely believes that he has extraordinary powers.** His delusions may cause him to take unnecessary or foolish risks because he believes he's indestructible.

—The victim may seem extremely anxious. All of us experience some stress and tension, but the victim in crisis will be almost overcome by anxiety. He may be filled with unreasonable dread or have feelings of impending doom. He will act restless, may sweat excessively, and will have a rapid heartbeat. He will probably appear to be very worried and upset.

—The victim may be depressed. Many times, the victim will convince herself that she is worthless, guilty, and deserving of the depression. She may become agitated, irritable, tense, and restless; she may wring her hands, cry easily and frequently, and have an extremely sad expression. In the extreme, depression can interfere with sleep and bring on deep feelings of hopelessness. A person who doesn't believe that the pain of depression will ever lift is a prime candidate for suicide.

—The victim may seem withdrawn. She loses interest in things that were previously important in her life; she seems apathetic and detached.

—The victim may become **manic:** he becomes almost hysterically happy, overly optimistic, almost giddy. Instead of concentrating on the crisis and what can be done, he escapes by forgetting it. This kind of blind optimism can result in foolish risk-taking and lack of judgment.

Don't Rule Out Physical Disorders[2]

One of the problems in recognizing psychiatric emergencies

lies in the fact that a number of physical disorders can bring on almost identical signs and symptoms. As you assess the situation, you may be convinced that the victim is undergoing an emotional crisis; in reality, he may be suffering from a life-threatening physical emergency.

If you encounter a victim who appears to be suffering from an emotional crisis, look for signs of the following:

—Multiple sclerosis. The victim may suffer depression, severe mood swings, and personality changes that result in inappropriate behavior. Physically, he may suffer from blurred vision, speech difficulties, and sensory losses that can mimic hallucinations. In the early stages, multiple sclerosis can cause hysteria similar to that suffered by victims of crisis.

—Delirium. Delirium, which causes altered mental states, can be caused by a broad range of factors, including alcohol intoxication, myocardial infarction, brain tumor, pneumonia, vitamin B-1 deficiency, typhoid fever, an overdose of digitalis, or disorders of the thyroid. Most commonly the victim of delirium loses the ability to concentrate. He may suffer from thought disorders, drowsiness, incoherent speech, loss of memory, chaotic or unusual behavior, hallucinations, and loss of a sense of reality. Emotionally, he may experience anger, euphoria, apathy, anxiety, fear, or deep depression.

—Delirium comes on rapidly and fluctuates unpredictably, with lucid periods in between. Delirium is often worse at night.

—Hypoglycemia. A condition known as "low blood sugar," hypoglycemia results when the pancreas produces too much insulin. Physical signs include dizziness, hunger, fatigue, tremors, and excessive sweating. The victim may be confused, agitated, and anxious; in some cases, he may feel dread or an impending sense of doom. Depression is a common effect of hypoglycemia. In severe cases, the victim may exhibit bizarre behavior or may act much like an alcoholic.

—Overactive thyroid gland. An overactive thyroid gland—one that secretes too much thyroid hormone—can mimic delirium, schizophrenia, psychosis, and extreme anxiety. The victim may feel tense, anxious, and distracted. She may develop shortness of breath, rapid heartbeat, heart palpitations, and tremors; a common sign is intolerance of heat.

—**Underactive thyroid gland.** In the opposite situation, not enough thyroid hormone is secreted, and the victim may become depressed, paranoid, belligerent, anxious, irritable, and unable to think clearly. She may suffer hallucinations and may appear to be "mad."

Look for physical clues if you suspect underactive thyroid. Common signs include swelling of the face, fatigue, stiff or aching muscles, constipation, and intolerance to cold. One of the most frequent clues is dry, thickened skin and brittle hair.

—**Diabetes.** A person who appears to be in an alcoholic condition or who appears to be extremely fatigued could be suffering from diabetes—the conditions of insulin shock and diabetic coma look much like emotional disorders. The victim may experience deep depression, irritability, profound confusion, and excessive mood swings. In addition, vision may be blurred, speech may be incoherent, and the victim may suffer loss of sensation. If not treated, the condition can lead to coma and death.

—**Cushing's syndrome.** A condition that results from chronic excess circulating adrenal cortisones, Cushing's syndrome can result in bizarre delusions, thought disorders, extreme excitability, loss of memory, delirium, hallucinations, and deep anxiety. Physical signs include excess body hair, wasting of the muscles, and obesity of the trunk and face.

—**Brain tumor.** Depending on the location in the brain, a tumor can produce a variety of signs and symptoms commonly manifest by people suffering from emotional crisis. Common effects include hallucinations, overwhelming fear, a sensation of strangeness, vast personality changes, euphoria, apathy, loss of memory, intellectual impairment, morbid depression, anxiety, and clouding of consciousness. Brain tumors may be extremely difficult to diagnose, because they may not produce physical symptoms until much later. When physical symptoms do occur, they may include nausea, vomiting, dizziness, and a distinct pattern of headaches.

—**Head injury.** Whenever you encounter a victim who seems to be suffering from a psychiatric emergency, quickly determine whether a head injury could have occurred. Head injuries can cause agitation, anxiety, irritability, profound confusion, loss of memory, restlessness, and aimless movement; some head injury victims act like they are intoxicated. They may be uncoordinated, and they may have slurred speech or blurred vision. Remember that even a minor head injury can produce these signs, especially if the victim is elderly or a child.

—**Infection.** Infection that is related to disease or illness (such as pneumonia, meningitis, or severe influenza) can result in severe confusion, agitation, hallucination, and bizarre behavior. In most cases, high fever is present.

—**Other physical diseases.** Other physical diseases that may manifest themselves in much the same way as emotional crisis include electrolyte imbalances (profound confusion); reactions to drugs (delirium, agitation, confusion, memory loss, bizarre behavior, and disorientation); epilepsy (confusion, disorientation, hallucinations, memory loss, and sudden anger); Korsakoff's disease (memory loss); cardiovascular disease (delirium, confusion, disorientation); Parkinson's disease (depression, dementia, intellectual impairment); Huntington's Chorea (paranoid behavior, personality changes, poor judgment, loss of memory, irritability); lupus erythematosus (delirium, hallucination, detachment, confusion, paranoia); and anemia (memory loss, confusion, depression, sense of worthlessness).

Two of the most common signs of emotional crisis—anxiety and depression—can result from dozens of physical disorders. Anxiety, for example, is a primary sign of disorders such as pulmonary embolism, hypoglycemia, high blood pressure, arteriosclerosis, internal hemorrhage, and drug intoxication. Depression is one of the major signs of problems ranging from hepatitis, encephalitis, cirrhosis, Alzhemier's disease, and syphilis to infectious mononucleosis, kidney failure, and alcohol intoxication. The watchword is this: **never assume that a person is suffering only from emotional crisis.** Take a few minutes to make a quick physical assessment to rule out obvious physical disorders.

Common Psychiatric Emergencies

The following are common psychiatric emergencies:

—**Acute anxiety or panic state.** Victims in this category usually experience extreme fear, sometimes accompanied by tremors, hyperventilation, diaphoresis (profuse sweating), agitation, palpitations, or the inability to swallow. Hysterical excitement is usually signalled by a victim who is overly dramatic or manipulative, and it is not usually serious. Organic brain syndrome (often called "senility") can bring on anxiety and restlessness, but the victim will also experience confusion and disorientation. The victim of senility will probably become even more confused if he is approached by strangers.

—**Schizophrenia.** A victim of schizophrenia is clearly disturbed and, when agitated, can be dangerous. Schizophrenics are usually tense, overactive, and unpredictable; most lose touch with reality. The schizophrenic is alone in his world and is usually detached, confused, and **very** paranoid. He may explode suddenly. He usually thinks that everything is directed at him, and he becomes extremely suspicious of others.

When schizophrenia advances to a catatonic state, the victim is slowed down to almost total detachment. He rarely speaks, may not move, and might assume some odd posture or curl up in a corner and refuse to move or communicate.

—**Mania.** A manic person cannot slow down long enough to eat, drink, or sleep. He is hyperactive; he speaks gibberish, exercises poor judgment, and moves quickly. Most manics are extremely strong and prone to attack or run away from those trying to help.

—**Psychoneurosis.** The psychoneurotic presents a complex picture of extreme anxiety, including crying, intense nervousness, and overactivity. They often become overdramatic or overdemonstrative; most become hysterical. Psychoneurotics look like they have no control over their actions; actually, they are in good contact with others but may become dangerous.

—**Old age and chronic illness.** Those who are chronically ill or elderly may suffer complications other than their physical illnesses. Many have memory problems and cannot identify people whom they have known for many years. Many are not quite sure what year it is or where they are. Some become suspicious. Because they are confused and cannot remember much, they become irrational and may wander away and get lost. Some may become violent; most are unpredictable and are generally uncommunicative.

—**Phobia.** The phobic is extremely frightened. All of his anxieties are focused on one situation or object. The intense fear may be one of heights, animals, or leaving the house. It is important to carefully explain each step of treatment or transport to a phobic.

—**Paranoia.** The paranoid person believes that everyone is out to get him. He becomes secluded, distrustful, and jealous. Many are hostile; most are uncooperative and difficult to handle. (Specific instruction on how to handle a paranoid person is given later in the chapter.)

—**Impaired consciousness.** Most victims of impaired consciousness are suffering from an organic disorder, usually of cerebral or systemic origin. At one moment, the victim may seem well oriented; at the next he may be disoriented or unconscious. The victim may be schizophrenic or have some kind of medical disorder; a person who is suffering from severe depression may also become stuporous at times. It is critical in cases of impaired consciousness to carefully rule out the possibility of a medical problem—and, if one is present, to treat it before worrying about the implications of psychiatric emergency. (As a rule, the medical problem will pose the more serious emergency.)

The Phenomenon of Conversion

Under serious emotional upset, such as that suffered during a psychiatric emergency, a victim may experience **conversion symptoms**—the phenomenon in which an idea or desire is expressed in bodily rather than verbal terms and is experienced as a physical, not mental, symptom. While conversion symptoms originate in the mind, then, they **seem to be physical** in origin. Mental thoughts ae literally "converted to" bodily sensations or feelings.

Conversion generally occurs in response to serious frustration, deprivation, need, or difficulty in responding to others. Internal conflict or the presence of a perceived life-threatening situation can also bring on conversion symptoms. The conversion symptom accomplishes four things for the victim:

—It allows him to express "forbidden" feelings (great anguish, fear, anger, frustration, hatred, and so on) in a way that is acceptable to society and in a way that he does not even recognize himself.

—It gives him a chance to punish himself for having such feelings (even though **he is not aware of the feelings or the need for "punishment"**).

—It allows the person to escape from the extreme psychiatric stress or the life-threatening situation. (For example, a person who is under extreme stress at work may get "sick" and have to go home, thereby escaping the stressful situation in a way that is understandable and acceptable.)

—Because the person becomes "sick," he can assume a new role and a new way of relating in the situation that has caused him so much stress.

Specific symptoms may develop in specific body parts as a result of past experiences, memories, various reinforcements (usually over a number of years), or feelings of rage and guilt. Common conversion symptoms include severe headache, backache, nausea, vomiting, gastrointestinal problems, skin lesions, dermatitis, hives, chest pain, shortness of breath, heart palpitations, nervousness, fatigue, weakness, severe anxiety, memory loss, and extreme fear.

Suspect conversion symptoms as part of a psychiatric emergency in the following situations:

—**The symptom can't be explained by normal physiological processes.** If a physical assessment of the victim gives no explanation for the symptom—or if the symptom is clearly inconsistent with what you find during physical assessment— the symptom may be the result of conversion. (If you find severe chest pain in a person who has a normal EKG, normal coloring, normal vital signs, and other normal findings, for example, you might suspect conversion symptom.)

—**The victim is obviously under some psychiatric stress.** Especially watch for the tendency to use the body for expression—to become extremely dramatic in both voice and gestures when describing something, for example. Watch, too, for the tendency of the victim to be fearful, forgetful, depressed, and extremely dependent. In taking a history, try to determine whether the conversion symptom was precipitated by extreme stress or some kind of psychiatric emergency.

—**The victim is in a situation where he saw someone else suffer the same symptoms.** In many cases, the victim might be reacting to what he **thought** the other person felt like or what he **thought** the other person suffered, rather than to what the other person actually experienced. In some cases, the victim experiences a symptom that he **wishes** someone else had suffered.

—The victim is bothered by but attached to the symptom. Watch out for the person who seems to be suffering and experiencing great upset over the symptom on the one hand, but who is obviously enjoying it or receiving some kind of gain or compensation from it on the other hand.

Managing Psychiatric Emergencies

Assessing the Victim[3]

Your assessment of the psychiatric emergency victim should begin as soon as you see him—you size up his appearance, quickly scan the surroundings for clues, and begin to talk to him. Your assessment should touch on the following areas:

—Thought process. Are the victim's thoughts coherent? Is he thinking at a normal pace, or does his thinking seem to be slow? Are his thoughts fragmented or repetitious? Listen to what the victim reveals about his thoughts. He may describe hallucinations, tell you that he feels empty or transparent, tell you about fears, describe a sense of impending doom, or talk about feelings of paranoia. He may tell you he is depressed. He may describe habits or obsessions. He may take great pains to tell you about his importance, his status, his possessions, or his special abilities.

—General intelligence. You can gauge much about the victim's intelligence as you talk to her. Pay attention to her abstractions, indications of judgment, and level of vocabulary. If the victim shows indications of being fairly intelligent but cannot relate her name, tell you what day of the week it is, or remember her problem, she is probably suffering from an emotional crisis.

—**General appearance.** Watch out for a person who is wearing clothes that are extremely soiled, in need of mending, or are inappropriate for the season. A man who wears heavy hiking boots, a thick sweater, a down coat, and a knit hat in July is probably disoriented and confused. Also note general grooming, body build, and the presence of any physical defects.

—**Motor skills.** Watch the way the victim moves. Motor movements should be smooth, coordinated, and frequent; emotional problems may manifest themselves in motor movements that are jerky, uncoordinated, awkward, infrequent, or twitching. Take note of the way the victim sits, the way she walks in and out of the room, and the way she shakes your hand.

—**Expressions and gestures.** Listen to the victim speak. Normal speech is easy, spontaneous, well paced, and not too loud or soft. Listen to determine whether the victim uses profanity, repeats information, or seems disoriented and confused. Facial expression can provide some clues: it should be congruent with the situation. A victim who is describing the terror of escaping from a burning building should have a terrified look in his eyes—not an expression of detached apathy. Watch to see whether the victim's expression changes as the subject and emotion change.

—**Orientation.** The victim should know who he is, where he is, what day of the week it is, what month it is, and approximately what time it is. As you talk to him, determine whether he is able to concentrate on the conversation and whether he is paying attention to what you are saying. He might seem irritated or hesitant or might require a great deal of effort to stay with the conversation. In asking him to tell you what led up to the crisis, determine whether his memory and recall are intact. You might find that he tells several different versions of the story and has trouble distinguishing what really happened.

—**Mood.** Try to determine the victim's mood. After assessing her physical appearance, watching her expression and gestures, and talking to her briefly, you should have some good clues as to whether she is generally happy, depressed, anxious, fearful, angry, or withdrawn.

As you talk to the victim, ask questions that will help you in your assessment. Avoid the temptation, however, to stray into unrelated areas. Concentrate on gathering information about the crisis, what led up to it, and how the victim is feeling now. **A person who seems seriously disturbed or who poses a danger to himself or others should be seen by a physician as soon as possible.**

What To Do In A Psychiatric Emergency[4]

Obviously, you will need to do certain things in specific crisis situations; you would respond to a woman who just lost her husband differently than you would to a teenager who is contemplating suicide. Despite these specific challenges, there are a number of general principles you should follow in managing victims of psychiatric emergencies.

—**Begin by clearly identifying yourself.** Verbally and nonverbally communicate confidence in your ability to be of help, and explain what you want to do: "I know that you are very upset about the fire. You must feel panic-stricken right now. I am here to help you, and I know that we can work this out."

—**Expect the best.** The victim will clearly read your attitude. She will watch the way you deal with her and will either think, *These feelings are temporary, and I'm going to be all right within a few hours,* or you will communicate to her, *Something is really the matter with me. I must be seriously ill. It's going to be a long time before I feel better.* (Learn to expect the best, but be prepared for the worst.)

—**Immediately calm the person down.** It's best if you can be in a quiet, peaceful place away from distractions and disorganization. If you can, remove the person from the crisis—get rid of all disturbing people or objects. If you're at the scene of a tragic car accident, take the victim a short distance to a more quiet place away from the flashing lights, screaming sirens, and investigating officers.

—**Be prepared to invest time with the victim.** Dealing with a psychiatric emergency isn't like splinting an arm. To gain the victim's trust and learn enough to be of help, you need to talk and listen.

—**Express confidence in the victim's ability to get control of the situation.** Most emotionally distraught people are afraid of losing control, and you can remedy that by saying something like, "I can understand why you're so upset, but you're stronger than you think. Let me help you figure out what to do next."

—**Don't rush the victim to the hospital unless he is posing immediate danger to himself or others or he has sustained life-threatening injuries.** He is probably afraid that there is something terribly wrong with him—and you'll confirm his fears by rushing to the hospital.

—**Work with the victim on a one-to-one basis; ask friends and relatives to move into another room so that you can have privacy.** In many cases, the friends and relatives precipitated the crisis, and the victim may hesitate to speak truthfully in front of them. Tell the victim that you respect her right to privacy and that you will guarantee her privacy. If you need to confirm parts of her story with others, do it at a different time when she is not present.

—**As you work with the victim, sit down.** Put yourself on his level. Never tower above him.

—**Encourage the victim to speak freely, ventilating his feelings and telling his story in his own words.** Don't try to direct the conversation; let it all spill out, even the parts that are unpleasant or painful. Resist the urge to stop the story midway in search of details—you can do that at a later time. Interrupt as little as possible. If the victim asks you a direct question, be as brief as you can in answering and let him continue.

—**Don't shower the victim with sympathy.** You should show

intense interest in what the victim is saying, and you can appropriately empathize with her, but don't be effusively sympathetic. If you show extreme pity, the victim may begin to believe that her situation **is** pretty grim. Throughout the conversation, maintain the attitude that you understand why she is having problems, but you know that she can feel better soon.

—**Do not deny the victim's feelings or experiences.** You can maintain honesty while you allow the victim his experience: a victim who is hallucinating might ask you if you see what he is seeing. You can honestly answer, "I don't see anything there except a car and some shrubbery, but you may certainly see a body."

—**Avoid arguments.** The victim may disagree with you; if so, calmly explain that there are many different ways of looking at things and that you could be wrong. Explain that it is his right to disagree. If you are afraid that something you say could offend or hurt the victim, remain silent; participate in the conversation by nodding your head, smiling, and giving other nonverbal responses. **That's a cardinal rule in working with troubled people: if you are afraid of the person's reaction, say nothing.**

—**Don't be judgmental.** The victim's feelings may seem ridiculous to you, **but they are real to him.** He doesn't need someone to discredit him, criticize him, or make fun of him. He needs someone who will listen and accept his right to have his own feelings.

—**Don't require the victim to make decisions.** Many victims of psychiatric emergency have lost the ability to make decisions, and if you expect a victim to do it she may feel overwhelmed and uneasy. Even a small, simple decision can seem impossible.

—**If the person is having a difficult time talking, do things that encourage him to relax.** Give him a cup of coffee or a soft drink; encourage him to sit in a comfortable position; encourage him to engage in a soothing motor activity, such as watering the plants, while you talk.

—**Don't be afraid of silences.** A victim may stop speaking temporarily because he is overcome by emotion; if you interrupt, you deny him the right to work out the emotion. Sit forward in your chair in a relaxed manner, smile softly, keep eye contact with the victim to indicate your interest in him, and wait quietly for him to resume.

—**If the victim doesn't start speaking again after a reasonable length of time, make a statement that will start things going again.** You might say, "You seem worried," or "You seem very angry. What are you feeling now?"

—**Guard against your own reactions.** Don't show negative reactions, and don't let the victim make you angry. She may say things that anger or upset you, especially if she directs her hostility and anger toward you. Remain calm—**remember that this hostility is not directed at you personally.** Remain kind.

—**Provide ordinary comforts for the victim.** Allow him to go to the bathroom, get a drink of water, get something to eat, or change clothing if he is wet or soiled. If the victim needs to leave the room, make sure he cannot (and does not) leave through a window.

—**Once you have started working with the victim, don't leave her alone.** Her safety is legally your responsibility. If she begs to be left alone for a few minutes, you might say something like, "I know you are capable of handling this situation on your own, but I would get fired if I left now."

—**Once the person has told her entire story, go back over it for details.** Relate parts of it in your own words to make sure you understand. Invite the victim to correct you if you are wrong or to add details she forgot the first time. This is the time to ask questions and get more information.

—**Never assume that it is impossible to communicate with someone until you have tried.** Be patient; be willing to get the ball rolling by making your own statements. Show that you understand. Say something like, "You seem very worried. I've been worried before, and I know how it can feel. Why don't you tell me what has happened. I want to help." Even a person who appears distracted, withdrawn, or detached may respond if approached the right way.

—**When you ask questions, make them open-minded.** As much as possible, avoid asking questions that the victim can answer with a simple "yes" or "no."

—**Don't give the victim false hope or build false expectations.** Be honest when you respond to his questions. Instead of saying, *I don't think you have anything to worry about,* you might say, *This has really been tough for you. You've got to work a few things out, but I know you can do it.*

—**Don't make promises you can't keep.** If you commit to doing something, follow through.

—**As soon as you can, talk to others who are involved with the person (such as family members, friends, or coworkers).** You might pick up missing details or gain a new perspective; even more important, you might learn valuable information such as a history of previous psychiatric problems, involvement with drugs or alcohol, or evidence of drastic behavioral or personality changes.

—**As soon as you figure out what the problem is, explain it clearly to the victim.** Uncertainty can be terrible. Be honest in explaining what the problem is, how it can be solved, and what the victim can expect. Remain optimistic and hopeful when you can.

—**Encourage the victim to go to sleep; sleep often helps restore psychological equilibrium.** Use tranquilizers only as a last resort and only when the victim is combative.

—**Make detailed notes about what you've learned about the victim.** Note carefully what you did for the victim and how he responded. These are important for medical **and** legal reasons.

Helping Someone Who Doesn't Want Help[5]

Face it. Not everyone who is having an emotional crisis **wants** outside help. Getting involved in someone else's problems is always a risky business, but not getting involved means risks of a different kind. As a rule, you've got a professional responsibility to get involved, so follow some of these suggestions:

—**Don't be surprised by resistance.** To admit that he needs help, the victim is forced into admitting that he is having problems, that he is too weak or too stupid to handle his problems on his own, and that his problems may overwhelm him. That's not easy for anyone to admit, especially someone in the midst of a crisis.

—**Try to get the person to talk.** She may be afraid of appearing vulnerable; she may be embarrassed. Make sure she has privacy, and encourage her with gentle phrases of nonjudgmental understanding.

—**State clearly the way in which you see the problem if the person is unwilling to admit to it.** Be specific, and talk in ways that will be difficult for the victim to deny. Instead of saying, *I think you're really having problems,* say something like, *I can tell that you are unusually afraid because of the way you are perspiring and trembling. I know that's how people act when they are afraid. What are you afraid of?*

—**Avoid the temptation to give simple advice.** The victim has probably already struggled with many solutions and found them inadequate. Empathize and agree with the victim that a problem exists; then enlist his help in figuring out options.

—**Don't be judgmental, and don't fix blame for the problem.** Exploring who is right and who is wrong in a situation can be interesting, but it rarely leads to constructive changes and solutions. Whatever happens, don't let the victim fix all the blame for his problem on someone else—his wife, his boss, his children. If you do, you "exonerate" him and remove his motivation to work through the crisis.

—If the victim is clearly in trouble and is still resisting help, be brutally honest in your forecast of the situation. You might say something like, "I know that you think you can work through this thing alone, but I don't think you realize the seriousness of the situation. Anyone in your shoes would need some help in getting back on their feet. I'm afraid that if you don't accept help, you will end up hurting yourself or someone else."

—If the victim becomes combative and resists efforts at help, you may have to restrain him and transport him to a hospital. As a general rule, in most states you can use restraint and force only if you are clearly convinced that the victim is posing a serious danger to himself or someone else. If you think that is the case, proceed with caution. Don't try to move in on the victim until enough rescue personnel are available to easily overpower the victim; count on at least four adults to overpower another adult. Place the victim on a stretcher and strap his arms, legs, and chest down with cloth or leather straps. Wrap the entire stretcher in a blanket. Then explain to the victim, "We are going to take you to the hospital, because we are convinced that you need some help. We know that you don't want to go, but we are afraid that you might hurt someone else or yourself if you don't go. The law gives us the right to decide that." Loosen any belts, ties, or other clothing that might restrict circulation or cause injury. Remove the victim's eyeglasses, jewelry, and other items that could cause injury.

—If the victim is armed or barricaded, surround him at a distance, try to get him talking, and wait for police to arrive.

—When you transport a person against his will, make sure that he cannot escape from the vehicle or injure the driver. If you are in a car, have someone sit on either side of him in the back seat and lock all doors. If you are in an ambulance, make sure that several rescuers are in the back with the victim.

Managing a Child[6]

When the victim of an emotional crisis is a child, you will need to use special techniques. You may be dealing with a child who is too young to clearly explain her feelings verbally, so you might need to let her draw pictures, tell stories, or act it out. You might also encounter a child who refuses to talk at all; in those situations, you need to watch how he interacts with those around him and try to gauge the seriousness of the situation.

In general, try some of these suggestions in dealing with children:

—It is critical that you gain the child's trust and convince her that you are a friend. One way to accomplish this is to offer the child food.

—Make it clear that you are strong enough to help her, but that you are not going to hurt her. Remember that people who are "strong" may have victimized or abused her in the past.

—Remember that a child's attention span can be extremely short. If you are working with a young child, keep the interview short. You might need to let him break several times during the interview to play with something, draw a picture, or engage in some physical activity.

—Never lie to a child. You will probably feel an overwhelming urge to protect him from unpleasantness, but you need to be honest with him. If you do need to tell him something unpleasant, do it gently and gradually.

—Use all the available resources to help bring the child out. Let her draw pictures, play-act, or tell stories to explain how she feels if she is reluctant to tell her story verbally. If you sense that the child is struggling with how to explain, offer some suggestions: "Did you feel upset then?" "Did that make you mad?" "Maybe you felt afraid then."

—If the child is not upset by his parents' presence, ask them to help you talk to the child and discover what the problem is. If the child is clearly upset by the presence of his mother or father, ask them politely to leave so that you can talk to the child privately. If the parent refuses, you might say something like, "I think there is a chance that your child sees you as some kind of a threat. I know that you're not, but I don't think your child will open up to me while you're here. Why don't you wait in the next room, and I'll see if I can get him to explain how he is feeling. We'll call you back in when we are ready."

—The rules of confidentiality are much more lenient when it comes to children. Since a child can't be responsible for himself, you can (and should) alert parents to the problem.

—Don't dismiss the possibilities of violence just because the victim is a child. Children have been known to murder and to commit suicide. Any threat of violence should be taken seriously, and you should take appropriate measures to protect the child and others around him. Work with parents to make them realize that a child who threatens suicide is not merely going through "a phase."

Managing the Elderly[7]

In working with victims who are elderly, follow these general guidelines:

—Realize that it may be more difficult for an elderly person to ask for help or receive help; many have fierce pride. Communicate verbally and nonverbally that it is certainly all right to need help and to ask for it.

—Elderly persons may have a sense of immediacy. They feel that something horrible will happen to them if you don't do something immediately. Many even fear that they will die. If the victim becomes demanding or threatening and appears to be overly frightened, do everything you can as quickly as you can to ease his fears.

—Be extremely patient. Remember that elderly people often can't hear or see well. You may need to repeat yourself several times or speak more loudly than you usually do. Use touch to reassure the victim that you are listening and interested.

—**Be prepared to listen for long periods while the elderly person recites details of his life.** You may think that it is senseless, but it's not. Often it's a way of resolving old issues and reviewing past successes. Don't interrupt unless absolutely necessary.

—**Be prepared to take plenty of action.** The elderly have a tendency to think that you are not helping at all unless you are **doing** something. Too many people have been "all talk and no action" during their lives.

—**Pay close attention to physical complaints.** While people of other ages may imagine their complaints or create complaints to attract attention, elderly people rarely report complaints that are not real. You can obtain important clues about possible physical disorders from a victim's descriptions.

—**Give the elderly person a clear explanation of what action you are taking.** Be extremely clear in what you think you can do to help.

—**If you decide to transport an elderly person to the hospital, be extremely sensitive.** Many older people die in hospitals, and the elderly person may become panic-stricken. Explain with kindness and gentleness, "Please don't let this trip to the hospital concern you. Your problem is a minor one, and I'm confident that you will be back home and on your feet within a few days."

Sharpening Communication Skills

As you talk to victims of emotional crisis, remember the principles of good communication:[8]

—Don't interrupt the victim while he is speaking.

—Listen courteously and attentively until the person has

finished speaking. Resist the temptation to break in before the victim has completed a thought or sentence.

—To make sure that you understand what the victim is telling you, occasionally repeat the information, using your own words. Be open to correction.

—Resist the urge to speak for the other person. You might ask questions or make statements to help the person begin, but you should leave them open.

—Don't try to pass your opinions off as fact. Instead of stating your opinion authoritatively, as though it is the last word, preface it with a phrase such as, "In my opinion..., I could be wrong, but I think that..., It seems to me that...."

—Spell out the specifics. As you explain a point, make sure that you are not being vague.

—If you and the victim have a genuine difference of opinion, stress your victim's right to disagree, and then move on to an area where you can agree and reach a mutual solution. In crisis situations, avoid arguments and resist the urge to always come out on top.

—Give the victim feedback as he relates his situation. You don't have to do it verbally; you might occasionally nod, smile, or touch his arm.

Certain groups will require special consideration as you try to communicate. Keep the following in mind:

—**Children.** Use simple terms and vocabulary that the child can easily understand. If you are trying to ask about a complicated issue, use a doll or toy to illustrate. A child may be shy, afraid, or unusually upset; allow her to keep a favorite blanket, toy, or doll to calm her and help her feel at ease. Move slowly, and give her plenty of chances to explain herself.

—**Elderly.** Before you begin talking, make sure that the victim is comfortable physically. Remember that hearing may be poor, so speak loudly and clearly; allow extra time for the person to respond. Use the victim's name and communicate respect and patience.

—Deaf. If you know sign language, use it. If not, try to determine if the victim can read lips; if so, position yourself so that she can clearly see your face as you talk. If you can get an interpreter, do it—you will have much greater success in communicating difficult or abstract concepts. If all else fails, resort to written messages.

—Blind. Take the time to carefully explain what you are doing and what is going on around the victim; a person who can't see may be extremely anxious over what is happening, and her anxiety may prevent her from communicating. Resist the temptation to shout. If you can see that there is no hearing impairment, speak in a normal tone of voice. If you need to move from one place to another, gently guide the victim and alert her to obstacles.

—Confused or developmentally disabled. Before you begin discussing the problem, take a few minutes to talk to the person about other things so that you can get some idea as to how well he is functioning intellectually. Once you have determined that, speak as you would to any adult, but speak on a level that can be understood clearly. Be patient; it may take the victim a little longer to respond. Take extra care in listening—it is easy to misunderstand.

—Non-English-speaking. Ideally, get someone to interpret. Realize that the interpretation process can be frustrating—not only to you, but to the victim and the interpreter as well. Be patient, and make sure that you are not communicating your frustration or impatience nonverbally. Listen carefully and repeat in your own words if you fear you have not understood completely. If you can't get an interpreter, try using gestures to communicate, or use drawings and illustrated charts to reach some kind of an understanding.

Paranoia

The paranoid victim is a special case because of his emotional state: he is hostile, distrustful, suspicious, and excitable. Unfortunately, a situation involving a paranoid victim can suddenly explode into violence. To protect yourself and the victim follow these guidelines:

—Maintain a certain distance from the victim, and act in a businesslike manner. A paranoid person may become violent if he fears that you are getting too close or are invading his personal space. Don't try to befriend him. He is distrustful and suspicious and will mistake your efforts for an attempt to overcome him.

—Clearly explain who you are and what you are going to do. Before you proceed, let the victim ask questions. If he starts to threaten you, back off.

—Before you start talking to a paranoid person, try to make sure that he is unarmed. Before you do anything, make sure that help is standing by in case of unexpected violence.

—If you need to talk to family members or friends, do so openly and in the presence of the victim. If you sneak off to another part of the room and speak in hushed tones, you will reinforce his fears that people are plotting against him.

—If you are unable to work with the victim and need to overpower him to protect him or others (including yourself), realize that he may react with incredible force and violence if he senses that he is about to be attacked. You will need to act swiftly and with great force; the struggle must be brief and painless. Most paranoid individuals will give up if it is clear they cannot win, but if they think they have a chance of overcoming their foes, they will fight with vengeance and violence.

—If the victim is armed and barricaded, let the police handle the situation. The best strategy is to surround him and secure the position, try to communicate with him, and listen carefully to his conditions for surrender. Instead of engaging in a shootout, it is better to isolate him and then give him time to think about things.

Depression

Depression deserves special mention because it carries with it a special risk: suicide. Severe depression fosters feelings of worthlessness, guilt sorrow, helplessness, and hopelessness. It is an emotional agony that is difficult to fully understand unless you have experienced it. When depression becomes severe, the victim often becomes convinced that there will be no relief from that agony—and the only solution is self-destruction. To him, it is the only way to end the pain.

Because of the distinct possibility of suicide, there are two specific guidelines in dealing with a depressed victim:

1. Ask the victim directly if she has had suicidal thoughts. (*Have you ever thought about killing yourself? Do you ever wish you were dead?*) If she says she has thought about it, ask her how she would plan on doing it. If she immediately relates a well-thought-out plan, her risk is extreme. She should be transported to the hospital immediately.
2. Do not leave the depressed person alone. If you do not transport him to the hospital, make sure that a family member or friend will stay with him until other help can be obtained. Stress to the helper the significance of staying. Explain clearly that the individual may hurt himself if he is left alone in this state of depression. Follow up by contacting the appropriate agency.

REFERENCES

1. Brent Q. Hafen and Keith J. Karren, *Crisis Intervention for Emergency Medical Personnel* (North Hollywood, Calif.: Creative Age Publications, 1980), pp. 17-20.

2. Jacquelyne G. Gorton and Rebecca Partridge, *Practice and Management of Psychiatric Emergency Care* (St. Louis, Mo.: The C.V. Mosby Company, 1982), pp. 30-42; J. Ingram Walker, *Psychiatric Emergencies: Intervention & Resolution* (Philadelphia, Penn.: J.B. Lippincott, 1983), pp. 21-39; and Hafen and Karen, pp. 22-23.

3. John L. Hipple and Lee B. Hipple, *Diagnosis and Management of Psychological Emergencies* (Springfield, Ill.: Charles C. Thomas Publishers, 1983), pp. 75-81.

4. Hafen and Karren, pp. 20-24; H.L.P. Resnik and Harvey L. Ruben, *Emergency Psychiatric Care: The Management of Mental Health Crises* (Bowie, Md.: The Charles Press Publishers, Inc., 1975), p. 50; and Diana Sullivan Everstine and Louis Everstine, *People in Crisis: Strategic Therapeutic Interventions* (New York: Brunner/Mazel, Publishers, 1983), pp. 31-52.

5. Paul G. Quinnett, *The Troubled People Book* (New York: Continuum Publishing Company, 1982), pp. 150-153.

6. Resnik and Ruben, pp. 45-46; and Hafen and Karren, p. 16.

7. Jeffrey T. Mitchell and H.L.P. Resnik, *Emergency Response to Crisis* (Bowie, Md.: The Robert J. Brady Company, 1981), pp. 157-161.

8. Douglas A. Puryear, *Helping People in Crisis* (San Francisco, Calif.: Jossey-Bass Publishers, 1979), p. 62.

9. Resnik and Ruben, pp. 46-47.

Suicide

Suicide—the "act of taking one's own life voluntarily and intentionally,"[1] as the dictionary defines it—can be one of the most painful, confusing, and hopeless of emotional crises. We can only guess at the depth of despair that drives a person to self-destruction. Its victims are among the most misunderstood people with whom we deal. And the crisis does not stop there: they leave behind survivors who must deal with the stress, guilt, and shattered psyche.

For most, suicide comes as a shock. The news (or discovery) that a friend or family member has committed suicide brings fear, agonizing self-doubt, and a vicious cycle of assumption. Most of the time, a suicidal person gives many clues about his impending act of self-destruction; in many cases, family members and friends fail to recognize the clues. Even so, survivors often feel guilty and "responsible;" they agonize over their possible role in the suicide and their potential to have stopped it.

If only I had been a better friend. If only I had listened that night. If only I had let her go back to school. If only I had refused to let him take the car.

Many of those who don't feel responsible try to rationalize. It's an attempt to ease out of the grief, shake off responsibility, soothe the hurt. The feelings associated with rationalization sound plausible and well-thought-out: *She never told me she was depressed; how could I have stopped her? It's not my fault her boyfriend deserted her. I had no idea her life was falling apart. She never shared her feelings with me.*

Out of all the hurt and confusion that suicide can bring, is it possible to make some sense? Is it possible to predict who might try to take his own life? Do the self-destructive leave clues that others can recognize? Can suicide be prevented, at least some of the time?

The answer to all of these is **yes**. It takes an understanding of what suicide is, a look at who its victims are, an analysis of what causes suicide, and a clear explanation of what clues its victims leave behind.

The Myths and the Realities

The first step toward a clear understanding of suicide is to identify and dismiss the popular myths regarding suicide. You've probably heard plenty of them, and may even believe some of them. Some of the most common misconceptions include the following:[2]

People who commit suicide always leave notes. Not true! Only a small percentage of those who commit suicide leave notes explaining why or telling that they intentionally took their own life. This misconception is a particularly dangerous one—many suicides are labeled "accidents" because friends, family members, or investigating officers did not find a suicide note.

People who commit suicide are psychotic or mentally ill. Some suicide victims are indeed psychotic; in fact, the risk of suicide increases if psychosis or mental illness is present. But many suicidal people are just severely depressed and can't figure out any other solution to their problems. So don't think that a "normal" person is beyond self-destruction.

Rich people commit suicide more often than poor people. That's not true, either. Suicide is pretty evenly distributed among the socioeconomic groups.

People who talk about suicide are just trying to get attention; people who really commit suicide don't talk about it first. This is probably the most unfortunate misconception of all. Eight out of ten people who commit suicide give definite warnings of their intentions; the other two usually give some kind of verbal clues. Almost no one commits suicide without first letting someone else know how he feels. A person who talks about committing suicide or who threatens to commit suicide is begging for help—he wants to be given an option so that he doesn't have to end his life. Listen! Pay attention! Never ignore a threat.

Suicide happens without warning. The clues may not always be verbal, but they are almost always there. People simply don't recognize them. Most suicidal people leave a host of clues and warnings of their intentions.

If someone has decided to commit suicide, there is nothing you can do to stop him. Sometimes that is true, but most of the time it's not. The majority of suicides can be stopped. Even a person who is severely depressed and seriously intent on suicide is probably torn between wanting to live and wanting to die—and you can push him toward the "living" side of it.

For suicide to happen, three things must happen: the person must want to die, the person must have the means to carry out his wish (a gun, for instance, or the knowledge and materials to hang himself), and the person must have energy enough to complete the act. Sometimes a person becomes so severely physically and mentally depressed that he can't carry out his own desire to kill himself.

A person who is once suicidal is suicidal forever. Most people who want to kill themselves are, in fact, suicidal for only a limited time. Many can go on to lead normal lives once the suicidal crisis is worked through. The best prognosis occurs for people who only **think** about suicide but do not actually **attempt** it.

If a person attempts suicide but survives, he probably won't attempt it again. The sad facts are these: four out of five people who succeed in committing suicide had made at least one previous attempt. Estimates say that about half of these who try will try again.

The secret lies in getting someone over the "hump;" if you can just pull someone out of a depression, he won't try to kill himself. Unfortunately, that's not always true. It can be baffling: most suicides occur within about three months of an apparent "improvement" in a severely depressed condition. Why? One reason was discussed above—a severely depressed person might not have the sheer energy to carry out his plans. Once he starts to "improve," he gets the energy to follow through.

Terminally ill people are the ones most likely to commit suicide. Knowledge of a terminal illness **can** lead to suicide in some cases—the person decides to take his own life rather than suffer the pain and disfigurement that will accompany a fatal disease. But terminally ill people are not as likely to commit suicide as are chronically ill people—people who are tired of suffering and who see no cure or end to that suffering other than self-destruction. The tendency increases among those over the age of sixty.

Suicide is hereditary. Suicide does tend to "run in families," which has given the mistaken idea that it is (or can be) genetically inherited. It is **not** a genetic trait. However, since members of families tend to share the same emotional climate, and since coping can be a learned skill, suicide can be more common in some families then in others. The suicide of one family member tends to increase the risk among other family members—a person who is suffering from a deep depression sees that her mother ended her suffering through suicide, and she does the same.

The most common method of suicide is drug overdose. That's not true. The leading cause of death among suicide victims is gunshot wounds; those who take drugs are less often successful.

Most suicides happen late at night. That's not true, for a very simple reason—most suicidal people don't really want to die.

The attempt at suicide is a plea for help in many cases, not an actual, intentional act of destruction. As a result, many suicides (and suicidal attempts) happen in late afternoon or early evening, when friends and family members are most likely to discover the victim and "save" him. A woman might overdose on sleeping pills at 4:30 p.m., for example, when she knows that her husband will be home by 5:15 and will be able to intervene and save her (but, of course, he will immediately stop doing whatever it is that has driven her to this extreme). Only those who are truly intent on dying attempt suicide late at night, when sleeping friends and family members aren't around to intervene.

You should never talk about suicide to someone who is depressed, because you'll give him ideas. Don't worry—those ideas probably already exist. If a person has not seriously considered suicide, your talking about it won't plant those ideas in his head. On the contrary: the act of talking about suicidal ideas helps a person work through them. It helps him bring them to the surface, where he can confront them and work through them with directness and honesty. Someone who is dropping clues, however subtle, will be relieved to talk about it.

The Incidence of Suicide

Recent estimates[3] suggest that approximately 30,000 Americans each year take their own lives, and that the number is rapidly increasing. Suicide among those aged fifteen to twenty-four seems to be skyrocketing: in the thirty years between 1950 and 1980, the rate for suicides in that age group increased 284 percent. In 1984, approximately 5,000 adolescents succeeded in killing themselves, and an additional quarter of a million tried unsuccessfully.

Unfortunately, suicide is like child abuse—it is probably grossly underreported. Sympathetic doctors and coroners want to save family members embarrassment, so many suicides are probably passed off as "accidents."

Suicide now ranks ninth among major causes of death;[4] it might rank as high as fifth, some experts believe, if reporting procedures were stricter. More people in the United States kill themselves than kill others—an average of eighty each day die at their own hands. Many experts think that those figures represent only the "tip of the iceberg" in suicide. For every 30,000 who commit suicide each year according to government-certified figures, they say, there are probably 70,000 others whose deaths are not correctly reported, 300,000 attempts, 3 million who threaten to commit suicide, 30 million who are engaged in indirect self-destructive behavior (such as alcoholism or smoking), and 120 million survivors.[5]

According to the latest figures released by the World Health Organization,[6] the United States ranks eighth in the incidence of suicide, with a rate of 12.5 suicides per 100,000 population. Hungary is first, with 45.6 suicides per 100,000; following it are Denmark, Austria, and West Germany. The lowest country reporting is Greece, with only 3.3 suicides per 100,000 population.

The Types of Suicide

Experts studying suicide have identified four general kinds of suicide that help to understand the reasons behind suicide. Those four general categories are as follows:[7]

Referred Suicide

Referred suicide is the type most commonly thought of: the person perceives himself to be a failure because he becomes overwhelmed by what he **imagines** others are thinking of him. He has a difficult time establishing and maintaining personal relationships, because he is convinced that he is of little value to himself or to others. He becomes fearful, lonely, and helpless.

He suffers a crisis in self-concept because he believes that he is not living up to the expectations of others. This kind of suicide is called a "referred suicide" because of the concept of "referred pain"—pain is actually experienced at some distance from its actual source. (An elbow injury may manifest itself as pain in the little finger, for example.)

Surcease Suicide

A surcease suicide occurs because the victim wants to be released from emotional or physical pain. This kind of suicide seems very logical and rational—who wants to endure pain? For some reason, life has become too great a burden to bear, too painful an experience. The woman who faces increasing pain and disfigurement from cancer may choose to end her own life. The teenager who battles drug addiction and becomes convinced that he will never be freed from it may choose to end his own life. The widower who is left without family or friends and who faces a bleak financial future in his sixties may choose to end his own life.

In almost all cases, there **are** alternatives to suicide, but the suicidal victim doesn't understand that. He truly believes that he has no other options. He may not know that those options are available, or he may believe that they are inadequate. So he chooses suicide as a way to end the suffering.

Cultural Suicide

In some cultures, suicide is accepted—or even expected. The **kamikaze** pilot intentionally flew to his own death to destroy the enemy; he was considered a brave hero for his sacrifice to his homeland. The ritual medieval Japanese **hara-kiri** or **seppuku** was a form of suicide that was expected when a warrior (samurai) was disgraced in battle or when he was instructed to use the suicide as a statement of protest. Certain classes in India were expected to practice **suttee**—the wife of a nobleman was expected to throw herself on his funeral pyre. Recently,

Buddhist monks protesting the Vietnamese War set themselves on fire to protest government policies. One of the most famous cultural suicides was the mass suicide of more than 900 people in Jonestown, Guyana, who drank cyanide-laced fruit punch in November 1978 at the directive of their leader, the Reverend Jim Jones.

Psychotic Suicide

Psychotic suicide, as the name implies, occurs in a patient who is psychotic—usually clinically diagnosed as having schizophrenia or manic-depressive psychosis. The suicide usually occurs without an intention to die, but instead as a desire to get rid of the psychosis or to "punish" himself for some reason. Because the patient is not rational, he cannot distinguish the fact that his attempts will indeed result in death.

Subintentional Suicide

Not one of the four categories, "subintentional suicide" is a fifth type of suicide that is often not recognized as a suicide. In subintentional suicide, the person plays a partial, covert, or subliminal (and often unconscious) role in his own destruction. But because of the circumstances surrounding the death, it can't really be classified as "natural" or "accidental."

There are many examples of subintentional suicide. Some people "experiment" or flirt with death (such as a person who experiments with a dangerous drug), even though they have no real intent to die. Others constantly take risks—speed down a narrow canyon, skydive in adverse conditions, swim in water that is too deep. Others hasten their own death by failing to safeguard their health (through proper nutrition and precautions against disease) or by getting involved in substance abuse (especially drugs and alcohol).

Subintentional suicide can occur when a person loses the "will to live," making it easy for death to occur by putting up little resistance to it. In other cases, a great fear of death actually leads to death (for example, a person who is terrified of being hospitalized because "people in hospitals die" could die as a result of being admitted to the hospital).

Characteristics of Suicidal People

What kind of a person is most likely to commit suicide?

No one particular kind of person commits suicide. Suicide crosses all ages, races, cultures, sexes, and creeds with seeming little respect. But there **are** certain characteristics that tend to make a person a higher risk for suicide, and those characteristics can be identified and studied. If we were to create a "profile" of a suicidal person, it would include the following:

Age. Generally, risk increases with age. Suicide is unusual in those younger than fifteen, although it does occur. It is highest among those over the age of sixty. Groups at particular risk include adolescents, college-age students, and middle-aged people of both sexes.

Sex. Women attempt suicide three times more often than men do, but twice as many men actually succeed in committing suicide (probably because men tend to choose more deadly methods).

Race. Blacks attempt suicide more often, but whites are more successful at completing the suicide. Among adolescents and young adults, the rate is about even between blacks and whites; as age increases, the rate among whites increases sharply. American Indians generally have the highest rate of completed suicides of any racial group in the United States, although the rate varies sharply from tribe to tribe.

Marital status. People who are married have a lower suicide rate than people who are not married (whether they have never been married, are separated, divorced, or widowed). Those who have recently lost a companion are at the highest risk for suicide. Among those who are single, the rate is highest among those who are divorced or separated and lowest among those who are widowed.

Health. Those who are ill are at a higher risk—especially if they suffer from an illness that is painful, pimiting, disabling, or chronic. Those who suffer from imagined illness are also at risk. Any illness or surgery that changes self-image (such as a mastectomy or hysterectomy) also increases the risk for suicide.

Stress. A person who is under significant amount of stress is at a high risk of suicide, especially if the stress stems from medical illness or the loss of a loved one.[8] In determining what kind of stress might make a person more prone to suicide, it is important to determine the person's needs and values and his reaction to the stress. A person who is strong and independent, for example, would probably be less prone to suicide following the death of a spouse than would a person who is passive, weak, and dependent. A person who places great value on physical appearance would be more at risk for suicide following a physically disfiguring illness than would a person who places greater value on intellect or personality.

Depression. The highest incidence of suicide occurs among those who are depressed—so much so, in fact, that depression is considered to be a major cause of suicide. Interestingly, suicide does not correspond with severity of depression, because suicide takes more energy than a severely depressed person can summon. As mentioned, the highest rates of suicide generally occur in the initial "recovery" phases from severe depression. Depression is especially indicative when it occurs in conjunction with insomnia, memory loss, restlessness, agitation, and feelings of helplessness or hopelessness.[9]

Approximately 70 percent of those who attempt suicide have been diagnosed as being depressed,[10] but remember that many depressed people never attempt or commi suicide.

Recent loss. The recent loss of something important to the person places the person at a higher risk for suicide. For men, the most significant is a loss in professional status (which includes the occurrence of retirement) or a change in financial status (which also often includes retirement). For women, the most significant loss is the end of a relationship. The loss may be real or imagined. It can include things such as the death of a loved one, the termination of a friendship, the loss of vitality or health, the loss of social status, or the loss of security.

Use of drugs and/or alcohol. There are several reasons why a person who uses drugs and/or alcohol is at highest risk. First, use of drugs and alcohol indicates low impulse control in general and a low tolerance for frustration and stress. Second, a person who is intoxicated or under the influence of drugs has significantly lowered control—he may act "on impulse" in a suicidal mood. Third, the alcohol and drugs themselves provide the means by which to end life.

Isolation. Those who are socially isolated run a much higher risk than those who have well-structured support networks. The recent loss of a companion makes those who are isolated at an even greater risk.

Previous suicide attempts. Those who have attempted suicide are likely to try it again; they are at a higher risk. Also at risk are those whose family members have attempted or successfully committed suicide—especially if the family member is of the same gender.

Social/religious activity. People who do not enjoy any kind of activity in social or religious organizations are at a higher risk, mostly because such inactivity increases their isoation and loneliness. The specific religious group does not seem to be as important in determining risk as the level of the individual's participation in the religion.

Profession. Members of some professions are at a markedly higher risk for suicide than members of other professions. Those at highest risk include medical doctors, dentists, lawyers, and members of the helping professions (including nurses, firefighters, policemen, paramedics, and emergency medical technicians, in addition to psychologists, therapists, and psychiatrists).

Sexual preference. Homosexuals are at a higher risk for suicide than are heterosexuals.

Ability to communicate. Traditionally, those at a high risk for suicide are those who are not able to communicate their thoughts and feelings freely with others. People who are conditioned and able to share their joys, frustrations, sorrows, ecstacies, and concerns are less likely to commit suicide than those who are afraid to become "vulnerable" through communication.

The Most Common Methods

The first decision that a suicidal person makes is to commit suicide. The second—and equally important—is the choice of a method. The method chosen determines how quickly death will occur and, therefore, how much time a helper has to intervene and prevent the death. The method also determines the seriousness of the suicide: a person who chooses a slow-acting, unsure method (such as slashing the wrists) is probably less intent on actually dying than is a person who shoots a loaded gun into his forehead.

While experts disagree as to the exact order of lethality of various methods, all experts agree that firearms and explosives (including gunshots) are the most lethal method—the method most likely to result in death. One of the most recognized experts in suicidology ranks the methods in order of lethality as follows:[11]

1. Firearms and explosives
2. Jumping from a high place
3. Cutting vital organs
4. Hanging
5. Drowning (if the person does not know how to swim)
6. Poison (both solid and liquid)
7. Cutting of nonvital organs
8. Drowning (if the person does know how to swim)

9. Poisoning (with gas, such as carbon monoxide)
10. Analgesic substances (pain medications)

A different ranking proposed by a different expert rates the following methods from most lethal to least lethal:[12]

1. Firearms and explosives
2. Carbon monoxide
3. Hanging
4. Drowning
5. Plastic bag (suffocation)
6. Jumping from a high place
7. Fire
8. Poison
9. Drugs
10. Gas
11. Cutting

Obviously, the lethality depends on the application. A gunshot wound to the head or heart will be much more lethal than one to the hand or foot. A deep slashing cut through the spleen or liver will be much more quickly lethal than a shallow cut to the arm or leg.

According to studies,[13] those who survive a suicide attempt with a highly lethal method are less likely to attempt suicide again than those who survive with a less lethal method. Those who tried to commit suicide by suffocating on a plastic bag, inhaling carbon monoxide, or drowning are most likely to try again; those who survived attempts with wrist-slashing drug taking, hanging, or burning are least likely to try again.

A number of facors influence the person's choice of method. An obvious factor is availability; a woman might have access to prescription sleeping pills but not a handgun. Experience and familiarity. are other factors; a policeman who has a handgun and knows how to use it might be inclined to shoot himself, and a pharmacist who understands the ways drugs act might be inclined to use drugs. Some people consider the impact on survivors when choosing a method. Those who want to avoid hurting their loved ones may choose a clean, quiet, less shocking method than someone who wants to communicate rage, hostility, and revenge.

Finally, an individual may choose a particular method because of symbolism or imagery. A woman may choose to overdose on tranquilizers because that's the way her mother committed suicide. A man may choose to drown because he envisions it as a fluid way of becoming one again with the universe. Another person may mimic the method chosen by a movie star or rock idol.

Suicide Methods Among Children

Most experts agree that the most common method used by children to commit suicide is drugs and/or poisons; obviously, the drugs must be available to the child, and the child must know something about the dangers of indiscriminate drug use. (Usually the drug was prescribed for an adult in the home, but sometimes a child will overdose on a drug that was prescribed for him. In many cases, drugs have been present in the home for a number of years.)

Obviously, children must choose methods that are accessible and possible; a child, then, chooses a method that he can carry off, such as running in front of a speeding car on a busy street. In one study encompassing a large number of child suicides, the most common methods were the following, in order from most to least common:[14]

1. Narcotic drugs (the overwhelming favorite)
2. Cutting
3. Hanging and strangulation
4. Poisoning with gas
5. Jumping from a height
6. Drowning (tied with jumping)
7. Running in front of a moving vehicle
8. Swallowing a sharp object (tied with running in front of a vehicle)
9. Shooting (children have less access to guns and less experience in how to handle them, which explains the popularity of other methods of suicide among children)

Use of narcotic drugs is the most common method among both boys and girls. Following narcotic drug overdose, boys prefer hanging; girls prefer cutting themselves. In third place among boys is cutting, and in third place among girls is poisoning with gas.

Suicide Methods Among Adolescents

The choice of methods among adolescents is different than the choice of methods among children. While the use of narcotics (mainly barbiturates) is the preferred choice among girls, boys do not demonstrate a single "favorite" method. Many studies show that adolescent boys tend to use a variety of active, fairly unique methods (such as jumping under a bus, electrocution, or decapitation). The results of one study[15] showed that gas poisoning was the most favored method among both boys and girls, but another study showed that male adolescents prefer firearms and hanging while female adolescents prefer poison.

Poison (including drugs, such as barbiturates) is the most frequent method of both attempted and successful suicides among adolescents.

Why People Choose Suicide

Almost everyone feels despair, hopelessness, frustration, or depression at some time or other in life. For most, it is a fleeting emotion; most people muster up their resources and deal with the situation at hand. Some people even contemplate suicide in a brief, inexact way ("I wonder what it would be like to kill myself?"), but never take the thought seriously or decide to act on it.

What, then, causes some people to go in a direction of self-destruction? What makes some people determined to go through with a suicidal thought? What makes some people unable to find other ways of coping with problems?

No single answer can explain all suicides. The decision to commit suicide comes about as an extremely personal reaction to a complex combination of thoughts, feelings, situations, and reactions. Each suicide, then, is intensely unique.

While suicide is personal and unique and stems from a countless variety of causes, researchers have been able to identify five basic patterns that explain some of the most common factors causing suicide:[16]

Suicide as a reaction to loss of a loved one. Suicide may follow the loss of someone who is important in the person's life; often the suicide follows a recent loss, but in some cases the loss may have occurred years earlier. Most often, the loss involves a spouse, parent, sibling, or extremely close friend; most often the loss is through death, but it can also occur through divorce, physical separation, or termination of a relationship. The person who is left behind decides that "life isn't worth living" without the loved one; life, in fact, becomes meaningless and overwhelmingly lonely. As time goes on, the feelings of loneliness and sadness intensify. The suicide is seen as a way of ending the loneliness and achieving some sort of magical reunion with the loved one. (Elderly people often commit suicide on the birthday or date of death of a deceased spouse.)

Suicide as a way to escape suffering. Suicide may be committed as a way to escape intolerable suffering. Sometimes the suffering is physical; the person may be stricken with a physical illness or disease that causes intolerable pain (suicide in this case is especially common if the disease is chronic, and is likely if the disease is terminal). But the pain doesn't always have to be physical; sometimes the suffering is emotional. A person who feels deep despair or emotional anguish may decide that things will never get better and may opt for suicide as a way to end the suffering.

Suicide as an impulsive reaction. In many cases, suicide is the result of a long, involved chain of events, and the suicide itself has been carefully considered, even down to the minute details of the method and execution. In some cases, however, the suicide is an impulsive act committed in reaction to a major disappointment or frustration. The person suffers a sudden and extensive blow to his pride, confidence, or self-esteem; it's too great to bear, and he reacts with suicide (the only way he can see to escape the humiliation and embarrassment). There are plenty of examples of impulsive suicide. A businessman faces communitywide humiliation when his business fails. A woman who has planned for years to be an attorney fails her bar exam. A man who wanted to be a doctor his entire life cannot get admitted to medical school.

Suicide as a way of controlling others. In this kind of suicide, the person doesn't really want to die—instead, he wants to change the way other people treat him. He's trying to communicate an important message. He makes a dramatic attempt on his own life as a way of telling his wife that he needs more attention, affection, and caring from her. A man may make a dramatic attempt on his own life to punish his father for being so stern and unfeeling. A woman who is rejected by a lover may attempt suicide to make him feel guilty. An adolescent who is angry at his parents may make a dramatic, public suicide attempt as a way of embarrassing and hurting them. Suicide can be used to communicate the need for sympathy, understanding, affection, or concern; it can also be used to express rage, anger, and hostility.

Suicide as a reaction to depression. As mentioned, depression is the most common cause of suicide. Because a person is depressed, he doesn't realize that his feelings are part of the depression—and that once the depression is under control, those feelings will disappear. To him, life becomes an intolerable burden, a painful and humiliating experience that is not worth enduring. Because depression also clouds the ability to reason, the person does not see any other alternative. He chooses suicide as a way of escaping his pain and discouragement.

It's important to realize that depression can vary in intensity and effect. Some depression is characterized by mild discouragement and downheartedness; its victims feel unhappy, discouraged, and pessimistic and usually lose interest in social interactions. On the other end of the scale is severe depression, characterized by utter feelings of hopelessness and despair; the victims of severe depression become preoccupied with their own worthlessness and weakness. People who are severely depressed often lose all initiative, suffer from physical complaints, feel disoriented or confused, and lose interest in living.

Depression also varies greatly in duration. Some people may be severely depressed for a month; others may be mildly depressed for years. Those most prone to suicide are those who have been moderately to severely depressed for a long period of time—they see no other way to escape their depression.

Critical to understanding depression and suicide is realizing that severely depressed people often become convinced that they need to be "punished" for some wrongdoing or for their own worthlessness. Their punishment is carried out in self-destruction.

Events That Lead to Suicide

In addition to the five patterns of suicide just discussed, there are often "precipitating events" that lead up to the decision to commit suicide. Obviously, some suicides occur without apparent reason. Many, however, follow a certain life experience or event that triggers suicidal thought and action. By recognizing these precipitating events, it is possible to take precautions that will help guide the person beyond the suicidal impulse.

In general, suicide may follow the threat of arrest or imprisonment, the diagnosis of major or terminal illness, economic loss (such as bankruptcy or foreclosure), the loss of a loved one (especially a spouse or child), and the termination of a close relationship. Less often, it can occur following the failure to achieve an important goal, a downward change in personal social status, or the occurrence of social isolation.

Men are most prone to commit suicide following the loss of a job (through termination, layoff, or retirement) or some kind of failure on the job (such as the failure to get an important promotion). Women, as stated, react most often to the loss of a personal relationship (especially that of a spouse or lover). The elderly react to financial problems, the fear of becoming a burden to others, forced retirement, the loss of a loved one (leading to loneliness and social isolation), and a feeling of being unwanted. Adolescents react most commonly to family problems; other precipitating events include humiliation with their peers, failure to be accepted by their peers, failure in school, and the loss of a loved one.

The Problem of Ambivalence

A particularly difficult problem associated with suicide is **ambivalence**—a situation in which the person wants to achieve two opposing goals or in which the person both wants something and doesn't want it. The result of ambivalence is extreme indecision and conflict. A woman may be torn regarding her marriage, for example: she may love her husband on the one hand, and want to stay with him; on the other hand, she may hate him and want to leave him. Her resulting anguish and inner conflict can lead to a suicidal state of mind.

Most suicidal people are ambivalent regarding the suicide itself: they want to die, but they want to live. They just don't want to go on living in the same situation. If some alternative came along, they would probably eagerly grasp it and go on living. For many, then, suicide is a way of saying, I don't want to die, but I don't want to go on living like this, either—and the only thing I can think of right now is to die.

Clues to Suicidal Behavior

Suicide usually comes as a great shock to the survivors—they may have had some inkling that the person was unhappy, but *they didn't expect suicide!*

Most often, they should have expected it. Experts believe that approximately 90 percent of all who commit suicide give clues about it first; unfortunately, people don't recognize the clues. They fail to respond.

Just as every suicide is intensely personal and unique, every suicide has its own set of clues. Sometimes a single clue will be given; in other cases, the person may give a host of clues before finally committing suicide. the following may occur alone or in combination with other clues:

—The person may become unconcerned about his personal welfare. He may fail to take necessary precautions, may not make moves to improve his own comfort, may not defend his position in a dispute at the office. He seems to be saying, "I don't matter; who cares about me, anyway?"

—Many people give verbal clues. Sometimes, they directly threaten suicide ("I think I'll just kill myself!"). Often, the clues are more subtle and more difficult to pinpoint. "You'll be sorry you treated me like that when I'm not around anymore." "You'd be better off if I were dead." "Soon I won't have to worry about that anymore." "Don't worry, I won't be making a mess of the family finances much longer." "I don't think we'll need to see a counselor. Things won't be like this for long."

—The person may seem unusually accident-prone. Take special note: they may only **seem** like accidents. In reality, they may be suicide attempts that failed, or they may be minor attempts at self-destruction with which the person is "practicing" in order to build up courage for the real thing. They may also be unconscious attempts at self-destruction.

—The person may undergo a sudden change in his habits, attitudes, or personality. A person who was once confident and aggressive may become passive and withdrawn; a person who was once talkative and happy may become sullen and quiet; a person who was a meticulous housekeeper may begin neglecting the house.

—The person may become depressed. Remember that there are various intensities and durations of depression, but you should watch for behavioral and physical clues that indicate depression. The person may suffer from sleeplessness or other erratic sleep patterns, apathy, anxiety, despair, loss of appetite, frequent headaches, irritability (especially toward others he once enjoyed), hostility (toward himself or others), constant debilitating fatigue, reduced sex drive, withdrawal, sadness, or frequent crying spells.

—A sudden or noticeable decline on the job or in school. Everyone suffers through a rough period once in a while, especially when starting to study a new subject or beginning a new area of responsibility. Watch for a person who doesn't change responsibilities but who suddenly begins to have problems keeping up.

—Be alert for signs of confusion, such as difficulty in concentrating or in thinking clearly. The person may either be deeply depressed or may be so preoccupied with thoughts of his suicide that he can't concentrate on anything else.

—Many suicidal people begin to neglect their appearance and hygiene; after usually being well-groomed and carefully dressed, they may suddenly become dirty, disheveled, or poorly groomed.

—Watch for signs that the person is "putting his affairs in order." He may suddenly draw up a will or purchase a large insurance policy. He may start to organize all his belongings and may clean out drawers or closets. He may suddenly organize or summarize all his projects at work. An especially acute sign is the person who begins giving away treasured possessions.

—The person may lose interest in people or activities that used to interest him. You may notice that he is becoming increasingly withdrawn socially; he may refuse to socialize with people he once enjoyed. He may look for excuses to avoid other people, especially in organized activities.

—The person may joke about suicide. But suicide is no

laughing matter; he may be trying to clothe it in humor while he "tries it on" and assesses other people's reactions to it.

—Many suicide victims become physically ill, are diagnosed as having serious or terminal illnesses, or suffer from physical symptoms of depression. Be especially cautious of someone who seems to have a number of illnesses (even minor ones) that affect different physical systems. Watch, too, for a person who seems to be taking an inordinate amount of time to recover from an illness or accident.

—The person may begin having difficulty in communicating with other people. He may have a difficult time expressing his thoughts and feelings; he may not have an interest in listening to others; he may have a difficult time concentrating. Suicidal people may especially have a hard time establishing or maintaining eye contact with others. Speech may be slow, faltering, or stumbling.

—The person may seem to develop an unusually intense interest in his own problems. He may seem preoccupied with what is happening to him, with little interest in what is happening to others or how others are feeling.

—Certain physical complaints are common in suicidal people. Watch for signs of sleep disturbances, anorexia (loss of appetite, with or without nausea), profound and rapid weight loss, fatigue, loss of energy, muscle weakness, constipation, headache, dizziness, numbness of the extremities, blurred vision, and burning of the eyes. Suicidal people often have convinced themselves that their discomfort is a permanent condition and that they will not recover from whatever is ailing them.

—A suicidal person may weep easily, with seemingly little provocation. (Usually such overemotional response is a sign of depression, but it can also be a sign of deep anguish or upset.)

—The person may become preoccupied with something that happened in the past, usually some wrongdoing or that she committed. She may express how "bad" she is because of it (even though, to you, she obviously has gone on to live an exemplary and productive life). Usually, the wrongdoing is of obvious minor significance to you but seems overwhelming in its severity to the suicidal person.

—The person may become preoccupied with a poor self-image; he may dwell on his faults, his failures, his betrayals, his errors, or his poor judgment. He may seem convinced that he is worthless or that he is a "burden" to someone else.

—A suicidal person may suddenly go on a spending spree, make donations to charities he previously ignored, gamble excessively, or take vacations he has been putting off. He may seem forced and almost desperate to squeeze in as much frenetic activity as he can.

—A suicidal person may be reacting to intense stress or a life crisis. Look for signs of unusually difficult problems that have occurred recently, such as foreclosure, death of a loved one, serious injury or illness, loss of religious faith, stockmarket reverses, bankruptcy, termination of an important relationship, loss of status on the job, threats of incarceration, or any other problem that could lead to stress. Especially look for a person who recently suffered the loss of a loved one to suicide.

—A suicidal person may become preoccupied with thoughts of death. He may talk excessively about death, purchase a funeral plot, talk about his funeral, wonder about a life after death, or read books about death. He is usually still torn between life and death and is trying to make the decision which way to go.

Assessing Risk: How Serious Is the Threat?

Once you've determined that someone may be suicidal, you need to ask him, directly and in a straightforward way, if he is considering killing himself or if he has thought about suicide. That may seem extremely difficult to do, but it is critical: the person is probably ambivalent about death, and you may be able to nudge him toward life if you can get it out in the open.

Some people worry about discussing suicide; they are afraid that they'll plant the idea in someone who wasn't considering suicide to begin with. That's not likely. The suicidal thoughts are probably already there—and if they're not, your simple question or suggestion won't plant them there.

What if the person admits that he is considering suicide?

Your job is to determine how serious he is. One point needs to be made: you should take **every** suicide threat seriously. Many people who commit suicide talk about it first. You should **never** ignore or dismiss a suicide threat. As you may guess, however, there are people who are much more capable of killing themselves than others. You can pinpoint those who are at extremely high risk by asking a few questions and considering a few factors:

—Ask the person if he has a plan for committing suicide. If he has vague, fleeting thoughts about suicide but no concrete plan, his risk is low; if he has more frequent thoughts and has had occasional ideas about a specific plan, his risk is greater. At high risk is the individual who thinks a great deal about suicide and has formulated a detailed, carefully thought-out plan. ("I am going to get Ed's rifle from the cabinet in the attic, drive down to the marshes near the lake, lock the doors, and shoot myself through my mouth. I'm going to do it on a Friday night when everyone is out late, so they won't miss me until the next morning.") The person is at a higher risk, obviously, if the method he has chosen is a highly lethal one (such as a gunshot) and if he has access to the equipment he will need to carry out his plan.

—The person is at extremely high risk if he has attempted suicide in the past, especially if the method he chose then was not a particularly lethal one.

—Ask the person if he plans on trying to commit suicide again. Ask him if he plans on using the same method, or if he has chosen a new one. If he has chosen a different one, ask him in detail about it. If, for example, he tried to slash his wrists before but is now planning on shooting himself, find out everything you can. Does he have a gun, or know where to get one? Does he have ammunition? Does he know how to use a gun? When is he planning on doing it? Where? If he has access to a gun and ammunition, knows how to use it, and can supply the details of a specific plan, he is at high risk.

—If the person attempted suicide before, find out how he feels about his failure to complete the act. Find out how he was rescued—and whether he intended to be rescued. A person who felt relieved about being rescued is at lower risk than a person who felt hostile and angry; a person who intended on being rescued is at lower risk than a person who was accidentally discovered and rescued. A high risk would be suffered by a person who took a bottle of sleeping pills while her husband was in another state on business and while her only child was away at camp, and who was accidentally discovered by unexpected visitors. She didn't intend on being alive; she is alive by accident. You can bet she'll be more careful this time.

—Ask the person how she feels toward the significant people in her life. Those who are at the highest risk will feel isolated, cut off, withdrawn, or unimportant to significant people in their lives; they may report that others don't care about them, that they are a burden, or that people would be better off without them. Those who have healthy, vigorous relationships at the time are at a lower risk.

—Ask the person about recent losses or troubling experiences. Those at highest risk will have suffered stressful incidents (such as divorce, failure in school, termination on the job, or loss of a loved one). Those at lower risk will probably still be feeling stress but may not be going through intense life crises.

—Ask the person if he is using alcohol or drugs. Those at highest risk are using one or both.

—Ask the person if he is physically ill or if he has been to visit a doctor within the last three months. Those at highest risk are suffering from chronic or severely painful illnesses; also at high risk are people who have a number of less serious illnesses that affect different body systems simultaneously. High risk is also suffered by people who imagine themselves to have various illnesses and who visit the doctor frequently in an attempt to get help.

—A person who lives alone (whether she is single, divorced, separated, or widowed) is at high risk; a person who lives with others, especially if she is a member of a large, active family, is at less risk.

—A person with hostile feelings is at a much higher risk than a person who is passive or has only a few hostile thoughts and feelings. The degree of hostility can usually be directly correlated with the success of a suicide attempt. (Those who are angry and hostile usually choose a dramatic, shocking way of committing suicide so as to have the greatest possible impact on survivors; a hostile person will probably outline details of that plan for you.)

—Ask the person how long he has had suicidal thoughts. If he's had them for a few days or a few weeks, he is at lower risk; if he has had them for a few months or for years, he is at higher risk. Generally, the longer the person has thought about committing suicide, the more dangerous his situation.

—Ask the person if she is taking medication. Generally, a person is at high risk if she is taking medication and does not feel as though the medication is "working" or having the desired effect (regardless of what the medication is for).

—Find out if the person has recently been discharged from the hospital. The period just following hospitalization for depression can be a critical time; doctors think that recovery has begun when, in reality, the person is just now getting enough strength to follow through with a suicidal thought.

—Determine whether the person seems cogent and in control

of his thought processes; a person who is disorganized, disoriented, or confused runs a much greater risk of following through with suicide.

—Are you talking to a man or a woman, and how old is the person? Generally, an older male is at the highest risk, while a younger female is at the lowest risk. (Obviously, this is a generalization; you need to consider other risk factors as well.)

—Find out whether the person knows anyone else who has committed suicide. If so, his risk is automatically higher. The risk is highest if a member of the family (especially a parent or spouse) committed suicide.

—Ask the person if he would consider getting help, or if he has tried to get help in the past. The highest risk is faced by those who do not believe they can be helped and by those who have had unsuccessful or dissatisfying experiences with therapists or therapy programs in the past. Consider the person an extremely high risk if he tells you that no help is available and that no one wants to be of help.

Suicide Notes

Suicide notes have traditionally prompted great curiosity and interest, even though, it is estimated that less than one-fourth of all those who commit suicide leave a written explanation of their act.[17]

Suicide notes often provide clues about the despair that was being suffered, and some suicide notes offer an explanation about what was going on. But most suicide notes are extremely disappointing because they rarely tell the whole story. Most suicide notes, in fact, raise more questions than they answer.

Survivors usually have a more difficult time with the suicide if a note has been left. Regardless of the tone, the survivor cannot respond. The dead person, in a very real sense, had "the last word." And many notes are full of hostility, blame, and hatred. Many notes are left, in fact, in an attempt to make the survivors feel guilty over the death.

Some notes are just the opposite: they stress that the suicide was "no one's fault," and they go to great lengths to absolve the survivors of any responsibility. Some notes attempt to explain the reasoning behind the suicide. A majority of notes, interestingly, contain instructions to family members or friends to be carried out after the suicide; sometimes these seem incredibly mundane ("remember to have the car serviced next week, and make sure to get the dripping faucet in the small bathroom repaired."). Some suicide notes contain instructions for distribution of the person's possessions. A few are nothing but philosophical ramblings, usually defending the right to commit suicide.

Genuine suicide notes usually have a few things in common:[18] they contain marked dichotomies in logic, they display a blend of hostility toward others and self-blame, they give specific instructions to survivors, they include specific names, and they communicate a sense of decisiveness about the suicide. Most contain references to ambivalence—usually a love-hate ambivalence toward a survivor or an ambivalence toward dying on the part of the suicidal person.

Suicide Among Children

As painful as it may be to admit, children do suffer the deep kind of despair that causes them to take their own lives. Unfortunately, we don't know exactly where we stand when it comes to suicide among children—the National Office of Vital Statistics does not compile statistics for suicide deaths in children under the age of ten. It was once believed that young children were incapable of committing suicide; we are gradually becoming aware that they **are** capable—and that they **do** take their own lives. Psychiatrists have found evidence of self-destructive behavior in children as young as two and a half.[19]

Psychiatrists working with preschoolers have identified

various suicidal patterns and methods in a group once considered too young to even comprehend death. Their most common methods? Running in front of fast-moving cars, jumping from high places, falling down stairs, and gulping pills—most of which are often mistaken for accidents.[20]

Those who have studied the problems associated with child suicide give a stern admonition: ask a child what happened. Most children will tell you. Following that philosophy, two poison control centers in Nebraska decided to ask children about the circumstances surrounding their ingestion of poison. Their chilling conclusion? Approximately 72 percent of the children who ingested poison did so as either a suicide gesture or a suicide attempt.[21] Today, suicide is finally recognized as one of the leading causes of death among children under the age of fifteen.

Why They Do It

Most adults commit suicide in response to feelings of despair, depression, hopelessness, or helplessness. The reasons are much the same for children. Experts have identified the following reasons for suicide in children:

—Children commit suicide to escape a situation of ongoing physical, emotional, or sexual abuse. Suicide is especially common in cases of sexual abuse: because the abuse is almost always kept quiet, the child feels helpless and despairs of ever being "rescued" from the situation by outsiders.

—A child may commit suicide in an attempt to manipulate his parents, especially if they are divorced, separated, or in the process of undergoing deep marital conflict.

—Children commit suicide in response to chaotic family situations. A child may be moved frequently from town to town, may have one or two alcoholic parents in the home, may have a parent who is emotionally ill, or may suffer disorganization because of divorce or separation of his parents.

—A child may commit suicide to escape feelings of deep despair. Those feelings can be brought on by a variety of things: failure to do well in school, failure to win an award in the science fair, rejection by a friend, loss of a parent or sibling, loss of a favorite grandparent, loneliness, the inability to make or keep friends, the loss of a favorite pet, rejection by parents, or the serious illness of a family member. Often, as with adults, these situations are real, but they are also often imagined. A child may be convinced that he is inadequate and that no one likes him, when in reality he is well-liked by most members of his class at school.

—Children commit suicide in response to a poor relationship with parents. In many cases, the child cannot communicate with her parents, does not feel as though her parents love her, is harshly disciplined by her parents, is constantly criticized by her parents, and is convinced that she can never "measure up" in their eyes. Again, this may be real or perceived.

—Just like adults, children may commit suicide as an act of anger or fear.

—A child may commit suicide in response to an acute conflict between him and his parents. (Some authorities believe that such acute conflict is the leading cause of suicide in children.[22]

—Children commit suicide in response to loss of a love object, such as a pet or a friend. For too long adults surmised that a child's infatuation was a harmless expression of puppy love, but nothing that was long-lasting or significant. Research now indicates that a child whose "puppy love" is crushed can indeed feel deep enough despair to cause suicide.

—A child who is convinced that she is not bright enough to handle the rigors of school may commit suicide to escape embarrassment, fear, humiliation, and degradation. Failures at school can lead to suicide, especially if parents consistently belittle the child for the failures or continue to hold unreasonably high expectations.

—Sexual conflict in children can lead to suicide; many suicide victims struggled with masturbation, menstruation, or homosexual feelings. Some children commit suicide when they learn they are pregnant.

—Children commit suicide to "punish" others, just as adults sometimes do. These children are usually extremely angry and are seeking revenge. Some children also seek to "punish" themselves because they have convinced themselves that they are worthless.

—While not common, some children who commit suicide are truly psychotic. Interestingly, psychotic children attempt or threaten suicide more often than they succeed at it.

Warning Signs Among Children

Children display many of the same signs as adults. Especially watch for children who have trouble sleeping, develop problems concentrating, suddenly begin having problems at school, develop a fear of going to school, become serious un- derachievers, or display signs of depression. Children who are depressed often cry frequently or show signs of hyperactivity.

Watch for a child who suddenly withdraws and who prefers to play alone for long periods of time instead of enjoying the company of friends. Watch for a child who has a difficult time making friends and who cannot seem to keep them. A child who believes she is "different" or "undesirable" is also at risk.

Children with behavioral problems are also at risk. Look for a loss of interest in previously interesting activities, loss of appetite, morbid ideas, severe separation anxiety, a sense of helplessness, antisocial activities (such as biting), aggressive behavior, hostile behavior, and signs of sadistic or masochistic behavior. Children who are suicidal frequently express surprisingly morbid ideas, and the majority of them suffer from serious nightmares.

Suicide Among Adolescents

As with children, official suicide figures are difficult to obtain for adolescents: suicides are underreported, usually to save the family from embarrassment, or are confused as accidents. Recent estimates, however, are disturbing: some feel that as many as 7,000 teenagers each year commit suicide, while an additional 400,000 try it.[23] Suicide among adolescents—those fifteen to twenty-four years of age—has skyrocketed, the fastest growing among any population. One expert believes that at least a million adolescents each year think seriously about committing suicide.[24]

Why They Do It

Adolescents suffer from many of the same problems as adults, especially in a society that has exposed adolescents to many adult pressures and stresses. Some additional factors can result in adolescent suicides:

—A void of meaningful relationships in the adolescent's life. In one study, 75 percent of those who survived a suicide attempt expressed extreme loneliness and the feeling that "no one really cared about or understood" them. Sadly, 88 percent of all adolescent suicides occur in the home, with parents in the next room, but those adolescents are convinced that their parents do not care.[25]

—Difficulty in maintaining friendships. The teenager may be extremely isolated, withdrawn, or lonely.

—The presence of physical or sexual abuse in the home. Sexual abuse is particularly at fault, as with children; the teenager may decide that suicide is the only way to escape the situation.

—Loss of a significant person (a parent, sibling, grandparent, friend, teacher, or favorite pet). Teenagers also commit suicide in response to a perceived loss of recognition, status, physical attractiveness, or control. An adolescent who feels that he has no control over his life may choose to end it.

—Acute problems with parents. Most teenagers have problems "relating" to their parents at one time or another, but a teenager whose parents are a constant source of grief, abuse, miscommunication, punishment, and degradation may not be able to cope with the breakdown of that most significant relationship.

—Sexual problems. A teenager may commit suicide because he fears he is a homosexual; she may end her life because she learns she is pregnant. She may not be able to deal with menstruation. Both boys and girls may commit suicide because of fear or confusion surrounding masturbation. Teenagers are particularly prone to commit suicide when they are rejected by a friend with whom they have had sexual intercourse.

—Problems in the family or the home. As with children, teenagers may react with suicide to problems such as marital conflicts, separation, divorce, or chronic chaos in the home.

—Severe depression. Depression ranks across the board as a leading cause of suicide. At special risk are adolescents who are convinced that they are worthless, those who suffer from low self-esteem, and those who have suffered a series of failures or rejections. To an adolescent, these may be overwhelming.

A Special Note

Pay special attention to an adolescent who asks for help. Adolescence is normally a period of increasing independence and a desire for self-reliance; asking for help is **not** a normal adolescent behavior. Most adolescents want privacy; most also want to make it on their own. You can consider an adolescent's plea for help as a serious sign of high risk.[26]

Suicide Among the Elderly

Even though there has been a decline in the suicide rate among the elderly over the past thirty years,[27] the tendency toward suicide increases with age. Major causes of suicide among the elderly include the following:

—An elderly person who has enjoyed independence may commit suicide because it becomes apparent that he can no longer be independent. He may fear becoming a "burden" to others.

—Suicide may seem the only option in the face of diminishing financial capabilities; many living on a fixed income can no longer provide their basic needs, such as food, shelter, and heat.

—An elderly person may commit suicide out of loneliness. In many cases, the loss of a spouse becomes overwhelming, even though the spouse died years earlier. The elderly react to loneliness and isolation more than other age groups.

—The elderly frequently commit suicide because of diminishing health and the diminishing ability to function. Elderly people may be disturbed because they lose their eyesight, hearing, mobility, memory, or intellectual function. Others may become crippled with chronic, painful disease; with no cure or hope for improvement in the future, they commit suicide as a way to end the suffering.

—An elderly person may commit suicide in response to a diminished sense of belonging or a diminished status in society. Once a flourishing, contributing member of society, he may now view himself as "driftwood."

—Elderly people may commit suicide because they feel they have been abandoned by their families.

—An elderly person may, because of advanced medical techniques, literally outlive his resources. He may live long beyond the point where he has the money, energy, and ability to live on his own. Many elderly people commit suicide rather than face the future in an institution.

A Special Note

Elderly people are usually the most stubborn when it comes to suicide. Even when attempts are made to reduce loneliness, isolation, withdrawal, pain, or financial destitution, those who have attempted suicide usually keep on trying until they are successful. The risk of suicide is generally considered to be high among lonely, isolated, or ill older people.

The Chronically Suicidal [28]

Most of what has been discussed has centered on suicide as a reaction to crisis—a person commits suicide to escape pain, to get away from abuse in the home, to seek revenge against someone who has hurt him, to east depression, or to avoid humiliation. Most cases of suicide are just that: the response to crisis. In most cases of suicide, it appeared to be the only alternative.

Occasionally, people will become what is known as **chronically suicidal.** Instead of attempting or committing suicide in response to a particular crisis (such as divorce or death of a spouse), they adopt suicide as a **habitual or chronic coping mechanism.** For these people, a suicidal attempt becomes a generalized coping mechanism; it is an adaptive response. In a normal person, the suicidal crisis is time-limited; in the chronically suicidal, it is a way of life.

Attempts to help the chronically suicidal are usually dismal failures. Why? It's a situation of reinforcement. When someone steps in to help, they are nurtured; in order to get nurturance again, they will attempt suicide again. Diagnosis of chronically suicidal people is difficult and time-consuming, and treatment is extremely difficult, usually requiring long-term care.

Suicide Prevention

Suicide prevention is as complex and individual as is suicide: for each person, unique kinds of things need to be done. A person who is committing suicide in response to devastating loneliness, for example, needs help in battling the loneliness. A child who attempts suicide to escape sexual abuse in the home needs to be removed from the situation (or needs to have the offending adult removed from the situation) followed by long-term therapy to cope with the situation.

In general, suicide prevention depends on the ability to recognize suicidal potential and the willingness to present alternatives to the individual. People desperately need to be educated about suicide—need to know that it is okay to feel depressed, and that help is available. The key to suicide prevention lies with people who are alert to the clues and willing to get involved.

A Special Note

Not all suicide is accomplished with guns, ropes, knives, or pills. Not all suicide takes place quickly. Not all suicide is even recognized as suicide. Why? There is an entire range of self-destructive behavior that leads to death just as surely as a shotgun wound to the head or a bottle of sleeping pills. Unfortunately, it is not often recognized as suicide—either by its victims or by those who associate with its victims. It encompasses things like drug abuse. Alcoholism. Cigarette smoking. Extreme obesity. Prostitution. Extreme risk-taking. Gambling. A diabetic's inattention to diet and exercise, or the failure to take insulin injections on schedule. A heart patient's refusal to walk a mile each afternoon, as instructed by his doctor. Driving while intoxicated. Involvement in high-risk sports, such a skydiving, hang gliding, and scuba diving. Committing crime.

Because such self-destruction is often unconscious or

subconscious, it is extremely difficult to diagnose and can present real challenges for treatment.

Responding to Suicide

While suicide is a complex, frightening, and difficult situation to confront, there is one basic principle that should guide your efforts: **always take every suicide threat seriously.** Never assume that an individual is just "overreacting" or "panicking" or "temporarily losing control." Always assume that the person genuinely wants to end his life—and take measures to protect him.

In responding to a suicidal person, follow these guidelines:

—**Never leave the person alone.** Make sure that someone else is with the person during response, during treatment for injury, during transport, and after you leave. Sometimes a person is doggedly determined to end his life—and a person who is that determined will usually succeed. But the overwhelming majority of suicide attempts are made by people undergoing a short-term crisis—people who don't really want to die but don't know how else to handle the crisis. Refusing to leave the person alone gives him a chance to figure out alternatives.

—**Treat life-threatening injuries.** Handle life-threatening injuries as quickly and expeditiously as possible; restore breathing and heartbeat, and control bleeding if necessary.

—**Treat other injuries if appropriate.**

—**Don't try to talk the person out of his feelings.** He's probably ambivalent: he wants to die, but he wants to live. Both of those emotions are real to him. Your attempt to talk him out of either one will increase his sense of isolation and loneliness. Instead, acknowledge his desire to die, and encourage his desire to live.

—**React with honesty to the victim.** Don't glibly say, "I know how you feel" if you've never felt like killing yourself. You might appropriately say something like, "I've felt discouraged before, and I know that it can be an awful feeling. I'm hoping I can get you some help so that you can overcome those feelings of discouragement." Be completely honest with the victim if he asks about his prognosis; don't try to predict what he wants to hear. If it is clear that he will not die from his injuries, you might say something like, "Your injuries are not serious enough to cause your death. You will probably need to be hospitalized for a few days, though."

Realize as you treat the victim that he may not be able to communicate with you; many suicidal people have lost the ability to communicate with others. Keep talking to him and reassuring him, even if he doesn't respond.

—**Be prepared for resistance.** A person who has just failed in an attempt to kill himself will probably be extremely upset; he may not want you to treat him or "save" him. Be prepared for that eventuality. Make sure there is enough manpower to subdue the victim if necessary; if he resists treatment and transport, call the police.

—**Collect the evidence.** When you are ready to transport a suicide victim to the hospital, find and transport the implement of self-destruction (the knife, the gun, the rope, the empty pill bottle). It is especially important for physicians to have any empty or partially empty drug containers so they can identify the substance that was used and initiate the appropriate long-term treatment for overdose. Check the scene for signs of possible alcohol ingestion as well.

—**Enlist the help of friends and neighbors.** Sometimes a person who has attempted suicide will be frightened, confused, and upset. She may resist treatment and may resist transport unless you enlist the help of people she knows and may trust. If a woman resists your efforts to transport her to the hospital, you might ask her if there is a neighbor or relative she would like to have come along; then let the person sit in the back of the ambulance with the victim. You might also ask if there is someone the victim would like to have present during treatment. Respect her wishes if they can be fulfilled.

—**As soon as you can, make the environment safe.** Immediately upon arrival, survey the scene for potential hazards. A person who has attempted suicide may react with fear and panic when help arrives, and she may not necessarily use the same implement again. (A woman who cut herself with a butcher knife, for example, may panic and try to strangle herself.) If you can, move the person to a quiet area away from noise and confusion; do whatever possible to reduce tension and provocation. Remove hazardous objects, such as guns, knives, ropes, razor blades, and glass objects that could be broken and used for cutting.

—**Avoid the temptation to moralize or analyze.** The last thing the victim needs is for someone to tell him he is stupid, wrong, shameful, or irresponsible. Your primary consideration should be in establishing a trust relationship; talk to the person about his suicide plan, what he did, why he did it, how he is feeling, and ahat he wants to do now. Let him talk and express himself if he needs to: encourage his open communication, but don't pass judgment. Don't try to analyze the reasons for the attempted suicide; without a detailed history, it's almost impossible to do. (It's often impossible even with a detailed history!)

—**Never promise anything you can't deliver.** Don't tell the person she'll feel better within a few hours; she may be suffering from severe clinical depression, and she will **not** feel better. Don't tell the person that things will look up. Don't promise a distraught man that his wife will come running back when she hears that he is in trouble. Stick to things you **can** guarantee, such as strict medical outlook or procedure.

—**Remember that there are "survivors" who may need help.** Family members are likely to react with hostility, shame, anger, embarrassment, or a combination of those feelings. Don't discount the family's feelings. Allow them to express what they are feeling. Answer questions honestly, and don't try to analyze what has happened. Family members will probably come to you for answers; be honest in your response. ("It does look as though your husband tried to take his own life, but I don't know why. I'm not sure how he is feeling now. I can put you in touch with some people at the hospital who can give you better answers to those questions than I can.")

If the suicide attempt is successful and the person dies at the scene, you will need to provide aggressive crisis intervention for the survivors.

—**Move slowly and take your time.** Try not to give the victim the impression that he is "just another case" and that you are eager to be done with him. Take your time; move slowly; be willing to talk. Let the victim know that you will stay there as long as he wants or needs you to.

—**Take care of yourself.** Responding to an attempted suicide can be a difficult, even devastating, experience. You may find yourself confused, frightened, and stressed afterward. Take the time to talk to a colleague who has had experience in dealing with suicides. Communicate your feelings openly.

Above all, remember this: the victim's life is his responsibility. Some people will succeed in their attempts to end their own lives, and you are not to blame. As devastating as it is, you may not be able to save people who are bent on their own destruction. If, despite your best efforts, the victim dies, rest with the peace that you tried your best.

REFERENCES

1. *Webster's New Collegiate Dictionary*, 5th edition.
2. Taken from Jeffrey T. Mitchell and H.L.P. Resnik, *Emergency Response to Crisis* (Bowie, Md.: Robert J. Brady Company, 1981), pp. 143-144; *Using Crisis Intervention Wisely* (Horsham, Penn.: Nursing 80 Books, Intermed Communications, Inc., 1980), p. 97; and Minni Allison-Tomlinson, "Adolescent Suicide," *Continuing Education*, September 1981, p. 35.
3. Interview with Ronald Maris, "Why 30,000 Americans Will Commit Suicide This Year," *U.S. News and World Report*, April 2, 1984, p. 48.
4. George Howe Colt, "The Enigma of Suicide," *Harvard Magazine*, September-October 1983, p. 47.
5. Colt, p. 49.
6. Maris, p. 50.
7. Categories were identified by Edwin Shneidman and Norman Farberow and are listed in Lynn Ann DeSpelder and Albert Lee Strickland, *The Last Dance* (Palo Alto, Calif.: Mayfield Publishing Company, 1983), pp. 353-357, 359.
8. J. Ingram Walker, *Psychiatric Emergencies* (Philadelphia, Penn.: J.B. Lippincott, 1983), p. 105.
9. Russell A. Whitworth, "Is Your Patient Suicidal?" n.d., n.s., p. 41.
10. Betty J. Carmack, "Suspect a Suicide? Don't Be Afraid to Act," *RN*, April 1983, p. 44.
11. Norman Farberow, quoted in Mitchell and Resnik, p. 146.
12. DeSpelder and Strickland, p. 364.
13. Ibid.
14. Syed Arshad Husain and Trish Vandiver, *Suicide in Children and Adolescents* (New York, N.Y.: SP Medical & Scientific Books, 1984), p. 67.
15. Husain and Vandiver, p. 158.
16. Mitchell and Resnik, pp. 146-148.
17. DeSpelder and Strickland, p. 366.
18. Ibid.
19. "'Accidents' Mask Kids' Suicides," *Medical World News*, June 13, 1983, p. 56.
20. Ibid.
21. Billie F. Corder and Thomas M. Haizlip, "Recognizing Suicidal Behavior in Children," *Medical Times*, September 1982, p. 26.
22. Husain and Vandiver, p. 59.

23. Jeannye Thornton, "Behind a Surge in Suicides of Young People," *U.S. News and World Report,* June 20, 1983, p. 66.
24. Ibid.
25. U.S. Department of Health and Human Services, *The Challenge for Nurses* (Public Health Service, National Institutes of Health, August 1981), NIH Publication No. 82-2308, p. 16.
26. Ibid.
27. Maris, p. 48.
28. Jacquelyne G. Gorton and Rebecca Partridge, *Practice and Management of Psychiatric Emergency Care* (St. Louis, Mo.: C.V. Mosby Company, 1982), pp. 133-135.

Death and Dying

One of the most basic human experiences—and the one most likely to cause crisis—is death. Death itself is not the crisis, but it becomes a crisis for the dying person and the survivors because of our nearly universal inability to accept death as a final stage in our growth process. Few people embrace death; many people deny it and fear it. Most people—even those in the helping professions—find it difficult to discuss death with a person who is dying.

Understanding death and the emotions it perpetrates can help create a more open society in which we can face death without fear, live our lives fully, and anticipate death with peace and acceptance. It will also help create a situation in which we can be of support to those who are going through the crisis of dying or of losing a loved one to death.

Signs of Death

Basic to any understanding of death is a clear understanding of the signs that indicate death—the cessation of life beyond the possibility of resuscitation. The early signs of death are absence of a heartbeat and breathing for at least twenty minutes; later conclusive signs of death include:[1]

—Changes in the appearance of the eye. The cornea becomes wrinkled and turns milky or cloudy, losing its transparency.

—A drop in body temperature. While the temperature may remain stationary or even rise slightly immediately following death, cooling soon occurs and the body temperature drops several degrees Fahrenheit each hour for the first eight or ten hours following death. Factors that can determine how quickly the body temperature drops include the amount of fatty tissue, the amount of clothing worn, the body temperature at the time of death, and weather conditions.

—Rigor mortis, or a stiffening of the muscles, usually appears within two to eight hours after death, and it lasts for sixteen to twenty-four hours. Rigor mortis, which is marked by rigidity of body tissues, usually starts in the face and extends gradually to the legs; it disappears in the same order. (Don't confuse rigor mortis with the rigidity that can occur following some accidents, such as electrical shock; in those cases, resuscitation efforts should continue.)

—Postmortem lividity, or gradual discoloration of the skin due to the settling of blood. Lividity occurs in the skin upon which the body rests—the back, shoulders, and buttocks in most cases—and lividity spots look like bruises. (Unlike bruises, however, they do not show considerable blood or clotting.) Lividity spots are considered a sure sign of death.

—Absolute proof of death is putrefaction (rotting decomposition), which occurs after rigor mortis has disappeared. It does not occur for at least one day after death and can be delayed longer, depending on the cause of death and the weather conditions.

Anticipated Death

In many cases, death is anticipated: a man faces death after a two-year struggle with terminal cancer. A woman lies in a hospital bed suffering through the final stages of congestive heart failure. A child checks into the hospital for the last time with leukemia. In those cases, the final stage of life for the dying person is a difficult challenge: he knows he is dying, and he must come to terms with that fact.

Elizabeth Kubler-Ross, renowned for her research on death, describes a five-part pattern that is experienced by the dying person and by those close to him:[2]

—Denial. At first, the dying person denies the fact that he is dying. Simply stated, the news is too overwhelming to accept all at once; denial is a valuable defense mechanism that gives him the chance to adjust to the death and absorb its inevitability slowly. There are many forms of denial. Some people simply ignore what they have been told. Others seek second opinions, ask for verification of medical reports, seek news of miracle cures, or otherwise cling to hope for life. Most peoply deny death to some degree simply so they can go on with the business of living from day to day.

—Anger. Once the inevitability of death is accepted, the most difficult emotion of all surfaces: anger. The dying person may lash out at those who are trying to help him; whatever they do seems to be wrong. While this is the most difficult time for those who are trying to help, it is a necessary stage for the dying person; he is reacting with anger that his life is being cut short, he is about to enter an unknown situation, and others are still being permitted to live.

—Bargaining. Once anger subsides, the dying person enters an almost frantic stage of bargaining, usually to try for an extension of life or a higher quality of life. Most of the "bargains" are secret, are made with God, and are rarely kept. A woman with lung cancer may promise to donate all her money to charity if only she can live long enough to see her first grandchild born; a man may promise to never sin again if he can live long enough to enjoy his daughter's wedding.

—Depression. This stage is characterized by inherent sadness; the dying person accepts the fact that she is dying, realizes that death is imminent, and prepares to say goodbye to everyone and everything she has ever known. Depression is a difficult stage for the dying person, who is being torn from everything she ever loved.

—**Acceptance.** At last, the person quietly accepts the imminent death, knowing that he has done everything he can to prepare to die. During this stage, the person seems calm; his most important wish is not to die alone. He probably needs less support at this point than do his survivors, who are close to losing him.

Not all people progress smoothly through all five stages in order. Some people skip from one stage to another; some regress to a stage they've already been through. Others get "stuck" in a particular stage (such as anger or depression); others move from one to another rapidly.

Sudden Death

Anticipated death can be prepared for; sudden death is a cruel occurrence that brings with it enormous, immediate emotional distress. Survivors are caught completely off-guard by the death. The sense of loss felt by survivors is intensified in a situation involving sudden death, whether it occurs by accident, homicide, suicide, or unexpected physical illness.

Survivors of sudden death characteristically experience some combination of the following reactions:[3]

—**Hostility.** Such hostility is, in reality, an expression of outrage that the death occurred. Unfortunately, it is usually directed at doctors, nurses, emergency medical personnel, or others who attempted to help the victim. A survivor may accuse a doctor, for example, of not doing everything possible to save the individual.

—**Guilt and self-blame.** The survivor may spend an inordinate amount of time pondering what she could have done differently—not only in the period immediately preceding the death, but throughout her life with the dead person. A woman may feel extreme guilt for being unfaithful to her husband, who was killed in an automobile accident on the way to work; a man may feel guilty that he never took his wife on the promised vacation to Europe. In some cases, a person blames himself for the death—"If only I had let someone else drive, this wouldn't have happened."

—**Preoccupation with the dead person.** A survivor may become preoccupied with the dead person, filling his days with thoughts about her or about their life together. For a period, the survivor is unable to function normally because of this preoccupation.

—**Disbelief.** If a person was murdered, committed suicide, or died in an accident, the news of the death may cause disbelief for the survivor—it is difficult to accept the fact that someone who left the house an hour earlier in the peak of health and vitality now lies crumpled on a roadside, devoid of life.

—**Physical distress.** The survivor may develop any number of physical complaints in reaction to the news of the death, including gastrointestinal problems, headache, dizziness, trembling, and weakness.

One study that involved those who lost a spouse to sudden death indicated that the survivors have certain needs that can help ease the shock of sudden death:

—**The need to see the person after he is admitted to the emergency department.** Many survivors feel that they need to see the person, even if he is already dead; some want to be with him during his "hour of greatest need," while others feel compelled to make sure he is really dead. Still others want a chance to say goodbye for a final time.

—**The need to make sure that prompt physical attention is given.** Even if the person is already dead when emergency personnel arrive on the scene or when the person arrives at the emergency room, he needs prompt and aggressive medical attention; if such attention isn't given, survivors may feel that something could have been done to change the outcome.

—**The need to immediately be told of the severity of the situation.** Survivors need to be told immediately how serious the situation is; a survivor needs to be told something like, "Your husband was critically injured in the accident, and we are doing all that we can to save him." Giving survivors this kind of information as soon as possible allows them a chance to see the victim, say goodbye, or do other things necessary to their peace of mind.

—**The need to express anxieties about the impending death.** A survivor needs the chance to express anxiety and concern over the victim's condition and the chance to express anxieties over the impending death. Health care workers need to be available to listen and talk to the survivors about their feelings.

—**The need for comfort and support from family members.** A survivor who is faced with news of the death has to gather her resources to sign legal forms, contact a mortuary, make funeral arrangements, and so on; it is critical that the survivor have the comfort and support of family members through this difficult period. If possible, hospital or emergency workers should contact other family members and arrange for them to meet the survivor at the hospital.

—**The need for concern and support of health professionals.** The survivor needs to know that health professionals who were involved in the death are concerned about what will happen. A doctor who tells a man that his wife has died should remain with the man, for example, and talk about the death; he should answer any questions the man may have, and should show concern about the man's loss.

Terminal Illness

The victim of terminal illness has a special problem with

which to cope: he is suddenly "different," no longer ordinary, suddenly separate from his friends and loved ones because of his "condition." He may not feel that he has changed, but others perceive him as being changed and unusual.

Most victims of terminal illness go through the steps associated with anticipated death—denial, anger, bargaining, depression, and acceptance. In the case of terminal illness, however, the denial, anger, bargaining, depression, and acceptance involve not only the inevitability of the death itself, but the existence of the disease.

Helping a patient cope with a terminal illness takes understanding, compassion, and empathy. Some doctors and experts disagree with the theory that a patient should be told he is dying, but most feel that a caretaker has a responsibility to be honest with the patient **if the patient indicates a willingness to learn the truth.** Keeping the fact of death away from a person who wants to know his condition removes some of his options and makes him a passive recipient of a medical program that someone else has designed.

It is essential to allow and encourage terminally ill people to maintain their sense of self-worth, to exercise choice about their treatment, to stay actively involved with their families, and to set goals and strive to reach them. Helping a patient do these things facilitates a will to live that will help him cope with the illness.

The Hospice Movement

One of the most significant advances in care of the terminally ill is hospice, a movement that grew out of the awareness that the needs of a dying person can't always be met in a hospital, which is forced to focus on the needs of people who are acutely ill. A hospital focuses on cure; a terminally ill patient who is facing death may be unconcerned about a cure but may have many other needs that desperately need to be addressed.

The main focus of the hospice is not in treatment and cure; instead, it is in control of pain and providing surroundings that will make the dying experience as pleasant and peaceful as possible. In a hospital, nurses and physicians frantically scramble for a cure, looking for a way to prolong life; in a hospice, nurses and doctors have accepted the fact that death will occur, and they try to make it as pleasant as possible for the patient.

Dr. Sylvia Lack, who brought the hospice concept to the United States from London, identifies ten components of hospice care:[4]

1. The hospice features coordinated home care with inpatient beds under a central administration.
2. The hospice seeks to control symptoms, including physical, sociological, psychological, and spiritual.
3. Because of the medical nature of physical symptoms, the hospice provides physician-directed services.
4. The hospice features care by an interdisciplinary team.
5. Services at the hospice are available twenty-four hours a day, seven days a week, with the emphasis on the availability of medical and nursing skills.
6. The patient and his family are regarded as the unit of care; family members are included in decisions, are offered support, and are treated along with the patient.
7. The hospice provides for follow-up during the period of bereavement following the death.
8. Volunteers are used as an integral part of the interdisciplinary team.
9. The hospice offers structured personnel support and communications systems.
10. Patients are accepted into the hospice program on the basis of health care needs rather than on the ability to pay.

While a hospital room is usually sterile and sparsely decorated, the hospice room is more like a warmly decorated bedroom. Flowers, pictures, and personal belongings fill each room; wallpaper, carpeting, lamps, and other personal touches make the hospice room pleasant. Most hospices offer extended visiting hours; some allow visiting around the clock. Family members are encouraged to stay with the patient as much as possible; even children and family pets are allowed in the hospice room.

Because death occurs frequently at the hospice, the staff knows how to deal with it. It is not a dreaded occurrence at a hospice. The hospice is a warm, cheerful place; even in the event of death, survivors are cheered and comforted by the knowledge that the patient was cared for not only physically, but psychologically and spiritually as well. Survivors are allowed to sit with the body for a time, and many hospices include a small chapel where survivors may go to pray or receive spiritual solace. Members of the clergy are welcome, according to the wishes of the family.

A Child's Understanding of Death

Most death situations involve a child—a parent dies, a sister dies, a grandparent dies. The child himself may face death because of a congenital or terminal illness. A child's understanding of death usually evolves gradually as he sees people die, sees pets die, or hears about death.

As adults, we take a knowledge of death for granted. We understand that death is irreversible and permanent. We know that death involves the cessation of all physiological functioning—that the heart no longer beats, the lungs no longer fill with air, the muscles no longer quiver with tension. We understand that death is universal (it happens to everyone at some point) and that it is inevitable (each of us is going to die eventually).

A child may not understand any of that; if he understands some of it, his impressions may be sketchy or riddled with misconceptions. Depending on a child's age, his cognitive development, and his previous experiences, he may have certain conceptions of death.

Preschoolers

Generally, children under the age of three are incapable of understanding death, even though they definitely react to it. A child who loses a parent to death will need to be reassured that her needs will still be met and that she will still be loved and kept safe.

Children between the ages of three and six start to develop some understanding of death, but their concept of death is filled with misinformation. A child in this age group, for instance, does not understand that death is permanent and irreversible; he thinks that dead people are "sleeping" or have "gone away." He may think that the person will come alive again as soon as he has gotten some rest. Children in this age group are also confused about the relationship between illness and death—they often do not make the connection that death is **caused** by an illness.

Anger plays a big part in the death experience for children in this age group. Many worry that the death was a result of their own angry feelings: a four-year-old may have been furious that his older brother wouldn't share a toy with him—and when the older brother is killed in a drowning accident, the four-year-old worries that his anger caused the death. Many children in this age group, too, react to death with extreme anger: a child whose mother dies is furious at her for deserting him. Children in this age group will displace that anger on anyone who is close to them, even though it is intended for the dead person.

Children between the ages of three to six think in concrete terms, so they are not able to detach themselves from places where the dead person was, the car the dead person drove, and so on. When a five-year-old passed the office building where his father worked, he started screaming, "Daddy! Daddy!" The office building **reminded** his mother of her husband, but for the child, it's the real thing.

A child between the ages of three and six who loses a parent may become extremely worried that her needs won't be taken care of—there will be no one to feed her, buy clothes for her, or provide a place for her to live. She begins to worry openly about her own survival and about the survival of others in the family.

(This can be especially true if the surviving parent is so overwhelmed by grief that he does not have the capacity to cope with his child's grieving.) The child may often express the wish for a replacement ("I want a new mommy!"), a wish that springs from the worries about the family's stability.

Children in this age group are harsh on themselves and on others. They may blame themselves for the death, as discussed, or they may lash out at the surviving parent for not preventing the death.

School-Age Children

Children between the ages of seven and twelve begin to realize that death is permanent and irreversible; they realize that a dead friend or brother isn't coming back. Many have nightmares about death.

Oddly, even though children in this age group begin to understand death, they do not understand (or accept) that they will die; to them, death is something that happens to other people. They are basically egocentric, so they may develop fears about disease, accidents, or suicide, depending on how a death close to them occurred; even so, they will not fully accept that death might happen to them.

Children in the middle years can't think abstractly, so they are detailed and specific in their reflections about death—even to the point of being macabre or morbid. They want to know what happens inside the body, what the undertaker does, what happens to a body after it is buried, and so on. By getting their questions answered, they are able to work out their own fears and concerns about death.

A child's grief at this stage has some similarities to an adult's grief. The child is likely to withdraw, deny the death, feel angry about it, feel guilty about the death or the dead person, and finally accept the death.

Adolescents

Children over the age of twelve definitely understand that

death is permanent and irreversible; during adolescence, most children start to form their own personal philosophies regarding life and death.

Adolescents, too, begin to realize that death can happen to them. If someone they know dies from an illness or accident, they tend to worry excessively about suffering the same fate; they develop intense fears of illness, disfigurement, pain, and sickness.

Children in this age group feel many of the feelings that adults do as they grieve and mourn; since adolescents tend to be quite self-centered, however, they may not feel the effects of grief as severely. Coping with death can be especially difficult for adolescents, since they are just beginning to shape their own lives.

Sudden Infant Death Syndrome

Sudden Infant Death Syndrome (SIDS) is the death of an apparently healthy infant that occurs suddenly and unexpectedly during the child's first year of life. [5] It brings with it a special kind of crisis—not only for the parents who lose a baby, but for parents who are expecting a baby or who bring a newborn home. Knowing that an apparently healthy baby can be robbed in its sleep without warning is tremendously frightening for most parents.

Approximately 7,500 babies die in the United States from SIDS each year; it is the major cause of death for babies between the ages of one month and one year.

Basic Facts About SIDS

Parents who are confronted with the death of their baby face extreme emotional upset and guilt. Did they cause the death? Could they have prevented the death? Did the baby suffer? Is the condition hereditary or contagious—will other children in the family die from it?

While there is still a great deal that we do not know about SIDS, we do know some basic facts:

—SIDS is not hereditary, and it is not contagious. The chances that another child in the same family will die from SIDS are no greater than the norm unless the child is the twin of a SIDS baby.

—SIDS is not caused by external suffocation, by vomiting, or by choking. The baby did **not** suffocate on a blanket, as many parents fear.

—SIDS cannot be predicted. Through extensive research we have been able to isolate some risk factors, but that is our only clue; no test can determine ahead of time which babies will succumb to SIDS.

—SIDS cannot, in most cases, be prevented. If there has been a previous episode in which a baby almost died, monitors can be attached that will alert the parents or caretakers in case the baby stops breathing; other than that, there is no way of preventing death.

—SIDS occurs rapidly and silently, usually during periods of sleep; there are usually no signs of struggle.

—SIDS babies do not suffer.

—SIDS can strike any family: it does not respect race, religion, economic status, nationalities, or geographies. (There is evidence that it occurred as early as Old Testament times, and it seems to have occurred as frequently in the eighteenth and nineteenth centuries as it does today.)

—SIDS is not predictable nor completely preventable, even by a physician; most important, SIDS is **not** anyone's fault.

Almost always, SIDS strikes babies between the ages of two weeks and one year; rarely, it has been known to strike babies as young as one week and toddlers as old as two years. The peak age range for SIDS seems to be two to four months of age. It strikes year-round but seems to be more prevalent during the winter months; it usually occurs during the night but can occur any time the baby is sleeping. It is more common in nonwhite babies and more common among boys than girls.

SIDS Risk Factors

Through extensive research, doctors have isolated some risk factors that seem to place a baby at higher risk for dying from SIDS:[5]

—Premature birth
—Low APGAR score
—Multiple-birth pregnancy
—Second or third in birth order
—Low birth weight
—Required oxygen or ventilatory assistance at birth
—Had a mild infection (usually respiratory) at time of death
—Has a history of feeding difficulties
—Is a boy

A number of factors involving the mother also may increase the risk of SIDS:

—Are narcotics abusers
—Have short spacing between pregnancies
—Are younger than twenty years of age
—Have inadequate prenatal care
—Smoke cigarettes during pregnancy
—Have had previous spontaneous abortions (miscarriages)
—Come from a low socioeconomic group
—Have another child who died from SIDS
—Are Black or American Indian (lower SIDS rates occur among whites and Orientals)

One of the most promising leads in understanding SIDS is research indicating that many victims of SIDS appear to have suffered from long-term underventilation of the lungs, possibly due to poor control of breathing during sleep and possibly caused by abnormalities within the brainstem.

Relationship Between SIDS and Apnea

Apnea—the temporary stoppage of breathing—has been shown to be related to SIDS; some SIDS infants suffer a high frequency of apneic episodes before their sudden and unexpected death. An infant may be at high risk for SIDS when apneic episodes are prolonged (between ten to twenty seconds in duration) or when there are frequent incidents of apnea when there is either no chest movement or there is chest movement but no air passes through the mouth or nose.

There is no conclusive data about how many babies suffered apnea prior to death from SIDS, but preliminary data indicate that only about 5 percent of SIDS deaths were preceded by apnea. Therefore, apnea cannot explain all SIDS deaths.

Apnea can occur in any infant between the ages of one week and four months; it is considered a problem only when the episodes are prolonged or when there are frequent episodes of mixed apnea (the situation in which the chest does not move or air does not pass through the mouth or nose where there is chest movement). Apnea can be caused by the sudden onset of disease, a severe infection, significant anemia, low blood sugar, cardiac abnormalities, or failure of the central nervous system mechanisms that regulate breathing.

Occasional periods of apnea appear to be part of the developmental pattern of all infants; it is considered to be a problem only when breathing stops for as long as twenty seconds or when the stoppage in breathing is accompanied by a bluish tint around the mouth and nostrils, pale skin color, or a slow pulse.

A Parent's Grief

After the initial shock of SIDS begins to wear off, parents often find that they are left with a prolonged depression; the depression can be triggered by a number of things, including thoughtless comments from people who don't understand SIDS or simply remembering that it is the same day of the week that the baby died. Parents of a SIDS baby commonly suffer the following:

—Difficulty in concentrating
—Sleep disruptions
—Extreme fatigue or exhaustion (even when sleep is not interrupted
—Loss of appetite
—Gastrointestinal distress
—A variety of physical symptoms, including a feeling of being tied up in knots inside; mothers often report that their "arms ache to hold the baby"
—Irresistible urge to escape
—Dread of being alone
—Unreasonable fears of danger
—Fear of the responsibility of caring for other children
—Extreme irritation and impatience with other children

While mothers tend to talk about their feelings and share their grief, fathers tend to grieve in silence. Both husbands and wives who work outside the home may be diverted from their grief by the demands of their work, while those who stay at home are surrounded by constant reminders of the loss.

A Child's Grief

Children who lose a brother or sister to SIDS are always affected by the death. Very young children often have frightening thoughts that they can't express verbally; instead, they cling to their parents or misbehave intentionally to attract and hold their parents' attention. Older children will likely understand the death and will have certain grief reactions. Many will feel extremely guilty about the baby's death, worrying that because they wished the baby would die they caused the death. Children may not display their grief in obvious ways but may instead deny it and seem unconcerned. Some may manifest their grief through increased insecurity, nightmares, bedwetting, difficulty in school, and other disturbances.

Distinguishing Between SIDS and Child Abuse

Only an autopsy can conclude definitely whether an infant's death is due to SIDS. You should know that the general appearance of the infant in the crib can be misleading: in many ways, the baby may look like the victim of child abuse. There are some ways in which you can distinguish between the two:

—A SIDS baby shows no evidence of external injury. A victim of child abuse will show distinguishable and visible signs of injury, including broken bones, bruises, burns, cuts, head injury, black eye, scars, welts, and wounds.

—The SIDS baby will exhibit the natural appearance of a dead baby, including lividity (settling of the blood that may resemble bruises), a frothy drainage from the nose or mouth, cooling (which takes place rapidly in infants), and rigor mortis (which also takes place rapidly within infants, usually within about three hours). Don't let these natural signs—such as lividity and frothing—confuse you and lead to possible misinterpretation.

—The SIDS baby appears to be well-developed, even though it may be small for its age; the victim of child abuse or neglect usually shows some signs of malnutrition.

—In cases of SIDS, other children in the family appear to be normal and healthy; in cases of child abuse, other children may show patterns of injuries that are commonly seen in child abuse and neglect cases.

—In cases of SIDS, the parents will tell you that the child was well and healthy when he was put down for his nap; in cases of child abuse and neglect, the parents may try to explain away certain illnesses or injuries with stories that don't sound quite right.

Remember: **it is the responsibility of the coroner or medical examiner to determine whether the child is a SIDS victim—not the responsibility of an emergency responder.**

Signs and Symptoms of SIDS

A baby who had died of SIDS will manifest the following postmortem signs and symptoms:

—Frothy, possibly blood-tinged mucus around the baby's mouth or nostrils; the secretions may have stained the bed clothes.

—Dependent pooling of blood to the underside of the body, with paleness on the upper side. A baby found lying on his or her stomach will probably have darkened areas on the undersides of the face, arms, and legs as well as the chest or abdomen.

—Livor mortis, or decomposition of the blood, which gives the skin a dark red, fixed color.

—Rigor mortis, or stiffening of the body, usually within about three hours.

—Evidence that the baby was very active just prior to death, such as rumpled bed clothes, unusual position, or location in the bed. (This activity is caused by muscular contractions of the body that occur with death, not because the baby was struggling.) An unusual position, coupled with dependent pooling of the blood, may produce pressure marks on the body where the pooled blood was pressed aside, such as by a crib slat.

—Disfiguration on the contours of the face of an infant who died on his stomach; the baby's face will look squashed because of the general relaxation of the body tissues in death.

Grief and Mourning

The survivors of death have a big job to do: they must progress through grief and mourning. If a survivor can progress through the normal grief reaction, he will eventually adjust to the death and regain equilibrium; a person who does not go through those normal phases of grief may develop long-term psychiatric problems associated with the death.

Normal Grief Reactions

Healthy and normal grief involves five distinct phases that eventually lead to healing and a cessation of mourning:

—**Denial.** At first, the survivor is shocked and stunned; he reacts to the news of the death with a numbed feeling of disbelief. Normally, this period of denial lasts anywhere from a few minutes to a few days; denial that persists more than a few days is a signal that something is wrong. During denial, the survivor acts in ways that indicate he does not accept the reality of the death—he accepts the fact intellectually but cannot accept it emotionally.

The period of denial is often a blessing to survivors, who rely on the feelings of numbness to get them through the difficult period of making funeral arrangements and burying their loved one.

—**Awareness.** Following the period of denial, the survivor goes through a period of awareness in which he emotionally acknowledges the death. It is during awareness that the individual begins to feel the anguish and emptiness of the loss; emotions and reactions can be easily triggered by comments, scenes, pictures, scents, and other seemingly small reminders. During this stage, the feelings of anguish and grief are most severe during the night.

Survivors during the stage of awareness may feel anger and self-blame. Specific behaviors that are common during the awareness stage include crying with tears, tearful longing for the dead person, preoccupation with the memory of the loved one, visual images of the dead person, irritability, restlessness, and inability to concentrate. Physical problems—including digestive problems, loss of appetite, insomnia, loss of sex drive, and weight loss—are also common during the awareness stage.

It is important that grieving individuals feel free to fully express their feelings during this stage; well-intentioned advice to "keep a stiff upper lip" or not to cry can wreak havoc and interfere with the normal process of grief.

—**Restitution.** During the period of restitution, the survivor is helped to clearly see and accept the reality of the death. The survivor is able to see the body, participate in the funeral services, and actually see the coffin lowered into the ground; for the survivor, this sequence of events is necessary and helps him cope emotionally with the loss. The practice of religion and social customs—regardless of how strange they seem to others—is an important part of the restitution stage and an important part of coming to terms with the death.

—**Resolution.** During the resolution stage, the person begins to "pick up the pieces" and determine how he is going to go on with life. He starts to visualize, for the first time since the death occurred, how he will function without the dead person. He progressively begins to regain an interest in the things that used to interest him, and he gradually begins to resume life as normal. (At first, this process can be excrutiatingly painful; not all people can resume normal activities as quickly as can others.)

During the fourth stage of mourning, the person moves from feelings of anguish and emptiness when he remembers the dead person to feelings of love, pleasure, and interest.

During the resolution stage, the survivor usually suffers from a number of physical sensations, particularly those that the dead person suffered from. (If the person died from cancer of the liver, for example, the survivor may develop symptoms of cancer of the liver, even though no cancer exists.) The development of these symptoms allows the mourner to suffer on behalf of the dead person and helps ease any guilt the survivor may feel about the death.

—**Idealization.** During the final stage of mourning, the survivor may experience brief periods of anguish and a sense of loss, but for the most part, the terrible anguish that characterized earlier stages of grief has disappeared. During idealization, the survivor represses all negative and hostile feelings toward the dead person and creates a positive, well-balanced image of the person that helps to soften the sense of loss. Thoughts of the death and the dead person can be tolerated with fewer feelings of anguish, hostility, guilt, or deep sorrow.

The normal period of grief usually requires a year or longer; those who are able to realistically remember both the pleasant and unpleasant aspects of their relationship with the dead person are able to heal more completely and quickly than those who cannot realistically do so.

Physical Reactions to Grief

Grief is quite literally a risk to health—those who are going through mourning are more susceptible to illness, tend to lose weight, take more medication than they should, tend to drink more than they should, and generally suffer some kind of deterioration in health.

Almost all survivors who progress through the grief cycle experience the following physical reactions:

—Tightness in the throat
—A feeling of choking or shortness of breath
—Loss of power in the muscles
—A feeling of emptiness in the abdomen
—Feelings of intense tension or mental pain

Other common reactions include the following:

—Insomnia
—Asthma
—Rheumatoid arthritis and bursitis
—Generalized body pain and reduced health
—Dizziness
—Blurred vision
—Chest pains, palpitations of the heart, and pounding heartbeat
—Nausea and vomiting
—Abdominal pain
—Constipation
—Frequent urination

—Menstrual problems, including painful menstruation and irregular menstruation
—Headache
—Fainting spells
—Skin rash
—Excessive sweating

Some researchers believe that acute grief interferes with the body's immune system, literally making the individual more susceptible to serious infections and less able to recover quickly. An unusual number of grieving people suffer subsequent heart disease, especially arteriosclerosis and coronary thrombosis, and a higher-than-normal number develop certain fatal diseases, such as stroke, blood cancer, and cancer of the cervix.

Abnormal or Unresolved Grief

In some cases, people fail to progress normally through the phases of grief and mourning; for them, the grieving process gets "bottled up" and proper healing does not occur. In severe cases, people are not able to mourn at all.

There are a number of reasons why the grief process may be interrupted. Sometimes the loss is uncertain; a woman may be told that her soldier husband is missing in action in a foreign country, and she may remain fixated in the denial stage, waiting for definitive news of a death or survival. Even if years go by, she may never be able to progress out of the denial stage because she lacks evidence of the death.

Other reasons for failure to progress through the normal grief process include the following:

—The death reawakens the memory of a previous loss with which the survivor never completely dealt; the feelings of frustration, guilt, and anguish that accompany the unresolved death make it impossible for the person to deal with the current crisis.

—The cause of death is an embarrassment to the survivor, so the survivor cannot face the death and does not receive support and encouragement from others. The death may have resulted from suicide, a drug overdose, an alcoholic emergency, or some other unacceptable situation.

—The survivor is acutely afraid of losing control, so he will not allow himself to confront the strong feelings associated with the death. He fears that if he **does** confront those feelings, he will lose control and never be able to regain it.

—The survivor is afraid to show signs of weakness; the normal behaviors that accompany grieving, such as crying, screaming, and sobbing, are unacceptable to him. He simply will not allow himself to display such behaviors—and, in the process, he interferes with his ability to progress through his grief. Some people stifle such feelings because they feel a responsibility to be stoic.

—The survivor has lost more than one loved one at the same time (usually as the result of an accident or disaster), and he is overwhelmed by the multiple loss. In some cases, he is unable to progress through the grief process because the people he relied on for support and encouragement have died, and he is left alone.

—The survivor may have been too dependent on the dead person; to grieve means he must admit that the person is gone forever and will no longer be able to support him. In cases of deep dependence, the survivor may not feel whole again and cannot confront the terrifying prospect of having to go on alone.

—On the other hand, the survivor may have ambivalent feelings toward the dead person. In some cases, the survivor may have felt intense feelings of both love and hatred toward the dead person; in order to grieve, he must confront those painful feelings. He may be afraid of uncovering even more feelings of hatred, which is unacceptable to him—so he refuses to grieve.

—The survivor may be geographically isolated from the death. There are several problems involved in this situation.

First, the survivor is not able to see the body, attend funeral services, and see the coffin lowered into the ground, so it is extremely difficult to emotionally accept the fact of the death. Also, in most cases of geographic separation, the survivor is isolated by distance from family members—his usual network of support—so he is unable to receive the support he needs through the difficult grieving process.

Signs of abnormal grief vary from person to person but may include the following:

—A significant change in personality; a person who was once peaceful and friendly may become hostile, angry, and antisocial.

—Adoption of the dead person's habits, behavioral traits, and obvious personality traits; in abnormal grief, these are much more obvious than subtle personality traits. A daughter may suddenly adopt her dead father's habit of going for a walk every evening before dinner.

—A breakdown in interpersonal relationships; the survivor may find himself facing even more loss as he suffers disintegrating relationships with other family members.

—An inability to talk about the dead person; even after a prolonged period, the survivor can't talk about the dead person without experiencing undue anguish, crying, and other signs of unresolved loss.

—A continued search for the dead person; after a prolonged period, the survivor may literally search for the dead person (traveling from place to place, making inquiries) or may emotionally search for him. In some cases, the survivor may wish for death or may contemplate suicide to effect a reunion with the dead person.

—A refusal to participate in the funeral services or to visit the grave; such refusal is a sign of acute denial.

—An overreaction to someone else's problems; a survivor who is unable to deal with his own grief may become hysterical years later when he hears about someone else's tragedy.

—Unaccountable sadness at certain times of the year; because the survivor is not able to express his grief at the appropriate time, he will do it at different times of the year, such as on his anniversary, on his birthday, or on a holiday.

—An agitated depression that is characterized by feelings of worthlessness, deep tension, severe agitation, and obvious desire for punishment.

—An expectation that someone else in the family will fill in for the dead person.

—A development of the dead person's symptoms; this is a part of normal grief, but in normal grieving it is temporary and passes quickly. In abnormal grief, the symptoms will persist and may become part of a dangerous syndrome.

—An exhibition of self-destructive behavior, such as excessive risk-taking, reckless gambling, foolish investments, reckless driving, excessive drinking, or the tendency to take up high-risk hobbies (such as skydiving). While the survivor doesn't recognize the reasons for his behavior, he is often subconsciously trying to punish or hurt himself.

—Withdrawal from the dead person, including a refusal to display any interest in the dead person's possessions, a refusal to attend the funeral, and the inability to cry over the death.

—The development of chronic grief reactions; normally, the five stages of the grief process are relatively brief, with grief and normal mourning usually being completed in about a year. Those who are suffering from abnormal grief may stretch this into a period of several years or more.

—Recurring symptoms of normal grief, such as the overwhelming feelings of anguish or the feelings of anger and denial long after the death has occurred.

—An obsession with loss; the survivor may equate all aspects of his life to loss and defeat.

—The onset of disease; especially common are emotionally

induced diseases and illnesses, such as migraine headaches, asthma, rheumatism, or ulcerative colitis.

The symptoms of abnormal grief should not be confused with those of **anticipatory grief.** Anticipatory grief occurs when the death was anticipated, and the individual moved through the stages of grief and mourning before the death actually took place. This kind of grieving commonly occurs in cases where a person dies from a terminal disease that lingered for some time. In this case, family members go through the periods of grief and resolve their feelings about the death before the person ever dies; as a result, they seem to be devoid of grief at the time of death. They may not cry, scream, feel deep anguish, or otherwise react as they are "expected" to. These people are not going through abnormal grief; they have simply done their grieving work already. In such cases, death may even seem sweet, since it signals an end to the person's suffering.

Coping With Death and Dying

Helping a Dying Person

Working with a person who is dying is awkward and difficult; you are often at a loss as to what to say and do. Obviously, you should take care of any physical problems and help relieve pain; beyond that, you can do a great deal to ease the person's emotional burden as he dies.

Follow these general guidelines:

—Even if the victim seems dazed or incoherent, make a real effort to orient him. Explain where he is, who you are, what you are doing, and what is happening. As you tell him what is happening to his body, be honest but tactful; be careful not to shock him.

—**Remember: even an unconscious person can hear and**

understand. Don't make negative comments about the victim's condition ("This one's a goner!"), even if you think he is in a coma. If he asks you if he is dying, allow for some hope. You might say something like, "I don't know. You and I are going to fight this out together! I'm not going to give up on you, so don't give up on yourself!" If the victim insists that he is dying, you might say, "Well, that might be possible. But let's keep trying!"

—Make every effort to find the victim's family before he dies; communicate the urgency of the situation to them and give clear, specific instructions about where they can meet you. If you can't find the family, reassure the victim that you will find them as quickly as you can and explain what has happened to him.

—If the victim tries to resist treatment or refuses to be transported to the hospital, do what is necessary to convince him of the seriousness of his situation. You might say something like, "I think you are making a mistake; I have real reason to believe that you will die soon unless you receive adequate care." If he still resists, you may need to have him declared incompetent so you can carry out life-saving care.

—If other family members have been involved in the same accident or disaster, be cautious about giving news of their condition to an unstable person who is dying. If the person directly asks you about family members, avoid saying things that might upset him and worsen his condition. You might say something like, "I haven't seen your mother, but I did see your wife, and she is doing fine."

—Continue resuscitation efforts until you have restored spontaneous circulation and respiration, until you have transferred responsibility to another person, until you have transferred responsibility to the medical facility where you transport the victim, or until you cannot continue because of disabling exhaustion. Do not give up because you think the victim is dead or will die anyway.

Helping Survivors Cope

The survivors of a death need special care, especially if the death occurred as the result of an accident and was unexpected. If the victim was in the accident, make sure that he is in completely stable condition before you tell him about the death of his loved one. **There is one important exception: if he asks you, be completely honest.**

In helping survivors to cope, follow these general guidelines:

—If you can, let the family member stay with the dying person in the ambulance and during emergency care. If family member arrive before the victim dies, **always** let them see the victim; they want to communicate their love one last time and may even have the need to ask forgiveness for some wrongdoing or take care of some unfinished business.

—Some family members want to see the body after death; you should let them do it if it is possible and if local protocol allows it. Before the family sees the body, clean it up as much as possible; wash away blood, secretions, and vomitus. Cover any mutilated body parts or bandage them. If there is mutilation, make sure that the family members know about it before they see the body.

—No matter what the situation, show the utmost respect for the patient who is dying; family members will be extremely sensitive about how the person is treated, what is said in his presence, and even unspoken messages. Be gentle and kind.

—Speak to an unconscious person as though he were fully conscious; carefully explain what you are doing before you do it. Explain those same procedures to the family; they are concerned about what you are doing.

—Encourage family members to talk to a comatose person. Explain that he still may be able to hear and understand, even though he cannot respond. Family members, especially those who arrive after the victim has lost consciousness, can gain great emotional relief from trying to communicate one last time.

—Encourage family members to express their emotions freely. **Let them know that it is perfectly all right to scream, cry, bang their fists against the wall, or do anything else they feel like —without being censored or judged.** Provide a quiet room where they can have privacy from other people, and make sure that someone (a friend, clergyman, or other trusted person) stays with them. Closely monitor any family member who does not seem upset, cannot cry, or does not express emotion over the death; he may need extra help in progressing through the grief process.

—Be prepared for an attack. It is common and understandable for family members to lash out in anger at you. Why didn't you save him? Why didn't you do more? How can this have happened? Remember—don't take the attacks personally. They are a normal part of the grieving process. Remain calm, and don't become angry or hostile toward them. (They may be extremely apologetic afterward; calm them by saying something like, "The way you were feeling is very normal in this kind of situation. I know that your comments weren't directed at me personally; I'm glad you vented your anger and frustration, because it will help you adjust to the death more easily.")

Helping the Parents of a SIDS Baby

The emotional distress of a parent who finds a lifeless baby can be terrifying and overwhelming. In helping the parent through the emotional crisis, follow these general guidelines:

—Even if you think the infant is dead, try to resuscitate him anyway; the parents will then know that everything possible was done to save the baby. If you don't make a heroic effort, the parents may be troubled for the rest of their lives, wondering, "If only they had tried, maybe she wouldn't have died."

—Don't give false hope, but be firm and clear that everything possible is being done.

—Take note of the baby's position in the crib, the baby's

physical appearance, the physical appearance of the crib, the presence of objects in the crib, the behavior of the parents, and the circumstances behind the discovery. You may need to report these in a legal report.

—Encourage the parents to talk about the situation and to tell their story; never be critical or judgmental. Never imply that the parents might have been at fault in causing the baby's death, and never imply that the baby may have died from child abuse.

—If local protocol allows it, let the parents ride with the baby in the ambulance. If not, explain exactly where you are taking the baby and arrange to meet them there. They will be extremely distraught, so encourage them to ride with someone else (a friend or neighbor) instead of driving themselves.

—Give the parents as much information as you can about SIDS. By telling the parents that SIDS is not preventable, not predictable, not caused by suffocation, not caused by choking, and not anyone's fault, you can save them a lifetime of distress. You may need to emphasize certain facts depending on the situation; for example, if the parents discovered the baby under a blanket, you may need to emphasize that SIDS is not caused by suffocation.

—Arrange for the parents to receive brochures or written materials on SIDS and to contact a support group.

—Encourage the parents to vent their feelings; let them know that it is all right to cry, scream, and express great anguish. Arrange for a room at the hospital where they can enjoy privacy, but **do not leave them alone**; stay with them or arrange for someone else (a friend, family member, clergyman, or doctor) to stay with them.

—Explain to the parents that you need to get certain information, but keep questions to a minimum. Ask only essential questions, such as whether the baby has been ill, whether the baby has been on medication, whether the parents have noticed anything unusual, and how old the baby is. Take special care not to ask questions that imply the parents are at fault or that criticize their parenting skills.

REFERENCES

1. Brent Q. Hafen and Keith J. Karren, *Crisis Intervention for Emergency Medical Personnel* (North Hollywood, Calif.: Emergency Medical Services, 1980), p. 75.

2. Ellen L. Bassuk, Sandra Sutherland Fox, and Kevin J. Prendergast, *Behavioral Emergencies* (Boston, Mass.: Little, Brown, and Company, 1983), p. 194.

3. Bassuk, Fox, and Prendergast, p. 193; and Julie Fanslow, "Needs of Grieving Spouses in Sudden Death Situations: A Pilot Study," *Journal of Emergency Nursing*, Volume 9, Number 4, July/August 1983, pp. 213-216.

4. Lee Ann Hoff, *People in Crisis*, 2nd edition (Menlo Park, Calif.: Addison-Wesley Publishing Company Nursing Division, 1984), pp. 376-377.

5. This and the following information from the National Sudden Infant Death Syndrome Clearinghouse.

6. Kevin R. Brown, "Sudden Infant Death Syndrome: Part I, Update for EMS Providers," *Emergency Medical Services*, Volume 12, Number 5, September/October 1983, p. 57.

Rape and Sexual Assault

It happens to a woman in this country once every eight minutes: she is forced to have sexual intercourse without her consent by means of force, threat, or fraud. Simply, it is called **rape,** and it has become one of the most debilitating and least understood of life crises.

Categories of Rape

In legal terms, there are several categories of rape. The one that most people associate with rape is **forcible rape**—intercourse forced against the woman's will. Penetration may be oral, anal, or vaginal; ejaculation does not need to occur to constitute rape. The two factors critical to defining rape are these: the rape must be forceful, and it must be committed against the woman's will.

But rape doesn't always start out that way. Sometimes there has been limited consent prior to the rape: the man and woman may be married, they may have been on a date, or they may be friends. The woman wants to terminate the sexual act or the relationship, but the man forces her (usually through physical force or verbal threats) into sexual intercourse.

A third category of rape is **statutory rape**—simply stated, a man takes advantage of a woman or child who is not able to use proper judgment. The woman may be under legal age, may be mentally retarded, may be inebriated, or may be on drugs. Even though the man does not have to use force, and even though the woman may seem to consent, it is legally classified as rape.

Kinds of Rape

Regardless of the category, there are several different kinds of rape:[1]

The Random Blitz Rape

This is the rape that conforms with most stereotypes. The blitz rape occurs "out of the blue." The rapist and the victim have had no previous contact: at one minute, the victim is enjoying her normal life-style, and the next the rapist forces himself on her with shattering speed. She is for him an anonymous target—he was looking for someone to attack, and she happened to come along. While some random blitz rapes occur in buildings, most occur outdoors (usually in parks or in streets). The rapist has carefully calculated his moves, but the victim happens to be in the wrong place at the wrong time.

The Specific Blitz Rape

The specific blitz rape is much like the random blitz rape: the rapist strikes suddenly, using the element of surprise, and has carefully calculated his moves. The rape seems to the victim to have occurred "out of the blue." There is, however, an important difference: the rapist has selected a specific victim. He probably does not know the victim, and has probably not said more than a casual "hellow" in the past, but he has observed her for some time. Maybe he has watched her walking her dog in a certain part at a certain time each night, or maybe he has seen her repeatedly in the parking lot of her building.

The Confidence Rape

The confidence rape is another matter completely. The rapist obtains sex under false pretenses from someone with whom he has had prior contact. He may strike up a conversation with the victim and "win her over" instead of using physical force to capture her; he may be a casual friend or acquaintance, or he may even be married to her. He may be a friend or relative or school teacher or date. Instead of using force, he uses the prior relationship to justify his presence—and then he betrays the woman's confidence by not honoring the bounds of the relationship.

The "acquaintance rape" (or confidence rape) accounts for about 60 percent of all reported rapes—and, unfortunately, a great number of them are **not** reported because their victims are so reluctant to press charges. The dynamics of "date rape," as it is called, set it apart from the less-common random blitz rape. Most blitz rapes occur outside or in the victim's home, are terrifyingly brief, involve lethal weapons, and occur at all times of the day on every day of the week. The "date rape" is different: most of them occur on the rapist's turf (in his apartment, in his car). They often last for hours, and few involve threats with lethal weapons—instead, the rapist uses verbal threats or sheer physical force to overpower his victim. Most occur on weekends between the hours of 10 p.m. and 2 a.m.

One of the most pronounced differences is in the reaction of the victim. Women who are raped by strangers often develop a fear of the unfamiliar; women who are raped by men they know or have trusted develop a triple-barreled crisis: they no longer know whom to trust, they doubt their own judgment (because they initially trusted the rapist), and they develop overwhelming guilt (because they initially wanted to be with the rapist).

Some disturbing attitudes and circumstances surround most confidence rapes. Victims say that their rapists seem to have a split personality—at one minute they are tender, loving, and charming, and the next minute they are hostile and aggressive. A surprising number of people almost condone the practice: men have come to believe that they "deserve" sex at the end of a date, even if the woman doesn't want it, and a disturbing percentage of women interviewed believe that forced sex is "permissible" under certain circumstances.[2]

Unfortunately, sometimes the rapist is the victim's husband. Only recently has this kind of rape been recognized, partly because men and women have been burdened with outmoded myths and beliefs. For example, many believed that a wife was "property" and that sex was a husband's "right," no matter what the wife wanted. Many believed that sexual relations—even forced ones—were between a husband and wife, and that "outsiders" (such as law enforcement personnel) shouldn't interfere. Women didn't resist because they believed sex was their "wifely duty," because they feared their husbands would leave them if they did, because their husbands threatened them, or because they somehow believed that their husbands would hurt the children if they were denied sexual intercourse. When it's all over, they stay with their husbands—because they honestly believe it won't happen again.[3]

White Collar Rape

A form of confidence rape, white collar rape occurs when a professional or semi-professional uses his position and influence to gain the confidence of a colleague or client, whom he then victimizes. The rapist lures his victim into a private place on the pretext of needing to discuss business—and she goes without fear or doubt because the prior relationship has been based solely on business. Once he gets his victim there, he forces her into sex by deceit, subterfuge, or betraying past interactions with her.

Power with Trickery Rape

In this kind of rape situation, the rapist relies on a position of power to gain control, and then he offers goods or services to lure the victim. (These goods and services are rarely monetary; usually they are in the form of candy, new clothes, toys, or intangible things, like "emotional security" or "pleasure." The rapist rarely follows through with the promised goods.) In many cases, the victim is a child or young adolescent who is "tricked" into the rape with the promised goods. In the majority of power with trickery rapes, the victim at first agrees to the sexual relations but changes her mind at the last moment, usually because of fear; her attempts to renegotiate usually fail. A large number of these rapes are not reported because the victim doesn't see it as a **rape**—she initially consented, so she figures she deserves what she got.

Contractual Rape

Contractual rape, somewhat like the power with trickery rape, involves initial consent. Usually, the victim is a prostitute; she contracts with the rapist, whom she views as "simply another client," a price is agreed on, and the sexual act begins. Then something goes wrong—and the prostitute changes her mind. In most cases, the rapist forces the prostitute to do something (such as oral or anal sex or some kind of perversion) that is definitely against her will, but he overpowers her, ties her up, or uses physical violence to subdue her. Often the rapist does not pay the agreed-upon price. Because a prostitute is in the "sex for sale" business, few of these rapes are reported—and the ones that are reported are rarely successfully prosecuted.

Ceremonial Rape

Sometimes, rape occurs as part of an initiation ceremony, ritual, or as part of black magic or mysticism; often more than one rapist is involved. Sometimes one rapist attacks one woman while other members of the group watch; other times, more than one group member attacks the woman, either simultaneously or in turn.

Situational Rape

In the situational rape, the rapist meticulously creates the "situation" in which he will rape the victim; he almost always uses others (without them knowing it) to lure the victim to the scene. The rape generally occurs in the rapist's car or at the rapist's home; the rapist and the victim generally know each other, at least for a few hours, before the rape occurs. The situational rape is carefully planned and created almost like a movie script.

Family Rape

Deliberate force is used in family rape, in which one family member rapes another—husband rapes wife, brother rapes sister, father rapes daughter, uncle rapes niece, grandfather rapes granddaughter, and so on. The rapist generally uses his role in the family to catch the victim off-guard in a situation in which she is isolated from other people. Interestingly, in most cases of family rape the victim and the rapist have not had a good relationship for some time; the rapist uses force, because mutual trust is lacking. Family rape is the most unreported type of rape, probably because the victim is afraid of her relatives' reaction. (In the case of a husband raping his wife, it has only been recently that such forceful situations have been defined as "rape," and they are still difficult to prove in court, which leads to a woman's natural reluctance to prosecute.)

Friendship Rape

Rape may occur between two people who are friends, who have had a good relationship (often over a period of months or years), and who have not had any kind of sexual relationship. It can also occur between friends who **have** had prior sexual experiences. The man often uses verbal abuse or verbal persuasion to coerce the woman, who goes along because she is fearful of what might happen if she resists. In some cases,

physical force is used. Victims of this kind of rape frequently do
not report it because of their previous relationship with the
rapist; they become guilty and assume that they somehow
"asked for it" after months of a good, stable relationship.

Interaction Between Rapist and Victim[4]

In the strict sense of the word, there is no **relationship**
between the rapist and the victim. During the rape, the rapist
neutralizes his feelings about the rape and depersonalizes him
from what he is doing to the victim; she is simply an object, a
means by which the rapist can act out his hostility. Because she
is not a "person" for him, there is no interpersonal relationship
during the rape—even if there had previously been a
relationship between the rapist and the victim. (The women
who were successful in dissuading a rapist did so by eliciting in
him some emotion—and once she is a person instead of an
object, the rapist has an extremely difficult time completing the
rape.)

While there is not a **relationship** between the rapist and the
victim, there is certainly an **interaction**—a situation in which
the rapist has an influence or takes action against the victim.
That interaction occurs in three specific stages: prior to the
rape, during the rape, and following the rape.

Prior to the Rape

—**Choosing the victim.** In most cases, the top qualification
for a rapist is that the victim is vulnerable: she might be
mentally retarded, intoxicated from drugs or alcohol, small,
sleeping alone, walking alone, divorced, separated, widowed, or
a person who is tired late at night. He wants a victim who is not
alert, not able to defend herself, and who is available. He will
choose a location where he is not likely to be discovered or

interrupted and a place that allows easy entry—a basement apartment, an all-night laundromat, or a building that is in disrepair.

Two kinds of women are at particular risk of being victimized: the woman who denies that rape can happen to her will not be alert to the clues, and the woman who tends to reach out to others and help them may unknowingly court disaster.

—**Testing the victim.** The rapist wants to know if the victim can be raped, so he "tests" her to see whether he can intimidate her. Usually he uses verbal threats, such as "Shut up!" or "Don't scream, or I'll kill you!" The rapist wants to make sure that he will be able to successfully subdue and intimidate the woman or he will not be able to complete the rape—or, even worse, he may get caught.

There is another kind of "testing" that goes on: the rapist wants to know how the woman will react to physical assault, so he begins caressing her or grasping at her. He may also test her submissiveness by doing something else first, such as robbing her.

—**Intimidating or threatening.** This stage represents the turning point in the rape: if the rapist is unsuccessful in intimidating or threatening the victim, he will abandon the rape.

The usual pattern involves the rapist both threatening and calming the victim: he threatens her with graphic descriptions of what he will do to her if she resists him, and he calms her down by telling her that everything will be all right if she submits to his demands. (He may tell her that he will kill her, kill her children, or some other terrifying penalty if she refuses to cooperate; then he may tell her that she will not be hurt if she cooperates.) During this stage of "negotiation," the rapist tries to get a guarantee of controlled behavior out of the victim. The victim, too, brandishes her own negotiation—she may agree to some things (oral intercourse), but not others (anal intercourse), or she may bargain for her escape by offering the rapist money or possessions.

One researcher notes that many of the victims who escape the rape do so at this stage by establishing some kind of interpersonal contact with the rapist—arousing his sympathy, openly showing distress, crying, showing signs of weakness, or protesting about physical difficulties. Rapists who approach with great physical aggression are most likely to respond to such a tactic.

Others who escape rape do so by demonstrating the unavailability or inability to be intimidated or threatened, but great danger exists from the potential of further angering the rapist and inciting him to greater violence.

During the Rape

—**Sexual act.** The sexual activity during rape is not always sexual intercourse—in fact, sexual intercourse occurs in less than half of all reported rapes. Many rapists fantasize about the rape beforehand and then play out their fantasies on the victim; oral and anal intercourse are common.

Remember—rape is not a crime of sex or passion, but a crime of violence. The sexual act is not a means to satisfaction sexually, but a means of exercising control or aggression over the victim. The rapist does not feel loving toward the victim; he feels hatred and contempt. He cannot feel affection, because he needs to exercise control; his need to conceal his identity to avoid being caught precludes his ability to establish intimacy.

—**Neutralization and depersonalization.** During rape, the victim becomes meaningless to the rapist; she is an object without equal rights, unique characteristics, or personality. Interviews with convicted sex offenders reveal that they often neutralize themselves from the rape—they convince themselves that **they** have been victimized by society or by women and that they could not help but lash out.

Through depersonalization, the rapist strips the woman of all human qualities; during the rape, it is as though he has never known her, even though they may have been acquainted for years (or even married). During those minutes of rape, she is a total stranger, an object.

Following the Rape

The rapist has one goal following the rape: he wants to do anything he can to delay the victim from reporting him. Simply stated, he doesn't want to get caught. Some will kill the woman to keep her from talking; some will knock the woman out so that she does not regain consciousness until the rapist has long fled the scene. Others will try to confuse the victim so she doesn't know the exact time when the rapist leaves. Still others will threaten to find the victim again and retaliate if she calls the police. Some try to bargain: they promise to go away and never come back if she will not call the police for an hour.

Some rapists feel guilty after the rape and apoligize to the victim; some plead with the victim for forgiveness, and some even try to establish a normal relationship (they ask for a date, as the victim to go out and eat, and so on).

Sexual Dysfunction

As stated, vaginal intercourse occurs in less than half of all reported rapes; one reason is because many rapists are plagued with sexual dysfunction during rape. The issue at hand is power and aggression, not sexual prowess, and it is estimated that about one-third of all rapists experience some kind of sexual dysfunction during the rape.

The most common dysfunction is impotence, the complete or partial inability to achieve or sustain an erection. Some rapists are not able to achieve an erection until they have become angry and aggressive; others demand that the victim stimulate them manually or orally to overcome their inadequacies.

The second most common dysfunction among rapists is retarded ejaculation, or the failure to ejaculate during intercourse even after prolonged activity—a complaint that is relatively rare among the general population. The result of retarded ejaculation can be extensive genital trauma for the victim.

The least common dysfunction among rapists is premature ejaculation, or ejaculation before penetration—usually as a result of rage or aggression.

In some cases, a rapist will suffer several different kinds of sexual dysfunction during a single rape episode, such as the inability to sustain an erection and then retarded ejaculation. Because of these kinds of dysfunctions, the presence of sperm cannot be relied on as the solitary legal evidence confirming rape.

Myths About Rape

A preponderance of myths exist about rape—myths that have added to the misery and guilt of the victims:

—It's not possible to rape someone: if a woman doesn't really want it, you can't force her. (Many women who are raped submit only when the rapist threatens their lives, usually with a knife or a gun. These women certainly don't want to be raped, but they see it as preferable to death.)

—Women "ask for it" by the way they dress or the way they act; they are so provocative that the rapist simply can't resist. (Rape is not a crime of sexual passion; it is a crime of violence. Rapists have been known to victimize infants and ninety-year-old women. The main thing a rapist considers is whether he can overpower the woman, not how she looks.)

—Nice women don't get raped; the woman who is raped is "cheap," unchaste, or "used goods." (Sometimes prostitutes are the victims of rape, but most victims are just the opposite. Rape affects women from all socioeconomic classes and in all age and racial groups.)

—Men can't be held responsible for rape, because they can't control their sexual desires. (Again, rape is not a sexual crime—it is a crime of violence. Sex is used simply because it is a way of exercising control and power over a woman.)

—Women enjoy being treated violently. (Women don't enjoy it any more than men do; it is a horrifying, terrifying experience.)

—Rapists are pathological perverts and criminals. (Not true—many rapists are "normal" married men who enjoy "normal" sexual lives, but they express their anger inappropriately through rage and violence. Many do not have criminal records and have not engaged in other criminal activities.)

—Blacks usually attack whites. (Only one in ten rapists attacks someone of another race; 90 percent of all rapes occur between members of the same race.)

—If sex were more available, such as from prostitutes, the incidence of rape would decline. (This can't be repeated too often: rape is a crime of violence, not a crime of sex.)

—Rape is a just punishment for being out alone at night; if women would stay home, they would be safe. (Many rapes occur in a woman's own bed because the rapist gained entrance into her home. Many other rapes occur between a man and a woman who were on a date, engaged in a business relationship, or married.)

—If the woman resists, the rapist will flee. Women who are raped were too "chicken" to put up a fight. (Just the opposite is true: because the rapist is trying to vent his violence and gain control over the woman, her acts of resistance can further anger him and may lead to increased violence, including murder.)

—Rape only happens to teenage girls. (Rape victims range in age from four months to ninety-two years; women of all ages in all neighborhoods and from all life-styles can be victimized by rape. Although it is less common, men and boys can also be raped.)

—Women are only raped by strangers. (As discussed, rapes can occur between members of the same family, between friends, between dates, and between business associates. Rapes in which a stranger acts on the "spur of the moment" are the least common kinds of rape.)

—There is no way to protect yourself against rape. (There **are** ways to reduce your risk; some of those ways are discussed at the end of this chapter.)

Why Men Rape

Many men rape to satisfy the desire for power. A little more than half of those who rape do it to gain power over a woman. In many cases, these men have come from homes that were dominated by women or they have been controlled by women (a girlfriend or employer, for example); they rape to gain control over women. In most cases, these men will use force to subdue the woman, but will not use force to hurt her. The power rapist usually suffers from low self-esteem and feelings of worthlessness, inadequacy, and vulnerability; he feels especially inadequate in his sexual abilities, which might explain why he chooses a sexual way of expressing his rage.

The power rapist is more likely to choose a stranger as a victim; he stalks her, much as a hunter stalks an animal, to make sure that he can conquer her.

Almost half of all rapists commit their crime out of anger; those rapes are characterized by force, intimidation, and physical brutality. The angry rapist does not usually choose a stranger for a blitz rape, but is more likely instead to win over a victim through confidence and then batter, hurt, and debase her. Angry rapes are characterized by actions that are true expressions of rage, anger, hatred, and contempt—the rapist will do whatever he can to degrade the victim, including insulting her, using vile profanity, or forcing her into particularly vile sexual acts. Through the rape, the rapist experiences a release of tension and anger.

The angry rapist often feels put down by women, and the rape is often preceded by an upsetting event (such as a fight with his wife or girlfriend). Most of the relationships in his life are characterized by irritation, aggravation, and conflict; he displaces his subsequent anger on the victim. The rape is explosive, and the rapist usually inflicts serious injury on the victim (which explains why more men in this category are convicted).

Only a few men rape out of a desire to be sadistic—to torture, abuse, and punish the victim. The victim of a sadistic rapist usually represents or symbolizes something he wants to destroy (such as the man who rapes a prostitute because he wants to wipe out prostitution). The rapes are characterized by pain, torture, abuse, bondage, bizarre ritualism, degradation, and punishment. Most sadistic rapists carefully plan their rapes to avoid discovery; the rapes are premeditated, and they are repetitive, with each rape increasing in the level of violence.

Most sadistic rapists are married, but most have problems in their marriages; they tend to masturbate with masochistic fantasies, or they collect masochistic pornography. The sadistic rapist generally views the world as a hostile place, and he has generally had problems developing mutually rich personal relationships.

While sadistic rapes are the least common, they are the most sensationalized by the press and attract the most curiosity; California's Hillside Rapist and Jack the Ripper are good examples of famous sadistic rapists.

In some cases, men rape because they are trying to defend against homosexual impulses; others rape to gain status among their peers (as in notorious gang rapes).

While rapists have some defects in their personality structures, most are not markedly mentally ill or retarded; most carry on what appears to be "normal" life-styles in normal families. Many use drugs and/or alcohol and may use them prior to the rape to either bolster their courage or help neutralize their feelings about the rape.

Fantasies About Rape[5]

While some adolescent women may fantasize about rape in response to heavy media coverage about rape, studies show that most women do not fantasize about being raped. The same studies show, however, that fantasies about rape—or about a master-slave relationship in sex—are remarkably common among men of all social classes. Interestingly, they are rare among adolescent boys.

But a distinction needs to be made. Sexual fantasies about rape (or about bondage or master-slave relationships) are just that—sexual. The titillation from such a fantasy usually comes from seeing the woman shake with fear or anticipation. **The** desire to inflict violence or pain is almost never a part of these fantasies.

The act of rape is entirely different: its motive is one of violence and the desire to gain control and power. Physical injury (or the threat of physical injury) is common.

The rape fantasies of adolescent boys, while not common, are even more removed from the actual scenario of rape. Adolescents envision older women ("like my mother") and concentrate on the erotic nature of the woman. Their fantasies, unlike rape, rarely contain visions of force, violence, or power.

Characteristics of the Rapist

Every rapist, obviously, is an individual. But studies have shown that rapists do have certain characteristics in common:[6]

—A man who rapes may have suffered repeated sexual rejection. He is raping now to prove his sexual prowess, but it is not a **sexual** desire—it is a motive of power; he wants to be powerful enough to attract and hold women. Many rapists are unable to enjoy relationships with women on a voluntary basis; instead, they must be forceful to maintain the relationship.

—Rapists are generally unable to control their impulses. They react to stress or tension with violent outbursts. They often have trouble managing many aspects of their life, such as employment or school. Their poor impulse control is often evident from their use of drugs and/or alcohol.

—Most rapists have a low tolerance for frustration: they want things **now** and cannot cope normally if their goals or desires are frustrated. Most have low self-esteem and feelings of worthlessness. They usually hate people in general and women in particular.

—Many rapists are demanding and self-centered; when obstacles appear, they react with sudden force and violence to remove the obstacles.

—The typical rapist is between fifteen and twenty-four years of age. There are some variations on that theme, however. Some rapes occur in the course of another violent crime—such as armed robbery—by a rapist who simply sees the opportunity and seizes it. Adolescents who have suffered sexual rejection and who are anxious over their ability to prove themselves sexually may use rape to prove themselves; they often choose elderly victims who represent a forgiving, symbolic mother. Gang rapists, usually between the ages of fifteen and twenty-two, perform the rape to gain status with their peers and to exert power.

One of the least understood situations is the child rapist. He has been portrayed as a sleezy pervert who lurks around school yards. In reality, he is usually someone in the child's own family; in 75 percent of all child rapes, the rapist was a member of the household, a relative that was not a member of the immediate household, or a friend with whom the child had frequent contact. Because the rapist has extreme feelings of inadequacy and a low self-esteem, he is fearful that he will not be able to subdue or overcome an adult.

Another frequently misunderstood situation is that of husband rape. Statistics show that one out of seven American women who has ever been married has been raped by a husband or ex-husband.[7] Compounding the problem, rape by a husband is considered a crime in only twelve states—California, Connecticut, Florida, Iowa, Massachusetts, Minnesota, Nebraska, New Hampshire, New Jersey, Oregon, Virginia, and Wisconsin.[8] Women who are raped by their husbands have specific rights, including the right to treatment of injuries without disclosing who assaulted them and the right to decide whether or not to report the assault.

Characteristics of the Victim

Any woman can become a victim of rape. But rape victims do share several qualities that make them more vulnerable:

—The rape victim is easily frightened when she is threatened.

—She is handicapped; she is not likely to be able to fight back, nor is she likely to be able to move quickly enough to alert police after the rape. The rapist is more likely to be able to escape without police detection.

—She is alone. She may be divorced, widowed, never married, separated, or simply by herself at the time of the attack. Widowed women and single mothers are most often victimized.

—She is young—less likely to fight back, easier to take advantage of.

—She is quick to respond to a friendly smile or a request for help.

Basically, the rapist is looking for a woman he believes he can overpower, intimidate, and threaten with success. He is looking for someone who will not scream or attract attention. He is looking for someone who will not move quickly to alert police once the rape is over.

A child who is raped is usually raped by someone she knows or by a relative. Most rapes occur during the daytime, but about one-third occur after dark, usually by someone who is left in charge of the child. Many cases of child rape do not involve actual vaginal penetration; many involve oral intercourse, rectal intercourse, fondling, or penetration of the vagina with a finger or other object. Few child rapes are reported; since brutality is not usually used, many go undetected. (In cases where brutality is used, the case is often reported as child abuse instead of rape.) Few children put up a fight; most are sworn to silence following the rape. Children who are raped suffer a broad range of physical, social, and emotional problems, such as social withdrawal, nightmares, bedwetting, repression, fear, and self-punitive behavior.

The most common victims involved in rape are adolescents; according to one study, slightly more than half had experienced sexual intercourse before being raped, and almost as many had been in trouble at home or in school (many are truants, runaways, or girls with criminal records). The normal developmental struggles that all adolescents experience are what make these girls vulnerable to rape: they are reaching out for new identities, trying to make new friends, loosening family restraints, challenging family rules, and testing all kinds of limits. Most are raped on weekends, after dark, and away from home, usually at a social event; gang rapes are common for this age group, and rapes usually last longer than an hour. About 86 percent of the time, vaginal-penile penetration occurs; most of the time, the rapist is someone the girl knows (even if she has known him only briefly, such as a few hours), and not as much brutality is involved as in adult rapes. Adolescent rape victims suffer intense emotional trauma, including problems such as regression, sustained unrest, and intense fear.

A special category of adolescent rape is incest: rape by a father, uncle, grandfather, or brother. Most are not reported—the girl is afraid of causing problems at home, afraid of breaking up the family, afraid of getting someone she loves in trouble. The family member who raped may be pressuring the girl to keep it quiet. He may even convince the girl that she somehow "deserved" it and that she is responsible for it. Such a victim does not realize that she is not to blame for what happened and that she needs—and deserves—to get help.

Adult victims are usually raped at night, indoors, by total strangers; the rape is usually brief but generally involves brutal violence. Many adult victims become angry with themselves, and most suffer extreme terror following the rape.

Children

Child sexual assault is three times more common than child battery;[9] unfortunately, up to 80 percent of those are estimated to go unreported. Usually, rape (or sexual abuse) of a child is not an isolated, one-time occurrence; it usually builds in frequency and intensity until it is stopped (usually by outside intervention or by the victim—the rapist usually doesn't stop on his own).

Because children are trusting and usually defenseless, they are perfect targets. Because they are easily frightened and threatened, they can easily be silenced afterward.

You should know one vital fact: children often fantasize and pretend about many things, but they rarely lie about being victims of sexual assault. If a child tells you that she has been touched or assaulted, believe her. Reassure her that it was not her fault, that **she** was not the naughty one, and that you want to help. Gently encourage her to tell you what happened.

Unfortunately, children are often too confused or frightened to tell anyone about the rape. Watch for physical or behavioral clues. Look for irritation, infection, or injury to the genital areas; watch for torn, stained, or bloody underwear. The child might be having trouble sleeping—she might be waking up with nightmares or might be wetting the bed. A child who has been raped might also develop behavioral problems, such as withdrawal, refusal to go to school, fear of being alone, increased anxiety, or sudden immature behavior.

Prostitutes

For years, no one acknowledged that prostitutes could get raped—everyone assumed that they "asked for it" and that they "deserved what they got." But prostitutes **do** get raped. Prostitute rape falls into two general categories:[10]

—**Rape.** The prostitute is an easy mark: she is often on the streets late at night or early in the morning, when there is little protection. She is almost always alone. The rapist knows, too, that he has little chance of being prosecuted—few prostitutes prosecute, and even those who report the rape rarely **appear** in court to testify.

—**Violation of contract.** Simply put, prostitution is a basic business transaction involving an agreement between the provider and the buyer. The prostitute agrees to render services in exchange for a certain price. But things can—and do—go wrong. Sometimes the man refuses to pay after he has received the agreed-on services. In other cases, the rapist may rob the prostitute of her money (prostitutes are easy prey for robbery, since they usually get paid in cash and they usually keep their cash with them until the end of the evening).

More often, a prostitute is made to do things to which she did not agree—things that are against her will. She may be forced through threats or physical force to engage in perverted sexual practices (such as anal sex or urinating on a man's face); in some cases, the man who contracted for the sexual acts becomes violent and brutal. Some are threatened with lethal weapons and fear for their lives; some get tied up and beaten with belts or other devices. These actions—committed forcibly and against the woman's will—easily fit the definition of rape.

Prostitutes who are raped suffer severe emotional damage; in a profession where they often feel exploited, they now feel used, degraded, and inhuman. Many feel revengeful but do not follow through with threats to go to the police. (In most cases of prostitute rape, the prostitute knows the rapist and can identify him or knows others who can identify him.)

Elderly Women

Elderly women become victims of rape for a simple reason: they are vulnerable, not likely to resist force, not likely to defend themselves, more likely to be alone, and not likely to summon help quickly enough to endanger the rapist.

Elderly women who are raped have special needs following the rape. Because of age, it often takes them longer to recover from injuries, or injuries may result in permanent disabilities; limited or fixed income may keep a woman from seeking medical help. They may be reluctant to tell others, especially their children.

Fear plays a great part in the elderly victim's reaction: she fears that she will no longer be able to protect herself, that she will be victimized again, and that she cannot survive. Intense fear associated with the rape may pervade other aspects of her life.

An elderly victim may also suddenly become dependent on others. She is too afraid to live alone; she is paralyzed by the thought that another rapist (or the same one) will come back. She desperately wants someone to "take care of her." The rape of an elderly woman can be the turning point that takes her from an active, independent life-style to one of fear, withdrawal, and dependence.

The Disabled or Handicapped Woman

Disabled people often think that they are immune to rape because they are unattractive or perceived as being "asexual." The contrary is true: because their disabilities often make them vulnerable, they are easy marks for rapists. (A rapist may choose a blind woman, for example, because he wrongly believes that she could never identify him; blind people, on the contrary, have often developed acute hearing, smell, and other senses that enable easy identification.)

Unfortunately, the disabled person has probably fought for her sense of independence, her ability to live alone, and her capacity to function well on her own; the rape may change all that, at least temporarily. She may react much like the elderly victim, fearful of venturing out alone, afraid to live alone. Compounding the problem is the typical reaction of those close to the victim: they tend to become overprotective instead of encouraging the victim to return to her life-style as quickly as possible. The disabled victim has a special challenge in trying to overcome feelings of helplessness, powerlessness, and fear.

Victims Who Are Men

Unfortunately, many people do not realize that men can be the victims of sexual assault—even a man who is raped may be startled and stunned by what has happened. Doctors, nurses, law enforcement officers, and paramedics may all be confused about what has happened and what they should do next. But the important thing to remember is this: no one deserves to be the victim of a sexual assault, and no one under any circumstance has the right to violate or control someone else's body.

Two dangerous myths about male rape may lead to unnecessary guilt for the victim and inappropriate questioning by authorities. The first myth is that **only homosexual men are raped.** The second myth is that **assaults against men are**

committed only by homosexual men.[11] Neither is true—you can become a victim regardless of your sexual orientation, and the sexual orientation of your rapist is not the issue. The issue, the focus, should be the physical assault.

Men may be reluctant to report the rape for several reasons. They may feel guilty ("Do I look gay? Why would that guy want to have sex with me? Did I provoke the attack?"); they may not realize that the rape had nothing to do with sex or passion. They may be stricken with doubts about their masculinity for the same reason. They may fear for their safety—they may become convinced that the rapist will retaliate with more violence (or murder) if they report the crime.

A man who is raped should request the help of a male counselor and should **always** be believed and treated seriously.

Defending Yourself Against Rape

Wouldn't it be nice if there was a clear-cut checklist of defense tactics that a victim could use in case of rape that would be guaranteed to work? It **would** be nice, but no neat little checklist exists. Every rapist is different, every rape is unique, and every victim must assess a number of factors to determine the best defense.

Authorities disagree about whether or not a woman should try to resist the rapist. In some cases, simply trying to resist will deter the rapist; in others, it makes him more determined than ever to go though with it. In still other cases, it enrages the rapist and leads to brutality or murder.

Only the victim can know—or guess—about the advisability of resisting, and a number of factors enter into that decision. Where is the attack taking place? Is the area deserted, or are people nearby? If she did manage to escape, where could she run to? Would there be people who could help? Does the rapist have a weapon? Might he use it? Almost all rapes involve threats of violence, but studies show that only about one in three rapists resort to violence or brutality; the rest confine the attack to the rape itself. But the threat is always there—and the danger intensifies if the rapist has a weapon. The victim has a choice to make: is it better to be raped and alive, or raped and dead?

Remember, the rapist has probably "tested" his victim to determine that she is vulnerable. In deciding whether or not to resist, the victim should realize that her attempts might not help her and might actually hurt her. Self-defense can be effective under certain circumstances, but sometimes it just further angers and provokes the rapist. Certain kinds of self-defense, or the use of certain kinds of weapons, is not advised because of the danger of the rapist reversing the attack:

—**Ordinary objects used as weapons.** You might have heard advice about grabbing an ordinary object—such as a rattail comb, hat pin, lighted cigarette, or umbrella—and using it as a weapon against the rapist. You run the risk of the rapist grabbing the object and using it against you instead. If you do decide to try, go for the throat or the stomach; blows to the head are usually ineffective because they are easily deflected and not forceful enough to stun the rapist.

—**Conventional weapons.** Conventional weapons, such as guns and knives, are of questionable value. First of all, they're usually not where you can grab them—if they were, the rapist would have seen them first and used them to threaten you. (Women usually drop their purses during an initial attack, so having a weapon in a purse usually doesn't help.) Second, you must be an excellent aim and be very practiced in using weapons to deter a rapist—if you fumble around, even for a second, you could be on the receiving end.

—**Martial arts.** Martial arts can be effective if a woman makes a serious commitment to the art and spends the time and self-discipline necessary to perfect the techniques. The skills must be polished and kept current to be of value. If martial arts techniques are performed wrong or hesitantly, they can do nothing more than aggravate the rapist to further violence.

—**Mace spray.** Mace, available in small aerosol spray containers, is illegal in many states; even where it is not illegal, it is difficult to use effectively. During the confusion and struggle of the initial attack, it is easy for the victim to mistakenly spray herself; it is easy, too, for the rapist to wrestle it away from her.

—**Whistles or pocket sirens.** Whistles are of questionable value unless you already have one in your mouth when the assault begins; you probably won't be able to wrestle one to your mouth after the attack begins. A battery-operated pocket siren that is immediately available and responds to touch will probably be a little more help—it may serve to scare away the rapist and attract help.

—**Screaming.** The value of screaming depends on the circumstances surrounding the rape. If the rape is occurring in an isolated area where there is little or no chance of someone hearing and responding, screaming is of little value—it may even further aggravate the rapist. If, however, the rape is occurring in an area where people are nearby and a means of escape is available, screaming may indeed help—the rapist doesn't want to be discovered, and he may flee to escape detection. Loud, persistent screaming may also startle the rapist and give the victim a few seconds in which to break away. You should always be aware of the fact that an extremely brutal or violent rapist may simply kill a victim to stop her from screaming and attracting attention.

—**Talking.** Many experts feel that talking can be one of the best tactics against a rapist—if a victim can establish some kind of relationship that forces the rapist to view her as a person instead of an object, he will probably be unable to complete the rape. Talking can also serve other functions—it can work as a bargaining tool ("I will agree to oral sex, but I cannot agree to anal sex"), can help the victim gain time if she is confident that help will arrive, or can sometimes distract the rapist from acts of violence.

There are a number of verbal tactics. You can try threatening the rapist, reasoning with him, bargaining with him, or stalling him ("Please just let me drink a cup of coffee first"). An interview with seven imprisoned rapists revealed some interesting things about conversation:[12] most agreed that it is unwise to threaten a rapist ("I'm going to call the police!"). Most said that conversation would work with some rapists, but that many are angered by it; one said he became "aggravated" when his victim persisted in talking. Interestingly, they all advised a woman not to fight back; one said, "When they gave me any trouble, that's when I cut them up good."[13]

—**Fighting back.** The convicted rapists answered the issue in a single word: don't. One of the rapists said, "One woman kicked me in the groin, but I had so much adrenalin going, I didn't feel it till the next day." In response to the fact that women are learning martial arts, one of the rapists said, "Men know that stuff, too. And they're better at it. Because when we're kids, boys learn to hurt each other. Girls don't learn that."[14] The authors of *The Woman's Bible for Survival in a Violent Society* agree that many of the martial arts and "self-defense" techniques work fine on a cooperative "assailant" but not in an actual attack situation. They advise against faking a fainting spell, assuming a karate stance (unless you are thoroughly trained and well-practiced), bending back the rapists's fingers, stomping on the rapist's instep, puncturing the attacker's eyeball, kicking the rapist in the groin, kicking the rapist in the kneecap, or blindly kicking, punching, scratching, or biting in an attempt to drive the rapist off. All of these, the authors say, are too difficult to pull off successfully and will likely further enrage the rapist.[15]

So what can you do to survive an attack? Experts vary in their opinions but advise some of the following:

—**Remain calm.** Remember, the rapist is interested in hurting you, not in having sex with you. If you struggle, you add to the cycle of violence; if you remain calm, you take some of the excitement out of it for him. Your goal is to get away with the least amount of harm possible. You might be able to increase your calm by mentally focusing on some other thought or situation or by praying. (By staying calm, you can also keep your wits enough to memorize details of the rape—the rapist's physical appearance, his license plate number, the unusual underwear he wore, and whether he used a condom, for example.)

—**Submit to the attack.** Too many women believe that submission is a form of consent. It isn't! You submit out of fear for your safety or the safety of those you love, not because you want to have sex. You should never feel guilty about submitting—it is still a crime, and the rapist is the criminal.

—**Resist without aggression.** Passive resistance works with some rapists, but not with others. The goal of passive resistance is to calm the rapist down, to diffuse some of his anger and hostility. You can do it by talking, reasoning, or pleading with him in a calm way.

—**Become the aggressor.** Refuse to be victimized! Remember—the rapist will "test" you before he chooses you as a victim. Show him, early on, that you will not be overcome. If you sense that someone is "sizing you up," make a few aggressive moves of your own to prove that you are not vulnerable. Take a few steps toward the rapist and speak to him. One woman on an elevator avoided an attack when she noticed that a man was looking at her in a threatening way. She took a few steps toward him and said, "Do you have the time?" She took a few more steps toward him and said, "What's going on in this building? I noticed three or four cops on the main floor." When the elevator reached her floor, she stepped out with confidence.

One of the convicted rapists who was interviewed recalled a situation when he confronted a woman on the street with the demand that she submit to him. She said, "Okay!" and began taking off her own clothes. He decided that she must be "nuttier than I am. So I ran like hell!"[16]

What Happens When It's All Over

If the rape does occur, what happens to the victim? She has plenty of psychological problems to sort through—but she must act quickly to alert law enforcement and medical personnel.

It is critical that the victim **not** change clothes, wash, douche, or touch her genital area until she has been examined by a physician; she is the evidence that the rape took place, and by washing or changing clothes, she could destroy that evidence.

The Police

The first thing to do is to call the police and report the rape. You are not obligated to file a criminal complaint, but the police are helpless in stopping the rapist if they don't have your help as a victim. Most rapists are repeat offenders—they rape again and again, victimizing countless women until they are stopped by someone who has the courage to prosecute. It may be extremely difficult to repeat the details of the rape or to "relive" the assault during questioning, but it is vital in apprehending the rapist.

The police will probably transport you to a hospital and will help you find out which community agencies can help you. (Most hospitals will contact the police if you come in on your own, but you are not obligated to file a criminal complaint if you don't want to.)

The Hospital

Medical help is essential, even if you don't think you are hurt: you may be in a state of shock and may not realize your injuries. You need to be examined to rule out injury or to treat injury; you need to be treated for unwanted pregnancy or venereal disease; and physicians and nurses need to collect medical evidence for possible future prosecution. It is vital that the evidence be collected **as soon as possible after the rape occurs.**

Commonly, the hospital will keep your clothing as evidence, including your underwear; you will need to call a friend and ask for a change of clothing. You may be asked to comb your pubic hair and collect the hairs in an envelope; you may be asked to tug out a few head hairs and place them in a separate envelope. If you have been battered, physicians may ask you to sign a consent form, and they may take photographs of your injuries. (If you plan on prosecuting, you should be aware that many bruises will not become visible for six to fourteen days after the assault; keep in touch with an officer so that pictures can be taken later.)

During a pelvic examination, the physician will collect specimens of vaginal secretions to detect the presence of sperm or semen in the vagina or the rectum. Tests for venereal disease and pregnancy will be done then and repeated two weeks later. (An initial followup appointment should be made two weeks after the rape, and a second followup should occur six weeks after the rape.)

The Courts

Unfortunately, fewer than one in five rape cases ever go to trial, and even fewer result in convictions.[17] This doesn't mean that you shouldn't try—it just means that you should do everything possible to collect as much evidence as you can and to cooperate fully with officials. To achieve conviction, there must be ample evidence to convict the rapist; without plenty of good, solid evidence, many prosecuting attorneys won't even take the case to trial.

Rape Trauma Syndrome

Regardless of the victim's age or circumstances, she is likely to pass through a five-stage reaction to rape known as rape trauma syndrome. The following reactions are characteristic of the syndrome:

The Rape

During the rape, the victim will feel terrified and may lapse into acute emotional shock; her consciousness may disintegrate. She may appear to be drugged; during the rape itself, she may have a number of physical reactions, including seizures, urination, paralysis, pain, hyperventilation, nausea, and vomiting.

The Acute Reaction Phase

Immediately following the rape, the victim may experience shock, disbelief, and incoherence. In most cases, as the reality of the situation occurs to her, she becomes visibly upset, shaken, agitated, angry, and restless. She may feel "dirty" and may blame herself in a wave of shame. Her general fears and feelings of anxiety may interfere with the reporting of the rape: she may not know who to tell, may fear that she will not be believed, may fear the physical examination by a male physician, and may fear that the rapist will retaliate against her if she reports him.

For the time being, she is unable to resume her normal life-style.

The Outward Adjustment Phase

For a period that may last for several months after the rape, the woman attempts to adjust to what has happened. She recovers from any physical injury but may suffer a number of physical problems, including nightmares, headaches, insomnia, loss of appetite, nausea, vaginal infections, and burning during urination.

The outward adjustment phase is one of fear. The victim is often jumpy and nervous; she feels anxious and insecure. She is afraid of crowds, of physical violence, of death, of being approached from behind, of the unexpected, and of intercourse (even with those she knows well, such as her husband). During this phase, she may become extremely anxious over impending medical treatments, over the possibility of venereal disease or pregnancy, and over the legal procedures that await her. Her normal life-style remains disrupted, and her usual sexual relationships suffer.

The Depression Phase

Previously successful defenses, such as denial, break down over the days and months following the rape. She loses her self-extreme and begins having both waking and sleeping nightmares about the rape. She is afraid that her life will never be normal again, tries to resolve her feelings, and needs help in removing guilt feelings about the rape.

The Integration and Resolution Phase

During the months and years that follow the rape, the victim takes the steps necessary to return her life to as normal as possible. She still experiences fear when she finds herself in a situation similar to the rape (on a sandy beach at night, for example, or in the alley between two buildings) and may feel anxious and afraid when confronted with situations that remind her in small ways of the rape. While she feels some sexual apprehension, it is during this stage that she is able to return to normal sexual function. She may continue to hesitate and avoid men and may not trust men. She may move (to get away from the rapist), change her telephone number (to ease her fear of the rapist finding her), take a vacation, or rely on close friends or a support group to successfully return to her normal life-style.

In some cases, the victim does **not** return to a normal life-style, despite the passage of time. In these cases, the victim suffers permanent psychic damage, a reaction more common among those who had a history of physical, social, or psychiatric difficulties. Common reactions include lesbianism, depression, suicidal behavior, alcoholism, drug abuse, psychotic behavior, and sexual acting out. The victim should receive professional counseling to help her deal with the rape experience.

—**Resuming normal sexual activity.** Unless a victim has been seriously injured, she can resume normal sexual activity as soon as she feels comfortable doing so. Some discomfort, fear, anxiety, panic, or frigidity may persist for weeks, months, or sometimes years following a rape, and it requires the compassion and understanding of the victim's partner to help her overcome those feelings.

A husband or lover may have a difficult time with the rape for several reasons. He may be indignant, eager to seek out revenge with the rapist, or preoccupied with the sexual aspects of the rape. Many men feel guilty because they were not able to stop or prevent the rape (even though they may have been miles away at the time), and they translate their guilt into overprotective behavior. Others may become angry at the woman for "putting herself in the situation" and may become concerned about "used merchandise;" for them, the rape represents an attack on their masculinity because the rapist violated their "property." Some may become concerned about their own rape fantasies, and others may not be able to understand the victim's special needs.

—**The silent rape reaction.** Occasionally, a victim will not adjust to the rape properly; instead of releasing and venting her emotions over a period of time, she becomes a "rock," dealing with her attack in silent suffering. She may succeed in consciously obliterating the rape, but the crisis continues. Look for the following clues: persistent violent dreams or nightmares; long periods of silence; minor stuttering; chronic loss of self-confidence or self-esteem; paranoia; physical distress of undetermined origin; increasing anxiety; sudden onset of phobias (especially fear of being alone or fear of going outside); marked changes in sexual behavior; and avoidance of relationships with men.

False Rape Accusations

While a vast number of rapes go unreported each year, sometimes a "rape" that did not occur is reported. Most often, reasons for false rape accusations fall into these categories:

—The woman accuses the man of rape as a way to get revenge or as a method of blackmail.

—The woman feels a need to protect her reputation; instead

of admitting that she willingly participated in sexual activities, she accuses her partner of forcing her.

—Rape is often used to explain a pregnancy in an unmarried girl, a divorced woman, or a married women whose husband is sterile or away at the time of conception. The woman is able to save face and preserve harmony in her marriage. Young girls who become pregnant use rape as the excuse to their parents to escape punishment for their own sexual promiscuity.

—Parents who discover that their young girl is engaging in sexual activity may accuse the boy of rape to convince themselves and others in the community that the girl wasn't willing—it wasn't "her fault."

—A schoolgirl crush may turn into an ugly rape accusation if the hysterical girl wants others to believe that her teacher "wants her."

—A child who wants to get rid of an unwelcome stepfather may accuse him of raping her, knowing that he will probably be forced from the home. (As already pointed out, however, young children rarely lie about sexual assault; only an older child or teenager would be likely to use this kind of tactic.)

—A woman who wants an abortion in a state where abortions are difficult to obtain except in cases of rape or incest may claim rape to get the abortion.

—A woman who agrees to sexual intercourse after prolonged courtship may become distraught when her boyfriend drops her; she feels resentment and claims she was raped.

—A woman may be embarrassed that her own husband assaulted her, so she may explain her injuries by claiming she was raped.

—A woman may claim she was raped if she pickes up venereal disease during a covert extramarital affair.

—False claims of rape may be made due to fear of losing welfare payments for illegitimacy or due to a desire to protect the woman's reputation during a child custody battle.

—A woman may claim she has been raped to elicit the sympathy of a lost husband or lover, whom she hopes will rush to her defense.

—A woman may want to attract publicity or attention.

—A woman who is anxious over her sexual relations may claim that she has been raped so that she can be examined for pregnancy or venereal disease; parents who are anxious over a daughter's sexual activities may also claim rape so that they can submit her to examinations to detect pregnancy or venereal disease without admitting that she has been promiscuous.

—When sexual activity is interrupted by the police or by parents, a girl may claim that she was being forced against her will in order to avoid being punished.

Unreported Rape

At the opposite end of the spectrum are the unreported rapes—cases in which rape genuinely has occurred but in which the victim does not report it to law enforcement or medical personnel. In many cases, she does not tell anyone—not even family members or friends. The major reasons for not reporting are the following:[18]

—The woman wants to forget all about the rape; she wants to forget that it even occurred. She believes that if she doesn't report it, no one will ever remind her of it and she will not have to be dragged through countless recalls in police stations, hospital emergency rooms, and courtrooms.

—The woman wants to avoid the general social stigma that comes along with being raped.

—The woman is afraid of how her family or husband will react (many men, as already discussed, have considerable difficulty resuming normal sexual relationships with their wives following a rape).

—The woman is convinced that the police will do nothing to help her or she is afraid that there is not enough evidence to convict the rapist anyway.

—The woman is afraid that the police or the courts will be hostile or that the ordeal will be too much to endure after the rape.

—The woman is afraid that the rapist will retaliate—that he will find her and murder her or brutalize her severely.

Protecting Yourself Against Rape

There are a number of things that you can do to protect yourself against rape:

—Don't advertise that you live alone. Keep your window shades or curtains drawn at night, and use only initials on your mailbox and in the phonebook (or add a dummy name).

—If you are alone and the doorbell rings, call out, "I'll get it, John." Use the peephole or intercom to identify who is at the door; never rely on a chain for identification (it is easy for even a moderately strong man to break a chain by kicking the door). If you don't know the person, don't let him in. If he claims to be a repairman, maintenance man, real estate appraiser, policeman, or person conducting a survey, require identification. If you are in doubt about the validity, check with the company by phone while the person waits outside.

—If someone comes to your door and asks to use your phone, refuse, even if the person claims it is an "emergency." Instead, offer to make the phone call for the person while he waits on the other side of your locked door.

—Make sure that your home always looks occupied. Use a timer for your lights and a timer for your radio (it sounds like conversation if you turn it to an all-news station or talk show). Don't pin notes to your door, and ask others not to. If you are going to be away for hours at a time during the day, unplug your telephone while you're gone (an incessantly ringing phone is the best clue to an unoccupied house). Use your porch light, and keep a bathroom light on at night. If you are leaving on vacation, ask you neighbors to take in your mail, and have your newspaper delivery stopped.

—Keep your doors and windows locked, even when you're in the house. If you are renting or have recently purchased your home, have the locks changed; have the cylinders changed when you lose your key. Never put your address on your keyring. Never hide a key on your property; if you need to know where an extra is, give your key to a friend.

—Have a phone near your bed, and keep emergency numbers near your phone (if you wear glasses, write the numbers large enough so that you can read them without your glasses on). Have a friend agree to call and check on you at the same time every day; work out a verbal code you can use to indicate if something is wrong (for example, you might ask, "Did Grace ever place that order for the tulip bulbs?"). Never reveal personal information on the phone, such as your name, address, plans, or the fact that you live alone. If you receive a series of obscene phone calls, report them to the police. When you receive an obscene phone call, do one of two things: either blow a shrill whistle into the phone receiver, or tap the mouthpiece sharply and say, "Operator, this is the call I wanted you to trace."

—Engrave your valuables with your social security number, and never keep large amounts of cash at home (deposit it in the bank). Keep valuables (such as your television and stereo) where they can't be seen from the window or door. Never display guns or other weapons on the wall.

—If you wake up and suspect that an intruder has entered your house, stay in your bedroom and pretend to be asleep; it may be a burglar who will not injure you if you don't startle him (most injuries and murders that occur during burglaries happen because the burglar has been cornered or startled). Try to get out of the house without being seen if you can. If the intruder confronts you, remain calm. If it is daytime, you might try providing him an "out"—try saying something like, "Oh, am I glad to see you! The landlady said you wouldn't be here for fifteen more minutes. Did you discover what was causing the leak?" Chances are, he'll be relieved for the chance to get away.

—Know your neighbors, and work out a procedure for alerting each other in case of emergency.

—Always have your keys in your hand before you reach your door or the entrance to a building; don't overload yourself with bundles, and prepare to drop them quickly if necessary. When you are alone, avoid going into deserted areas of a building, such as the stairway, laundry room, trash room, and storage area.

—Avoid getting into an elevator with a strange man. If you have to, stand near the controls; if he begins to confront you, press the alarm button. If you get nervous, return to the lobby or the main floor before getting off the elevator.

—If you think that you are being watched as you leave your apartment, call back to a mythical companion, "Remember to take the cake out in ten minutes, John." If you approach your apartment and think it has been entered, **do not** go in yourself. Return to the lobby or go to a neighbor's and call the police.

—If you are assaulted in a building, yell "fire" instead of "rape," and make as much noise as you can. Avoid serious injury by using nonaggressive self-defense, as discussed earlier.

—When you are outside, never walk alone; always walk with a companion or in a group. Even when you are with someone else, don't shortcut through parking lots, vacant lots, or alleys. Walk on the sidewalk next to the curb; avoid walking near doorways or shrubbery, where an assailant could be lurking. If you are uncomfortable walking on the sidewalk and the traffic is light, walk in the street. If you are walking near the curb, go in the direction opposite the traffic; if a car pulls up alongside you going in the same direction in which you are walking, abruptly change direction.

—Avoid talking to strangers on the street. If someone asks

you for directions, maintain a safe distance. Never walk through a group of men; walk around them or, if they look threatening, cross the street.

—If you can, avoid carrying a purse. If you have to carry a purse, keep a minimal amount of cash in it and carry it between your body and something else (such as a package) on the side away from the street. If you can, carry your money inside your bra, your shoe, or in a hidden pocket instead of in your purse. If you think that someone might try to take your purse, drop it in the nearest mailbox; the postal service will return it to you if identification is in it. If someone does try to grab your purse, throw it into the street into heavy traffic or turn it upside down, dumping out the contents. If someone does snatch your purse and you get a phone call telling you where to retrieve it, call the police and have them accompany you or get the purse for you. Avoid twisting your purse strap around your wrist—an assailant could use it to pull you down.

—If you carry a whistle, keep it on a key chain, not on a chain around your neck. If you start to feel uneasy, put the whistle in your mouth.

—If you travel a regular route, know where you can get help. Know where there are doormen, police call boxes, all-night convenience stores, and so on.

—When you are going to visit, tell the people which route you are traveling and when you expect to arrive; when someone drives you home, have them wait until you are inside and flash a light for a signal that you are safe. (You should even ask a taxi driver to wait for you.)

—When you travel, try to go with a companion. When waiting for a bus or subway, stand in a confident, erect position, balanced with your feet slightly apart. At a bus or subway stop, stand against the wall to avoid being approached from behind, and have your token ready. Sit near the driver or the conductor; on a subway, choose a busy car and avoid the last car. If you suspect that you are being followed, don't get off at your regular stop; get off at a busy stop and tell the attendant at the change booth that you are being followed.

—When you do your banking, deposit your checks soon after you receive them. Put your cash away before you leave the window. If you can, arrange for direct deposit. If you do need to walk to the bank, don't go alone; vary your route and the time of your deposits.

—When you are driving an automobile, approach the car with your keys in your hand; keep car keys on a separate key ring from your house keys. Never put your name and address on your keyring. Always have at least one-quarter of a tank of gasoline in your car, and drive with the doors locked and with windows at least three-quarters rolled up. Put packages on the floor or in the trunk, not on the seat, where they can be seen.

—Never pick up hitchhikers.

—If your car becomes disabled, raise the hood, tie a white cloth to the radio antenna or door handle, get inside, and lock the doors. If someone comes along to help, stay in the car and ask the motorist to call the police for you.

—At night, always park in a well-lighted, busy area and ask a friend to escort you to your car. Keep your car locked, and always check the back seat and floor before you get in the car.

—Never leave personal papers or credentials in your car.

—If you see a motorist in distress, don't stop to offer help. Note the location of the car and stop as soon as you can to call the police and alert them to the motorist's troubles.

Responding to Rape

In responding to the scene of a rape, follow these guidelines:

—Immediately check the victim's vital signs, and take appropriate corrective measures. Take appropriate steps to control bleeding, and treat the victim for shock.

—Replace fluids if necessary.

—Splint any fractures or suspected fractures.

—Treat any minor injuries.

—**Do not cleanse the victim, and keep her from cleansing herself.** If the allegations of rape are to be proven in a court of law, certain evidence must be collected. Explain to the victim gently that you realize that she feels dirty and that she wants to cleanse herself, but that she needs to let hospital personnel collect specimens so that the rapist can be caught and punished. Explain to her that following a brief exam at the hospital, she can be cleaned up. The victim may insist that she does not want to press charges; **tell her that the hospital wants to collect the evidence and keep it in case she changes her mind later.**

—Prepare the victim for transport to the hospital by wrapping her securely in a clean white sheet and placing her, still wrapped in the sheet, on the stretcher. The sheet will trap pieces of evidence, such as buttons, pubic hair, bits of clothing, and other fibers.[19]

—Prior to transport, radio the hospital and let staff members know that you are transporting a rape victim; ask them to be prepared to handle her as soon as she arrives and ask that they deal with her in a gentle, calm, reassuring way. If possible, a female physician should be assigned to examine the victim at the hospital.

Be sensitive to your obligation for collecting evidence at the scene of the rape. Follow these guidelines:

—Look for blood or semen stains on the ground, bedding, furniture, clothing, or auto upholstery; semen is fluorescent and can be seen with a Wood's lamp. Take photographs where appropriate.

—If the victim used tissues or pieces of cloth to wipe semen from her body before you arrived, collect the tissues or pieces of cloth and place them in a paper bag; seal the bag and label it. **Do not place evidence in plastic bags; the moisture can cause evidence to deteriorate.**

—Photograph the victim if she is still wearing the clothing

that she was wearing during the rape. Then explain to her that you will need the clothing as evidence. Allow her to change her clothing, if a change of clothing is available, and instruct her to handle her clothing as little as possible. Carefully fold each article of clothing, place each in a separate paper bag, and label each. (Remember—plastic bags can cause semen to mold and deteriorate.) **This and the next two steps to be performed by assigned law enforcement personnel only.**

—Photograph the victim's injuries if she will consent to it.

—Photograph the area where the rape occurred if there are visible signs of a struggle (such as overturned furniture, rumpled bedding, forced locks, or strewn leaves and dirt). Photograph any evidence of forced entry.

—Find out if the victim scratched the rapist or pulled out any of his hair. If so, keep the victim from washing her hands; the hospital laboratory can get valuable identifying evidence from under her fingernails.

—If the victim was photographed by an accomplice or by members of a gang, confiscate any camera equipment of film that you can find in the area.

—If you are trained and equipped to do so, dust the area for fingerprints.

—Examine the area surrounding the rape scene carefully and collect anything that might be used for evidence, such as buttons, pieces of cloth, bits of clothing, fibers, hairs, and so on. Bag each one separately in a paper bag and label each with complete information.

—Note on the victim's report any evidence of bruises, punctures, stains, burns, lacerations, abrasions, teeth marks, fractures, swellings, redness, or bleeding; make note of any foreign material on the victim's body, and record whether you took photographs of the injuries or the area.

In working with rape victims, be calm and gentle; speak in a low, quiet, reassuring tone of voice, and avoid making sudden or aggressive movements. Take the time to explain to the victim what you are doing so that she does not feel as though you are moving in and "taking control." Where possible and appropriate, allow her to make decisions and approve treatments. On the way to the hospital, explain carefully and gently what she can expect when she gets there (she may be apprehensive about any kind of examination). Explain the necessity of examinations such as the pelvic examination, and explain to her why it is critical that she receive medical attention **even if she does not intend on pressing charges against the rapist.**

Remember: the victim has the right to choose against pressing charges. Respect that right, and help her protect it.

Special Note

You can be the first to help the patient begin to overcome the stigma of the attack and readjust to her normal life pattern. It is critical that you be neither callous nor judgmental; speak softly, answer questions simply and directly, and explain everything that you can to the patient. Do not be surprised if the patient seems uncooperative or angry with you. Do not take it personally—it is a normal response under the circumstances. Do not force emergency care on the patient if she is resisting due to fear or embarrassment. Care for her as you would any critically ill or injured person. She has been critically injured emotionally.

References

1. Paul R. Wilson, *The Other Side of Rape* (St. Lucia, Queensland: University of Queensland Press, 1978), pp. 34-43; Ann Wolbert Burgess and Lynda Lytle Holstrom, *Rape: Victims of Crisis* (Bowie, Md.: Robert J. Brady Company, 1974), pp. 14-19; Rochel Grossman, ed., *Surviving Sexual Assault* (New York, N.Y.: Congdon & Weed, Inc., 1983), pp. 57-58; and Jean Seligman, "The Date Who Rapes," *Newsweek*, April 9, 1984, p. 91.

2. Seligman, p. 91.

3. Grossman, pp. 59-60.

4. Theresa S. Foley and Marilyn A. Davies, *Rape—Nursing Care of Victims* (St. Louis, Mo.: The C.V. Mosby Company, 1983), pp. 37-44.

5. Wilson, pp. 85-86.

6. (Reference #24 in violence chapter)

7. Grossman, p. 59.

8. Ibid.

9. Grossman, p. 47.

10. Burgess and Holstrom, pp. 287-292.

11. Grossman, p. 51.

12. Rita Rooney, "A Shocking Report: Rape, The Battle of the Sexes Turns Violent," *Ladies' Home Journal*, September 1983, p. 140.

13. Ibid.

14. Ibid.

15. Thomas P. McGurn and Christine N. Kelly, "What To Do (and What Not To Do) If You're Attacked," *New Woman*, September 1984, pp. 99-100.

16. Rooney, p. 140.

17. Grossman, p. 18.

18. Wilson, pp. 57-58.

19. Michael L. Antoline, "Sexual Assault," *JEMS*, May 1981, p. 48.

Child Abuse

Its victims are the young, the innocent. In most cases, its perpetrators are charged with protecting those young and innocent. It happens with startling frequency in a surprising number of homes throughout this country. It leaves in its wake permanent physical and psychological damage.

It is child abuse, and it is one of the most difficult aspects of medicine to deal with. **Any** emergency involving a child is emotionally exhausting; when the injuries were purposely inflicted by an adult on a helpless child, it can be almost impossible to avoid feeling intense anger.

Too often, we think only of the physical aspect of child abuse—the child who has been physically battered or beaten. In actuality, there are five categories of child abuse:

—**Physical abuse.** Physical abuse occurs when physical harm is inflicted on the child; often, the child is maimed or permanently injured. The most common kinds of physical abuse include beating, slapping, punching, burning, scalding, and shaking.

—**Sexual abuse.** Although laws vary from state to state, sexual abuse generally involves the forceful molestation of a child, including forceful intercourse. In most states, sexual abuse includes incestuous relationships between an adult and a minor.

—**Emotional abuse.** Emotional abuse occurs when parents, over a long period of time, consistently deprive their children of normal emotional nurturing and love. As a result, the child feels worthless and may develop long-term feelings of self-hatred.

—Neglect. While most other kinds of child "abuse" deal with what the parents do, neglect involves what the parents do not do. In cases of neglect, the parents do not provide adequate food, shelter, clothing, or medical/dental care for the child; a child may be sent to school in bitter cold wearing a short-sleeved shirt and no shoes, for example.

Unfortunately, many cases of child abuse never come to the attention of the authorities, so it is impossible to offer firm statistics about how many children are abused each year in the United States. The National Center on Child Abuse and Neglect has wagered some estimates: more than 1 million children are reported victims each year. The center estimates that for each child who is reported, two are not—resulting in an estimated 2 million children who are unreported victims. (Some estimate that these figures may be closer to 4 million.) Two-thirds of these children suffer substantial harm; about one in five needs hospitalization.

One child every four hours—an average of six a day, or 2,000 every year—die as a result of their injuries.[1]

Understanding the problem of child abuse and neglect necessitates an understanding of what kind of parent abuses a child, what kind of child tends to be abused, and ways in which abuse can be prevented.

Profile of an Abusive Parent

The tragic thing about child abuse is this: any human adult, given the right child and the right set of circumstances, has the potential to be abusive. Each of us likes to think that we would never strike out at an innocent child. The truth is, you might—if you are under unique kinds of stress and if you are confronted with a certain kind of child.

Because any parent has the potential for abuse, it is difficult to come up with a set "profile" for an abusive parent. It is possible, however, to pinpoint some characteristics that many abusive parents seem to have in common:

—Women tend to be abusive more often than men. That could be explained, though, by the fact that women are more often the ones that are at home for long periods of time with the children, while men tend to be away from home because of employment obligations.

—Parents who abuse were likely abused themselves when they were children. It's a vicious cycle: violence breeds violence. A woman who lashes out at her children may be behaving in the only way she knows: when her mother got frustrated, upset, or angry, she lashed out, too. She is reacting to her children the way she herself was taught to react.

—Abusive parents tend to be isolated; they have few opportunities to socialize with family members, friends, and others in the community. The more support a person gets from family members, friends, or others in the community, the less likely he will be to abuse his children.

—An abusive parent generally has a difficult time trusting other people.

—Abusive parents tend to have poor coping skills. The pressures and problems that are part of most families can actually cause a crisis for an abusive parent, simply because her frustration tolerance is so low. The morning she receives an overdue notice for the electric bill and the toilet in the main bathroom gets clogged with a diaper, she feels like she's going to snap.

—An abusive parent has the tendency to be unsatisfied in marriage; she is in a relationship that does not fulfill her basic needs for love, affection, and attention. Sadly, she expects her child to supply her with the kind of love and attention she needs from other adults; when her child is unable to do it, she strikes out.

—Most child abuse begins as simple discipline: a man spanks his son for rifling through his tool box, a woman slaps her son's hands after she finds him drawing on the bedroom wall. Somewhere along the way, "discipline" gets distorted; parents get carried away, and "discipline" becomes "abuse."

—Many abusive parents suffer from devastatingly low self-esteem. Many are crippled by low opinions of themselves; as children, they were battered emotionally by parents who told them they were bad, worthless, or stupid. Men and women who do not like themselves have a difficult time genuinely liking someone else, even a child.

—An abusive parent tends to have unrealistic expectations about his child's behavior. He might truly think that a three-year-old child can sit perfectly quiet and still for the two hours they wait at the mechanic's shop. When the child doesn't live up to the parent's expectations, the parent "punishes" the child.

—Abusive parents tend to have a poor understanding of the child's needs. When a child's needs aren't met, the child may become fussy, restless, or difficult to deal with; the parent, who has poor coping skills anyway, can't tolerate the situation.

—For whatever reason, an abusive parent tends to be "disappointed" in her child. The child may not be attractive enough, bright enough, well-mannered enough, or athletic enough to please the critical parent.

—A particular psychological pattern tends to present itself in cases of abuse.[2] A child whose parents had extremely high expectations found that affection and approval were measured out selectively: he had to "earn" his parents' love. He grew up and sought out a mate who had the same family background. The two of them have children and expect the children to become a source of gratification. Obviously, a child can't be expected to meet a parent's needs. So, when the child fails, the parent reacts with anger and hostility.

—Many abusive parents feel helpless. They feel ill-prepared for parenthood and do not know how to seek outside help. (Many, too, are convinced that outsiders simply can't help.)

—An abusive parent tends to have poor impulse control. Drug and/or alcohol abuse is common among abusive parents.

—Abusive parents tend to identify their children with negative parts of their own personality. ("Susan really has problems in school, just like I did," or "Justin never can seem to make friends—that's just how I was at his age.")

—An abusive parent tends to suffer from depression.

—Many abusive parents genuinely think that their child has adult thoughts and motives. When a child tracks mud across a newly scrubbed floor, an abusive mother thinks, "She's trying to get even with me for not letting her have any popcorn after lunch!" instead of realizing that the child is preoccupied and simply careless. The mother of a baby who has been crying for half an hour decides that the baby is purposely trying to anger her—when, in fact, the baby is uncomfortable because of a severe diaper rash.

—Younger parents have a higher incidence of abuse than do older parents. Much of that tendency may stem from the fact that older, more experienced parents have a better knowledge of what kind of behavior is appropriate for children in a specific age group; older parents tend to have sharpened their parenting skills, too, and are more confident and secure in the job of parenting.

—Many abusive mothers are battered wives.

—Abuse is less frequent in large or extended families than in small ones. Several things explain this tendency.[3] First, children who grow up in a large family have the opportunity of seeing children at various stages of development; when they grow up and become parents, they have more realistic expectations. These children, too, get practice caring for their brothers and sisters—so many of the basic skills that come along with parenting (such as feeding, diapering, and dressing) come naturally. In large or extended families, a large social network is available for times when the mother is feeling stressed or frustrated—instead of striking out at her child, she can ask an older child to care for the younger child, giving her a break from her responsibilities.

—Many abusive parents are highly motivated, upwardly

mobile people who drive themselves with fierce competition. The job of being a parent becomes an impossible one in view of the many other stresses that are part of the parent's life.

—An abusive parent tends to have problems communicating with a child. The parent may fear that the child is trying to "trick" him or is not telling the truth. Because of poor parenting skills, a parent may not be able to understand what a toddler is trying to say or communicate—and the parent may be frustrated by the toddler's repetitive pleas.

—Many abusive parents lost their own parents at an early age, due to either death or divorce.

—Poverty tends to occur more frequently in abusive homes. Because of economic and financial problems, parents are unable to meet daily demands; frustration and stress result, breeding violence. Approximately three-fourths of the time, abusive parents are blue-collar or unskilled workers; only about one-fourth of the time are they white-collar or professional.[4] **(While abuse is more common among blue-collar or unskilled workers, it can and does occur among white-collar workers and professionals.)** Many abusive families are plagued by un-employment, which further aggravates financial problems.

—Those who have not completed high school have a greater tendency to abuse their children than those who have graduated from high school and pursued some postgraduate education. Many abusive parents had a history of problems in school and deficient academic skills.

—Many abusive parents have records of juvenile offenses or criminal activities.

—Many abusive parents have some degree of mental or emotional illness. Only a few have serious psychotic problems, but many have milder dysfunctions.

—A number of abusive parents suffer from medical problems. (Frequent pain or discomfort can increase stress levels and cause outbursts.)

—Abusive parents tend to believe that harsh physical

punishment is necessary to control or train children; they lack the parenting skills that would expose them to alternate forms of discipline.

—Many abusive parents set inappropriately rigid standards of behavior and performance for their children; when the children do not measure up and perform as expected, the parents respond with harsh physical discipline.

—Parents who are guilty of neglect can be suffering from a number of problems. The parents may be intellectually deprived or actually mentally retarded and may be incapable of properly caring for children. In other cases, profound poverty may make it impossible for the parents to care properly for the children, even though they know how and would do so if they were financially able. In many cases, the parents are profoundly depressed and the family unit is chaotic and disorganized; in these cases, the parents are so totally absorbed with meeting their own needs that they cannot concentrate on caring for their children.

—Those guilty of neglect may also live in overcrowded or run-down housing; many suffer from social, racial, or cultural discrimination.

—Sometimes abuse occurs among parents who are fundamentally able to cope but who are temporarily overwhelmed due to periods of stress. The signs among these parents are different:[5] they have a history of caring for their children properly and enjoy emotional support from a network of family members and friends. They have adequate employment with a regular income and possess average problem-solving abilities. Although a major crisis or a series of crises have temporarily overwhelmed them, they are usually very cooperative in receiving help and are likely to regain their parenting abilities once the crisis has been resolved.

New Mothers At Risk

Several characteristics of new mothers tend to occur among abusive women. Women who have handicapped children tend to abuse them, as do women who deliver premature babies. (Somehow, the woman perceives these problems as reflections of her own inadequacy to deliver a "normal" baby; she then strikes out at her baby in anger over her supposed inadequacies.)

Mothers who abuse their babies tend to believe that the baby does not feel love for the mother. The mother may handle the baby roughly, holding it at a distance and failing to support its head. The mother may refuse to pay attention to the baby and may even feel that the baby is unattractive.

Abuse is more common among mothers who have injured previous children, who are addicted to drugs or alcohol, and who are single (especially if they have been abandoned by the baby's father, since he represents a critical support).

What Brings on the Breaking Point?

Among parents who are prone to abuse their children, what brings on the explosion? Often, it's simply a matter of timing— an event that would not normally cause a crisis comes along at just the wrong time, when coping abilities are at their lowest. The kinds of events that are most commonly linked with the explosion of violence in child abuse include the following:[6]

—Family situations, such as physical attacks on a spouse, marital separation, divorce, desertion, or abandonment.

—Developmental situations, such as childbirth, children starting school, adolescence, children leaving home (the "empty nest" syndrome), marriage, menopause, retirement, and death.

—Economic situations, such as loss of employment, loss of money (through theft), termination of public assistance, missed support payments, repossession of cars or furniture, eviction, termination of utilities (such as water or electricity), or financial pressures arising from debt.

—Community situations, such as arrest of a family member, trouble in school, social isolation, and disagreements with neighbors.

The Special Case of Sexual Abuse

Parents who engage in sexual abuse share many of the characteristics of abusive parents in general. However, some special characteristics of sexually abusive parents have also been identified:[7]

—Sexually abusive parents tend to have low self-esteem, stemming in part from their own experiences as children; many suffered as children because their emotional needs were not met by their parents.

—Many sexually abusive parents have inadequate coping skills.

—Sexually abusive parents may have lost their spouse through either death or divorce, or may be having marital problems that cause one spouse to seek affection from a child rather than from the other spouse (sometimes the "denying" husband or wife finds the situation acceptable).

—Many sexually abusive parents are geographically isolated or lack social and emotional contacts outside the family.

—Homes in which sexual abuse occurs tend to be over-crowded.

—Sexually abusive parents have cultural standards that determine the degree of physical contact that is acceptable; many abuse alcohol.

—Many sexually abusive fathers are rigid disciplinarians who need to be in control of the family.

—Sexually abusive fathers tend to be passive outside the home and rarely have police records or histories of public disturbances; few sexually abusive fathers engage in social activities outside the home.

—Many sexually abusive fathers are jealous and protective of the child they victimize; many have distorted perception of the child's role in the family, and they often pay special attention to the child (resulting in sibling jealousy).

—In many cases, sexual abuse from a father begins with hugging and kissing; over time, the sexual contact develops into more caressing, genital-genital contacts, and oral-genital contacts.

—Wives who know or suspect that sexual abuse is taking place between a husband and a daughter rarely report it or try to stop it. Why? There are a number of reasons. A wife may hesitate to report it for fear of destroying her marriage and being left on her own. She may decide that the activity between her husband and her daughter is better than the husband having an extramarital affair. She may also feel "relieved" of the pressure to satisfy her husband sexually and may think that the activity will guarantee that her husband and daughter will be close. Most of these mothers feel a combination of jealousy and guilt toward the daughter who is being victimized in the relationship.

Profile of the Abused Child

Developing a profile of an abused child is as difficult as developing a profile of a child abuser: **any child who relates to an adult has the potential of being abused or neglected.** What's more, the abuse is the adult's fault, not the child's fault. We do know, however, that certain children run a higher risk of being abused than others—not because they are bad or "worthy" of abuse, but because they may aggravate a parent with a low toleration for frustration.

Children who run a higher risk include the following:

—Physical abuse is more common among boys; sexual abuse is more common among girls. Why? Girls tend to be more submissive; boys tend to be more active and competitive, which can frustrate their parents.

—Abused children tend to be children who, for some reason, are difficult to manage; children with behavioral problems, such as hyperactivity, run a special risk, as do children who have special needs that place demands on their parents' time and resources.

—Children who are separated from parents at birth run a higher risk because bonding may not have occurred. Birth separation may be due to prematurity, illness in the infant, or illness in the mother.

—Any child with special needs that make him demanding is at a higher risk. This includes children who are handicapped, mentally retarded, gifted, or premature.

—A child who falls short of his parents' expectations runs a high risk. For example, a couple may have been dreaming of a girl; when a boy is born, there is higher risk; they may have hoped for a vivacious, gregarious child and may begin to abuse their quiet, shy one.

—A child who does not communicate openly with her parents runs a higher risk. She may simply be shy or quiet, but her parents may assume that she is lying, withholding information, or purposely frustrating them.

—A child who is difficult to satisfy runs a higher risk.

—A child who is illegitimate runs a higher risk because of the changes in life-style that his mother is forced to undergo due to the birth. She may have to stop her education or may be forced to interrupt her career; the baby may place too much strain on her financially. She begins to resent the baby and rarely has emotional and physical support from the baby's father.

—A child who is unwanted runs a higher risk. (Especially high risk is faced by children who are products of incest, rape, or dissolved parental relationships.)

—Children who are born to very young mothers or older mothers who are extremely emotionally immature run a higher risk. The risk increases if the mother does not have a good emotional base of support from family members, relatives, and friends.

—Children who suffer from medical problems, especially

repeated illnesses, run a higher risk.

—A child who is perceived as "bad" or "evil" runs a higher risk. (This is more prominent in members of fundamental religious faiths, who tend to believe that God expects them to vigorously punish their children.)

Signs of Physical Abuse

It seems as though it would be easy to pinpoint a victim of physical abuse: you can see the injuries and make positive identification.

Unfortunately, it's not always that easy. Sometimes you can see obvious physical injuries that can't be satisfactorily explained by parents or by the child; but in many cases you need to rely on behavioral clues to physical abuse.

Watch for the following:

—You might notice obvious bruises on the child's skin. Many children are careless and might bruise themselves during rough play; those bruises usually occur on boney prominences, such as the forehead, the shins, or the arms. **Children rarely bruise themselves in places such as the abdomen, small of the back, or the buttocks.** Particularly watch for bruises that are in the shape of a discernible object or in the shape of a hand (these result from forceful slapping). You might notice bruises on the arms, face, or buttocks that resemble finger and thumb prints. Watch, too, for cases where there are numerous bruises in various stages of healing.

—You might see obvious burns or welts on the child's skin. You might also see evidence of an adult bite mark (the arch will be much higher than that in the bite mark of a child, and there will be marks from more teeth, including molars). It's difficult to confuse a human bite with an animal bite—animals tear the flesh, but humans compress it, often causing bruising.

How to Date Bruises

You can tell the approximate age of a bruise by the following:

Swollen, tender, and red in color: Less than 2 days old
Red, blue, or dark purple in color: 1 to 3 days old
Green in color: 4 to 7 days old
Yellow in color: 7 to 14 days old
Brown in color: More than 2 weeks old
Most bruises take from 2 to 4 weeks to disappear.

Burn injuries are quite common in children, but most accidental burns occur between the ages of eighteen months and five years.[8] You can usually determine whether a burn was accidental by its location and severity. Parents who purposely burn their children often use cigarettes; the burns are circular, punched-out areas, often on the hands, soles of the feet, or buttocks. Some parents use hot appliances or objects, such as irons; the burn will be in the shape of the object. Scalding is also common: a parent will forcibly immerse the child's hands, feet, or buttocks into scalding water as a punishment; you will notice a distinctive burn line where the water stopped. (A child whose buttocks are scalded probably didn't fall into the water accidentally, or his legs, feet, arms, and hands would be scalded, too.)

—Injuries to the face are common in child abuse. Look for missing teeth, loosened teeth, bruising or lacerations of the lips and soft tissues inside the mouth, or burning of the tongue or soft tissues of the mouth. A single forceful blow to the ear can cause the eardrum to rupture; repeated blows can cause a condition known as "cauliflower ear." The child may have a nosebleed or broken nose and may suffer a black eye, dislocated lens, detached retina, or other eye injury.

—Abdominal injuries are the most frequent cause of death among abused children—damage to the abdominal organs can result in massive hemorrhage, shock, and death. Look for tenderness of the abdomen, discoloration or bruising, swelling or distention, or recurring vomiting. (These injuries often cause an absence of bowel sounds.)

—Children who are punched in the chest may suffer broken ribs. Look for misshapen chest, severe pain in the chest when the child moves or breathes deeply, or the signs of a punctured lung.

—Coma, seizures, paralysis, bruising of the scalp, and swelling of the scalp may indicate head injuries. Look for a child who has bald patches—his hair may have been pulled.

—Watch for the signs of fractures; look for swelling, deformity, paralysis, or limitation of movement in an extremity. Any infant with a fracture of a long bone should be suspected of abuse—infant bones are too pliable and rarely break unless they are subjected to excessive external force.[9]

—A child who has been tied up as punishment will have rope burns on his wrists, ankles, neck, or chest. Look, too, for scratches from fingernails.

—Look for behavioral clues, whether or not there are obvious physical injuries. A child may become withdrawn and passive; he may appear to be almost dazed, as though he were daydreaming. He might begin to avoid other people, even other children, and may avoid physical contact of any kind with adults.

—A child who is a victim of physical abuse may become demanding, aggressive, destructive, disobedient, and generally difficult to get along with. He may begin to cause trouble or interfere with others when he has not done so in the past. He may begin to throw terrible temper tantrums. (He may have decided that the only way to get attention is to invite abuse, so he misbehaves—even to the point of deliberately breaking the law.)

—The child may develop problems at school; he may have difficulty concentrating and may seem too anxious to please. Watch out for children who are habitually late or absent from school or children who consistently arrive too early and resist going home at the end of the day. Children who lose their sense of curiosity and who become rigid and too controlled may be victims of abuse.

—A child who is abused may become frightened of his parents; even a young child may show little or no distress when separated from his parents. Other children express an excessive concern about their parents' well-being and whereabouts. A child may try frantically to get affection from adults who are not his parents, because he cannot seem to earn affection from his parents. (Children who are consistently too affectionate with strangers may be desperately attempting to "Get what they can" from the relationship before it sours.)

—A child abuse victim may cry persistently; attempts to comfort her are usually in vain. (An infant with a head injury has a characteristic high-pitched, shrill cry and usually can't be quieted.)

—The child may be dressed inappropriately for warm weather—his long sleeves and long pants are an attempt to hide bruises or other signs of physical injury.

—One of the most reliable clues to physical abuse in the absence of obvious injury can be the explanations of an injury that **could** have been accidental. When you ask a young child how he got hurt, he will probably tell you that his mother or father hurt him; very young children usually do not lie and usually do not make up stories to explain their injuries.

—Older children, on the other hand, may very well create a story about how they were injured in order to protect their parents. Look for discrepancies in explanations about how the injury occurred—the parents may tell a different story than the child. Question parents individually, away from the child, and question the child privately. See if the stories match.

—Watch out for injuries that are inconsistent with the explanation. Watch out, too, for parents who refuse to explain how the child was injured or who are vague in their descriptions. (If the child has not been abused, the parents will usually display genuine concern about how the injury happened and will go to considerable lengths to discover how the injury occurred; beware of the parents who shrug and tell you that they "just found him like that.")

—Look for discrepancies between the injury and the explanation. A parent may tell you that the child tripped down the stairs; you may notice that the bruises are along his back instead of his legs and chin, and that they are in the shape of a belt or loop of wire.

—Be careful of parents who insist that the injury was inflicted by a third party—a sibling, a babysitter, a friend, or a neighbor. That **could** be the case; ask the parents for the name of the third party, and check out the story completely. If the parents refuse to tell you the name of the third party, suspect abuse. (Parents who are not abusive will be outraged that someone else injured their child, and they will not be afraid to disclose the person's name.) Be careful, too, of parents who tell you that the child's injuries are self-inflicted—children who are emotionally healthy rarely inflict injury on themselves. (It might also be obvious that the child could not have injured himself—a parent may insist that a two-month-old rolled over in the crib and broke her arm, but you know that an infant's bones are too pliable and that the baby could not have exerted enough force to break her own arm.)

—Suspect parents who bring in a child with repeated injuries, and a parent who waits twelve to twenty-four hours before seeking medical attention for a serious injury. (Parents who inflict the injury may be fearful of being discovered; on the other hand, a parent whose child has an accident will usually seek immediate care.

Signs of Emotional Abuse

Emotional abuse is extremely difficult to diagnose. The child may develop what is known as "failure to thrive syndrome;" he may fail to gain weight, may develop learning disabilities, and may suffer emotionally and mentally. Because you can't readily see the child's injury, it is much more difficult to diagnose.

The child may become overly compliant, following instructions and complying with demands without any protest. He may be inappropriately submissive and may continue to put up with unpleasant behavior from other adults or children. Many victims of emotional abuse become shy, withdrawn, passive, and overly anxious to please.

Some victims of emotional abuse go in the opposite direction—they become hostile, demanding, angry, and difficult to get along with. They may suddenly begin to cause trouble, may get into trouble with school authorities or law enforcement officers, and may begin to throw particularly violent temper tantrums. (They key here is change in behavior; watch for a child who was sweet, generally easy to get along with, and well-behaved who suddenly and without explanation develops problems.)

A child who is victimized by emotional abuse may seek affection and attention from adults outside his home; be especially aware of children who are inappropriately friendly and affectionate with strangers.

Children who endure emotional abuse tend to fall at either end of the spectrum as far as emotional maturity is concerned. Many are extremely immature for their age and will show signs of regression (such as bedwetting, thumbsucking, pants-wetting, and baby talk). Others seem overly mature for their age.

Signs of Sexual Abuse

Approximately half a million children are victims of sexual abuse in this country each year; victims of child abuse may also be victims of sexual abuse. Like child abuse, sexual abuse is rarely an isolated condition; sexual abuse tends to begin gradually and persist over long periods of time, usually years.

There are two general kinds of sexual abuse.[10] In the first, the child is forced into sexual activity; the parent or guardian uses threats and physical force to guarantee that the child complies. In this kind of abuse, the danger of physical injury is great. In the second kind of sexual abuse—in which a child is seduced or enticed into sexual activity—the danger of physical injury is reduced, but the danger of long-term psychological injury is great.

Young girls are not the only victims of sexual abuse. Boys can be victimized, too, as can infants. On occasion, the child may be sexually abused by someone outside the family (a relative, neighbor, or babysitter, for example), but it is most often by a parent or other close relative.

Research has shown that children rarely make up stories about sexual abuse; if a child tells you that he has been abused sexually, believe him. (Older children may invent tales in order to get attention or to seek revenge, but young children are usually reliable sources.) Sexual abuse by a stranger is usually a single episode that occurs most frequently during warm weather and in a public place; a child who is habitually abused and who tells you that the abuse is occurring at home is almost always a victim of abuse on the part of someone she knows.

It seems amazing that a child would cooperate with an adult who involves her in sexual activity, but it happens all the time. Many children cooperate out of a need for love, affection, attention, or out of a sense of loyalty to the adult. Even when the abusing adult is a stranger, a child is an easy target—adults don't often have to use force, because children are naturally trusting, dependent, and obedient.[11]

Incest is the most emotionally charged and socially intolerable form of sexual abuse and, for most people, the most threatening and difficult to understand and accept. It is also the most difficult form of sexual abuse to detect: incest, by its very nature, tends to remain a family secret. The most commonly reported types of incest are father-daughter (or "father-figure" and daughter); mother-son, mother-daughter, and father-son are believed to be more rare. Sexual activities between brothers and sisters or cousins are believed to be the most common unreported type of incest and do not seem to carry the long-term psychological damage of sexual abuse from adults.[12]

Look for the following signs of sexual abuse.[13]

—Torn, stained, or bloody underclothing

—General injuries to the genital area (such as bruises, lacerations, swelling), bleeding from the vagina or rectum, foreign bodies in the vagina or rectum, signs of penetrating wounds in the vagina or rectum, signs of penetrating wounds to the bladder, or vaginal or penile discharge

—General itching and/or discomfort in the genital area

—Diagnosis of venereal disease or pregnancy in a child

—The presence of blood in the urine or stools, or the presence of semen in the rectum, mouth, or vagina

—Difficulty in walking or sitting

—Complaints of vague medical problems, especially headache, lower backache, stomach ache, and abdominal pain

Watch for the following behavorial indicators:

—The child may become withdrawn and begin to suffer poor relationships with other children; he may refuse to participate in physical activities and may be particularly guarded around other adults.

—A victim of sexual abuse may blatantly tell others that he has been abused, or he may make indirect allusions to the situation; if he determines that sexual activity is a way of gaining attention from adults, he may become inappropriately seductive when around adults.

—The child may withdraw into fantasy or babylike behavior.

—The child may refuse to go home, may run away from home, or may deliberately break the law to be removed from his home by the courts; he may begin to use drugs or alcohol to escape.

—Children under the age of five may experience night terrors, extreme nightmares, clinging behavior, inappropriate fear, and developmental regression. Grade-school-age children may begin to fail in school, become consistently truant, suffer from extreme anxiety or depression, and develop an unexplained weight gain or loss. Adolescents usually suffer from severe loss of self-esteem, depression, and suicidal behavior; some become delinquent, some run away, and some become extremely rebellious against the parent who failed to protect them from the abuse.[14]

—The child may become sexually promiscuous.

—The child may display bizarre, sophisticated, or unusual sexual behavior or knowledge that is inappropriate or extremely unusual for his age.

The most serious and long-range emotional effects of sexual abuse occur among children who are young, children who have had no prior sexual experience, children who are emotionally immature, children who were abused by someone they knew, and children who were subjected to repeated incidents that involved some amount of force or injury.[15]

Some children are victimized by adults who use them in "sex rings" and for child pornography. There are three basic kinds of these offenders:[15]

—**The solo offender.** The solo offender works alone to victimize children into child molesting, child pornography, and/or child prostitution. Most solo offenders gain access to the child in ways that appear to be legitimate—many have connections with the child because of occupation (including teachers, camp counselors, school bus drivers, and scout leaders). In other cases, the adult uses his status in the neighborhood to entice children—he is usually a well-respected member of the neighborhood who is well liked, and he invites children to his home. Parents seldom suspect. In other cases, the adult will find a child who is willing to draw his friends into the sex ring in return for favors; the adult may also draw children in under the guise of legitimate purposes (he may advertise for girls to help with housework, for example).

—**Transition sex rings.** In transition sex rings, offenders communicate with other offenders, exchanging stories, photographs, and experiences. In some cases, a network is established by which offenders can share common interests (such as a preference for young boys or a playing out of certain fantasy scenarios).

In transition sex rings, photographs are often exchanged, including pictures of children being victimized in bondage, sadomasochism, and beastiality. When the children who participate in these rings grow older and the offenders lose interest, they often move the child into prostitution or adult pornography.

—**Syndicated sex rings.** The syndicated sex ring involves a well-organized, structured organization that recruits children, delivers direct sexual services, publishes pornography, and develops an extensive network of customers.

Signs of Neglect

Children who are victims of neglect look it: they are usually dirty, unkempt, unbathed, or smelly. The child may be extremely tired and lack the energy to do what other children his age love to do. Many victims of neglect come to school without eating breakfast; they do not bring a lunch nor any lunch money. Many suffer from signs of malnutrition—they are pale, extremely thin, small for their age, lacking in muscle tone, and lacking in normal endurance or strength; they may have a distended abdomen, dull eyes, sore gums, or skin infections.

The child may be ill frequently and may suffer from obvious medical and dental neglect. He may have a severe diaper rash or skin disorder. He may be left alone for long periods of time and may not know where his parents are when he is questioned. He may be unable to concentrate, may be irritable, or may seem extremely anxious or depressed. He may be disruptive, may seem antisocial, and may fall asleep frequently in school. Many victims of neglect are frequently absent from school. Some beg or steal food.

When all the children in the family are neglected, some of the children (usually the older ones) will assume "parent roles," mothering the younger children trying to provide nurturing and care. Some neglected children get involved in delinquent behavior or begin using drugs and alcohol.

Most neglected children develop feelings of hopelessness, apathy, and helplessness; many feel isolated, and the majority develop an inability to trust others.

Preventing Child Abuse and Neglect

The key to successfully preventing child abuse and neglect is to identify the **potential** for child abuse and neglect. Is the parent at high risk for abusing or neglecting the child? Is the child at a higher-than-normal risk of being abused or neglected? Once the potential, or risk, is identified, steps can be taken to help both parents and children.

Information at the beginning of this chapter gives a general profile of an abusive parent and an abused child; from that information, it is possible to construct a profile of a person (adult or child) who is at risk. Additional risk situations include the following;

—A mother who repeatedly brings her new baby (obviously healthy) to the clinic or pediatrician may be at high risk for abuse. Why? While she may be overprotective or may need reassurance that she is being a good mother, it is also possible that she is trying to tell people that she can't cope with being a parent.

—A woman who complains excessively during her pregnancy about the burden of being pregnant or being a parent may be at risk.

A woman who voices extremely high expectations for her child during pregnancy may be at risk, as are parents who continually drive their children out of unreasonably high expectations.

A high risk may exist when parents harbor unreasonably high expectations throughout a pregnancy and the child is born with a mental or physical handicap.

—Illness or death surrounding the pregnancy or birth of the child can signal a high-than-usual risk.

—Watch the mother's attitudes during the pregnancy. In addition to those clues already cited, watch out for a mother who seems particularly depressed about being pregnant or a mother who insists that this child will be "one too many" for the family. She may insist throughout the pregnancy that the baby was a "mistake" or an "accident" and may not be looking forward to the birth. She may deny the pregnancy. She may suffer repeated illnesses during the pregnancy, or she may develop emotional problems during the pregnancy. Also be concerned with a woman who seems overly concerned about her baby's sex.

—A mother who wanted an abortion but waited too long should be considered a high risk, as should parents who carefully considered giving the baby up for adoption but changed their minds. (They may still desire to relinquish the baby but may be responding to tremendous pressure from friends and family members to keep the baby.)

—A high risk may be indicated by a mother who frequently expresses doubts and fears during her pregnancy about her ability to be a parent, rear a child, care for a child, and so on. Such a mother is at special risk if repeated attempts to help instruct her, explain parenting skills to her, and ease her fail to dissipate her fears.

—Higher risk exists for a woman who is extremely ill during her pregnancy; she may resent the baby for "putting her through" the physical and emotional demands of pregnancy and labor. Also at risk is the mother who has an extremely difficult labor and delivery.

Risk exists for the mother who does not want to hold her baby following birth and who expresses little or no interest in the baby; she may hold the baby at a distance, may seem withdrawn from the baby, may actively resist breastfeeding, and may show extreme apathy about the birth.

—A family who has moved frequently or moved just before the birth of a baby is at risk: moving always introduces stress into the family, so the family's toleration and resistance have been compromised already by the move. The addition of a family member can be the factor that precipitates crisis.

—When a baby is born during a period of high stress in a family (such as the period just following the death of a family member or during a period of long-term unemployment), there is risk: the family may already be under too much stress to deal with the arrival of the baby, too.

—Watch the way the parent interacts with the baby. Higher-than-normal risk is indicated when parents do not establish eye contact with the baby, when parents do not seem to enjoy the baby, when parents are negative or critical toward the baby, and when parents seem extremely upset by the baby's crying.

—High risk is signalled if the partners named the baby after someone they did not like or if the baby was not named for some time after birth.

—A parent who is overly disgusted by dirty diapers or by the baby spitting up is at risk, as is a parent who does not want to feed the baby or seems upset by the baby's demands to be fed. Watch out for the parent who seems repulsed by the mess involved in feeding, changing, or caring for a baby.

High risk is indicated by parents who are initially **extremely** disappointed by the child's sex and who remain disappointed.

—Parents may be at high risk if they consistently voice unrealistic expectations regarding the child or if they make unrealistic complaints about the child. (A mother may tell you, for example, that her six-week-old daughter wakes up during the night "just to bug me" or to get back at her for something.)

—Watch how the parent reacts to the child when she is brought in for checkups. A high risk may be indicated by a parent who brings the baby in and immediately relinquishes her to the care of the doctors and nurses, refusing to take any responsibility for her care. Watch, too, how other family members react to the baby; do brothers and sisters exhibit an unusual amount of jealousy or hostility toward the baby Is the husband overly jealous of the baby's demands on his wife?

The ideal time to help a parent is during those first few weeks and months—or, if you can detect risk, during the pregnancy. Allow a mother to build her relationship with her baby slowly if she needs it; bring the baby for brief periods, and take the baby away when she starts to get distressed. Never force an unwilling mother to breastfeed; if she is reluctant because she fears she will fail, however, help her enroll in classes or support groups where she can learn how to successfully breastfeed.

If a mother seems disturbed about a new baby, take the time to talk to her in a nonthreatening way to find out what concerns her. Concentrate on the mother's feelings and needs (or on the father's, if he is the problem) instead of concentrating on the baby. If the parents seem at risk, increase the number of office calls or help them get involved in a support group.

Parents who are at risk should be given plenty of information on how to parent, on what kinds of discipline are appropriate for various age levels, on what kinds of behavior to expect at various age levels, and on basic care (including nutrition). Parents should be complimented on accomplishments and improvements and should be encouraged in positive ways.

In situations where high risk has been identified, arrange for health visitors to visit the parents regularly to provide support, help, and encouragement; new parents may also need to arrange for a sitter so they can enjoy some time away from the baby. Parents can also enroll in support groups where they can exchange joys and frustrations with other parents.

Families who seem unusually stressed or at risk for child abuse may need advice and help regarding family planning. Sometimes the stress may result from too many children spaced too close together, or children who arrive at periods of high stress (such as the husband's final year of law school). These families may well be able to cope with a child at a better time marked by less stress.

A Word of Caution

In an effort to identify child abuse and neglect or to identify high-risk families, mistakes can be made. Sometimes the symptoms commonly associated with child abuse occur in association with other conditions. For example, a child who is vomiting may not have been punched in the abdomen by her father—she may simply be overly excited about an upcoming birthday party or may have eaten too much candy at the amusement park. Child abuse usually manifests a combination of symptoms and should not be immediately assumed on the basis of one sign or symptom.

Even when a child is brought to the emergency room with multiple injuries, you shouldn't necessarily immediately assume that child abuse has occurred. The child may have been in a traffic accident, may have fallen off a bicycle, or may have been in some other kind of accident. The key is to question the parents and the child about what happened: if the explanation is clearly consistent with the injuries and if all parties involved tell the same story, child abuse may not be the problem. It is often necessary to look for extenuating circumstances when you suspect child abuse.

Be cautious, too, that you do not confuse Sudden Infant Death Syndrome (SIDS) with child abuse. There are some important distinctions:[17] the parents of a SIDS victim will be extremely distressed. The baby will appear to have been well cared for, with no signs of neglect or maltreatment; there will not be any lacerations, bruises, swelling, or other marks that would indicate abuse. SIDS **can** cause pooling of deoxygenated blood in the tissues that may look like bruises, but a diagnosis of SIDS should explain the appearance. Accusing parents of SIDS baby of child abuse can cause severe long-term psychological damage—they were not responsible for the baby's death, and even under good circumstances may require help in overcoming feelings of guilt over the baby's death.

Responsibility for Reporting Child Abuse

Every state has laws requiring those who suspect that a child is abuses or neglected to report their suspicions to authorities. While the specifics vary from state to state regarding details of the reporting, the laws are generally designed to protect the child from further injury and to identify families who need help.

In most states, authorities conform to provisions of the Child Abuse Prevention and Treatment Act of 1974. Those provisions include the following:[18]

—Individuals are bound to report known or suspected cases of child abuse or neglect, even those that occur in institutions. In most states, teachers, physicians, and others who work with children are especially charged with the responsibility of reporting.

—Law enforcement agencies, the courts, and human service agencies are bound to cooperate in the protections of victims of child abuse and neglect.

—Law enforcement agencies, the courts, and human service agencies are bound to cooperate in the protection of victims of child abuse and neglect.

—Those who report child abuse and neglect or suspected child abuse and neglect are given immunity from prosecution under the law.

—All child abuse or child neglect records are guaranteed to be kept confidential.

—Under the law, guarantees are made that once a report is received, an investigation will be made promptly and appropriate steps will be taken to protect the child and any other child impacted by the situation (including removal from the home if necessary).

Under the law, an effective system will be established within the state to reach children who are in trouble, help the children and the families, and implement the state child abuse laws.

Responding to Child Abuse and Neglect

When you respond to a call involving child abuse or neglect, **your first and primary responsibility is to guarantee the safety of the child.** That isn't always easy; you may have to forcefully remove the child from the home against the parents' wishes, and you may have to confront parents who are defensive, hostile, and panic-stricken about what will happen if they are discovered.

—Do not try to collect "evidence" at the scene; do not photograph the child for proof of battering or abuse. Only law enforcement personnel who are responsible for gathering evidence should take photographs. You may further endanger the child's safety by taking photographs, since the parents may become overly concerned and stressed.

—Be as sympathetic and compassionate toward the parents as you can. Your first impulse will probably be outrage; it's not easy to deal with a situation in which an adult has purposely harmed a child. Realize that there may be many stresses at work and that the parents probably don't like what they've done, either. Be courteous to the parents, and carefully explain what you are doing. If you need to remove the child from the home to protect the child's safety, carefully explain in a nonthreatening way that the child has possibly sustained an injury that needs to be looked at by hospital personnel. Explain where you are going, and offer to let the parents follow you in their own car and meet you at the emergency room.

—Resist the temptations to remove all of the child's clothing in a search for further indications of abuse. You should remove only as much clothing as necessary to assess and treat obvious injuries.

—If parents refuse to cooperate with your examination of the child, or if they refuse to let you take the child to the hospital, call the police.

—If you suspect that the child is a victim of abuse, say nothing about your suspicions to the parents; do not record your suspicions in your report, either. Report your suspicions to appropriate hospital personnel when you transport the child in a private and confidential place. Make sure that you record only factual information.

—Approach the child slowly, and conduct a visual assessment first. Be gentle and kind; the child is probably extremely frightened and under a great deal of stress. Take the time to establish rapport with the child before you touch him, **unless you must perform a life-saving first aid treatment**. If the child's life is not in danger as a result of his injuries, establish a rapport before you do anything at all.

—Use a soft tone of voice and talk gently to the child. Place yourself at the child's level when you talk to her: kneel, crouch, sit, or bend over so that you can establish direct eye contact on her level.

—As you perform first aid, do it as gently and slowly as you can. Explain each thing that you are doing to the child in simple words, even if the child is very young. ("I think your bone might be hurt, so I am going to put something stiff on your arm to keep your bone from moving around. This stiff thing is called a 'splint.' It will help hold your bone still until the doctor can X-ray your arm.")

—Treat any obvious injuries. If you suspect that further,

hidden injury may have occurred (such as blunt injury to the abdomen) conduct a quick assessment and treat if necessary.

—Transport the child to the hospital, **even if you don't think the child's injuries will require followup hospital care.** It is important to remove the child from the home if he is in danger there until a team of child protective workers can assess the danger and provide appropriate support. You also need to take the child where he can receive a complete physical checkup: doctors need to rule out the possibility of other injuries, and they may need to collect evidence of abuse.

—Be on the alert for two associated problems: the child may have been sexually abused as well as physically abused, and the parents may have given the child drugs prior to or during the abuse episode. If genital injuries are not apparent, do not persist with an examination, but mention your concern to emergency room personnel.

—During transport, allow the child to sit on the seat next to you unless the severity of his injuries dictate that he ride in the back of the ambulance. If the parents insist on riding with you (for example, if they have no car), ask that the parents ride in back with an ambulance attendant while the child rides in front with you. During transport, the child should be able to see only emergency personnel, not his parents.

—During transport, continue to talk to the child in a gentle, soft way. Tell him you know that he is hurting but that the pain should stop soon. Touch him gently on the arm, or maintain other gentle, caring contact. Avoid quick, jerky movements that may startle the child or remind him of the abusive situation.

Interviewing the Parents

It is essential when you respond to a call of suspected child abuse that you interview the parents and learn their side of the story. Give them a chance to explain what happened to the child by following these guidelines: (**follow local protocol**)

—Once you have given the child basic first aid treatment and have taken care of any pressing injuries, ask the parents to talk with you in a separate room. **Never interview the parents in the presence of the child.**

—Ask the parents to describe how the injury occurred. Try to remain open; do not be threatening or accusatory as you question the parents. Maintain eye contact with the parents, but be careful not to glare at them.

—Simply record what the parents tell you; do not respond in disbelief to what they are telling you.

—If there was obvious delay between the time the injury occurred and the time the parents called for help, ask them why they waited to call. Record what they tell you.

—Don't bombard the parents with questions that will threaten them, but gradually try to find out information about their relationship with the child. Ask whether the child presents special problems in the family, whether the child has been the source of extra frustration, how the parents react or feel when the child cries or makes other demands. Try to find out how many other children are in the family, where those children are, and whether any of them are ill or injured.

—If the parents become defensive and accuse you of suspecting child abuse, react with calm and cool emotion. You might say something like, "In any case of injury to a child, child abuse is a concern that needs to be ruled out. I am simply giving you the chance to share information with me that would help rule it out."

—**Never leave the child alone in the next room while you interview the parents.** Have someone else stay with the child, and don't leave the child until his injuries have been attended to and he is reasonably comfortable. Tell him where you are going, what you are doing, and that you will return to the room in just a few minutes.

Interviewing the Child

—Do not ask the child questions about what happened until you have finished treating him.

—If you can, wait to interview the child until you are transporting him to the hospital; he may be extremely stressed if he is still at the scene of the abuse, and you may cause psychological damage by asking him to relive the situation there.

—It will probably be painful and difficult for the child to tell you what happened, so pay careful attention to what he says so that he won't have to tell the story more than once. If the child tells you the story, relate the facts to hospital personnel so that the child doesn't have to repeat his story.

—Never make accusations, and don't interrogate the child. Don't accuse the child of lying or withholding information; he may be afraid to tell you what happened, or he may feel that he has to lie to protect his parents. (Even in the most brutal abuse situations, children have been known to lie to protect their parents.)

—If possible, interview the child alone. He will not be likely to admit any wrongdoing on his parents' part if they are in the room.

—Avoid the temptation to ask too many questions. Keep your questions confined to the information you need to learn to assure the child's safety and health.

—Don't make promises you can't keep. Don't say to the child, "Well, everything will be okay and your mom won't hit you again." Instead, say, "I am really sorry that your mom hit you; she must have been unhappy and frustrated. I am going to take you to the hospital so that the people there can help you get better, and I am going to talk to them about getting some help for your mom so that she won't be so unhappy anymore."

—Never accuse a parent to a child, and do not be judgmental. Remain calm, and seek the facts. If a child tells you that his father beat him with a wire loop, don't react with disgust and anger; say something like, "That must have hurt you. I think the doctors can help you so that it won't hurt."

Dealing with Sexual Abuse

When you are responding to a call of sexual abuse, take the same measures to gain the child's trust and confidence; move slowly, gently, and do not touch the child until you have established a rapport. Follow these specific guidelines:

—Conduct the examination in a gentle, thorough way. Explain the procedure to the child as you go along in words that she can understand. Include genital, rectal, and oral examinations.

—Interview the child and parents separately, as described above, to find out as much as you can about the situation.

—Explain to both the parents and the child what medical procedures will be necessary once the child arrives at the hospital. A child who has not reached adolescence may not require a pelvic exam, but physicians there may need to get swabs. Explain what will happen and why.

—If someone other than the parents has assaulted the child, be open and honest with the parents. Include them in your assessment; assure them that if the situation is dealt with properly, the child will not suffer long-term effects. Encourage them to return to a normal life-style as quickly as possible. Explain that their attitudes and the way they react to the child will determine her own feelings and recovery.

—If someone other than the parents assaulted the child, encourage them to be open in venting their anger, hostility, and feelings. It is most appropriate for them to do it, but it should be done away from the child to avoid traumatizing her further.

References

1. Ellen L. Bassuk, Sandra Sutherland Fox, and Kevin J. Predergast, *Behavioral Emergencies* (Boston, Mass.: Little, Brown and Company, 1983), p. 176.

2. Eugene Kennedy, *Crisis Counseling* (New York, N.Y.: Continuum Publishing Company, 1981), p. 94.

3. Diana Sullivan Everstine and Louis Everstine, *People in Crisis: Strategic Therapeutic Interventions* (New York, N.Y.: Brunner/Mazel, Inc., 1983), p. 105.

4. Blair Justice and Rita Justice, *The Abusing Family* (New York, N.Y.: The Human Sciences Press, 1976), p. 91.

5. Robert Borgman, Margaret Edmunds, Robert A. MacDicken, *Crisis Intervention: A Manual for Child Protective Workers* (U.S. Department of Health, Education, and Welfare, National Center on Child Abuse and Neglect, 1979), DHEW Publication No. (OHDS) 79-30196, p. 6.

6. Borgman et al., p. 9.

7. James W. Lauer, Ira S. Lourie, Marsha K. Salus, and Diane D. Broadbent, *The Role of the Mental Health Professional in the Prevention and Treatment of Child Abuse and Neglect* (U.S. Department of Health, Education, and Welfare, National Center on Child Abuse and Neglect, 1979), DHEW Publication No. (OHDS) 79-30194, pp. 21-22.

8. Margaret C. McNeese and Joan R. Hebeler, "The Abused Child: A Clinical Approach to Identification and Management," *Clinical Symposia*, Volume 29, Number 5, 1977, p. 18.

9. Jeffrey T. Mitchell and H.L.P. Resnik, *Emergency Response to Crisis* (Bowie, Md.: Robert J. Brady Company, 1981), p. 135.

10. Mitchell and Resnik, p. 133.

11. National Center on Child Abuse and Neglect, *Child Sexual Abuse: Incest, Assault, and Sexual Exploitation* (U.S. Department of Health, Education, and Welfare, Office of Human Development Services, 1978), DHEW Publication No. (OHDS) 79-30166, p. 6.

12. National Center on Child Abuse and Neglect, pp. 6-7.

13. Taken in part from Brent Q. Hafen and Keith J. Karren, *Crisis Intervention for Emergency Medical Personnel* (North Hollywood, Calif,: Emergency Medical Services, 1980), pp. 48-49.

14. Kennedy, p. 106.

15. Everstine and Everstine, p. 127.

16. Kenneth V. Lanning and Ann Wolbert Burgess, "Child Pornography and Sex Rings," *FBI Law Enforcement Bulletin*, January 1984, pp. 10-20.

17. Mitchell and Resnik, p. 140.

18. Hafen and Karren, pp. 52-53.

Violence

We are a violent society; indeed, the United States has been called the most violent society in the Western world.[1] Some of that violence occurs on the streets between total strangers, but much of it occurs in the home between family members. A national survey conducted in 1980 revealed that most Americans believe in using physical punishment for rearing children—and that almost 4 million children are abused every year. Nearly 2 million wives are beaten each year—one every eighteen seconds—and one-fourth of all married couples are violent with each other. Up to 1 million elderly U.S. citizens each year suffer from physical, psychological, sexual, or financial abuse, usually from their relatives. And FBI statistics reveal tht more than half of all the murders committed in the United States occur in family relationships.

The tide of violence is disturbing, and its roots are not exact. Violence has no single "cause;" instead, there are complex reasons why some people are violent and others are not. Because of those reasons, some people turn to violence as a way of reacting to stress and resolving personal crises. For some, violence is a way of life.

While there is a great deal we do not know about violence, we do know something about its causes, about the people who are more prone to violence, and about how to assess a violent person.

The Causes of Violence

Violence is **not** hereditary; we have no evidence that the tendency toward violence is genetic. However, violence **can be a** product of the environment—including the home—which explains why violence seems to "run" in families. When violence occurs on a common basis in the home, family members are conditioned to accept violence as a normal pattern of behavior.

But what causes people to be violent in the first place? Most often, a number of factors combine in a complex, interrelated network to result in violence. Some of those factors may include the following:

—**Brain damage or dysfunction.** Violence that is the result of brain disease is generally explosive and rarely isolated; a person suffering from brain dysfunction that results in violence usually has a long history of violent behavior. (A history of sexual assaults and traffic accidents is also common.) In these cases, the violence is accompanied by feelings of panic, memory loss, epileptic seizures, and impaired vision. Even small amounts of alcohol can trigger a violent episode.

—**Alcohol and drugs.** Violent behavior is usually an impulsive response to stress or crisis, and many drugs (including alcohol) work to diminish self-control. For that reason, the use of drugs and/or alcohol can cause a violent outburst in a person who does not have a history of violence. Violent behavior can also be characteristic of drug or alcohol withdrawal.

—**Threat.** Threat—whether physical (such as the threat of injury) or psychological (such as the threat of embarrassment or rejection)—can cause a person to react with violence in an attempt to defend himself. Sometimes the threat is real, but many times it is imagined. Violent behavior usually occurs when the person believes that the threat is real and imminent. The violence is not always directed at the object of the threat, either: a man who feels that his job security is threatened may not feel that he can direct a violent attack against his employer, so he turns it on his wife instead.

—**Frustration.** Normal, everyday, temporary frustrations do not usually result in violence. But a violence-prone individual may have a low tolerance for frustration, and she may react with rage when her needs are not immediately met. Constant frustration has an even greater likelihood of breeding violence. In such cases, the person uses violence to remove whatever is preventing him from achieving his goals.

—**Cultural acceptance of violence.** A child who grows up exposed to violence begins to accept and embrace it. A child may be punished with violence; she may see violence every day on television. Before long, she learns that violence is a way of solving problems and dealing with personal feelings.

—**Fear of being helpless.** Think about the typical scene of a parent punishing a child: the parent is strong and willful, and the child is usually weak and helpless during the episode of punishment. Such a situation can become embedded in a child's mind. As he grows, he wants to be strong—not weak and helpless. So, to avoid those feelings of being helpless, hopeless, and passive, he becomes strong and aggressive. He becomes violent.

—**Need for power.** Somehow, we as a society have developed the idea that to be powerful is to be accepted; we have fostered the idea that the more powerful a person is, the more he will be respected, liked, and admired. For some, violence is a way of gaining power. The rapist is a perfect example: he interprets his ability to overpower, intimidate, and induce fear as a way of gaining power.

—**Desire for wealth, prominence, and influence.** With some exceptions, the attainment of great wealth, prominence, and influence involves aggression: those who are aggressive tend to climb the social ladder, while those who are passive usually do not. When the attainment of goals begins to involve frustration and intense competition, violence can erupt.

—**Role models.** While the women's movement has made some impact on the concept of "male" and "female" roles, many families still hold out certain role expectations for their boys. Boys are expected—and encouraged—to get involved in a few fistfights while they are growing up. In the athletic arena, they are expected and trained to be tough and aggressive. Patterns of aggression that are firmly established can lead to a violence-prone personality.

—Marital disagreement. Certain issues—such as money, sex, discipline of children, and social issues—tend to breed conflict in some marriages. In some situations, married couples find that they **always** disagree on some issues, such as how to discipline the children or how to spend the money. The greater and more prolonged the conflict, the greater the chance for violence.

—Child-rearing. The demands, frustrations, and pressures associated with rearing children can result in domestic violence as one or both parents try to meet all the challenges involved. If violence was a factor in a child's home, that child is more likely to react to his own frustrations and problems with violence. According to studies, the highest incidence of child abuse occurs in families with five children;[2] families with more than five children are at a lower risk because the children tend to share in child-rearing duties. Violence is more likely to erupt in homes where there are financial problems, outside commitments that require transportation, and limited privacy.

—Stress. Some common stressors have been identified that, when chronic, can lead to violence. They include:[3] arrest of a family member, unemployment, work-related problems, inability to increase family income, increasing inflation rates, foreclosure on mortgage loans, relocation (of either home or school), disciplinary problems with a child at school, a child suspended from school, a child involved in drugs or alcohol, serious illness or accident, medical expenses, pregnancy, sexual problems, separation or divorce, death in the family, or problems with relatives.

—Disruption in balance of power. Ideally, both parents in a marriage should share in the decision making for the marriage and the family. When one partner makes all the decisions, that partner holds all the power; the other partner becomes powerless, submissive, weak, and vulnerable. In such a situation, the partner with the power tends to use violence and aggression in dealing with the vulnerable, weak partner.

—**Panic.** A person who feels that he is losing control over himself or his situation may begin to panic; as his panic escalates, he finds that he **does** start losing control over his own behavior and perception. In an attempt to regain control, he may lash out in violent, erratic, and unpredictable behavior.

—**Systemic disorders.** Aggressive and/or violent outbursts can be caused by a systemic disorder; common culprits include connective tissue disorders, electrolyte imbalance, pulmonary insufficiency, diminshed cardiac output, diabetes, hypoglycemia, anemia, uremia, vitamin deficiency, and other nutritional deficiencies.

—**Neurological disorders.** As already mentioned, brain disease or dysfunction can cause violence or aggression; so can head injury, cerebrovascular disease (stroke), epilepsy, dementia, meningitis, intracranial hemorrhage, and central nervous system infections.

—**Mental illness.** Various psychoses or other forms of mental illness are hallmarked by episodes of violence or the tendency toward violence. People plagued by mental illness may become detached from reality, lose control over impulsive behavior, and misinterpret their environment. They may sincerely believe that they are being persecuted and may react with violence in an effort to regain control or power. Some may "hear voices" that command them to perform violent acts that they would not otherwise try. Some who have periods of mania or hysteria may become quite easily provoked and may respond with aggression or violence.

Likely Candidates for Violence

Certain experiences and characteristics can combine to make a person more prone toward violence:[4]

—Profound depression, which increases the risk of both suicide and homicide

—Alcohol intoxication or withdrawal
—Drug intoxication or withdrawal
—Certain kinds of physical illness, especially anemia, electrolyte imbalance, epilepsy, and delirium
—Certain kinds of mental illness, especially schizophrenia and mania
—Seizures, which can cause confusion that leads to violence; in certain seizure disorders, behavior such as biting, kicking, and scratching is characteristic, and the slightest provocation can cause violent outbursts
—Antisocial personality traits
—Paranoid personality traits
—Drug addiction
—A history of violent behavior, especially a history of fighting, drunk driving, drunk and disorderly behavior, or violent behavior in the military
—A poor record in school or on the job, whether or not the record specifies involvement with violent behavior
—A conviction of criminal homicide or a history of making homicidal threats, especially if the person has never attempted suicide or threatened to attempt suicide (lack of suicide attempts signals a greater likelihood of homicide)
—A history of physical assault, especially fistfights
—A history of symbolic acts of murder (such as firing a gun at a person's photograph)
—The presence of weapons, either in the home or carried
—A history of being abused as a child (abused children often become abusive parents)
—A dehumanizing view of mankind, in which people are viewed as mere objects
—A combination of bedwetting, fire setting, and cruelty to animals during childhood has been associated with violent behavior in adulthood
—A plan to injure or kill someone
—Latent homosexuality
—Emotional coldness
—Loud, rapid, and aggressive speech
—Restless, tense posture (such as the person who sits on the

edge of a chair, gripping the armrests, or a person who paces nervously back and forth)
—Threatening, abusive gestures, such as slamming doors, shaking a fist, or using threatening language
—A tendency to startle easily
—Conflict in significant relationships, especially someone who is coping with infidelity or divorce
—Expression of a strong desire to control others or to "get even" with someone else
—Poor concentration, poor coordination, and memory difficulties
—Preoccupation with sexual thoughts or fantasies
—A childhood history of brutality, neglect, seduction, or emotional deprivation in the home
—A childhood history of brutality, neglect, seduction, or emotional deprivation in the home
—A childhood history of frequent exposure to death in the family combined with little personal fear or apprehension about death
—Refusal to talk to others
—Illogical thought processes
—Intense, irritable, agitated behavior
—A dull, unresponsive, blank expression
—Extreme anger or hostility

In addition to these personality and situational clues, look for the following, which can be signals of impending violence:[5]

—**Demographics.** Young, single, black males between the ages of fifteen and thirty have the highest incidence of violence. (The incidence is highest for all men between the ages of fifteen and thirty, and blacks have a slightly higher rate.) Although people without spouses or children are more prone to violence, spouses and children are often targets of violence when they do exist.

—**Home environment.** A person who comes from an antagonistic home atmosphere with family members who are aggressive or prone to violence will be more likely to be violent; so will a person who is taking medication, who possesses a knife or gun, and who has identified someone as a target of his hostility, especially if that person is available to the aggressor.

—Recent history. A violence-prone person will probably have manifest clues of potential violence: a woman may have driven recklessly at high speeds through a residential area following an argument with her teenage son. A man may have strangled his wife two or three times in the past week and threatened her with a gun while he was drunk. An eighteen-year-old may have thrown away all the medication in the house because she was afraid of hurting herself. A father may have thrown his crying baby into the crib and run from the house in a fit of rage.

—Family conflicts. As stated, one-fourth of all murders are between family members; half of those are between spouses. (One study revealed that 41 percent of all women killed were murdered by their husbands.) Arguments over infidelity, separation, divorce, financial pressures, sex, or discipline of children can erupt into violence.

—Early history. Look for clues that demonstrate a low tolerance for frustration, anger, and anxiety. Children who were victims of emotional deprivation or rejection are more likely to become violent adults, as are children who come from chaotic family environments (including foster homes). Other childhood experiences that can lead to violence include child abuse, uncontrollable temper tantrums, truancy, excessive fighting, cruelty to animals, and parental seduction leading to incest.

—Mental status. Impending violence may occur if the person is confused, irrational, angry, frustrated, or panic-stricken. Watch for rapid breathing, twitching eyelids, muscle tension, nervous pacing, and threatening gestures.

Violence and Hostage Situations

A special kind of situation develops when a violent individual takes a hostage—an innocent bystander who is caught up in the vicious cycle of anger, frustration, and violence. The taking of hostages has increased over the past few years, so much so that law enforcement agencies and banks have begun training employees in how to handle themselves in hostage situations.

Knowing what kind of person is motivated to take a hostage and knowing how to deal with the hostage situation can reduce the chances for violence and enable the hostage to survive with dignity.

In essence, three kinds of people tend to take hostages:[6]

The Criminal

Two basic kinds of criminals take hostages. The first is the antisocial personality—usually an armed robber who has been trapped at the scene of the crime because of rapid police response. Once he finds out that the police have him cornered, he takes a hostage as a bargaining tool. With the hostage at bay, he can dicker with the police to let him keep the money, get him more money, let him escape unharmed, and so on. He makes logical demands—food, money, freedom. Almost always, the hostage is a stranger to the criminal, and studies have shown that this kind of criminal is usually an experienced felon with an above-average education.

The second kind of criminal who takes a hostage is the inadequate personality—to put it simply, he goofs. Because of poor planning, he seriously miscalculates his ability to rob an establishment; he makes childlike errors, and he ends up taking hostages to protect himself. While the antisocial criminal makes logical demands, the inadequate personality criminal makes foolish, almost impossible demands, such as bargaining for a million dollars in gold bricks. He may begin by stating his demands with conviction, but he usually backs down, offering several options and becoming almost apologetic.

The Mentally Ill

Two types of mentally ill people most commonly take hostages. The first is the paranoid schizophrenic, the most common; the demands are frequently bizarre. One bank robber in California demanded that authorities turn off the moon, that all people in Los Angeles walk to the ocean to be cleansed, and that a truckload of birdseed be delivered to every bank in California. [7]

The second most frequent type of mentally ill person who takes hostages is the one who is profoundly depressed; he will speak in quiet tones with slow speech patterns. He will probably be extremely negative, and his demands are laced with references to depression and death. This type of person may be suicidal, and he may threaten to kill (or may actually kill) the hostage to force the police to shoot him. The hostage is usually known to him. He takes the hostage because he wants to be punished, and he is crying out for help; he can usually be talked out of his plans for the hostage.

The Politically Motivated

The politically motivated individual usually selects the hostage situation very carefully, planning out every detail of the place, time, and hostage. While this situation is much more common in Europe and South America than in the United States, it does occur—and it provides the greatest challenge, since it is carefully planned and since the person is likely to have killed hostages before. The hostage is taken and held in exchange for promises of political favors or as an avenue for the expression of political convictions. The hostage is usually a public figure who holds some value to society.

The Four Stages of the Hostage Situation[8]

Any hostage situation involves four basic stages. There are no common time limits for each stage; the time frame varies greatly with each situation.

ALARM. The first—and probably most traumatic—period is the alarm stage. Emotions are high. The hostage-taker reacts with desperation; he wants to buy time, and he succeeds by taking a hostage. He will probably be extremely aggressive during the alarm period, even if he carefully planned the hostage situation; he works to terrorize the hostage into submission, often with abuse, threats, and harassment. During this stage, the hostage runs the greatest risk of injury or death. The hostage-taker usually shoots at anyone he believes to be a policeman.

The alarm stage is difficult for the police: they arrive on a scene of mass confusion. It's often difficult to determine what is happening, who is taking the hostage, and who else might be involved in the crime.

The hostage may experience nearly paralyzing fear—he goes from a routine situation into one of life and death. Many hostages react by denying reality. Some hostages report that they believed they were dreaming and would soon wake up; others sleep for up to 90 percent of the time they are being held hostage. Those who do realize what is happening tend to react with confusion, defenselessness, and overpowering fear; they panic when they perceive that the police are doing nothing and that the chances for a favorable outcome are dim.

CRISIS. During the crisis stage, the hostage sets up a pattern of relating to the hostage-taker that can determine survival. While some continue to emotionally deny the situation, many hostages recover during the crisis stage and begin to act as they do under normal circumstances. Three great psychological hazards occur to the hostage during the crisis stage:

—He loses his sense of time. The only knowledge the hostage may have is what the hostage-taker chooses to relate.

—He has to struggle with claustrophobia. Many hostages are confined in small, dark spaces for the length of the hostage situation—a condition that creates considerable stress. Even normally sedentary people become stressed after a few hours of confinement.

—He has to cope with isolation. A hostage may either be left totally alone during the hostage situation, or he may be exposed to the hostage-taker—someone who is hostile. The isolation element is the most difficult for gregarious hostages to cope with.

During the crisis, law enforcement officials are extremely busy: they fortify their position, control the crowd, establish the command post, and try to determine the identity of the hostages and the hostage-taker and what the demands are.

During the crisis situation, the hostage-taker is still dangerous and unpredictable. He may become extremely frustrated, especially if the hostage situation was not planned; early dialogue with the police may be marked by emotional outbursts and excessive demands. Hostage-takers use this time to secure their position—they may move the hostage around or move furniture and cover windows to barricade themselves. Some collect personal belongings from the hostages as still another bargaining chip.

—ACCOMMODATION. The longest and most peaceful of the stages, the accommodation stage is marked by a long bargaining period between the hostage-taker and law enforcement personnel. The criminal concentrates on bargaining—he is trying to strike a deal with the police to achieve his goal (more money, freedom, and so on). The criminal usually tries to guarantee his escape, and the police concentrate on getting him in a position where they can capture him without risking injury to the hostage. The mentally ill hostage-taker uses the bargaining period to ventilate his frustrations ands—he wants to talk about his problems, and he wants someone to listen. The mentally ill usually wind down after several hours and can be talked into surrendering.

By the end of the accommodation phase, the mentally ill hostage-taker is usually working out the details of the surrender; the criminal or terrorist is still bargaining for freedom. During the last phases of the accommodation stage, however, the hostage-taker usually makes more reasonable demands and begins to show a willingness to settle for saving face instead of holding out for the initial demands.

During the accommodation phase, the police are busy: SWAT teams are usually established, and sniper teams report the hostage-taker's movements. While officers talk with the hostage-taker, detectives gather background information that will help in negotiations. It is common for policemen to work on short shifts and to switch off frequently in order to stay rested; in the meantime, the hostage-taker and the hostage are worn to a frazzle. During the accommodation phase, the police work out the fine details of their tactical plan.

During the accommodation phase, the hostage experiences long periods of boredom punctuated by terror; hours seem to stretch into days. The fluctuation of such intense emotions brings on incredible fatigue.

Hostages who survive may develop the Stockholm Syndrome during the accommodation stage. If the Stockholm Syndrome does develop, the hostage is more likely to survive. Simply put, the Stockholm Syndrome has three stages:

1. The hostage develops positive feelings toward the hostage-taker.
2. The hostage develops negative feelings toward the police.
3. The hostage-taker develops positive feelings toward the hostage; this spells the difference between life and death.

While it is not entirely clear how the Stockholm Syndrome develops, it appears to be a coping mechanism on the part of the hostage; the hostage might develop feelings of compassion and affection because he is anticipating death, and the hostage-taker represents continued existence. Most hostages resist those feelings of compassion at first but relent as the hostage situation drags on. The hostage suppresses the fact that he might be killed and concentrates on the positive occurrences: he is being given food, blankets, and so on.

Another factor in the Stockholm Syndrome is the apparent uselessness of the police: the hostage may begin to view the police as the cause of the problem. The hostage may believe that the entire ordeal would end if the police would just leave.

Still another factor is the powerful reaction to helplessness: a hostage who is totally helpless may develop a kind of parent-child relationship with the hostage-taker.

—RESOLUTION. Finally, the hostage situation ends, either because the hostage-taker surrenders or he is captured or killed.

The hostage-taker may react in a number of ways. Most experience a great sense of loss; the situation is a failure. He began with a great feeling of triumph, believing that all things were possible, and now he faces the ultimate defeat.

The most dangerous of the hostage-takers at this stage is the inadequate personality criminal. He may view this as an unbearable failure and may want to commit suicide. But he can't pull the trigger on himself, so he tries to force the police into shooting him instead. He may walk calmly out of the door and suddenly start shooting at the police, or he may walk out quietly and calmly and then shoot the hostage so that the police will shoot him. Or he might come out according to the agreement and then purposely disobey police instructions. Some may actually commit suicide.

If the hostage-taker surrenders, the police will take him into custody during the resolution phase; it will seem quiet and almost anticlimactic. But if the hotage-taker does not surrender, the SWAT team and police officers will be forced into executing their well-rehearsed plan for capturing the hostage-taker. The primary goal during the resolution stage is to preserve the life of the hostage.

The hostage will probably emerge with mixed emotions: there will be relief, exhaustion, fear, hostility, and gratitude. If the Stockholm Syndrome has developed, the hostage will feel gratitude toward the hostage-taker and hostility toward the police. Many hostages suffer a variety of physical and emotional problems long after the siege is over; some live with the acute fear of being taken hostage again.

The Homicidal Person

Homicide is a special crime that bears a specific definition. According to the Uniform Crime Reporting Program,[9] an **aggravated assault** is the unlawful attack by one person on another for the purpose of inflicting severe bodily injury; usually a weapon or some other means is likely to produce death or great bodily harm. The difference between aggravated assault and homicide? In aggravated assault, the victim lives. In homicide, the victim dies. The difference, then, is not in the intent, but in the outcome.

Homicide—or murder, as it is commonly called—is on the increase in the United States; so is aggravated assault. Both the offenders and the victims of aggravated assault and homicide bear striking similarities. If you could arrive at a composite of the offender and the victim, it would be this:[10]

Sex: Male
Race: White
Age: Between twenty and thirty-nine
Location of crime: In a building, usually a home
Circumstances leading up to crime: Argument
Weapon: Firearm, knife, or other cutting instrument

Even though we have isolated a stereotypical composite, there are some clues about homicide—the kinds of threats that are most likely to result in homicide, early signs of homicidal aggression, and ways to determine the potential to kill.

Homicidal Threats: How Real?

A homicidal threat is like a suicide threat—it should always be taken seriously. Even so, there are ways to tell how likely a threat is to result in homicidal behavior. Look for the following signs of a serious threat:

—The person admits that he has caused loss of life or serious harm to another person.

—The person admits that he feels responsible for the death of another person.

—The person admits that his threat is designed to frighten someone into submission. (If so, find out what will happen if he does not get his way!)

—The person has a concrete plan about how to carry out his threat; be especially cautious if he has access to a weapon.

—The person admits that he has injured another person (whether or not it was intentional).

—The person admits that he has entertained thoughts about injuring or killing someone.

—The person is making the threats in a paranoid or jealous rage; a person who has been involved in a relationship that includes threatening behavior over a long period of time is less likely to act on the threats than someone who does not have such a history and is suddenly aggravated.

—The person admits to having tied someone up with rope, straps, wire, or some other material.

—The threat is directed against a specific person. (A general statement, such as "I'm going to kill someone" usually indicates that the person has lost control and is crying out for help.)

—The threat is an expression of rage or extreme anger, especially if it is directed at a specific individual instead of an innocent person.

—The threat is not being made in a clearly open way. If the person is making the threat in an open manner, he is usually inviting someone to step in and prevent him; the person who makes the threat in a secretive or covert way is most likely to carry out the threat and is most serious in making it.

In assessing how real the threat may be, take into account other signs of violence-prone behavior, as listed earlier.

Early Signs of Homicidal Behavior[11]

The following can indicate impending homicidal aggression:

—The person has been through an emotional "crescendo;" he seems to have undergone a tidal wave of energy, agitation, restlessness, anxiety, excitement, or panic. Many experience crying or sobbing spells that indicate a breakdown in the ability to control emotion.

—The person has experienced a significant loss; sometimes the loss is symbolic or perceived rather than real. For example, a man may have tried to help his lover with a problem; to him, his failure to help indicates his loss of the lover.

—The person has undergone mood shifts characterized by self-hatred and deep pessimism.

—A man may have endured threats to his manhood; this can especially occur when a woman taunts him or challenges him to perform some specific task at which he subsequently fails. In his embarrassment and humiliation, he may become enraged at the woman and either beat her up, kill her, or hurt someone who is close to her.

—A man has been involved in either open or secretive homosexual activities.

—The person has been complaining of medical problems that are chronic and recurring; most frequent are problems with sleep, persistent aches and pains, and severe headaches.

—The person has begun using drugs or has increased his use of drugs significantly.

Such signs should be taken more seriously if the person has stated a specific plan by which to kill a specific person, has access to the weapon he plans on using, and seems hostile or destructive. Immediate danger can be assumed if the intended victim is helpless or seems to be provoking the person (even though such provocation is innocent).

Additional danger can stem from a situation in which the

person does not have a strong support network, has an unstable life-style, has a poor employment record (especially if he has recently quit is job), seems unwilling to try to change his lie or solve his problems, and has been aggressive or extremely violent before.[12]

Domestic Violence

Domestic violence is generally defined as **behaviors among family or household members that threaten to cause or do cause serious physical harm.**[13] Domestic violence was once almost a taboo subject: it didn't happen in "nice homes" or in "nice families."

Attitudes have changed. We are finally recognizing—openly—that nice homes and nice families are indeed plagued by violence. A spokesman from the U.S. Attorney General's Office and head of the Task Force on Family Violence maintains that domestic violence may now be "the most prevalent form of violence in America."[14]

Dr. Richard J. Gelles, professor of sociology at the University of Rhode Island, agrees, stating, "The family is the most violent group in society, with the exception of the police and the military. You are more likely to get killed, injured, or physically attacked in your home by someone to whom you are related than in any other social context. In fact, if violence were a communicable disease, like swine flu, the government would consider it an epidemic."[15]

In a broadened definition, domestic violence is not confined to incidences of physical abuse; it also encompasses abusive mental, emotional, or psychological treatment and verbal or nonverbal threats of abuse.

Unfortunately, the problem of family violence crosses all socioeconomic, geographic, age, race, and sexual boundaries. Recent statistics—which probably only hint at the real extent of the problem—indicate that as many as 16 million Americans are assaulted by members of their own families. Children are bitten, kicked, punched, beaten, and threatened with guns and knives—not only by parents, but by brothers and sisters. One out of every five children assaults or threatens to assault a parent. Nearly half of all marriages are marked by violence between spouses, and more than one in ten include incidents of severe batterings.

The Victims of Family Violence

Sadly, every member of the family is a possible target. A two-year-old toddler, an executive husband, a tottering grandfather, a teenager, and a mother are all at danger. Certain characteristics have been identified that may place a family member at higher risk to become a victim of violence:[16]

—**Child.** A child from a broken home is more at risk of violence, as is a child whose mother is battered or whose father is not his biologic father. A child who is socially or developmentally retarded is at high risk, as is a child who has been labeled a "juvenile delinquent." Other risk factors include neglected health and chronic physical complaints, such as insomnia, headache, asthma, bedwetting, gastrointestinal complaints, and a fear of going to school.

—**Wife.** A woman who was beaten as a child, married as a teenager, pregnant prior to marriage, or reared in a broken home runs a higher risk of being victimized by violence. She is also at risk if she is married to a man who is unfaithful, alcoholic, or a gambler. Other risk factors include drug abuse, depression, anxiety, suicidal behavior, or refusal to comply with her husband's demands. The high-risk wife may suffer from a number of physical complaints, including headache, insomnia, back pain, pelvic pain, chest pain, gastrointestinal distress, a choking sensation, or hyperventilation.

—**Husband.** A husband who is elderly, disabled, or self-righteous runs a higher risk of being abused or battered. Other risk factors include extreme passivity, dependence, depression, or fear of hurting his wife.

—**Parents.** Parents who are in poor health, who are elderly, or who are disabled are more likely to encounter violence from their children. So are parents who are experiencing marital discord or midlife crisis. Other risk factors include ambivalence and permissiveness.

Domestic violence is given a fertile breeding ground because of certain cultural and societal factors: one of the primary ones is the long-standing dominance of men in society. While women's rights advocates have succeeded in challenging many of these so-called "sacred" beliefs, one factor can never be changed by legislation: women are smaller and often weaker than men. Some of the most common factors that contribute to the cycle of violence include the following:[17]

—The criminal justice system is predominantly male, and the system has offered little or no protection to women who are battered.

—Society has traditionally defended the notion that men are authority figures and women are subject to that authority.

—Economic constraints work against women. The pay scales in many professions place women in a position of dependence on men for support of themselves and their children. Women who do go to work are faced with the burden of child care expenses and the guilt of worrying about "leaving" their children.

—Women are pressured into staying with men who abuse them not only out of economic necessity but out of the myth that a single-family household is not a viable family unit.

—Some federal laws exist and many states have laws that place men in positions of authority over women; these laws imply a covert "right" for a man to be violent toward his wife and children.

—Society has preached that a woman's most important role is that of "wife and mother," while a man is left free by society to invest as little time as he wants to in his "husband and father" role. In addition, society has tended to magnify the achievements of men while it has downplayed the achievements of women; therefore, women who do achieve tend to experience less positive self-image than men who achieve.

Battered Wives

The term "wife abuse" or "battered wife" actually refers to women who are maintaining an intimate relationship with a man—the woman may be the man's wife, or she may simply be his lover, his girlfriend, or his ex-girlfriend. The words "abuse" and "battered" don't refer to the typical stress and conflict that occur in any relationship; instead, they refer to violence that causes serious injury or death. The figures relating to battered wives are sobering.[18] Approximately 4 million women each year are beaten in their homes by their husbands, lovers, boyfriends, or ex-boyfriends. Those beatings are responsible for one-fourth of all suicide attempts by women (half of all attempts made by black women), and half of all the rapes that occur in women over the age of thirty are part of the battering syndrome. Up to half of all the murders in this country are committed within the family; 13 percent of those occur between spouses.

A typical cycle occurs in cases of wife abuse. The first stage is marked by a buildup in tension between a husband and wife—usually the result of a series of minor occurrences or irritations. The wife may fail to keep the bathroom as clean as the husband wants it; she may spend too much money on groceries for the weekend; she may ask for new shoes; she may burn the porkchops. The husband begins his response with verbal abuse—screaming, yelling, name-calling, threatening.

What follows is inevitable: physical abuse. The wife may be choked, kicked, punched, slammed against the wall, thrown down the stairs, shoved to the floor, bitten, knifed, or even threatened with a gun. The husband may use objects such as belts, household objects, or small items of furniture in the attack. In 85 percent of the cases, the wife leaves, but in the overwhelming majority of cases, she comes back.

What happens when she comes back? Initially, there is reconciliation. The husband feels guilty; he showers his wife with affection, profusely apologizes, and assures her that he will never do anything violent toward her again. During the period of reconciliation, he probably truly believes that he will be able to make good on his promise—that he will control himself. During reconciliation, the wife **wants** to believe in her husband—she wants to believe that if she stays, he will not hurt her again.

Unfortunately, most husbands and wives then move into the next stage of the cycle: rebuilding of tension. The cycle continues, often despite professional help.

Men Who Batter

Every marriage—indeed, every relationship—involves stress and tension. Some are able to deal with their tension in nonviolent ways, while others turn to violence in response to stress and tension. What makes the difference? Why do some men batter?

Characteristics of men who batter their wives include the following:[19]

—They were the products of violent homes. A man who batters his wife was probably the victim of child abuse, and he likely saw his father beat his mother; he may have seen violent exchanges between other significant people in his life.

—He may be childlike when he is not being violent; he may be passive, dependent, and yearn to be "cared for." He may perceive this to be a "weakness" and may translate his anger toward himself into a physical attack on his wife.

—He may be extremely possessive and jealous of his wife and may react with violence if he senses that other men are paying attention to her. The wife usually cannot convince this kind of man that she is being faithful to him, even though he monitors her every move—sometimes to the extreme of following her to the bathroom, reading her mail, and listening in on her phone conversations.

—He may be unemployed or may be extremely dissatisfied with his present job; he may not have a job that challenges him or that pays him well enough.

—He is probably a traditionalist who believes that men are superior, that men should be the authorities, and that men should have the option of beating their wives if deemed necessary to inflict punishment or guarantee good behavior.

—He may frequently abuse or injure family pets, and he may hunt for the pleasure of killing.

—He may accept violence as a viable way to solve problems, and he may seem preoccupied with weapons.

—He sees sex not as a form of loving communication between a husband and wife, but as an act of aggression during which he can build his self-esteem (especially in the face of doubts about his virility); he may be bisexual.

—He has a dual personality. On the one hand, he is sweet, considerate, loving, affectionate, attentive, caring, and repentive; the next day he may be violent, hateful, abusive, angry, and domineering. This kind of dual personality presents a difficult situation for the woman: it is extremely confusing to be beaten up one day and showered with love the next. There's another hazard to this kind of behavior—the public may see only the sweet, kind, considerate husband, while the wife has to put up with the man only she knows in private.

—He blames others for his actions; he wouldn't be this way if it weren't for her, for the boss, for a friend who cheated him, and so on.

—He uses alcohol and/or drugs and frequently uses them just prior to episodes of battering. (The alcohol may be consumed in an effort to calm the man down, or he may use it to bolster his courage.)

—He does not believe that his violent behavior should have

negative consequences; he sincerely believes that he is "above the law," that he should not be punished, and that he is acting like all other men act. To him, abuse is simply part of being married—it's his "right."

Why Women Stay

Just like men who batter, women who are battered have various characteristics in common. Most have low self-esteem; she may be convinced that she somehow deserved the attacks, and she may feel guilty over alleged misdeeds (such as burning the porkchops). She, too, has a dual personality: she presents a positive, optimistic face to the world but lives in terror and anger; she seems passive to outsiders but may be strong enough to resist further violence and avoid being killed. She is a traditionalist, holding strong beliefs in the "woman's place" and other female sexual stereotypes; she tends to use sex as an attempt to establish an intimate relationship with her husband. She is under an extreme amount of stress and suffers a number of physical complaints as a result.

To those who are not battered, it seems astounding that a woman wok around and endure the abuse.

Why do women stay? There are a number of reasons:[20]

—The woman is afraid of loneliness and isolation. A woman who is abused typically suffers from low self-esteem, and her husband does nothing to boost her sagging ego. She fears being alone and is afraid that if she leaves she will not be able to make friends or establish close relationships.

—She is afraid that she is being abused because she is "crazy" or "insane." She feels a constant sense of impending doom; she is often unable to sleep and is driven by panic and anxiety. She fears that because of her assumed "illness" she will be unable to survive alone.

—She is afraid of what her husband will do if she leaves. Most battering husbands make extreme threats: that if she leaves, he will prove that she is an unfit mother and will take the children;

that he will maime her so that no other man will ever want her; that he will kill the children; that he will kill her. The woman has every reason to believe, based on his violent nature, that he will carry out his threats.

—She is not prepared economically to survive on her own. She does not have her own savings account, does not have training that enables her to get a good job, or may have let her former training and experience stagnate over the years of her marriage. Without her own money and without a place to go, she has few options. Most women in this situation are unaware of community resources. Even battered women who work rarely have control over their own incomes; their husbands seize their money and spend it as they wish. Women who do think that they may be able to scratch out a living end up staying with their husbands because they don't want to deny their children the social, educational, and cultural opportunities that come with the husband's income.

—She feels guilty: she has been reared to believe that she is the foundation of the home and that any malfunction in the family unit is somehow her "fault." She blames herself for the battering.

—She would be too embarrassed to leave. Friends would ask questions. She would have to explain her reasons for leaving to her parents, her siblings, her friends, her neighbors, her associates at work—most of whom have no idea that she is battered and most of whom would be shocked to find out. Because she blames herself for the battering, she presumes that others will blame her, too—and she can't face that kind of embarrassment.

—She has "learned" to be helpless. She truly believes that she cannot escape her husband's violence, so she has learned to be passive and accepting and does not seek to escape.

Clues to An Abusive Situation

Several clues may help identify husbands and wives who are

caught in the cycle of wife abuse:[21]

—The woman may have multiple injuries (there are relatively few ways other than a beating to sustain multiple injuries).

—When asked what happened, the woman may not try to explain; the husband may do all the talking, including answering the questions that are directed toward the woman.

—The husband and wife may be angry and obviously frightened; they may toss accusations back and forth or may constantly interrupt each other.

—The house may be disheveled, giving evidence of a struggle.

—The husband may show little or no concern over the wife's injuries; the wife may seem guilty or sheepish about them.

—The explanations for the injuries are inconsistent or illogical with the appearance of the injuries.

—There may have been previous episodes of violence between the man and woman.

Battered Husbands

The problem of battered husbands is still largely unexplored. There are many reasons for our lack of information, the chief one being that a man who is battered by his wife is not likely to admit it—it would crush his ego too severely.[22] Statistics do indicate that about as many wives beat their husbands as husbands beat their wives.

There are some important differences, though, that make the problem unique. First, when women use violence against their husbands, it is usually in self-defense; when they kill, it is usually after enduring years of harsh battering and abuse themselves, and the murder is committed in an attempt to end the cycle of violence. (Interestingly, the criminal justice system tends to be harsher on women who kill than on men who kill.) Finally, a woman's attacks usually level less harm and result in much less serious injury than a man's.

Dealing with Violence

Intervening in a violent situation involves considerable danger for you: a person who is directing his violence at someone else may turn on you as you try to intervene and gain control of the situation.

The following suggestions should be used in intervening with violent individuals:

—Talk to the person about what is bothering him and what has lead to the situation he is in now; help him to quickly think of alternatives for venting his frustrations.

—Encourage the person to honestly express his feelings; if he feels like crying, then that is what he should do.

—Try to help the person maintain an element of hope, but don't offer false reassurances; don't guarantee him that the police won't take him into custody when they arrive, but keep reminding him that there are plenty of people who want to help him work through the problem.

—As difficult as it may be, remain calm yourself. The violent person is out of control and is terrified by his feelings of being out of control; if you come into the scene in a state of panic and terror, you will reinforce his fear of losing control completely.

—It is normal and necessary to be afraid of a violent person, but do not let your fears upset you. Express your fears to your partner or other emergency personnel, but do it in a calm way.

—Remember that it takes time to deal successfully with violence. Don't rush right in to settle the situation instantly. Take your time; move slowly and speak slowly; don't make any sudden moves. (The exception is when someone's life is in immediate danger and you must intervene to save it..)

—Don't try to immediately disarm the violent person. Instead, concentrate on lessening his violence potential first; he will be more prone to surrender the weapon on his own if you succeed.

—Engage in calm, continuous conversation with the person. Listen intently, maintain eye contact, and repeat some of the things he tells you in your own words. Show him by your response that you understand how he feels and that you are interested in helping, not hurting, him.

—Offer the violent person food, nonalcoholic drinks, or cigarettes.

—To avoid confusion and panic that may precipitate more violence, choose a spokesman who will do all the talking with the violent person. Resist the temptation to have several emergency workers trying to communicate with him. The spokesman should keep up a smooth, calm, unhurried dialogue and should **not** be interrupted by other emergency workers.

—Don't let the person start talking about unrelated issues; concentrate on the "here and now" and on what can be done to resolve the current problem. Avoid being judgmental, and be careful not to take sides.

—As you help the violent person explore solutions, help him discover nonviolent ways of solving his problem that will allow him to "save face." Enlist the person's cooperation by saying something like, "I'd really like to help you. I think the two of us can come up with something that will work. We can handle this better if we work together. I'm not here to fight you, I'm here to help you."

—Never touch a violent person, and keep an appropriate distance. If he thinks that you are "closing in" on him, he may react with fear and panic.

—Call for extra manpower as soon as you determine that a situation of violence exists, but don't use the extras immediately. The violent person should be aware that you have come backups, but don't overwhelm him with an army; he might panic and carry out his threats of violence.

—Don't draw a weapon unless there is a clear threat to life (if you carry a weapon in the first place).

—If you have to take a person by force, make sure that you have enough manpower to accomplish it. Work quickly, using cloth or padded restraints or wide leather straps; don't use ropes, handcuffs, or wires of any kind. Your aim is not to hurt the person, but to subdue him. **Never** remove the restraints once you have taken a victim by force; transport him to the hospital and let medical personnel there remove the restraints.

—Acknowledge the person's feelings of fear, anger, and hostility. You might say something like, "I can see that you're very angry. What has happened?"

—Don't trap the violent person in a room or in an area, and, by all means, don't cut off your own route of escape. If you are in a room, leave the door open and don't stand between the person and the door; you don't want to appear to be aggressive. Avoid other aggressive behaviors, such as speaking with a loud voice, yelling, staring at the person, or making threatening facial gestures.

—Never make promises you can't keep.

—It will be difficult to do in a tense situation, but remember: the violent person has rights. Ask his permission to talk to him; ask his permission to help him. If he feels helpless or abused, he will react with violence.

—If the person seems to be disoriented, carefully explain who you are and what you are trying to do. You might need to repeat the most basic things over and over.

—Ask your partner to survey the surrounding area quietly and subtly for others who may be part of the violence situation. Ask him, too, to look for potential hazards and to quietly remove them if he can. Try to get rid of things like broken glass; look around yourself and be aware of things like low-hanging pipes (you might bump your head), litter on the floor (you might trip), or anything else that could disrupt your conversation.

—Try to figure out (with the person's help) what triggered

the violence and what is reinforcing it. Work toward removing those factors. If you discern that the arrival of the police might trigger or agitate the person, ask them to stand nearby but remain out of sight while you work with the person.

—If you suspect that the person has a weapon, take immediate steps to verify your suspicions. Come right out and ask, "Is that a gun? What are you going to do with it? Do you intend to use it on me? It makes me feel uncomfortable. Would you promise not to use the gun on me?" Ask the person to surrender the gun. He doesn't need to give it to you, but he should be willing to put it in a closet, put it in a drawer, or toss it across the floor. If he refuses, **leave immediately**. A person who refuses to surrender a weapon should be left to the police.

—Check around the area for less obvious items that could be used as weapons, such as broken glass, pens and pencils, broken furniture, and so on. Stay alert to objects that could be used to hurt you.

—Never argue with a violent person. You can't win.

—To restrain a combative patient, see p. 253.

Protecting Yourself[25]

Your first responsibility in a violence situation is to protect yourself. If you end up being sucked into the violence and injured or killed, you won't be effective at all. In responding to a possible violent situation, follow these safeguards:

—If you approach in a car, don't park immediately in front of the house; go down the block a little ways and take a minute or two to size up the situation from a distance.

—If you can, leave your car unlocked so that you can get away quickly.

—Approach the door with caution. Never stand directly in front of the door; the violent person might shoot through the closed door.

—Before you knock on the door, listen carefully for sounds

that indicate violence; try to assess what might be happening inside.

—Knock firmly, but don't pound on the door with undue authority.

—If someone tells you to come in, pause before you do so. When you do go inside, quickly scan the entire room and look for potential hazards; then try to establish eye contact with the violent person.

—Try to get the person to sit down and talk about what is happening; sit down with him. Never stand over the person in an authoritarian way.

—If you can, keep the person out of the kitchen or the bedroom; most weapons are most easily available in those two places.

—If necessary, separate the people, but as soon as things have calmed down, bring everyone back together again. Don't let the separation continue for too long—it will breed suspicion, fear, and panic.

—If the person is armed, work toward having him put down his weapon. If he won't, leave.

—If the person seems unduly upset and panic-stricken, calmly tell him that you have medication that can help him regain some feelings of control and that will help him feel more calm.

Handling a Hostage Situation

If you are confronted with a hostage situation, don't try to be heroic. Innocent lives-including your own—are at stake. The most difficult part of the hostage situation is the first stage, or the alarm; emotions are highest, the hostage-taker is the most panic-stricken, and he is the most likely to do something violent.

During the alarm stage, keep a low profile. One man who

survived a two-month hostage ordeal gave remarkably good advice: "Lie very close to the floor."[26]

Hostage situations should be handled by trained policemen and federal officials. Once you sense that the immediate danger is over, calmly back out of the situation if you can. Immediately notify tactical police teams and other backup personnel, including specialists who are trained to manage hostage situations.

If you are taken hostage, remain calm. Keep a low profile. Don't try to escape or do anything heroic. Cooperate with the hostage-taker's demands. While every hostage situation is unique, most specialists agree that it is risky to resist.

Handling a Homicidal Person

If you arrive at the scene of a homicidal situation and you determine that the homicidal threat is real, notify the police immediately. While the police are arriving, follow these guidelines:[27]

—Listen to the person carefully. Let him know by your eye contact, your nonverbal expressions, and your calm speech that you are interested in what he has to say. Invite him to express himself, and show your interest in his responses.

—When and if he does respond, validate his feelings. You might say something like, "I can understand how you could feel that way," or, "No wonder you are so angry."

—Confront the individual's urge to kill; don't try to whitewash it. Then help him explore some alternatives. You might say something like, "I understand that you want to kill your wife. I can understand why you feel that way. But I'm not sure that will solve the problem. Can you help me think of some other way to handle this that won't get you into trouble?" Don't be afraid to point out possible consequences of the homicide, but be careful not to threaten the person.

—Give the person positive reinforcement as he struggles to

come up with alternatives. You might say something like, "That sounds good to me. I knew you could think of something. What else can you come up with?" Praise him and work to help him regain some self-control.

—When the police arrive, explain to them in front of the person that you are pleased with him. You might say something like, "Ted was feeling very angry a few minutes ago, but he has really thought things over. I'm really impressed with what he has come up with. I think he has come up with a few alternatives. Why don't you talk to him about them?"

—Remain calm and back away slowly as the police take over the situation.

Helping Victims of Domestic Violence

If you respond to the scene of domestic violence, follow these guidelines:[28]

—Before you do anything, call the police. Make sure that they understand that the situation involves domestic violence.

—Identify yourself and explain that someone called because they were afraid someone had been hurt. Don't probe into the causes of the conflict; instead, stress the fact that you are there to treat any injuries. Specifically ask if someone is hurt.

—If any person is badly beaten, treat the severe injuries immediately and arrange for transport to the hospital.

—While the more severely injured person is being treated, talk to the spouse. Explain in a low, quiet, calm tone of voice that you understand that sometimes things can get out of hand. Explain calmly that you need to know what happened because you must file a report.

—Never take sides in a dispute at any time. Ignore accusatory remarks.

—Above all, remain calm and in control. Ask that family

members sit down, away from each other. If either person strikes the other while you are there, insist in a sharp voice that they stop and that they go back to their seats. Treat minor injuries.

—If there is a threat of homicide, let the police handle the aggressor; confine yourself to treating any injuries. If the aggressor has a gun and refuses to put it down, don't try to treat even severely injured people.

—Let the police handle the aggressor.

Restraining A Combative Patient

—The angry, combative patient is ready to fight with anyone who approaches. Convey a sense of helpfulness rather than hostility or frustration. Present a comfortable, confident, and professional manner.

—If a possibility of danger exists, the patient should be interviewed with another emergency worker present. Identify yourself and let the patient know what you expect.

—Avoid reacting with anger; do not threaten or make physical gestures until sufficient help is available to saely restrain the patient.

—If necessary, create a safe zone and wait for the police. **Follow local protocol.**

—Place the patient on an ambulance stretcher and apply ankle and wrist restraints.

—Pull the arms tightly across the patient's chest and tie them on opposite sides of the stretcher frame.

REFERENCES

1. This and the following statistics are from Lee Ann Hoff, *People in Crisis*, 2nd Edition (Menlo Park, Calif.: Addison-Wesley Publishing Company, Nursing Division, 1984), p. 227.

2. Carmen Germaine Warner, *Conflict Intervention in Social and Domestic Violence* (Bowie, Md.: Robert J. Brady Company, 1981), p. 40.

3. Warner, pp. 41-42.

4. J. Ingram Walker, *Psychiatric Emergencies: Intervention & Resolution* (Philadelphia, Penn.: J.B. Lippincott, 1983), pp. 153-156; Hoff, pp. 260-263; John L. Hipple and Lee B. Hipple, *Diagnosis and Management of Psychological Emergencies* (Springfield, Ill.: Charles C. THomas, 1983), pp. 32-33; and Gail Pisarcik, "Violent Patient," *Nursing81*, September 1981, p. 63.

5. James T. Turner, *Violence in the Medical Care Setting* (Rockville, Md.: Royal Tunbridge Wells, 1984), pp. 64-66.

6. Turner, pp. 184-186.

7. Turner, p. 185.

8. Turner, pp. 189-201.

9. Jacquelyne G. Gorton and Rebecca Partridge, *Practice and Management of Psychiatric Emergency Care* (St. Louis, Mo.: C.V. Mosby Company, 1982), p. 139.

10. Gorton and Partridge, p. 140.

11. Warner, pp. 136-139.

12. Turner, p. 28.

13. Ellen L. Bassuk, Sandra Sutherland Fox, and Kevin J. Predergast, *Behavioral Emergencies* (Boston, Mass.: Little Brown and Company, 1983), p. 171.

14. Roberta Roesch, "Violent Families," *Parents*, September 1984, p. 75.

-15. Ibid.

16. Richard M. Viken, "Family Violence: Aids to Recognition," *Postgraduate Medicine*, Volume 71, Number 5, May 1982, p. 117.

17. Warner, p. 48.

18. Figures taken from Geraldine D. Greany, "Is She a Battered Woman?" *American Journal of Nursing*, June 1984, p. 727.

19. Warner, pp. 49-50.

20. Warner, pp. 52-57.

21. Corlis Taylor, "Domestic Violence: The Medical Response," *Emergency Medical Services*, Volume 13, Number 5, September/October 1984, p. 36; and H.L.P. Resnik and Harvey L. Ruben, *Emergency Psychiatric Care* (Bowie, Md.: The Charles Press Publishers, Inc., 1975), p. 132.

22. Hoff, p. 250.

23. Ann Wolbert Burgess and Lynda Lytle Holmstrom, *Rape: Victims of Crisis* (Bowie, Md.: Robert J. Brady Company, 1974), pp. 4-11.

24. Theresa S. Foley and Marilyn A. Davies, *Rape: Nursing Care of Victims* (St. Louis, Mo.: C.V. Mosby Company, 1983), pp. 44-45.

25. Hipple and Hipple, pp. 39-40.

26. Turner, p. 201.

27. Gorton and Partridge, p. 145.

28. Resnik and Ruben, pp. 133-135.

29. Brent Q. Hafen and Keith J. Karren, *Crisis Intervention for Emergency Medical Personnel* (North Hollywood, Calif.: Creative Age Publications, 1980), p. 56.

Drug and Alcohol Emergencies

Drugs and alcohol are misused and abused by people spanning all socioeconomic groups, all classes of people, and almost every age group. It is estimated that there are 10 million alcoholics in the United States today. Alcohol is directly involved in approximately 30,000 deaths and 500,000 injuries every year as a result of automobile accidents. Because of its deleterious effects on the liver, pancreas, central nervous system, and other body organs, alcohol reduces the average life span of an alcoholic by ten to twelve years.

Drug and alcohol abuse is an extremely complicated problem. Why? Because a serious drug or alcohol habit can be maintained only through a vast array of interpersonal and external reinforcements.[1] To help a person overcome a drug or alcohol habit, it is necessary to remove (or neutralize) all of those reinforcements—those that come from the outside (such as peer acceptance, peer pressure, and social approval) as well as those that come from the inside (such as relief from pain, boredom, fatigue, or frustration).

There's another important reason why drug and alcohol abuse is such a complicated problem: the drug and alcohol abuse is rarely **the problem**. Drug and alcohol abuse is often a sign of other crises—medical problems, financial worries, marital stress, or other problems, are usually the real crisis; drugs and/or alcohol are used to temporarily relieve the problems. Because temporary relief **is** gained, the user is reinforced; the problem becomes compounded as the drugs and alcohol are part of a vast network of emotional need.[2]

General Terminology

The scope of drug and alcohol abuse may encompass everything from habitual use to physical addiction, and the specific phases of dependence vary, depending on the individual, the drug, and the patterns of use.

Drug abuse is defined as the self-administration of drugs (or of a single drug) in a manner that is not in accord with approved medical or social patterns. Compulsive drug use refers to the situation in which an individual becomes preoccupied with the use and procurement of the drug. Compulsive drug use usually leads to addiction characterized by physical or psychological dependence.

Physical dependence is defined by the appearance of an observable abstinence syndrome following the abrupt discontinuation of a drug that has been used regularly. Physical dependence signs and symptoms are different for different drug classes (such as narcotics, depressants, or stimulants), but physical dependence can always be identified by the presence of abstinence syndromes.

A physically dependent person will usually have one set of signs and symptoms due to drug use and an opposite set when the drug is withheld. Opiates, for example, reduce gastrointestinal activity. When a person who is physically dependent on opiates is denied the drug, he suffers the opposite effect of increased gastrointestinal activity.

Physical dependence is not a "normal" physiological condition. It represents adaptation by the bodily systems to the presence of the drug. When a person becomes physically dependent, then, the absence of the drug has a significant physiological impact.

Psychological dependence refers to a condition in which the patient experiences a strong **need** to experience the drug repeatedly, even in the absence of physical dependence. The state of psychological dependence is sometimes called habituation.

While most drug therapy has traditionally centered on treating physical dependence, psychological dependence is often more compelling and critical. Some drugs produce no physical dependence at all but produce intense psychological dependence.

One of the difficulties with psychological dependence is that the patient is "rewarded" for taking the drug. He becomes motivated, feels good, and thinks that he is capable of doing marvelous things. In many cases, the drug is used to escape feelings of depression.

Tolerance refers to the situation in which, after repeated exposures to a given drug, achieving the desired effect requires larger doses. The magnitude of tolerance can be measured by comparing the results obtained from the initial dose of the drug with those obtained from subsequent doses.

In many instances, tolerance works within a drug class, i.e., tolerance to one barbiturate produces a tolerance to all barbiturates. In addition, tolerance may develop in response to only some actions of a particular drug. Tolerance to the different effects of a drug does not necessarily develop at the same rate or with the same degree.

The extent of tolerance and the rate of its development depend on the individual, the drug, the dose, the frequency of dose, and the method of administration. Most tolerance results from frequent and continuous exposure to the drug. An increase in dosage will again produce the desired results. With some drugs, however, the patient reaches a plateau, and the desired effect cannot be obtained with **any** dosage.

Addiction involves physical and psychological dependence, tolerance, and compulsive drug use. It is characterized by overwhelming involvement in the use of a drug.

Signs and Symptoms of Drug Abuse

Different classes of drugs produce different signs and symptoms and have varying potential for tolerance and addiction; a summary of each group and its effects follows. Despite those differences, some signs and symptoms are characteristic of a victim of drug abuse:[3]

—Insomnia
—Change in appetite; some drug classes cause a marked loss of appetite and a significant disinterest in food
—Reduction in sex drive
—Chronic fatigue
—Agitation
—Irritability
—Mood alteration
—Isolation and apathy
—Change in pupil size (either enlargement or constriction, depending on the drug used)
—Rubbing and irritation of the nose and eyes
—Yellowing of the skin, indicative of jaundice (a common complication resulting from dirty needles or shared equipment)
—Facial rash, frequently accompanied by scratching
—Fever, usually of short duration
—Blood-spotted clothing at injection sites
—Hostile, verbal outbursts
—Slow, halting speech
—Indifference toward work or other projects, accompanied by a poor ability to concentrate
—Unexpected and unexplained absences from school or work or the unexplained ability to keep appointments
—A change in the usual life pattern
—A decline in physical appearance, grooming, and dress
—A shift in language use (a user may suddenly become profane, for example)
—Rejection of old friends and secrecy about new ones
—Sudden tendency to steal
—Peculiar or unwarranted use of sunglasses (to hide unusual appearance of pupils)
—Inappropriate or unwarranted wearing of long-sleeved shirts (to hide needle marks in arms)
—Skin tracks and related scars on the neck, armpit, forearm, wrist, hand, foot, under the tongue, or on the dorsal vein of the penis
—Needle puncture marks located directly over a vein (because these marks usually disappear within a week, their

presence indicates recent injection)
—Pop scars (from "skin popping") located on the arm,
abdomen, thigh, and shoulder (pop scars are permanent)
—Abscesses, infection, or ulceration in areas where injection
or skin popping may have occurred, usually on the arm,
thigh, shoulder, abdomen, chest, hand, or finger
—Gangrene of the skin in any of the above areas
—Severe swelling of the hand and reduced flexion of the
fingers (results from injecting drugs into the hand)
—Thrombophlebitis in any unusual area that might also be
the site of an injection
—Unusual and obviously accidental (unpatterned) tattoos, a
result of carbon from flaming a needle and usually seen at
an injection site; these tattoos gradually disappear
—Bullae at the site of a possible injection, resulting from a
too-hot liquid drug
—Toxic dermatitis at the injection site
—Purpura, urticaria, and pruritis as a result of allergic
reactions to drugs
—Ulcerations or perforation of the nasal septum
—Wrist scars(resulting from suicide attempts)
—Unusual pigmentation differences in the skin around
possible injection sites
—A poorly defined linear mark of pigmentation that appears
above a possible injection site, usually resulting from a
cordlike or beltlike material used as a tourniquet during
injection
—Impetigo
—Cracking of the skin at the corner of the mouth
—Cigarette burns, usually between the fingers, due to drug-
induced drowsiness while smoking
—Dental disorders, due to neglect
—Trench mouth, due to neglect
—Goosebumps, usually a complication seen during
withdrawal

Specific Signs and Symptoms of Drug Abuse

Each of the drug classes has unique effects of use, symptoms of withdrawal and overdose, and patterns of tolerance, as follows:

DRUG CLUSTER	MOST COMMON DRUG OF ABUSE	CONSEQUENCE OF ABUSE
STIMULANTS AND APPETITE SUPPRESSANTS	AMPHETAMINES Caffeine Cocaine Ephedrine Methylphenidate Nicotine Over-the-Counter Preparations	Moderate dosages cause increased alertness, excitation, euphoria, increased pulse rate and blood pressure, insomnia, loss of appetite. Overdoses can cause agitation, increase in body temperature, hallucinations, convulsions, possible death. Although the degree of physical addiction is not known, sudden withdrawal can cause apathy, long periods of sleep, irritability, depression, disorientation.
CANNABIS PRODUCTS	Hashish Marijuana THC (Tetrahydrocannabinol)	Moderate dosages cause euphoria, relaxed inhibitions, increased appetite, disoriented behavior. Overdoses can cause fatigue, paranoia, possible psychosis. Although the degree of physical addiction is not known, sudden withdrawal can cause insomnia, hyperactivity, and decreased appetite is occasionally reported.
DEPRESSANTS — NARCOTICS AND OPIATES	Codeine Heroin Methadone Morphine Opium	Moderate dosages cause euphoria, drowsiness, respiratory depression, constricted pupils, nausea. Overdoses can cause slow and shallow breathing, clammy skin, convulsions, coma, possible death. Sudden withdrawal results in watery eyes, runny nose, yawning, loss of appetite, irritability, tremors, panic, chills and sweating, cramps, nausea.
DEPRESSANTS — SEDATIVES AND TRANQUILIZERS	Alcohol Antihistamines Barbiturates Chloralhydrate, Other Non-Barbiturate, Nonbenzodiazepine, Sedatives, Over-the-Counter Preparations, Diazepam and Other Benzodiazepines, Other Major Tranquilizers, Other Minor Tranquilizers	Moderate dosages can result in slurred speech, disorientation, drunken behavior without odor of alcohol. Overdose can result in shallow respiration, cold and clammy skin, dilated pupils, weak and rapid pulse, coma, possible death. Sudden withdrawal results in anxiety, insomnia, tremors, delirium, convulsions, possible death.
PSYCHEDELIC DRUGS	DET (N, N-Diethyltryptamine) DMT (N, N-Dimethytryptamine) LSD (Lysergic Acid Diethylamide) Mescaline MDA (3, 4 Methylenedioxyamphetamine) PCP (PHENCYCLIDINE) STP (DOM-2, 5-Dimethoxy, 4-Methylamphetamine)	Moderate dosages, can result in illusions and hallucinations, poor perception of time and distance. Overdose can result in longer, more intense "trip" episodes, psychosis, and possible death.
INHALANTS	Medical Anesthetics Gasoline and Kerosene Glues and Organic Cements Lighter Fluid Lacquer and Varnish Thinners Aerosol Propellants	Moderate dosages cause excitement, euphoria, giddiness, loss of inhibitions, aggressiveness, delusions, depression, drowsiness, headache, nausea. Overdoses can cause loss of memory, confusion, unsteady gait, and erratic heart beat and pulse are possible. Sudden withdrawal results in insomnia, decreased appetite, depression, irritability, headache. Death can result from suffocation.

Phencyclidine (PCP)

One of the most dangerous hallucinogens—and one that deserves separate treatment—is phencyclidine, better known as angel dust, killer weed, supergrass, crystal cyclone, hog, elephant tranquilizer, PeaCe Pill, embalming fluid, horse tranquilizer, mintweed, mist, monkey dust, rocket fuel, goon, surfer, KW, or scuffle.

Nothing has so bewildered and amazed researchers as phencyclidine (PCP)—a drug that is cheap, easy to make, and easy to take and that is related to horrible psychological effects (some of which can last for years).

Physical signs and symptoms of moderate PCP intoxication include extreme agitation, involuntary horizontal and vertical movement of the eyes, unresponsiveness to pain, severe muscle rigidity, production of excessive bronchial and oral secretions (leading to choking in some cases), and hypertension. Signs and symptoms during moderate intoxication tend to come in spurts—a patient may seem to have no reaction and may suddenly flare into frantic activity (physical and mental).

All the physical and psychological signs and symptoms present with a moderate dose will be present with a high dose but in a much exaggerated state. A high dose of phencyclidine—ten to twenty milligrams—can lead to death. Physical signs and symptoms include disruptions in heart rhythm; marked increases in blood pressure; marked decreases in blood pressure; decreased urinary output; convulsions; respiratory arrest or decrease in respiration; coma; and vivid visual hallucinations. A user may be intermittantly in and out of a coma for weeks and months following severe intoxication. Acute muscle rigidity occurs, and eyes are often fixated open with a blank stare. In some cases, laryngospasm (spasm of the throat muscles) may occur. Excessive sweating, drooling, and vomiting are characteristic of severe intoxication.

Three of the most severe reactions stemming from high doses of PCP are psychological ones: schizophrenia, paranoia, and memory loss (amnesia)—in some cases, permanent.

Cocaine

Another drug deserving of separate mention is cocaine—currently the most desired and most expensive drug in America. According to a survey in *Time* magazine, 11 percent of all U.S. adults have tried cocaine; every day, 5,000 new users try cocaine for the first time through intranasal use (snorting). Cocaine in North America today is a $25 billion industry, bringing in more consumers and three times as much money as the recording and movie industries combined.[4]

Cocaine—commonly known as blow, C, charlie, coke, corine, flake, dynamite, gin, girl, gold dust, heaven dust, leaf, joy powder, snort, snow, stardust, sugar, toot, and white girl—is usually "snorted," or sniffed into the mucous membranes of the nose. Less frequently it is injected intravenously or subcutaneously. A vegetable alkaloid derived from the leaves of the coca plant found on the eastern slopes of Peru's Andes Mountains, cocaine currently costs $2,200 an ounce and is the drug of choice for millions of upwardly mobile, status-seeking people. Once used only by the rich (obviously because of its price), it has now invaded the middle class and blue-collar workers: statistics indicate that 20 million Americans have used cocaine at least once, 4 to 5 million use it at least once each month, and of the forty-five tons of cocaine smuggled into the country each year, at least part of it ends up in junior high schools.[5]

Effects of Cocaine Use

Within a few minutes, cocaine produces euphoria and a sense of well-being; those psychological effects disappear entirely within twenty-four hours. At normal doses, cocaine produces physical effects much like those of amphetamines—anxiety, high blood pressure, and a racing heart, Paranoia is common. Those who "snort" cocaine regularly suffer from inflamed, swollen, and/or ulcerated nasal membranes.

As the dosage is increased, the brainstem functions are affected; the user may develop depression of the central nervous system, respiratory collapse, cardiovascular collapse, vomiting, hyperthermia, and nerve conduction blockage. At high doses, seizures and tremors can result.

If cocaine is used regularly, it can result in psychological disturbances (including the inability to concentrate and severe irritability), and it can disrupt sleeping patterns. Cocaine psychosis—characterized by paranoid delusions, manic-depression, confusion, and incoherent speech—rarely occurs and is short-lived when it does, so few victims have the time to seek medical help before the episode is over on its own. One of the most common hallucinations that occurs with cocaine psychosis is a sensation of crawling on the skin (called "formications").

While cocaine does not produce physical dependency, its psychological dependency is severe. Withdrawal, or letdown, can be remedied only by more cocaine in higher doses.

Special Problems Associated with Cocaine Use

One of the most serious and potentially lethal problems associated with cocaine use is "body packing"—smugglers swallow a number of small packages of cocaine in an attempt to cross international borders. Most packages contain about five grams of cocaine; one "body packer" swallowed 180 packages. Commonly, toy ballons, condoms, or the fingers of latex gloves are used as packages; other packages are made of multilayer tubular latex. The problem? The packages can break, releasing a massive dose of cocaine into the stomach or intestines, where it is absorbed and can produce toxicity or death. Even packages that don't break almost always leak. Surgical removal of the packages may be necessary if leakage or rupture is indicated.

Another problem occurs when users try to get quick results by "freebasing," a practice in which the cocaine is smoked. Cocaine salts are extracted in ether, placed on a glass plate, heated gently (usually with a propane torch), and smoked in a glass pipe designed especially for freebasing. Freebasing is extremely dangerous because of the risk of explosion and fire, especially the danger of respiratory tract burns. (Comedian

Richard Pryor suffered severe facial burns in a freebasing accident.)

Effects of Drug Abuse on the Newborn

Many drugs cross the placental barrier; among those are common drugs of abuse. Such drugs increase the baby's chance of being born early and/or at a lower birth weight. Approximately half of all babies born to women who are addicted to narcotic drugs are smaller than average (including a number who are born prematurely). But the more serious problem is that babies of addicts are likely to be born addicted to the same narcotic drug. Shortly after birth, when the baby's supply of drugs is cut off, the baby goes through withdrawal—in serious cases, it can cause death.

Withdrawal symptoms in a newborn addicted infant normally include shrill, high-pitched crying; muscular rigidity; trembling leading to convulsions; gastrointestinal disorders; and a bluish coloring. The child will seem unable to sleep and may scratch at himself.

Treatment for neonatal narcotic withdrawal involves a ten-day period in which the drug of addiction is administered to the baby in gradually decreasing doses while other medical support is given.

Related Illnesses and Diseases

Most related illnesses and diseases are, curiously, not caused by the drug itself, but by the conditions in which the drug is used. Common medical complications include the following:[7]

—Increased infections and diseases due to a lowering of the body's natural immunity system
—Severe infections of the reproductive system, gastrointestinal system, skeletal system, and genitourinary tract

—Diabetes (drug abuse precipitates diabetes)
—Epilepsy (drug abuse precipitates epilepsy)
—Cellulitis (stony deposits at injection sites)
—Gangrene (usually in the hands from hand and/or finger injection)
—Tetanus (the unsterile conditions of drug use have accounted for 90 percent of all tetanus cases recorded since 1955)
—Malaria
—Reduction in testosterone levels
—Endocarditis (bacterial infections of the heart valves)
—Blindness
—Bilateral deafness
—Septic pulmonary emboli
—Peripheral nerve lesions
—Cerebral atrophy (wasting of the brain tissues)
—Myocardial disease and cardiac arrhythmias
—Thrombophlebitis
—Embolisms and blockages of the arteries
—Cardiorespiratory arrest
—Strokes resulting from blockages of the arteries in the brain
—Chronic liver disease and cancer of the liver
—Serum hepatitis
—Convulsive seizures, usually grand mal
—Parkinson syndrome
—Menstrual dysfunction
—Pneumonia
—Acute meningitis
—Various disorders of the skin surrounding injection sites, such as needle-track scars, tattooing, carbon deposits in the skin, and abscess formation at the injection site

The Addictive Personality

With all of the unpleasant side effects of drug use and the common medical complications, why do people abuse drugs?

Researcher Sidney Cohen identified twelve situations in which susceptible people might abuse drugs:[8]

1. An inadequate personality might seek a quick or magical solution to problems that result from immaturity, depression, psychosis, or other emotional/mental problems.
2. Those with the money and opportunity to try drugs might do so to satisfy curiosity.
3. Those who are bored with their everyday life might try drugs to bring life and excitement.
4. A compliant person with a strong need to belong to a group might start using drugs if the rest of the group does, usually as a result of strong social or peer pressure.
5. An artist might use drugs to refuel his inspiration.
6. A person who feels that he needs to escape from a certain situation—whether that need is real or imagined—might try to do so through drugs.
7. Some people become "accidental" addicts—they become hooked to drugs either at an age when they don't know better or under circumstances in which they are not able to discriminate (such as the individual who becomes dependent on pain-killing drugs used following surgery).
8. A person might start to use drugs if she is persuaded to by a "significant other" in her life (a lover or a family member, for example).
9. A person who is suffering from actual stress (either from overwork or as a result of unpleasant life circumstances might turn to drugs to relieve the stress.
10. An impulsive or poorly controlled person who is willing to "try anything" might turn to drugs with little realistic regard for his health or safety.
11. A person who used to abuse drugs but seemed to quit can return to the habit.
12. A person who is seeking some kind of religous experience or personal insight might try to achieve it through drugs.

Experts in the drug abuse field cannot agree on whether there is an "addictive personality"—a personality more prone to becoming addicted (whether it be to drugs, alcohol, food, or something else). Some feel that people with specific personality traits are markedly susceptible to drug abuse; others disagree on the specific traits or dismiss the notion altogether. Most experts do agree, however, an **inadequate personality**—a personality that is not well-formed, regardless of the reasons—is much more susceptible to drug abuse. (This theory explains why so many adolescents get caught in the drug abuse trap.)

Alcohol Emergencies

The alcoholic syndrome usually consists of problem drinking, during which alcohol is used frequently to relieve tensions or other emotional difficulties, and the stage of true addiction, in which abstinence from drinking causes major withdrawal symptoms. The form in which alcohol is ingested is irrelevant; the heavy beer drinker may be as much an alcoholic as the patient who indulges in too much hard liquor. Frequently, alcoholics are dependent on other drugs as well, especially those in the sedative, barbiturate, and tranquilizer categories.

Alcoholism occurs in all social strata. The alcoholic differs in many significant respects from the true social drinker. The alcoholic usually begins drinking early in the day, is more prone to drink alone or secretly, and may periodically go on prolonged binges characterized by loss of memory ("blackout periods"). Abstinence from alcohol is likely to produce withdrawal symptoms, such as tremulousness, anxiety, or delirium tremens (DTs). As the alcoholic becomes more dependent upon drinking, his performance at work and relationships with friends and family are likely to deteriorate. Absences from work, emotional disturbances, and automobile accidents become more frequent.

The Stages of Alcohol Dependency[9]

Alcohol dependency progresses through specific, ordered stages: the earlier intervention occurs, the better the chance of recovery from the addiction.

—**Stage One.** The first stage begins somewhat innocently with social drinking; as the drinker notices that alcohol can bring on a pleasant, euphoric mood, he tends to drink more often to duplicate that mood. The drinking increases, and so does the denial, until the drinker becomes dependent. At this point, he participates only in activities during which he can drink; if he knows that he won't be able to drink in a certain situation, he avoids it. During the first stage, the drinker starts to develop problems in his social behavior.

—**Stage Two.** During the second stage, outsiders start to realize a problem exists. The drinker starts to suffer blackouts—starting with brief blackouts that last only a few minutes, but progressing to periods of days, weeks, and even months in which he cannot remember conversations or behavior. Simply stated, these blackouts are chemically induced amnesia, and they occur only when the drinker is chemically dependent on the alcohol.

—**Stage Three.** The third stage is characterized by a loss of control. The drinker still has a choice about whether or not to take the first drink—but once he takes that first drink, he continues to drink; there is no longer a choice. He may be able to abstain from drinking for a while but will return to drinking— inevitably with disastrous effects. He can't control the number of drinks he takes or the amount he drinks; he drinks to achieve a sense of well-being. If he is denied the alcohol, he suffers withdrawal symptoms (sometimes serious enough to require medical treatment).

—**Stage Four.** Stage four is characterized by acute, chronic dependency—the drinker's entire life revolves around drinking. The drinker suffers critical deterioration and impairment of thinking; one in ten suffer chemical psychosis. When deprived of alcohol, the drinker cannot think or act; he can't even tie his shoes. The drinker's values are affected; things he used to value (such as his family and regular employment) are lost, and he begins to associate only with others in his same circumstance.

Signs of Alcohol Intoxication

The following signs indicate alcohol intoxication or dependency:

—The odor of alcohol on the breath
—Swaying, unsteadiness, and a broad-based, foot-slapping walk
—Slurred speech
—Gastrointestinal distress, including nausea, vomiting, diarrhea, and loss of appetite
—Flushing or swelling of the face
—Poor coordination
—Visual disturbances, such as bloodshot eyes, blurred vision, and hallucination
—Sleep disturbances, most commonly insomnia
—"Green tongue syndrome" (a green coloring of the tongue that results from overuse of breath mints containing chlorophyll in an attempt to mask the odor of alcohol)
—Cigarette burns on clothing (the result of smoking while intoxicated)
—Drowsiness in varying degrees, ranging from sleepiness to coma
—Inappropriate displays of emotion, such as laughing, crying, or becoming suddenly hostile and aggressive
—Problems indicating physical neglect, such as bruises, sores, bleeding, or broken bones
—Sudden seizures or blackouts
—General indications of poor health, such as generalized infections, chronic cough, or vague gastrointestinal discomfort
—Generalized anxiety
—Persistent depression
—Tendency toward accidents (accidental falls, automobile accidents, and so on)

The Stages of Intoxication

Blood alcohol content is used pretty uniformly as a way to

measure the stages of intoxication. After drinking one drink (or its equivalent), blood alcohol level usually registers approximately 0.03 percent, and there is usually no noticeable effect. Beginning with two highballs (or their equivalent), however, the blood alcohol level rises to 0.05 percent and brings with it the first effects of alcohol ingestion. The various stages proceed as follows:[10]

—**Mild high.** With blood alcohol between 0.05 and 0.12 percent, the mild high produces a variety of effects from person to person. Some feel drowsy, warm, relaxed, mildly fatigued, and overwhelmed by a feeling of peace; others feel excited, elated, enthusiastic, or mildly aggressive. Reaction time is slowed, and fine motor coordination is impaired. Some people feel a little unsteady, and others experience some nausea or vomiting. In most cases, the mild high wears off within two or three hours if no additional alcohol is consumed.

—**Alcohol intoxication.** WIth blood alcohol level at 0.15 percent, acute alcohol intoxication brings on gross impairment of both physical and mental functions. The intoxicated person usually experiences wide swings in mood—one minute he is laughing wildly, the next he is morbidly depressed, the next he is openly violent. He experiences blackouts. His speech is slurred, he is profoundly uncoordinated, he walks with an unsteady sway, and his vision is blurred. If no more alcohol is ingested, he can usually return to normal within twenty-four hours.

—**Alcoholic stupor.** If a person who is intoxicated keeps drinking, driving his blood alcohol level above 0.15 percent, he may enter an alcohol-induced stupor. He may be conscious but will stare blankly ahead; he won't respond to questions, can't remember who he is, and doesn't know where he lives. Most often, he is unconscious. Many victims of alcohol-induced stupor fall, incurring head injuries. In a full coma, the alcoholic will suffer from respiratory depression, cardiac problems, and other life-threatening situations.

—**Death.** A person who is not unconscious during a stupor and who keeps drinking can drive his blood alcohol level so high that death results. Blood levels of .55 percent are usually considered fatal.

The Effects of Alcohol Intoxication

Some of the most common effects include the following:

—Impaired judgment
—Blurred vision and hallucination, "spots" before the eyes, "snowfield" vision
—Impaired reaction time
—Loss of balance and coordination
—Shock
—A Parkinson-like syndrome, encompassing tremors, spasticity, and hypokinesis
—Permanent loss of vision or hearing
—Permanent heart disease
—Permanent liver disease (including cirrhosis)
—Permanent kidney disease
—Multisystem failures
—Central nervous system disturbances, including headache, seizure, dizziness, lethargy, confusion, and coma

If you encounter someone who seems stuporous, walks with an unsteady gait, or is confused, don't immediately assume he is intoxicated—even if you can smell alcohol on his breath. A diabetic in insulin shock mimics the intoxicated drunk; a person with severe hypoglycemia can suffer many of the same symptoms and effects.

Also be alert to the possibility that the victim may have taken a combination of alcohol and sedative drugs—a situation that can significantly complicate the picture. Always check the victim's pockets and surroundings for signs of medication or drugs. A person who has taken aspirin with alcohol, for example, will suffer from exaggerated gastric irritation; used with sedatives, alcohol can lead to rapid sedation, respiratory depression, and death. A patient who is on nitroglycerin and who drinks alcohol can suffer cardiovascular collapse. An alcoholic in a coma should be given life-supporting emergency care (including establishment and maintenance of an airway), should be monitored carefully, and should be transported to a hospital immediately where the presence of other drugs or complications can be determined. An alcoholic who lapses into respiratory depression, cardiac arrhythmias, or shock should be treated as if he were any other patient with those problems.

The following signs indicate that you should obtain medical attention **immediately**:

—Signs that the nervous system is depressed: sleepiness, coma, lethargy, decreased response to pain, and so on
—Impaired reflexes, coordination, and judgment
—Tremors (especially if the victim is suffering from withdrawal)
—Extremely low blood pressure
—Withdrawal that is accompanied by severe pain
—Inappropriate behavior, especially if it is aggressive
—Digestive upsets, including gastritis, vomiting, bleeding, and dehydration
—Excessively slow or absent breathing
—Grand mal seizures
—Delirium tremens (terrifying mental confusion, constant tremors, fever, dehydration, rapid heartbeat, and fumbling movements of the hands)
—Disturbance of vision, mental confusion, and muscular incoordination
—Disinterested behavior and loss of memory
—Injury to bones and joints, even in various stages of healing

Alcoholic Withdrawal Syndrome

The alcoholic withdrawal syndrome encompasses a wide spectrum of signs and symptoms, ranging from acute anxiety and tremulousness to delirium tremens (usually occurring within twenty-four to seventy-two hours after the last drink, but sometimes not occurring until seven to ten days later). The stages of alcohol withdrawal include the following:[11]

Tremulus Stage

The mildest of the alcohol withdrawal states, the tremulous stage is usually characterized by agitation, mild muscle tremors, headache, flushed face, and nausea. It can be marked by nightmares and hallucinations (visual or auditory). If complicated, seizures can occur.

The tremulus stage starts within several hours after the person stops drinking, and symptoms usually persist for five to seven days; this stage often progresses to include the more serious symptoms of later stages.

Acute Hallucinosis Stage

Two to three days after a very heavy drinker stops drinking, he may enter the acute hallucinosis stage, in which he suffers all the symptoms of the tremulous stage but also suffers extremely vivid visual and auditory hallucinations. The drinker also becomes extremely fearful, suffering from paranoid and persecutory delusions; he may suffer excessive sweating and marked agitation. Some drinkers become combative or suicidal.

Most cases of hallucinations clear up within about a week, but there have been cases that have lasted as long as several months.

Delirium Tremens (DTs)

Within one to seven days after a serious drinker takes his last drink, he may experience delirium tremens—DTs as they are commonly called—which comprise the most severe stage of withdrawal. The drinker is generally disoriented as to time (he loses all concept of time), place (he doesn't know where he is), and person (he cannot remember who he is). In addition to vivid hallucinations, he may suffer marked agitation, tremors, paleness, sweating, seizures, terror, high fever, rapid heartbeat, and delirium. In advanced stages, he may lose consciousness.

Delirium tremens constitute a true medical emergency and call for immediate transport to a hospital. (A person suffering DTs should **not** be put in jail!)

Related Illnesses and Injuries

Heavy alcohol use is related to the following illnesses and injuries:

Subdural hematoma. Impaired clotting mechanisms and frequent falls render the alcoholic more susceptible to subdural hematoma. Clotting is impaired because alcohol damages the liver and interferes with its synthesis of clotting factors.

Subdural hematoma, or a blood clot in the brain, occurs when blood vessels rupture and bleed into the subdural space. This is dangerous because it increases intracranial pressure and, left untreated, can create pressure on the lifesustaining brainstem.

—Cardiovascular system injury. Long-standing cardiac changes may affect the alcoholic's ability to respond to the stress of injury.[12] Heavy drinkers are subject to cardiomyopathy, EKG changes, and heart failure; drinkers are also subject to blood loss through hemorrhage, altered platelet function, dysfunctions in clotting, and anemia. Alcohol also affects the outcome of blunt injury to the chest; 90 percent of those who ingested alcohol prior to blunt trauma to the chest died.

—Liver disease. Liver damage may result in cirrhosis and may impair glucose metabolism, which can lead to hypoglycemia. Other liver diseases common to alcoholics include hepatic coma, acute alcoholic hepatitis, and esophageal varices.

—Pancreatitis. Alcoholics suffer a high incidence of

pancreatitis, or inflammation of the pancreas. Other common gastrointestinal diseases include gastritis, peptic ulcers, and bleeding ulcers.

—**Upper gastrointestinal hemorrhage.** The alcoholic is prone to upper gastrointestinal bleeding from gastritis, ulcers, and tears in dilated esophageal veins.

—**Central nervous system disorders.** Memory loss, brain damage, cerebellar degeneration, dementia, depression of the thought processes, loss of concentration, lack of discrimination, nerve damage, convulsions, seizures, and elevation of the pain threshold are common among alcoholics. The result? Many alcoholics are unable to recognize and avoid danger and can't tell when injury has occurred.[13]

—**Increased infections.** The alcoholic is prone to increased infections, especially tuberculosis and viral pneumonia.

—**Nutritional disease.** Malnutrition, Wernicke-Korsakoff syndrome (a result of thiamine deficiency), anemia (a result of iron deficiency), folate deficiency, and combined neurologic degeneration as a result of B-12 deficiency are common among alcoholics.

—**Risks of anesthesia.** Alcoholics who require surgery face magnified risks from anesthesia. Respiratory complications are likely because of depressed cough and gag reflex, increasing the probability of vomiting and aspirating. Alcoholics usually can't tolerate blood loss, so transfusions may become necessary; in addition, liver changes in chronic alcoholics affect the ability to detoxify and eliminate anesthesia. Alcoholics may also require additional, aggressive warming because alcohol increases loss of body heat.

—**Incidence of injury.** Alcoholics are much more prone to injuries such as falls, burns, and fractures. The relationship between alcohol ingestion and automobile accidents, violent crimes, drownings, and falls has been well documented. More than half of all injuries in automobile accidents in the United States involve intoxicated drivers.

Fetal Alcohol Syndrome

Because alcohol passes freely and easily through membranes, alcohol can cross the placenta and enter the baby's bloodstream in the same concentration as in the mother's bloodstream. In other words, if the mother is drunk, so is the baby.

The problem for the fetus centers around the liver: while the adult liver can metabolize about an ounce of alcohol every hour, the fetal liver is not fully developed and is incapable of rapid metabolization. Most of the alcohol that reaches the fetus eventually returns to the mother's bloodstream after crossing the placenta again. The fetus, like a sponge, absorbs and holds the alcohol until the mother's liver has successfully metabolized her own alcohol.

In a mother who is continually drunk—or whose blood alcohol level is always high—the fetus cannot release the alcohol, and fetal development is adversely affected. Defects may involve any organ, depending on the stage of pregnancy when the damage occurs. In cases of heavy maternal drinking, fetal alcohol syndrome may occur.

Fetal alcohol syndrome symptoms differ from baby to baby, but a generally common pattern includes the following defects and abnormalities:

—**Central nervous system dysfunctions.** The brain is almost completely formed during the first trimester of pregnancy, but fine brain cell division and maturation continues to take place during the entire term of the pregnancy. Maternal alcohol consumption at any time during pregnancy, then, can cause brain damage. Most of those affected by fetal alcohol syndrome are mentally retarded; even those who are not have lower-than-average mental abilities. (These conditions are permanent, not temporary.) Additional brainstem dysfunctions are common, including poor sucking and swallowing reflexes, apathy, and problems with eating. Small head size is extremely common among victims of fetal alcohol syndrome.

—**Alcohol withdrawal.** A baby who develops in an environment of alcohol will suffer withdrawal when the alcohol supply is cut off at birth. Soon after birth (sometimes as early as three hours after delivery), fetal alcohol syndrome babies display signs of irritability, tremors, seizures, depressed respiratory rate, increased muscle tone, arching of the back, abdominal distention, and vomiting. Initial symptoms disappear within about twenty-four hours, and most other symptoms last approximately one week. In some cases of fetal alcohol syndrome, the symptoms of withdrawal last up to six months.

—**Growth deficiencies.** In addition to having a small head, almost all fetal alcohol syndrome babies suffer from growth and weight deficiencies throughout life.

—**Facial malformations.** One of the most common symptoms of fetal alcohol syndrome is facial malformation. Babies tend to be born with thicker-than-normal hairy growth dovering the face; other unusual facial features that commonly accompany the syndrome include a narrow, flat head; a flat midface; a short, upturned nose with upturned nostrils; a low nasal bridge; a broad space between the nose and the upper lip; a wide mouth with an extremely thin upper lip; slantlike eyes with heavily folded eyelids (similar to those of mongoloids); a small jaw; smaller-than-normal eyes that are set wide apart; asymmetry of the face; and large, protruding ears. While the nose is almost always much smaller than normal, it is usually the most prominent feature because of the smallness of the eyes, the narrowness of the upper lip, and the broadness of the nasal bridge. Many victims have crossed eyes.

—**Skeletal malformations.** Most characteristic of fetal alcohol syndrome is a markedly altered pattern of creases on the palms of the hands; many victims have smaller-than-normal fingernails and toenails, with some nails being abnormally formed. Joint malformations are also characteristic, especially immobility of the elbows and knees.

—**Heart malformation.** Heart murmurs, defects in the septum, and abnormal muscular formation of the heart occur frequently in association with fetal alcohol syndrome. Some infants develop serious congenital heart lesions that lead to critical cardiac conditions throughout life.

—Other abnormalities. Other abnormalities include abnormally pigmented skin; small, raised, strawberrylike birthmarks scattered over the body; excessive hair growth on the face and other areas of the body where hair growth is normally sparse or absent; deformities of the external genitals; defects of the kidneys; club foot; dislocated hip joints at birth; repetitive self-stimulating behavior, such as head-banging, head-rolling, or masturbation; deformities of the toes; poor eye-hand coordination; and abnormal liver structure and function.

Dealing With Drug and Alcohol Emergencies

Crisis intervention is by definition short term; it involves alleviating the pain and confusion of a specific event or circumstance. The conscious patient with drug or alcohol-related emergency problems is often experiencing severe emotional stress. In such instances, the most important crisis intervention tools are the verbal and nonverbal communication skills of the attending emergency worker.

The goal of crisis intervention is to establish and maintain rapport, create trust, and build a short-term working relationship that will lower anxiety, produce a clearer understanding of the problem at hand, and identify the resources necessary to cope with it.

The following guidelines may be helpful in reducing emotional overraction by helping the patient make sense out of what is happening to him:

1. Provide a reality base.
    Identify yourself and your position
    Use the patient's name
    Anticipate the concerns of the patient, family, and friends. Based on the patient's response, introduce as much familiarity as possible, e.g., persons, objects, newspapers, TV programs.
    Be calm and self-assured.

2. Provide appropriate nonverbal support.
   Maintain eye contact.
   Maintain a relaxed body posture. Be quiet, calm, and gentle.
   Touch the patient if it seems appropriate.

3. Encourage communication.
   Communicate directly with the patient, not through others.
   Ask clear, simple questions.
   Ask questions slowly, one at a time.
   Try to ask questions that require a "yes" or "no."
   Tolerate repetition; do not become impatient.

4. Foster confidence.
   Be nonjudgmental. Do not accuse the patient.
   Help the patient gain confidence in you.
   Listen carefully.
   Respond to feelings; let the patient know you understand his feelings.
   Identify and reinforce progress.

Obtaining a history may also be helpful. You should ask the following questions:

—What was taken? The bottle and all its contents should be brought to the emergency department. Its label may help identify the drug, and the number of pills remaining may give a clue to how much was ingested.

—When was it taken?

—How much was taken?

—Was anything else taken (other drugs or alcohol)? Particularly among today's drug culture, overdoses are rarely "pure," and usually represent a combination of agents.

—What has the patient or bystanders done to try to correct the situation? Has vomiting been induced? Street resuscitation procedures are frequently as dangerous as the overdose itself, and exactly what has been done for the patient is very important. The most common form of street resuscitation is "stimulation"—cold showers, vigorous slapping, and so forth. Check for broken teeth, blood in the mouth, or other signs of injury. If the patient has a barbiturate overdose, the patient's friends may have tried to reverse this by giving the patient speed (Methedrine or Dexedrine). There is also a myth prevalent on the streets that salt or milk given intravenously will reverse an overdose. In fact, salt may cause pulmonary edema, and milk can induce lipid pneumonia. All of these street remedies will complicate the picture, so you should learn as much as possible about what has been done.

Factors Impeding Effectiveness

The following factors make a drug or alcohol emergency more difficult to manage and may impede effectiveness if not recognized:[14]

—The victim may deny that he has used drugs or alcohol.
—The victim may resist treatment because he fears police retribution.
—The victim may deny drug use and resist treatment because he fears retaliation on the part of his drug source.
—The psychological and physical effects of some drugs cause the victims to deny use and resist treatment.
—The victim may suffer impaired motor reflexes and motor skills.
—The victim may deny drug or alcohol use because of social reasons (fear of job loss, loss of credentials, loss of driver's license, or fear of embarrassment).

Managing the Victim with Delirium Tremens

Long-term management of delirium tremens requires hospitalization; in the field, try the following prior to transport:

›   —Try to provide a calm, nonstressful environment while you assess the victim's injuries; keep crowds away and keep the noise level at a minimum. If the victim can be moved, move him to a quiet room or area where there is a minimum of confusion.

—Reassure the victim that his hallucinations are only imaginary and temporary; explain that they will stop once he has completed his withdrawal.

—Maintain fluid and electrolyte balance.

—Do what you can to control nausea and vomiting during treatment and transport.

—Restrain the victim as necessary and appropriate; victims of delirium tremens are out of touch with reality and can pose a danger to themselves and others.

—Transport the victim to the hospital.

Managing the Violent Drug or Alcohol Victim

1. Do not approach a potentially violent patient alone. Do so only with a sufficient number of people to control an outbreak of violence. Emergency workers should not create a situation in which they may be injured. It is important to protect the patient as well as the potential victim.
2. Avoid aggressive actions unless there is the immediate possibility of serious injury. In all other circumstances, only defensive techniques, e.g., holding the arms or legs, or rolling in a blanket, should be permitted.
3. If the emergency worker is assaulted, it is possible that he ignored the many signals of impending loss of control presented by the patient. These include high degrees of agitation, sweating, and excessive talking while struggling with violent impulses, etc. Control your own anxiety, be alert to such signals, and take evasive action (leaving the room or calling in other people) before the patient's impulses are translated into action. There is nothing wrong with running from a room occupied by a physically threatening patient, armed or unarmed.

4. If you can, transport the patient to the hospital immediately. If at all possible, keep something familiar with the person—a family member, a friend, a coat, or some other possession.
5. Let the person sit near the door of the room; do not place any obstacle (person or furniture) between the person and the door. In other words, do not block his route of escape. A person who feels that he is being trapped will likely become more anxious, which will exaggerate his hostility and violence.
6. If the patient is armed, the police must be called. If there are not enough personnel to ensure control of an unarmed but violent patient, the police should also be called. Once they have neutralized the threat, assessment and emergency care activities can be resumed.
7. The patient must be protected while in the environment of the emergency setting. Needles, sharp instruments, drugs, etc. should not be in the immediate proximity of the patient. Also, the patient should be observed at all times while in transport.

Emergency Treatment of Alcohol Emergencies[15]

Basic guidelines in treating alcohol emergencies that are not complicated by drug use include the following:

1. Establish and maintain a clear airway; remove anything that might pose a hazard from the throat and mouth, including false teeth, blood, or vomitus.
2. Turn the victim's head to the side and downward toward the ground; his mouth and throat will drain more easily following vomiting in this position. If vomiting does occur, hold the victim's tongue down and forward.
3. Monitor the victim's vital signs carefully and frequently (cardiac and respiratory complications can occur suddenly).
4. Speak firmly to the victim, but never ridicule or criticize him.
5. If the victim is conscious, offer him small amounts of fluids (preferably juices) by mouth.

6. Obtain a brief history to determine how much alcohol was consumed; perform a brief examination to rule out complicating injuries or illnesses.
7. Transport to the hospital as quickly as the victim is stabilized.

Observation and Assessment

The most important information to be gathered from the emergency drug/alcohol patient concerns the level of consciousness and vital signs. Describe the severity of the intoxication by observing:

1. Whether the patient is awake and will answer questions.
2. Whether the patient withdraws from painful stimuli.
3. Whether respiration is intact.
4. The circulatory system as it relates to blood pressure, pulse, and cyanosis.

Typically, most patients will fall into one of three categories:

1. Awake, claiming to have ingested a medicine—the patient may be questioned and not fall asleep when not disturbed.
2. Semicomatose—the patient will respond appropriately to verbal or noxious stimuli but fall asleep when the stimulus is removed.
3. Comatose—the patient cannot be aroused to consciousness by verbal or noxious stimuli.

Supportive care should be initiated as soon as possible. It is obvious that many of the procedures can and should be carried out simultaneously by various members of the emergency team. In any case, the immediate objective is to assess cardiopulmonary functioning and to stabilize basic life support functions. If you are confronted with a comatose patient who is not breathing and whose pulse is absent, emergency CPR must be started immediately.

Once the patient's vital signs have been obtained and stablized, a brief primary and secondary survey should be completed.

Dealing With Hyperventilating Patients

Hyperventilation is a common emergency situation in drug abusing patients. It can be a manifestation of acute anxiety, but it also may indicate metabolic acidosis, severe pain, drug withdrawal, or aspirin poisoning.

Hyperventilation in a drug emergency should be cared for as a medical disorder and **not** as anxiety hyperventilation. **Do not** have the patient breathe into a paper bag.

Often it is difficult to provide a quiet, reassuring environment in an emergency setting. The hyperventilating patient should be removed from the crisis situation as soon as possible. Hyperventilating patients should not be left alone. Listen (in a nonjudgmental way) to the problems of the patient and respond to the patient's questions regarding his condition in a calm, professional manner.

How To Determine If An Emergency Is Drug/Alcohol-Related

Because abuse of drugs and alcohol produce signs that mimic a number of systemic disorders or diseases, it is often difficult to properly assess a condition as a drug or alcohol emergency. This is especially true if the patient is unconscious.

If you suspect that a patient might be experiencing a drug or alcohol emergency try the following:

—Inspect the area immediately around the patient for evidence of drug or alcohol use—empty or partially filled pill bottles, syringes, empty liquor bottles, and so on. Be sure to check the patient's pockets.

—Check the patient's mouth for signs of partially dissolved pills or tablets that may still be in his mouth. (If present, remove.)

—Smell the patient's breath for traces of alcohol. (Be sure that you do not confuse a musky, fruity, or acetone odor for alcohol—all three can be indicative of diabetes.)

—Ask the patient's friends or family members, if they are nearby, what they know about the incident.

—Ask any witnesses who might have seen the patient lose consciousness if they can offer any suggestions about what might have happened.

—Remember—many serious diseases (such as diabetes and epilepsy) resemble drug overdose. Do not make the mistake of assuming that a stuporous, slurry-speeched person has ingested drugs. **Never jump to conclusions.**

Other Causes of Coma

Remember, there can be a number of causes of coma other than alcohol or drug ingestion:[16] before you dismiss them, consider hypoglycemia, head injury, intracranial hemorrhage, hyperglycemia, ketoacidotic coma, malignant hypertension, cerebrovascular accident (stroke), hepatic coma, uremic coma, meningoencephalitis, and other disease conditions.

How to Determine if an Alcohol/Drug Emergency is Life-Threatening

If you suspect drug or alcohol ingestion at a dangerous level, observe the patient briefly for these six signs and symptoms that indicate that the patient's life is in danger:

—**Unconsciousness.** The patient cannot be awakened, or, if you can awaken him, he lapses back into unconsciousness almost immediately. He appears to be in a deep sleep or coma.

—**Breathing difficulties.** The patient's breathing may have stopped altogether, may be weak and shallow, or may be weak and strong in cycles. The patient's exhalations may be raspy, rattling, or noisy. The patient's skin may have a bluish or purplish color, indicating that he is not receiving enough oxygenated blood.

—**Fever.** Any temperature above 100° F. (38° C.) may indicate a dangerous situation when drugs and/or alcohol are involved.

—**Abnormal pulse rate or irregular pulse.** Normal range for pulse rate is between 60 and 100 beats per minute for an adult; any pulse that is below or above that acceptable range may indicate danger, as does a pulse that is irregular (not rhythmical).

—**Vomiting while not fully conscious.** A person who is stuporous, semiconscious, and who vomits runs a high risk of aspirating the vomitus back into his lungs, creating serious breathing difficulties.

—**Convulsions.** An impending convulsion may be indicated by twitching of the face, trunk, arms, or legs; muscle rigidity; or muscle spasm. A patient who is experiencing a series of violent jerking movements and spasms is experiencing a convulsion.

General Procedures for Overdose

An overdose of almost any drug can cause poisoning and should be cared for at once. Emergency care is limited for a person suffering from drug poisoning, but the following procedures can be done. Most of the time, you will be unable to tell exactly which drug a patient has been using. These are guidelines that apply to treatment in all alcohol and drug emergencies:

—Do not panic. Treat the patient calmly. Squelch your impulses to throw cold water on the patient or to move him around. Of course, you should move a patient if he is inhaling a harmful substance of if he is in immediate danger (for instance, a patient who has lost consciousness near a burning building).

—Quickly assess the situation. Because symptoms of drug abuse resemble those of other diseases, it is important that you obtain as much information as possible. If the patient is conscious, ask him what he has taken. If the patient is unconscious, ask friends or family members who may know what has happened. Whatever you do, do not spend a lot of time finding out what has happened at this stage; there may be life-threatening symptoms that need to be handled directly. You can always come back for further assessment once the patient is under control.

—Establish and maintain a clear airway. Remove anything from the mouth or throat that might pose a breathing hazard, including false teeth, blood, mucus, or vomitus.

—Administer oxygen and artificial ventilation if the patient needs ventilation.

—Turn the patient's head to the side and downward toward the ground; in case of vomiting, the patient's mouth and throat will drain more easily in this position.

—Should vomiting occur, suctioning may be necessary. Use great care to prevent aspiration of vomitus.

—Monitor the patient's vital signs frequently. In case of respiratory or cardiac complications, treat the life-threatening situations immediately.

—Watch overdose patients carefully; they can be conscious one minute and lapse into unconsciousness the next.

—Reestablish proper body temperature.

—Take measures to correct or prevent shock. If shock is present, consult your base physician about possible use of the MAST apparatus. Be alert for allergic reactions.

—If the patient is conscious, induce vomiting, particularly if the drug has been ingested within the last thirty minutes. This course of action depends, however, on where the crisis occurred. If the patient can be taken to a hospital within minutes, inducing vomiting is unnecessary. On the other hand, in an isolated setting where medical care is not promptly available, inducing vomiting is useful. Of course, if the drug has been taken intravenously or by inhalation (sniffing), induced vomiting is meaningless. Nor should vomiting be induced in stuporous patients who may become comatose within minutes.

The danger of aspiration of vomitus is too great.

—If the patient is conscious, reassure him of his well-being, and explain thoroughly who you are and that you are trying to help him.

—If the patient is convulsing, protect him from hurting himself by holding his head in your lap so that he will not bang it against the ground.

—Speak firmly to the patient. Be understanding and assuring. **Never** ridicule or criticize the patient.

—Obtain a brief history so that you know what kind of drug or alcohol was consumed. Perform a brief physical assessment to eliminate possibilities of complications or other injuries.

—Transport the patient as soon as his condition is stabilized.

—If there is time prior to transport, search the area around the patient for tablets, capsules, pill bottles or boxes (especially empty ones), syringes, ampules, prescriptions, hospital attendance cards, or physician's notes that might help you identify what drug the patient has taken. Have any such evidence transported to the hospital along with the patient.

—If the patient is agitated, move him to a quiet place where he can be observed and where he will have little interaction with others. It is critical that you calm the patient who seems to be agitated or paranoid. Carefully explain each step of care so that you can help reduce his paranoia.

—If the patient becomes increasingly excited and approaches or reaches a delirious phase, be firm but friendly in dealing with him. Some patients will be in an excited phase when the emergency team arrives. This is a common problem with overdoses of amphetamines, antidepressants, and some over-the-counter medications. This excitement period, often a prelude to coma, may last for several hours. If necessary, make proper efforts to restrain the patient to protect him from himself, and try to obtain help, especially en route to the hospital.

—DO NOT jump to conclusions—do not make decisions based solely on the patient's personal appearance, the fact that you detect an alcoholic odor, or the patient's companions.

—DO NOT accuse or criticize the patient.

—DO NOT leave intoxicated patients alone; make sure that they are attended and observed at all times. They should not be left alone even in a jail cell.

The Talk-Down Technique

The dangers associated with the hallucinogens and with marijuana are primarily psychological in nature. These may be evident as intense anxiety or panic states ("bad trips"), depressive or paranoid reactions, mood changes, disorientation, and an inability to distinguish between reality and fantasy. Some prolonged psychotic reactions to psychedelic drugs have been reported, particularly with persons already psychologically disturbed.

The "talk-down" technique has been established as the preferred method for handling bad trips. This technique involves nonmoralizing, comforting, personal support from an experienced individual. It is aided by limiting external stimulation, such as intense light or loud sounds, and having the person lie down and relax.

The goal of talking-down is to reduce the patient's anxiety, panic, depression, or confusion. Follow these steps:

1. Make the patient feel welcome. Remain relaxed and sympathetic. Because a patient can become suddenly hostile, have a companion with you.
2. Reassure the patient that his strange mental condition is a result of ingestion of the drug and that he will return to normal. Help him realize that he is not mentally ill.
3. Help the patient verbalize what is happening to him. Review for the patient what is going on in his trip; ask him questions. Outline the probable time schedule of events.)
4. Reiterate simple and concrete statements. Be absolutely clear in letting the patient know where he is, what is

happening to him, and who is with him. Identify yourself clearly. Help him identify objects around him that will probably be familiar to him, a process that helps with his self-identification.

5. Listen for clues that will let you know whether the patient is anxious, and, if he is, discuss those anxieties with him. Help him work through them. Help him conquer guilt feelings.

6. Forewarn the patient about what will happen to him as the drug begins to wear off. He will probably be confused one minute, and will experience mental clarity the next. Again, help him understand that this is due to the drug, not to mental illness.

7. Once the patient has been calmed, transport him to the hospital.

Antabuse Emergencies

Antabuse, or Disulfiram, is a drug used to treat alcoholics; antabuse helps the victim control his drinking by interfering with the breakdown of alcohol. If a victim is on antabuse and takes a drink of alcohol, the following symptoms may occur.:

—Severe nausea and vomiting
—Severe drop in blood pressure (it may be sudden and severe enough to cause death)
—Difficulty in breathing accompanied by chest pains
—Rapid heartbeat and breathing
—Flushed face and excessive sweating
—Bloodshot eyes
—Severe headache

The violent illness and reaction will last as long as there is alcohol in the blood.

Follow these general guidelines for treatment:

—Ask the victim to lie down on his side with his face directed toward the ground; vomitus will drain more easily and freely from his mouth and throat should he vomit.
—Ask the victim how much alcohol he ingested. Less than

two ounces is not cause for alarm; if he ingested more than two ounces, coma is likely.

—Elevate his legs to help prevent shock.

—Closely monitor breathing and heartbeat; respiratory and circulatory problems are common in antabuse emergencies.

—Transport immediately.

Emergency Response for PCP Overdose

The PCP patient may be combative and require restraint. It is critical that you provide reassurance that will not frighten or further upset the patient. Most patients will be confused and upset; adverse emergency care efforts can increase psychological harm already inflicted. Keep the patient in a quiet, nonstimulating environment. **"Talking down"—a method recommended for other victims of hallucinogenic drugs— should not be used with PCP patients, since it will probably further aggravate them.**

Since PCP acts as an anesthetic, the patient will probably be unaware of any injuries sustained. Check quickly to determine whether there are any injuries that need attention. If there are, administer emergency care before continuing with psychological care. Restrain a patient who attempts to harm others. If there is a great deal of confusion going on around the patient and it is impossible to move to a quiet atmosphere, plug the patient's ears with cotton or with commercial earplugs. Keep the lights in the room as dim as you can (they will need to be bright enough, however, for medical personnel to monitor signs and otherwise care for the patient). Do whatever you can to minimize the confusion. Most PCP patients will require medical care, and vital signs will need to be monitored regularly. Therefore, you should transport the patient as quickly as possible while you work to calm him.

REFERENCES

1. Eugene Kennedy, *Crisis Counseling: The Essential Guide for Non-professional Counselors* (New York, N.Y.: The Continuum Publishing Company, 1981), p. 78.

2. Kennedy, p. 79.

3. List taken from Helen I. Green, Michael H. Levy, *Drug Misuse.* .*Human Abuse* (New York, N.Y.: Marcel Dekker, Inc.), p. 472; C.J. Frederick, "Emergency Mental Health," unpublished manuscript in possession of the author, pp. 26-27; Patti Lowery and John Schulz, editors, *Diagnosis and Evaluation of the Drug Abusing Patient for Treatment Staff Physicians, Volume 1, Number 1, pp. 29-31; and The National Drug Abuse Center, Rosslyn, Virginia, November 1976.*

4. Ron Rothenburg, *"Cocaine," Emergency Medical Services,* Volume 13. Number 2, March/April 1984, p. 29.

5. Rothenburg, p. 33.

6. Brent Q. Hafen and Keith J. Karren, *Crisis Intervention for Emergency Medical Personnel* (North Hollywood, Calif.: Emergency Medical Services, 1980), p. 30.

7. Hafen and Karren, pp. 40-41.

8. Kennedy, p. 82.

9. John P. Eddy, David M. Lawson, Jr., and David C. Stilson, *Crisis Intervention: A Manual for Education and Action* (Lanham, Md.: University Press of America, Inc., 1983), pp. 20-21.

10. Jeffrey T. Mitchell and H.L.P. Resnik, *Emergency Response to Crisis* (Bowie, Md.: Robert J. Brady Company, 1981), pp. 76-78.

11. Mitchell and Resnik, pp. 78-79; and J. Ingram Walker, *Psychiatric Emergencies: Intervention & Resolution* (Philadelphia, Penn.: J.B. Lippincott, 1983), pp. 76-78.

12. Judy Stoner Halpern and James W. Davis, "Effects of Ethanol in Trauma," *Journal of Emergency Nursing,* Volume 8, Number 5, September/October 1982, p. 261.

13. Ibid.

14. Billy M. Turner, "Drug Use: Myths, Reality, and Problems for EMS," *Emergency Medical Services*, Volume 12, Number 4, July/August 1983, pp. 50-51.

15. Hafen and Karren, pp. 40-41.

16. Walker, p. 41.

Psychological Aspects of Disaster

Disasters vary in kind, length of warning period, number of people affected, duration of impact, intensity of the catastrophe, extent of property damage, number of casualties, and recovery period. The problems that are encountered as a result of a disaster also vary. A disaster like an earthquake is usually marked by little or no warning, sharp impact, and sometimes lengthy recovery. A natural disaster such as a flood or volcanic eruption gives some warning and has a longer duration. Regardless of the disaster, however, people will suffer to some extent or another—both physically and psychologically.

A disaster is generally defined as something that occurs in one location and results in injury or death to one or more victims. Depending on the number of victims involved, various rescue measures will be needed.

Kinds of Disasters

—**A mass-casualty disaster**, the least common kind of disaster, is one in which a large number of people are killed; existing community resources are overwhelmed, and help from adjacent communities (or even adjacent states) must be summoned.

—**A multiple-casualty disaster** usually results from a natural disaster (such as a hurricane, blizzard, flood, tornado, or minor earthquake), but it can also be the result of a manmade disaster—such as a train collision, airplane collision, riot, or dam break. The multiple-casualty disaster involves fewer than one hundred victims and, depending on size, may require the help of emergency personnel from surrounding communities.

—**A multiple-patient incident** involves ten or fewer victims; it may be the result of a minor explosion, an apartment building fire, an automobile accident, or a bus accident. In most cases, emergency personnel within the community can handle this situation without calling for outside help.

Regardless of the scope of the tragedy, however, coordination is needed between all emergency personnel (including fire departments, police departments, hospitals, and emergency medical workers) in order for the situation to be handled smoothly. Regardless of the scope of the tragedy, too **it is critical that psychological injuries not be overlooked in the rush to treat physical injuries.**

General Principles of Psychological Care During Disaster

Several basic principles should guide all efforts in treating psychological injuries in a disaster:[1]

—**Survivors are primarily normal, not psychiatric cases.** Disaster victims are usually normal persons, generally capable of functioning effectively in normal situations. They have just been subjected to severe stress, and some of the reactions they have may manifest themselves as emotional strain. This is usually a temporary condition, it is to be expected, and it does not imply mental illness. Most often, the survivors need concrete help—information about available services, how to get insurance benefits or loans, how to apply with government agencies, help with health care, help with babysitting, transportation, and so on. Often the most important help for someone who has just suffered a disaster is to simply listen with interest and concern.

—**People are seldom shattered by disaster.** Considering the amount of stress that people endure during disaster, they usually perform quite capably. However, frustrations may mount, and feelings of helplessness and anger can result. Again, these are to be expected and are almost always temporary; with help and support, victims can get back on their feet again.

—**People respond to active interest and concern.** People undergoing great stress and pressure—regardless of the source—often feel isolated and alone, even if it is obvious that many others are suffering from the same disaster. The person's ability to cope may be jeopardized. Someone who shows an interest in the victim's concerns helps him restore a sense of identity and forestalls much more severe subsequent emotional distress. People almost always respond in a healthy way to interest and concern; pathological responses are much less likely to occur if yo **expect** a healthy response.

—**Victims may reject help if it implies that they are crazy or weak.** Many people are unable to accept—and will even actually refuse—help for anything that is identified as an emotional problem. It is critical that you not use words that imply mental illness—words such as "counseling," "therapy," "psychiatric," "psychological," "neurotic," and "psychotic" should be strictly avoided. If you suspect that the victim is suffering from emotional problems that will need help, discuss with him the possibility of seeing a "human services worker."

—**People may reject help because of pride.** Some people might feel disgraced because they need help; others might no want help from "outsiders." Helping people in these situations requires great tact and sensitivity, especially if the disaster is large and people from outside communities have been called in to help.

—**People are likely to display great ambivalence.**

Ambivalence is a universal human characteristic in which conflicting—even opposing—feelings may be present in an individual at the same time; it is most likely to occur during periods of emotional stress. You should expect some ambivalence and not be confused when people give you mixed messages: "I don't want help, but I can't go on like this." "I hate you, but I need your support." "I'm depending on you, but I can make it on my own."

—**Respect everyone's right to his own feelings.** You probably won't feel the same way that many of the victims feel; you might have different values systems, and you might be convinced that you would act differently in the same situation. Remember: this victim's feelings are real to him. Don't judge. Don't censor. Don't ridicule. Try to understand how the victim is feeling (even if you don't agree with his feelings) so that you can help him in the best way. Don't try to figure out **why** someone feels the way he does—just accept that he feels that way and try to figure out how you can help him.

—**Remember that emotional disability is just as real as physical disability.** That might be hard to remember when you are faced with multiple casualties involving real (and sometimes terrifying) physical injuries. But consider this: if a man's leg was ripped off in an automobile accident, you would not expect him to get up and walk away from the scene of the accident. Too often the person who is undergoing tremendous emotional crisis is expected to just walk away. You need to realize that the emotional crisis or disability is real, is difficult for the victim to handle, and requires help and support. Be patient, and help the person work through the problem. He will resolve his problems as quickly as he can; no one likes to be upset and confused.

—**Remember that every physical injury is accompanied by a psychological one.** Emotional crisis isn't the lone property of those who somehow miraculously escaped physical injury. Any victim of physical injury will have a strong emotional reaction to that injury, even if the injury is minor; the injured person will be upset, and the more severe the injury, the more upset the victim will become. You need to care for emotional injuries as well as physical ones; don't ignore a victim just because you have finished splinting her leg and she is breathing normally.

The Phases of Disaster

Any disaster can be broken down into seven basic phases—warning, threat, impact, inventory, rescue, remedy, and recovery.[2]

—**Warning.** Not all disasters are preceded by a warning phase; disasters like earthquakes, flashfloods, major explosions, and train collisions involve little or no warning. Others are marked by gradual onset, so they allow for warning; a flood, for example, may be preceded by weeks of heavy rainfall and swelling lakes and rivers. When warning is present, people react with anxiety and apprehension. Some people react to the warning as though the disaster had already occurred, especially if they have been through a similar disaster earlier in their lives.

—**Threat.** During the period of threat, the disaster becomes imminent. It is obvious that the disaster will occur, although some factors about the disaster still remain unknown (how severe it will be, for example, or exactly how many victims it will claim).

—**Impact.** During the impact stage, the disaster actually strikes. People then know exactly what the disaster is going to involve and exactly how they will be impacted. Impact is the hurricane, the tornado, the tidal wave, the fire, the collision. It is generally followed by confusion and some panic, but most people will experience fear rather than panic at this stage. (The movies that show wild panic, with thousands of people running through the streets, aren't too accurate.)

—**Inventory.** During inventory, people quickly assess the situation and figure out what resources are available for dealing with the disaster. Immediate inventory helps to prevent further injury, prevent disability, reduce abnormal reactions, and generally reduce confusion. During inventory, victims and rescuers alike determine exactly what has happened and what needs to be done.

—**Rescue.** During the rescue phase, resources are put into action. Because the disaster has passed, people are generally safe; they need to be reassured of that fact. Rescuers help people deal with not only their physical injuries, but with the shock of the disaster and other emotional trauma.

—**Remedy.** During the remedy phase, rescuers repair the stricken community; in many disasters, the physical damage is severe and requires extensive repair. While physical structures are undergoing repair, victims are going through rehabilitation and healing. The remedy phase is the longest of the phases and requires the most work.

—**Recovery.** During the recovery stage, the community as a whole and the individual victims finally regain their sense of equilibrium.

There are four distinct phases of emotional response to disaster:[3]

—**The heroic phase.** The heroic phase occurs at the time of the disaster, usually immediately after impact. During the heroic phase, people realize what has happened and begin to recognize the serious nature of the problem. The heroic phase is characterized by a great effort to work together to save each other and property. Excitement is intense, and people are concerned with survival.

—**The honeymoon phase.** The honeymoon phase is usually brief—lasting anywhere from two weeks to two months—and occurs after people have had some success in adapting to the demands of the crisis. There is a sense of closeness among the victims, who are pleased that they survived; they feel buoyed and supported by each other and by helpers, and they see the future in optimistic terms. During the honeymoon phase, losses are determined and people make plans to reestablish what was lost.

—**The disillusionment phase.** Eventually, the honeymoon phase breaks down, giving way to disillusionment, depression, anxiety, and frustration. Where the victims looked toward the future with hope and optimism at first, they now see a gloomy picture. During the honeymoon phase, they expected to be able to return to normal quickly; during the disillusionment phase, they realize that unexpected delays and failures will impede progress. During the disillusionment phase, which generally lasts anywhere from several months to a year or more, people work to rebuild their lives and solve their problems.

—**Reconstruction phase.** During the reconstruction phase—which may last for several years—people continue to suffer from the disaster and the losses it involved, but they work to rebuild, reorganize, and restructure. This phase is characterized by cooperation between individuals and the community in rallying to reestablish normal functioning for everyone.

Emotional Responses to Disaster

Emotional responses to disaster depend on a number of factors—how large the disaster was, how many people were involved, how long the disaster lasted, and how intense the catastrophe was. The reactions of individuals also depend on the general emotional makeup of the person, the amount of stress he was under prior to the disaster, and whether or not he has been through similar disasters before. Considering the variables involved, you can expect certain reactions from individuals, emergency workers, and the community as a whole.

Individual Reactions to Disaster

In general, the individual's reactions to disaster will vary and will coincide with the stage of the disaster—reactions will be different, for example, during impact than they will during recovery.

Reactions During Various Phases of Disaster

During warning, most people react with anxiety and apprehension; many people react as though the disaster had already occurred. People who generally react to any crisis with helplessness and extreme fear may become hysterical or paralyzed by fear. During threat, anxiety and apprehension continue; many people tend to emotionally deny the impending disaster as a way of coping with their extreme emotions.

During impact, most people will experience fear but will not panic; many will experience anger, disorientation, agitation, confusion, and feelings of helplessness or hopelessness. During the inventory phase, when people are really realizing the extent of the disaster, they will start to feel isolated, depressed, and apathetic; many will feel overwhelmed and afraid. Initial responses may include withdrawal from reality, nightmares, chronic anxiety, fantasy, delusions, and complaints of many physical problems (headache, indigestion, and so on). Many of those feelings will persist into the rescue phase, which is marked by depression, regression—especially crying and trying to hide—and anxiety.

During the remedy phase, people experience heightened morale, a cooperative spirit of helpfulness, and the desire to make a contribution toward rebuilding (either for an individual or for the community as a whole). During recovery, most people achieve equilibrium; a few will sustain long-term or permanent psychological damage as a result of the disaster.

Long-Term Reactions to Disaster

Some reactions may linger for several years; those may include:[4]

—Separation anxieties (a fear of being abandoned by others, a reaction that is especially common among children)

—Nightmares

—Withdrawal from others and from reality

—Irritability

—Apprehension

—Feelings of resentment toward those who came out of the disaster in a better condition, and feelings of guilt and shame for having survived when others died; some people suffer long-term feelings of guilt and shame because they did not lose as much property as others or because their injuries were not as severe

—Sexual impotence and loss of sex drive

—Loss of appetite

—Feelings of isolation and deteriorating relationships with family members and friends

—Excessive concern over person well-being

—Feelings of hopelessness, helplessness, and meaninglessness

—Unresolved grief

—An increase in smoking and/or drinking

—Irrational fears, often unrelated to the disaster

—Loss of memory or disturbed memory, not necessarily related only to the events surrounding the disaster

—Sleep disturbances, including insomnia

—Deep depression

Despite the tendency for people to suffer some long-term emotional effects of disaster, these do not translate into destructive behaviors. In one study, researchers followed a community for eighteen months following a serious flood that affected 550 families; in that time, there was no significant increase in suicides, attempted suicides, juvenile delinquency, citations for driving while intoxicated, automobile accidents, infant mortality, prescriptions written for tranquilizers, or the rates of scarlet fever, strep throat, and hepatitis.[5]

Stress Response Syndromes[6]

The stress response syndrome is a characteristic set of

psychological and physical reactions or symptoms that follow a crisis or disaster. First identified during the Civil War among American soldiers, it even affects rescue workers. Some of the signs and symptoms include nausea and vomiting; diarrhea; muscle tremors and muscle tension; excessive fatigue; restlessness; insomnia and other sleep disturbances; irritability; anxiety; the startle reaction; depression; moodiness; difficulty in concentrating; and suspicion. Some people will experience general tremors, excessive sweating, heart palpitations, hyperventilation, and crying spells. Others will experience confusion, distractability, combativeness, withdrawal, denial, hysteria, amnesia, and aimlessness (people will often walk or run aimlessly).

Fewer than 10 percent will experience panic, and fewer than 25 percent will become hysterical.

Classic General Reactions[7]

Some psychological reactions are common to any kind of disaster. They include the following:

—**Grief.** Most disasters involve a loss (loss of a loved one, loss of property, loss of financial security, loss of status, loss of employment, and so on); people react with the classic grief syndrome. First they deny the loss, then become angry, and then depressed before finally accepting the loss and working to compensate for it.

—**Guilt.** Even those who fare well in a disaster may suffer severe emotional reactions; they are guilty and feel ashamed that they fared better than others, and feel guilty in some cases that they even survived.

—**Anger.** The anger that follows a disaster can take many forms; some people become angry at God (for allowing the hurricane to happen in the first place), while others become angry at rescue workers (for not doing an adequate job) or the government (for not providing enough money, for not making loans, or for delays and red tape).

—**Anxiety and vulnerability.** Even after a disaster is over, many people feel anxious and vulnerable to further hurt; many people suffer from nightmares about the disaster, fantasies about additional disasters, and crippling fear that disaster will strike again. Increased drug and alcohol use is common among people who become paralyzed by the fear that they will be involved in another disaster.

—**Isolation and problems in relationships.** Even when a number of people are involved in a disaster, victims tend to feel isolated and alone; they are not convinced that anyone else knows what they are going through and can adequately share their hurt. Because people are so wrapped up in the disaster and their emotional problems, their interpersonal relationships tend to suffer; old marital problems surface, and new ones appear. Women tend to care for others and neglect themselves, and tend to think that men are callous and unfeeling; men tend to think that women are hysterical and overreacting to the disaster.

—**Depression.** Almost everyone who is involved in a disaster will feel depressed at some point. At person may be depressed because of the scope of the disaster, over losing a loved one, over losing property, because they have been financially wiped out, or because they have lost their means of support. Many people feel depressed because they are overwhelmed by the disaster.

—**Reemergence of old problems.** In many cases, problems that people thought were resolved reappear; such a reaction is a normal part of extreme stress, such as that suffered in response to a disaster.

Factors Affecting How Well People Recover[8]

A number of factors determine how quickly survivors will recover emotionally. Those factors include the following:

—Whether or not a warning was given, and whether the warning was followed by specific instructions on what to do. If a warning is followed by specific instructions, people mobilize and do what they can to minimize loss and injury. If a warning is given but no instructions are given, people tend to become extremely anxious; some even emotionally deny that the disaster is about to occur.

—Whether or not family members are able to stay together. People (especially children) suffer less severe emotional injuries and recover much more rapidly if they are able to stay together as family units; those who are separated, especially during the most acute phase of the disaster, are more likely to suffer long-term problems.

—How much outside help is available to the individual. Someone left to deal with the disaster on his own will obviously have more emotional stress than someone who knows that a number of outside resources are available.

—Whether or not someone took leadership, made decisions, and gave directions. Those who are part of an organized and coordinated effort are much less likely to suffer long-term effects than those who are part of a group that is not headed up by a strong leader (or leaders).

—Whether or not those in charge kept in good communication with the victims. When good communication is not maintained, people become worried and anxious, rumors fly, and rescue efforts are often hampered. When good communication is maintained, people are less likely to act impulsively and irrationally.

—Whether or not aggressive steps are taken to reorient people; it is especially important in a mass-casualty or multiple-casualty disaster to register survivors and help them locate their relatives and friends.

—Whether or not an evacuation took place. People who are forced to leave their homes and communities will suffer more stress than those who are not. If an evacuation does occur, it is critical that it be orderly, planned, and well executed instead of chaotic; in a confused evacuation, delays and blockages are common.

Response of Workers to Disaster

Emergency workers who respond to disaster are subject to a host of emotional reactions, many of them similar to the reactions that the victims are suffering. Common reactions include loss of objectivity, feelings of helplessness, feelings of being overwhelmed, apprehension, anxiety, confusion, frustration, irritability, anger, apathy, and emotional callousness (usually a defense mechanism that occurs in cases of extreme death and injury).

Response of the Community to Disaster

Obviously, disaster involves the disruption of normal social patterns on which all community members depend; the community suffers a type of social paralysis as people are separated from family members, friends, public services, and public resources. In some disasters, the community loses water, electricity, heat, food, and shelter; accidents occur because traffic control tends to be confused, and hospitals are overloaded and overwhelmed.

Disasters tend to bring out the very worst and the very best in people. In a situation in which schools and businesses close, communications are poor, telephone lines are down, and chaos persists, people may be either heroic or hysterical. The goals for a community should be to preserve life and health, conserve and distribute available resources (such as water, food, and emergency supplies), conserve public order, and maintain morale among community members.

Abnormal Reactions to Disaster

It is normal for people to react to a disaster by doing something about it—they band together, cooperate in achieving goals, and work to rebuild what was lost. Even though they are extremely afraid, trembling, confused, and nauseated, they work toward a rebuilding. As they work to rebuild, their physical and psychological stress is reduced, and they are able to cope better with the disaster itself.

It is **not** normal for people to react in the following ways:[9]

—It is normal to experience some physical stress reactions, such as nausea, vomiting, trembling, rapid heartbeat, rapid breathing, and excessive perspiration. However, these symptoms should be temporary and should not occur until the disaster actually occurs. It is not normal when these symptoms occur before the disaster actually strikes, when they become prolonged or severe, or when efforts of helpers are unable to relieve the symptoms.

—It is normal to be afraid, but it is not normal to experience blind panic. Less than 10 percent of those involved in disasters panic; they lose control, cry profuse, run around aimlessly (without any regard for safety), and become too exhausted to care for themselves or others.

—It is normal to experience some confusion following a disaster, but it is not normal to overreact. People who overreact actually add to the confusion—they become overly confident, cannot carry out instructions, will not follow directions, talk excessively, become demanding or critical, and tell stupid jokes.

—It is normal to feel depressed at some point during the disaster, and it is normal to feel dazed, shocked, or numbed after the disaster occurs. Most of those feelings are temporary and should disappear quite quickly. People who are not able to shake those feelings are having an abnormal reaction: look for those who are extremely withdrawn, unduly isolated, unable to respond, completely helpless, unaware of their surroundings, or unable to display any emotion.

Special Risk Groups in Disaster

Certain groups are at special risk of developing deep emotional problems during disaster. Those groups, as defined by the National Institute of Mental Health, include the following:

Special Age Groups

Some age groups appear to be vulnerable in unique ways to the stresses of disaster. In general, children will suffer from problems such as sleep disturbances, night terrors, persistent fear, fear of future disasters, loss of interest in school, and a loss of personal responsibility that includes regression. Adults generally experience anxiety, depression, hostility, resentment, loss of ambition, sleep disturbances, and psychosomatic symptoms. Age groups at particular risk include:

Children, Preschool Through Adolescence

Children below the age of six tend to suffer physical problems (loss of appetite, indigestion, vomiting, diarrhea, constipation, and sleep disorders) as well as emotional problems that include nervousness, irritability, disobedience, speech difficulties, and extreme separation anxiety from parents. Children of all ages (including adolescents) display regressive behavior: preschoolers regress to thumbsucking, bedwetting, and fear of darkness, while older children regress to competition with younger brothers and sisters for the attention of parents, school phobia, failure to perform assigned chores, and disappearance of earlier responsible behavior.

Older children also suffer physical and emotional problems, including headache, visual loss, hearing loss, persistent itching, sleep disorders, loss of appetite, bowel problems skin rash, withdrawal, school phobia, unusual social behavior, loss of interest in hobbies and friends, difficulty in personal relationships, sharp resistance of authority (with both parents and teachers), and problems with concentration.

Middle-Aged Adults

Middle-aged adults tend to develop a variety of psychosomatic problems, including ulcers, diabetes, and heart trouble. In addition, they suffer withdrawal, anger, suspicion, irritability, apathy, loss of appetite, sleep problems, and loss of interest in everyday activities.

Elderly Adults

Elderly adults who are not institutionalized have usually settled into pretty routine habits; when the familiar routines are upset by the disaster, especially if they are forced from their home or apartment, they develop extreme despair, grief, depression, confusion, and disorientation. They may also suffer apathy, agitation, anger, suspicion, memory loss, and an accelerated physical decline, which may also be accompanied by an increase in physical complaints.

Socioeconomic Groups

Lower-income people will be willing to accept medical help for physical injuries, but will not be likely to accept help for psychological distress. Middle- and upper-income people are more likely to accept help because they both realize the potential for problems and desire to prevent them by taking early measures. Upper-income people might be resistant to outreach programs, however, while those in lower socioeconomic brackets would be more likely to accept the help from public agencies. Lower-income people also face a greater likelihood of more serious psychological problems because they may have less insurance coverage, more precarious job situations, fewer job skills, and less knowledge about available help.

Culturally and Racially Unique Groups

Cultural differences (especially those involving race and language) make it more difficult for people to accept help; they feel suspicion about the help that is being offered to them by "outsiders" and ignore or reject such help when it is offered.

Cultural and racial groups have a tendency to "close ranks" and accept assistance only from family and close friends. But in a large disaster, family members and close friends will probably also need help and will not be in a position of assist. Feelings of helplessless, hopelessness, resignation, apathy, and depression are common among these groups following a disaster.

Institutionalized People

Those who are in institutions when a disaster strikes may experience extreme frustration, anxiety, and panic because of their limited mobility and their complete dependence on their caretakers. Common reactions among these people include anger and a desire to "escape."

People Requiring Emergency Medical Care

Those who are in need of immediate medical and surgical treatment and those who suffer from physical shock may also experience severe anxiety due to separation from loved ones or a lack of information about the extent of damage to their home, place of business, or community. The degree of anxiety suffered by the victim may aggravate his physical condition and his response to medical treatment.

Emergency Workers

Emergency workers in all phases of disaster relief expose themselves to incredible demands that can lead to burnout—a state of exhaustion, irritability, and fatigue that markedly decreases the worker's effectiveness and capability. Symptoms common to burnout include mental confusion, slowness of thought, inability to make judgments and decisions, loss of ability to conceptualize alternatives, loss of objectivity, depression, irritability, anxiety, hyperexcitability, excessive rage reactions, physical exhaustion, loss of energy, gastrointestinal distress, appetite disturbances, hypochondria, sleep disorders, tremors, hyperactivity, excessive fatigue, and the inability to express thoughts and feelings verbally or in writing.

Help and Seek-Help Behaviors

In a disaster, as in any crisis situation, some people will be able to recover with minimal support even though they may seem to be upset and distressed; others will need aggressive help in overcoming emotional crisis. The behaviors have been termed "help and seek-help"—the National Institute of Mental Health has defined them as behaviors that indicate when you should feel confident in being able to help someone, and behaviors that indicate when you should refer the victim to someone else for aggressive treatment.

In a disaster, keep these guidelines in mind:

—**Alertness and awareness.** You can probably handle the situation if the victim is only slightly confused or dazed or shows slight difficulty in thinking clearly or concentrating, but is aware of who he is, where he is, and what has happened. Seek aggressive help for the victim if he is unable to give his own name or the names of people with whom he is living, cannot tell you the date, cannot tell you the state where he is, cannot tell you what he does for a living, cannot recall the events of the past twenty-four hours, and complains of memory gaps.

—**Actions.** You can probably handle the victim if he wrings his hands, clenches his fists, appears stiff and rigid, has sleep difficulty, has rapid or halting speech, and is restless, mildly agitated, or excited. Seek help if he shows agitation, restlessness, or pacing; is apathetic, immobile, or unable to rouse himself to movement; is incontinent; mutilates himself; uses alcohol or drugs excessively; is unable to care for himself (doesn't eat, drink, bathe, or change clothes); or repeats ritualistic acts.

—**Speech.** You can probably handle a person who has appropriate feelings of depression, despair, or discouragement; has doubts about his ability to recover; is overly concerned with small things but neglects more pressing problems; denies his problems; says that he can take care of everything himself; blames his problems on others; or is bitter about his being a victim. Seek help for someone who hears voices, sees visions, or has unverified body sensations; states that his body feels unreal and fears he is losing his mind; is excessively preoccupied with one idea or thought; has the delusion that someone or something is out to get him and his family; is afraid he will kill himself or someone else; is unable to make simple decisions or carry out everyday functions; and shows extreme pressure of speech, with talk almost overflowing.

—**Emotions.** You can probably handle a person who is crying; constantly retelling the details of the disaster; has blunted emotions or little reaction to what is going on around him; shows excessive laughter or high spirits; or is easily irritated or angered over trifles. Consider getting help for the person if he is excessively flat, unable to be aroused, or completely withdrawn; or is excessively emotional, showing inappropriate emotional reactions.

Mental/Emotional Problems Following Disasters

Many victims of disaster will "recover" from the disaster, eventually rebuilding and achieving an equilibrium so that they can conduct themselves much as they did before the disaster occurred. Unfortunately, some victims will suffer long-term mental or emotional problems that will require professional help. As a general rule, the more severe the symptoms, the more likely it is that the individual will need professional help in order to resume normal function.

Victims who are likely to suffer long-term problems requiring professional help may display the following signs or symptoms:[10]

—Psychosomatic illnesses, including vomiting, diarrhea, insomnia, loss of appetite, headaches, allergies, ulcers, bladder problems, extreme fatigue, weakness, and rashes; these illnesses are not due to some physical problem and are not physiological in origin.

—Social stresses, including divorce, separation, delinquency, alcoholism, drug abuse, family discord, and other social problems that manifest themselves in late periods after the disaster has occurred.

—Psychological problems, including nightmares, unreasonable anticipation of another disaster, difficulty in concentrating, nervousness, crying spells, hopeless feelings, and irritability. All of these reactions are normal to some extent in the immediate period following the disaster, but in normal situations they are temporary and resolve themselves quickly.

—Severe depression; the victim may feel hopeless, can't get out of bed, won't eat, cries uncontrollably, is apathetic, is unable to engage in usual activities, suffers from sleep disturbances, and has unshakable feelings of helplessness, hopelessness, and feelings of worthlessness.

—Severe disorientation; he is so confused that he does not know where he is, what is happening, or what time it is. He may be dazed, stuporous, unaware of his surroundings, or unable to remember recent events.

—Hysteria, including uncontrollable crying, screaming, agitation, and possible paralysis or numbness of the body.

—Psychosis, including marked personality changes, irrational thinking, and highly unusual behavior. The victim may report sensations for which there is no determined cause, may have delusions of grandeur, or may have delusions of persecution.

Psychological Care in Disasters

Psychological care for those involved in disaster is crucial—it can make the difference between a person who recovers and goes on to resume normal function and a person who suffers long-term psychological problems requiring profession help.

Assessment

As mentioned, victims of disasters go through a wide range of psychological and emotional reactions. In assessing a victim's condition, you can generally categorize him in one of the following three groups.[11]

The "Adequately Functioning" Victim

About one-fourth of the victims will appear to be fine; they will not be manifesting any physical or emotional problems, and they may even be assisting in rescue operations. Looks can be deceiving: these people may **appear** to be fine, but they are still suffering emotional crisis; the symptoms just haven't appeared yet. Eventually, they will need support and help in dealing with those problems. Most of them will eventually break down and display clear symptoms of distress.

To treat a person who appears to be fine, follow these guidelines:

—As soon as you reasonably can, relieve the person of any rescue or helping work. In a calm and reassuring way, ask him to move to a quiet area where you can check him over for any signs of physical injury. If there is minor injury, provide appropriate care.

—As soon as the most serious cases have been transported, transport the "adequately functioning" person to a hospital or other medical facility where he can be further evaluated and given psychiatric care if needed.

—If the person insists on continuing to help and will not agree to go to a quiet area, assign him simple tasks. In some cases, keeping busy and having the feeling that he is helping may keep him from breaking down emotionally.

The Hysterical Victim

While wide-range panic is not common at the scene of a disaster, hysteria can be; a hysterical victim may be crying uncontrollably, losing control, screaming, running around aimlessly, or fainting. A victim of hysteria also suffers physical signs and symptoms, including convulsions, amnesia, limb paralysis (that is not accompanied by injury), dizziness, confusion, incoordination, nausea, and a tingling sensation in the fingers and toes. Hysterical victims are dangerous: they can interfere with rescue efforts, distract rescuers' attention, run into danger themselves without being aware of it, or become combative. And there's an additional danger: hysteria tends to spread. A hysterical person can enter a group of people who are coping pretty well, and before long, they will start to scream, cry, and panic.

To treat a hysterical victim, follow these guidelines:

—**Never** use unusual or unnecessary force in dealing with the victim; stay calm and in control. Slapping the person or using other force will agitate him and contribute to his hysterical behavior.

—Transport him to a hospital as quickly as possible; he needs to have psychiatric evaluation, even if he does not have physical injuries. If you cannot transport him immediately, at least get him away from the scene of the disaster and isolate him from other victims.

—If you can't transport him or move him away from the scene, ask a responsible person (even a bystander) to stay with the person and keep him˙ under control until he can be transported. If this is not possible, try giving the hysterical victim calm, direct orders, such as "stop moving now." Try telling him in a commanding but calm voice, "You are safe now. Just do what I tell you to do."

The Subdued Victim

At the opposite end of the spectrum is the subdued victim—

the one who is quiet; the subdued victim often shows little emotion, may show signs of shock, and may be paralyzed by fear. He may seem quiet, but usually an emotional storm is raging inside. Such a victim may have low blood pressure, shallow breathing, profuse sweating, pale skin, numbness, trembling, dizziness, nausea, thirst, and weakness. Movements are aimless, random, and uncoordinated.

The subdued victim is the most common at the scene of the disaster. To help, follow these guidelines:

—If you can, immediately transport the victim away from the scene of the disaster; if you can't, block his view of the disaster by placing an object between him and the scene.

—Ask the victim to lie down, keep him in a shock position, and keep him warm. Elevate his feet if there is not head or chest injury, and give him nothing by mouth.

—Never leave a subdued victim alone. If there are not enough emergency workers to stay with him, ask a bystander to stay with him until he can be transported.

Helping Survivors Cope

There are a number of general principles to follow at the scene of a disaster that will help ease psychological and emotional problems for the survivors. Follow these general guidelines:

—Provide accurate information about the disaster to the survivor, but make sure that you provide only as much as the person is ready or able to assimilate. Share good news as it becomes available, and concentrate on the things that are most relevant to the survivor.

—Provide honest, complete information to the survivor about his medical condition.

—Encourage the survivor to be active in helping himself cope with the disaster. Encourage him to talk about his feelings and to formulate a plan for coping, and ask him to think about problems he has solved successfully in the past. Provide continual positive reinforcement when you see signs that he is trying to deal with the problems.

—Provide information to survivors about where they can go for help of various kinds; clearly identify any support network and agencies.

—Let the victim talk about his feelings of fear, panic, loss, and grief. Acknowledge those feelings, and let the victim know that you accept those feelings. Encourage the victim to fully explore his feelings and to accept them.

—Listen with concern and great empathy. It may be difficult for you to do, since you may not have any idea of how the victim is feeling or you may be convinced that you would feel much differently in the same situation. Never criticize, judge, or demean the person for his feelings. Allow the victim to cry and express feelings of frustration and despair.

—Arrange for someone to stay with the victim through the first stages of the disaster while he realizes gradually the reality of what has happened. Help the person to gradually make that realization. If necessary, arrange for the person to be accompanied back to the scene of the disaster, where he can see for himself what has happened and how it will impact him.

—Help a victim get in touch with relatives, friends, or immediate family members; if necessary, make telephone calls for the victim. If many people are involved in a mass-casualty or multiple-victim disaster, start a survivor's list and help oeple locate each other.

—Mobilize capable survivors and let them help with simple but necessary tasks.

—Reassure the victim that what he is feeling is normal, and that it is temporary. Tell him that most victims of disasters feel that way, and that within a few hours or a day or so, his feelings will disappear. If necessary, help the victim understand what he will be feeling over the next few weeks, and reassure him that help is always available for times when he needs support.

—Reassure victims that the disaster is over and that they are safe. It is critical to help people realize that they will not be endangered again soon.

—Never give false reassurances to a person when you don't know the facts or can't learn the information. If a person is worried about a friend or family member and you can't locate the person, don't say, "Oh, I'm sure she's just fine." Instead, say something like, "I don't know where your sister is right now, but I will be happy to do everything I can to help locate her. As soon as I find her, I will be back to tell you how she is."

—Don't make promises that you can't keep. Don't tell someone who just lost his home that the government will give him a low-interest loan to rebuild it. Don't tell someone who has lost a relative that he'll feel just fine within a few days.

—If a family member wants to stay with the victim and even accompany him in the ambulance, make arrangements for him to do so.

—If the victim has died and family members want to see him, allow them to. Clean up the body beforehand as much as you can; cover any body parts that are disfigured or mutilated. If there is disfigurement or mutilation, prepare the family members ahead of time ("Your son's left arm was twisted off by the force of the collision").

—Establish a rapport with the victim; maintain eye contact while he talks to you, and give occasional responses as you listen. Avoid interrupting him. Be tolerant and accepting of what he tells you.

—If the disaster has involved large numbers of people, grou the victims with their family members and neighbors; grouping will reduce their fear, anxiety, and feelings of isolation.

—Tell the victim exactly what is happening to hi,, tell him that he is likely to recover rapidly, tell him that he is suffering a temporary setback, and tell him exactly what you expect of him. Ask him to perform simple tasks, and give him simple, clear instructions. Follow up to make sure that the victim is doing what you instructed him to do.

—Reassure victims that by accepting help they are not displaying weakness. Make sure that the victim understands that the help is only temporary and that as soon as things are under control, he may even be needed to help someone else.

—Work to minimize the chances of burnout among rescuers by following set schedules and making sure that each rescuer takes a rest break. If a rescuer develops signs of undue stress, remove him from the disaster scene, allow him a longer-than-usual rest period, and return him to a less stressful situation.

REFERENCES

1. National Institute of Mental Health, *Human Problems in Disasters: A Pamphlet for Government Emergency Disaster Services Personnel* (Rockville, Md.: U.S. Department of Health, Education, and Welfare, 1978), DHEW Publication Number (ADM) 78-539, pp. 3-5.

2. Brent Q. Hafen and Keith J. Karren, Crisis Intervention for Emergency Medical Personnel (North Hollywood, Calif.: Emergency Medical Services, 1980), pp. 78-79.

3. Norman J. Farberow and Norma S. Gordon, *Manual for Child Health Workers in Major Disasters* (Rockville, MD.: U.S. Department of Health and Human Services, 1981), DHHS Publication Number (ADM) 81-1070, p. 3.

4. Jeffrey T. Mitchell and H.L.P. Resnik, *Emergency Response to Crisis* (Bowie, Md.: Robert J. Brady Company, 1981), pp. 171-172.

5. National Institute of Mental Health, *Crisis Intervention Programs for Disaster Victims in Smaller Communities* (Rockville, Md.: U.S. Department of Health, Education, and Welfare, 1979), DHEW Publication Number (ADM) 79-675, p. 35.

6. Jeffrey T. Mitchell, "When Disaster Strikes," *jems*, January 1983, pp. 36-37.

7. Beverly McLeod, "In the Wake of Disaster," *Psychology Today,* October 1984, pp. 54-57.

8. Lee Ann Hoff, *People in Crisis,* 2nd edition (Menlo Park, Calif.: Addison-Wesley Publishing Company Nursing Division, 1984), pp. 285-286.

9. Hafen and Karren, p. 77.

10. National Institute of Mental Health, *Field Manual for Human Service Workers in Major Disasters* (Rockville, Md.: U.S. Department of Health, Education, and Welfare, 1978), DHEW Publication Number (ADM) 78-537, pp. 12-14.

11. Mitchell and Resnik, pp. 173-176.

Burnout and Emergency Personnel

Burnout.

It's a word you're probably hearing quite a bit to describe a wide range of conditions. You hear it from the factory worker who can't face punching the time clock at the beginning of the shift. You hear it from the teacher who sits in a corner of the faculty lounge and regales the other teachers with tales of her students' misdeeds. You hear it from the nurse who feels pulled in a hundred different directions by patients and their needs. You hear it from the emergency medical worker who doesn't have the energy to go out on another run.

Basically, burnout is what happens when you've endured prolonged stress.[1] It is marked by disillusionment, frustration, apathy, and a loss of idealism. Energy wanes; motivation dissolves.

The dictionary defines **burnout** as "to fail, wear out, or become exhausted by making excessive demands on energy, strength, or resources." Often, burnout occurs in reaction to job-related stress, and the result of burnout is detachment from the job.[2]

But burnout is often very difficult to recognize: just as individuals vary in their ability to cope with stress and to withstand its effects, individuals also vary in their vulnerability to burnout. A woman who reaches her breaking point and becomes a victim of burnout may work beside a colleague who handles the same job stress with ease. The ability to cope with job stress can also very from time to time within the same individual—a person who does well during the week may find that the added pressures of family demands on the weekends lowers her coping abilities.

There's another reason why burnout is difficult to identify. The demands that result in burnout are not always negative in nature[3]—you may be thoroughly enjoying the challenges of your job, but those same challenges may be leading to burnout.

The result?

Where once you were productive you become preoccupied and careless. Where once you were healthy, you begin suffering from illness. Where once you were energetic, you become fatigued. Where once you looked forward to each new day with vigor and enthusiasm, you become apathetic and detached.

A Vulnerable Profession

Members of the helping professions are particularly prone to burnout for a number of reasons:[4]

—**The idealistic expectations of helpers are frustrated.** Those who enter the helping professions most often do so out of a simple desire to help others—they want to do good, and to do it on a grand scale. They want to help people who are sick or injured or in trouble. But the very nature of the profession leads to a frustration of those goals. The cancer patient dies no matter how valiant the nursing staff. The auto accident victim suffers permanent paralysis as a result of injury, even though the paramedics were thorough and precise in emergency treatment. The troubled teenager suceeds in taking her own life after hours of therapy with a concerned social worker. Soon, those in the helping professions find that their dreams are shattered.

—**It is difficult to measure accomplishment.** An advertising executive knows that she has succeeded when the client signs a hefty advertising contract with the agency. A realtor knows that he has succeeded when he sells the apartment building. The contractor knows that he has succeeded when he hammers the last nail into the two-story home on the shaded avenue. But measuring accomplishment isn't that easy for many of the helping professions. A patient who is severely depressed may seek therapy for that depression; his therapist may have to wait for months or even years before progress is apparent. The patient might continue to be depressed but might experience gradual improvement in other areas of his life—improvement that might not be apparent to the therapist.

—**Pay is often low.** Those at the highest levels of the helping professions—such as psychiatrists—are often paid well, but many at lower levels are not. Those who are paraprofessionals are often subject to the same job stresses as professionals at a fraction of the pay. When the stress becomes intense and the rewards seem meager, the individual might sigh, "It's not worth it."

—**The natural desire to advance in status can conflict with original job goals.** The desire to advance is a normal and natural one—no one dreams of getting a job and staying at exactly the same level forever! But in the helping professions, a strange thing happens: you enter the profession because you want to help people. The more you advance in status and the higher you go in the hierarchy, the farther you move away from the people and the opportunity to be of direct help. A member of the helping profession is often faced with a particularly bitter dilemma: to remain in a position where he can enjoy the job satisfaction of helping but where he is a powerless and low-paid worker, or to increase pay and power but sacrifice satisfaction.

—**Sexism, while present in all professions, can be particularly pronounced in the helping professions.** Sexism, with its attendant frustrations, seems especially pronounced among the helping professions. Women are often relegated to clerical positions in other professions, but in the helping professions even the nonclerical women are often in positions of structural inferiority. Schoolteachers are women; principals and administrators are men. Family relations personnel are women, attorneys and judges are men. Nurses are women, doctors are men. Of course there are exceptions, but the problem of sexual stereotyping is a difficult one industry-wide.

—Funding is often inadequte to accomplish important goals. An energetic and motivated staff may envision a number of programs to help better serve clients or patients only to find that funds simply won't support the proposed programs. Members of the helping professions suffer continual frustration when funding is habitually cut back or denied; recommendations are disregarded, decisions are reversed, and proposals are ignored.

—The realities of case management call for the abandonment of some patients or clients. You remember "triage"—it was ushered in during World War I when medics couldn't possibly attend to all the casualties, and it is still used in cases of accidents or disasters involving more than a few people. The basic principle of triage requires a "rating system," and care is given first to those whose injuries are life-threatening but treatable. Those whose injuries are so severe that death is likely despite treatment are a lower priority, as are those whose injuries are not life-threatening.

Triage exists in the helping professions, too, but it's called "case management." Case management forces helpers to face up to reality: with limited staff and funds, patients who do not show progress or who do not respond should be gradually weaned out of the system. Instead, too many helpers don't understand the principle of case management. They end up spending a disproportionate amount of time on those who probably won't respond and get better. Those who are teetering on the fence, who could be helped by intervention and aggressive therapy, are often not given adequate attention because the therapist is so caught up in trying to salvage the unsalvageable.

Even when a helper understands the principle of case management and is responsible in the handling of her cases, frustration can occur—it's a terrible frustration to "abandon" and patient when you feel that you have not done everything humanly possible to help.

—**There is a high degree of public misunderstanding, distrust, and hypocrisy toward the helping professions.** Consider the stories that reach the public in newspapers, news magazines, and television news programs. It's not often that journalists report on the steady day-to-day progress or the constructive work being done. Instead, journalists seize the sensational, the occasional abuse, the drain on the taxpayer. The result? Few understand the real purposes and functions of the helping professions.

—**The demands of administrative personnel sap valuable time and energy from working directly with patients.** A person who entered a helping profession to provide service can be extremely frustrated by paperwork and other administrative duties that take away from the amount of time available for helping.

—**Hours in the helping professions tend to be long and consecutive.** A sad characteristic of the helping professions is the number of people needing help and the few people who can give it. As a result, helpers tend to work long hours, to be "on call" during off-hours, and to spend long consecutive hours during emergency situations. When coupled with low pay, long hours can breed resentment and frustration.

—**The feeling of not being appreciated packs a punch with people who are trying to help.** By the very nature of the profession, many of those who need help are incapable of fully expressing appreciation. The result? A helper may knock herself out in an effort to be of help, working long hours and robbing herself of free or leisure time, without getting the feedback or appreciation she so desperately needs. Before long, she asks herself, "What's the use?"

—**Many members of the helping profession are thrown into situations for which they are inadequately trained or prepared.** A nurse who was drilled in the techniques of how to give an injection may suddenly find herself cornered in the hospital room by a violent patient who is threatening to kill her. A paramedic who is well-trained in emergency medical procedures may be at a loss when confronted by a suicidal woman threatening to jump from the ledge of a building. A teacher prepared to teach science or math may not know what to do with a student who is abusive or rebellious in class.

—**Helpers may be overloaded.** A drug counselor may be forced by staff and funding restrictions to handle twice as many clients as he should. A paramedic may be faced with covering twice as much geographical territory. A therapist may have to take on another therapist's patients when funding cutbacks necessitate layoffs. A teacher's class may swell to thirty students instead of the ideal eighteen.

—**Some in the helping professions, especially those who are paraprofessionals, may be in career deadends.** Most professions offer advancement and reward—a woman who begins as a clerk in a national convenience-store chain can work hard and be promoted to assistant manager, manager, supervisor, district manager, and so on. With each promotion comes increases in pay, status, and power. A counselor, though, will probably always be a counselor. A teacher will probably always be a teacher. A nurse will probably always be a nurse. For paraprofessionals, the plight is worse—the limited scope of their training prohibits much career movement. The result can be incredible stagnation. The result can also be frustration from wanting to gain enough power to make positive changes in the department or institution.

—**Members of the helping profession may be required to earn academic degrees that have little application to their work.** A woman who is skilled at working with people may be required to earn an MSW (Master of Social Work) degree before her skill can become marketable; the time and expense simply take her away from the people she wants to help. For many, clinical training is much more valuable than academic training, but no options are available.

—**Feelings of powerlessness can become rampant in the helping professions.** A counselor may have all the skill in the world but cannot compel her alcoholic client to keep his appointments. A teacher may propose enriching extracurricular programs for gifted students in his class but cannot convince school administrators to implement the programs. A paramedic may know that a certain technique would save lives but is prevented from using it because of local ordinances.

—**Sometimes the system doesn't seem geared toward meeting the needs of the people it sets out to help.** A drug abuse counseling program is so wrapped up in quotas and numbers that counselors resort to the quickest, most inexpensive, highest-volume treatment method—methadone maintenance—without determining what is best for the individual patient. The emphasis at a prison may be on keeping staff employed instead of rehabilitating criminals. A school may place all its emphasis on test scores instead of on enriching the students. The hospital corporation may make decisions based on fiscal considerations instead of patient consideratins.

—**The idealism that prompts a person to enter the helping profession can also lead to despairing disappointment over peers or colleagues.** An idealistic young woman who decides to become a nurse may be shattered a few weeks into her first job when she realizes that the other women on the staff are interested mostly in meeting handsome doctors, not soothing the patients. A young man who enters the teaching profession armed with enthusiasm and idealism may be disarmed by the attitudes of other teachers who are jaded and unwilling to explore new ideas.

—**The training a helper receives may not mesh with reality.** A counselor may spend years in training learning the fine points of psychotherapy, but when he's thrown on the front-line of an alcohol abuse center, he finds himself confronted by people who have primary needs for the rudest basic necessities in life. Exploring an alcoholic's relationship with his mother is certain to be meaningless when the alcoholic is frantic over where he will sleep that night.

—The helping professions are difficult. An architect works with contractors who try to share his vision. A paramedic may work with a patient who is abusive, unmotivated, resentful, nonverbal, and resistant to change.

—Because of the nature of the helping professions, the helper often is not able to see a case through to completion. Everyone likes to take pride in a job well done. Sadly, many helpers must turn clients over to others midway through the treatment process so that clients can receive different or more specialized help. Even more devastating are the cases that must be abandoned because of heavy caseloads, lack of funding, or arbitrary deadlines—the helper is faced with "getting rid of" clients as soon as minimum standards have been met.

—Working conditions can be poor, uncomfortable, or unpleasant. A child protective services worker may have to conduct interviews in homes that reek of garbage or swarm with flies. Others may have to work with clients in places that are filthy, infested with rats, or littered with human waste. Some middle-class workers have to go into decaying slums where they are obviously intruders.

Who Is At Risk for Burnout?

Are members of certain professions at a higher risk of developing burnout? Yes, as far as we can tell. Are people with certain characteristics at a higher risk as well? Yes, as far as we can tell.

If you fall into one of those categories, you should realize that you are at a higher risk. That is **not** to say that you will suffer from burnout—only that you are more prone than others.

Professions at Risk

Members of the following professions have a greater tendency toward burnout:[5]

—**Education professionals**, including school counselors, teachers at all grade levels, staff development instructors, and continuing education personnel.

—**Health care professionals**, including nurses, emergency care personnel, physicians, chaplains, social workers, health care administrators, patient representatives, and therapists (respiratory, occupational, and physical).

—**Mental health professionals**, including outreach workers, social workers, counselors, psychologists, and psychiatrists.

—**Legal professionals**, including attorneys, public defenders, advocates, and judges.

—**Law enforcement personnel**, including chaplains, counselors, police officers, and prison guards.

—**Social welfare professionals**, including counselors, social workers, and administrative personnel.

—**Human resource management professionals**, including human resource coordinators, human resource trainers, and personnel directors.

—**Executive management professionals**, including department managers and chief executive officers.

A professional who is just entering the job market has a high risk for burnout when the demands of a new job bring him face-to-face with the shock of reality. Fresh out of college or graduate school, he finds himself facing the need to be responsible, accountable to others, and productive; he expects perfection from himself, hopes to gain the respect of his superiors, and plans to benefit from interpersonal contact. What he is actually faced with can come as a shock that leads to burnout: on the job he encounters lack of support, incredible time pressures, constraints in reaching out, and constant blows to his self-confidence.[6]

Professions that involve contact with people—such as clients or patients—involve a high risk for burnout. Why? Interpersonal relationships can become intense; patients or clients can become overly dependent, and helpers can be drained by the constant demands for giving.

Personal Characteristics at Risk

Ironically, it's not the lazy or the unmotivated or the mediocre workers who usually burn out. Instead, the burnout victims are generally the "cream of the crop"—the best and brightest in any given profession.

The very characteristics that help a person embark on a successful career can later actually promote burnout. Many of these characteristics are positive; a few are negative. Obviously, each individual differs slightly, but the following list of characteristics has been shown to be indicative of those who are at risk of burnout:[7]

motivation
ambition
enthusiasm
independence
self-starting abilities
self-sufficiency
sensitivity
compassion
energy
high expectations
high goals
idealism
dedication
commitment
impatience
low frustration tolerance

There's an important distinction, too, that can help identify the risk of burnout. Ostensibly, those in helping professions entered the profession because they wanted to be of help to others. But that encompasses two very different kinds of people. One has a desire to help others solely because he truly wants to help; his is a mature kind of commitment and involvement. He is able to accept the frustration of people who don't want to be helped or the impatience that comes along with wanting rapid progress.

The other kind of person wants to help because he thinks it will make him feel accepted and liked. His commitment and involvement are not mature; he often goes overboard in a desperate attempt to prove his self-worth. The more he helps, he reasons, the better person he is.

A person who has a true **need** to give to others is in danger of burnout. Why? Most people who seek help have been withstanding poor living conditions—whether from their poverty, their mental illness, their abusive personalities, or their desertion and loneliness. They tend to take all the help they can get, almost desperately; they would consume a helper if they could. A person in a helping profession must guard against giving to excess, or he can be consumed and drained— leaving little to exist on himself.

Job Environments at Risk

Combine a profession that leads to the risk of burnout with a person whose characteristics make him a burnout risk, and you've got an explosive combination. But there's still another factor that can increase risk even more: the situations or environment in which the person works.

Situations or environments that lead to stress and subsequent burnout include the following:[8]

Erratic hours, especially shift work
Constant deadlines
Shifts around the clock, twenty-four hours a day
Professions where "the customer is always right"

Seeing people die
Making life-and-death decisions on a regular basis
Working with customers or clients who complain
Listening to or mediating arguments
Being a "sounding board"
Listening to people's problems
Being a working mother (especially a single parent)

Recognizing Burnout

Like any other physical or emotional problem, burnout manifests itself with a battery of physical, emotional, and social/behavioral signs and symptoms. Each individual differs, so not all people will experience the same signs and symptoms. In addition, each burnout situation is unique, and each burnout situation determines how the individual will react.

Bearing those differences in mind, consider the following as possible signs and symptoms of burnout:

Physical Signs and Symptoms

—Exhaustion and fatigue that are not remedied by sleep or resting
—Insomnia, including the inability to fall asleep easily or the tendency to awaken frequently during the night
—A number of minor illnesses, especially the common cold, that linger on
—Gastrointestinal disorders, including loss of appetite, nausea, and heartburn
—Frequent headaches
—Sudden weight loss or gain
—Increase in blood pressure
—Shortness of breath
—Lowered resistance to infection, marked by frequent, stubborn, or persistent infections or illnesses

—Muscle and backaches
—Skin rashes
—Development of ulcers
—Loss of sexual drive or desire
—A general run-down or "wiped out" feeling

Emotional Signs and Symptoms

—Depression, ranging from mild but persistent depression to severe, disabling depression
—Feelings of hopelessness
—Feelings of helplessness
—Feelings of being "trapped"
—Self-doubt about the ability to perform necessary duties and be an effective worker
—Increases stubbornness and rigidity, including resistance to change
—Shortness of temper and tendency to become angry over seemingly insignificant occurrences
—An overwhelming attitude of pessimism and cynicism where once there was optimism and hope
—Loss of control over basic drives, such as hunger and sex
—Decreased ability to reason and judge
—Distrust and suspicion
—Withdrawal and/or isolation
—Stagnation
—Feelings of boredom or restlessness
—Inability to act or think quickly in emergencies
—Inability to properly establish priorities
—Resentfulness
—Discouragement
—Frustration
—Anxiety over personal safety or about professional competence
—Inability to control emotions
—Feelings of apathy
—Inability to concentrate or express thoughts clearly
—Forgetfulness

—Tendency toward emotional outbursts or uncontrolled crying spells
—Carelessness, with an accident-prone tendency
—Feelings of hostility
—An unwarranted feeling of importance or indispensability

Social/Behavioral Signs and Symptoms

—Tendency to take risks, usually from a belief that he has "been through it all" and can take chances that others can't take
—Drug use, especially tranquilizers
—Increased alcohol use
—The tendency to spend longer hours at work while accomplishing less
—Severing of long-term relationships (such as marriage)
—Excessive bonding with other staff members in an attempt to satisfy basic human needs for friendship and recognition

—An increase in the number or frequency of interpersonal conflicts, both at home and at work
—Excessive dedication to the job (defending excessive hours and preoccupation as being "dedicated" or a superior employee)
—Remaining at the place of work after hours without a specific purpose
—Delaying or cancelling scheduled vacations because of a feeling of indispensability
—Failure to take scheduled breaks or lunch hours
—Inability to recognize, enjoy, or compliment the successes of others on the staff
—Tendency to find fault with other staff members
—Tendency to make many minor errors
—Excessive defensiveness when confronted about errors, attitudinal problems, or necessary changes
—Consistently putting in extra hours at the sacrifice of personal considerations and leisure time

—Tendency to limit or reduce the amount of time spent with clients or patients

—Turning excessively to other staff members for help in coping with professional responsibilities or personal problems

—Increase in emotional outbursts, even outbursts directed at clients or patients

—Tendency to use "textbook" solutions instead of working to determine appropriate individual therapies or solutions

—Tendency to categorize or label clients or patients

—Tendency to avoid the work situation by calling in sick frequently, arriving late at work, taking excessive compensatory time, or spending frequent time away from the work environment "on business"

—The feeling that you are the only one on the staff that is doing a good job

—Tendency to concentrate on one aspect of your job while neglecting other aspects

—Tendency to socialize more with staff members than is appropriate

—Tendency to categorize or "label" patients or clients, using technical and dehumanized descriptions instead of names ("The gallbladder case in 619," "The welfare mother from the inner city")

An important characteristic of burnout is the tendency to rationalize. You may read the above list of symptoms and signs and recognize more than a few—but, you say, "I have a good reason to think that," or, "It's different in my case." If you find yourself rationalizing that way, take a good hard look at your situation. You may be using rationalization as an attempt to cope with the stress that is causing the burnout.

The Stages of Disillusionment: How Burnout Develops[9]

Researchers who have studied the problem of burnout

generally conclude that there are four basic stages of disillusionment that lead to burnout:

Enthusiasm

Enthusiasm is the hallmark of the initial period: you have high hopes and a high level of energy to devote to the job. You feel as though your job will provide you with everything you need in life—so you don't mind spending hours (and most of your energy) fulfilling the demands that your job places on you. For you, your job promises everything.

You have chosen a helping profession because you truly desire to be of help and service to others. Generally, you will be put to work in situations that are "safer" or easier to solve because you're new at the job—so you have the heady experience of early satisfaction and success. (It's only later, when you are faced with tougher, more demanding situations, that you realize how easy you have it now.)

At this point, it's easy to believe that all satisfactions and rewards stem from your job—your excitement over your job has, however, simply obliterated some of the personal needs and concerns and deficiencies in other aspects of your life. Your job may not be providing that much satisfaction, but it may be helping you forget sources of dissatisfaction.

While most of this first stage is bliss, a few characteristics begin the road toward burnout. First, your natural enthusiasm and energy may lead you to spend too much time and energy on the job; you are likely to voluntarily overwork, putting in extra hours out of sheer enjoyment. The extra hours don't seem to be taking their toll, so you keep on investing the time and effort—and before you know what has happened, you are sapped of energy and enthusiasm.

Another characteristic of this first stage quickly leads to burnout: you tend to identify too much with the problems and situations of your clients or patients. You find yourself "taking your work home"—you are unable to forget the battered wife, the young alcoholic, the small and timid victim of incest. It's extremely easy during this period of enthusiasm, dedication, and high hopes to emotionally take on the problems of others.

During the period of enthusiasm, your challenge is to walk a fine line between coping with discouragement and losing idealism. You need to realize that you can be an effective counselor without making yourself available by phone all hours of the day and night (at the cost of harmony at home). You need to realize that you can be a tremendous nurse without agonizing over every patient's pain. You need to realize that you can be an effective emergency medical technician without necessarily saving every life.

Stagnation

As the stage of enthusiasm wanes, you enter the stage of stagnation. You're still doing your job, but your job has lost some of its thrill. You've lost the momentum, the burst of hope and desire that kept you going through those hectic periods of enthusiasm.

One of the initial elements of stagnation is realizing that it's not easy to identify progress in the helping professions. A teacher may put his all into working with a child who can't comprehend math, and the child's improvement might not show up until the next year—when she has moved on to a new teacher. A psychologist may work with a client for months before any progress at all is apparent. An emergency medical technician may exert all her energies for an accident victim only to surrender the victim to emergency room personnel—often without knowing the outcome.

During the stage of stagnation, you become bewildered: why isn't the job what it once seemed to be? Minor annoyances start to nag at you. During the enthusiasm stage, money wasn't an issue—you knew you weren't being paid all that well, but it didn't matter. You didn't join the profession for the money, but to be of help and service.

During the stagnation stage, all these things combine; enough reality has come through to impress you that it really would be nice after all to have a little leisure time. A little money to spend. A home. A family. Some friends you could do things with away from the job.

Suddenly, issues like low pay, long working hours, deadend career situations, casework overload, and low respect on the job become important.

Frustration

Is it any wonder that those feelings lead to frustration?

You started with the idealistic notion of providing for other people's needs; now you realize with acute clarity that you have needs, too, and they're not being met.

Your overwhelming feeling during this stage is, What's the use? Why bother anymore? Why pour your energies into a job when no one appreciates you? Why continue to work with people who resist your efforts to help them? Why agonize ver the alcoholic's plight when you can't even get him to keep his appointments with you? Why keep rushing to the scene of accidents when the victims die anyway? Why batter yourself trying to influence students when they don't respect you and don't care about what they're studying? Why expend all this time and energy on other people when you yourself have so many needs?

It is during the stage of frustration that most of the physical, emotional, and social/behavioral signs and symptoms manifest themselves. Before, you looked at the limitations of the job and realized that they detracted from your satisfaction; now those same limitations loom on the horizon as a real threat— threatening to defeat what you are even doing.

The stage of frustration provides a pivotal point in the burnout process: your reaction to the frustration determines whether you pull out of the burnout or not.

Why?

Frustration, by its very nature, creates energy. How you use that energy determines the outcome. You can use it to take responsibility, confront the issues, and take action that will bring about positive changes, enabling you to keep working within the profession. Or you can use it to become frenzied and hysterical over the perceived shortcomings, eventually letting it defeat you. Or you can use it to completely withdraw from the situation—to avoid clients or patients, to develop dislike or resentment, to foster feelings of despair over your inability to really make an impact, or to become physically exhausted.

During the stage of frustration, some people lose their idealism, walk away from their jobs, and then become angry and assertive, diving back into the center of things with renewed vigor. Some never muster up that anger and assertion, and they never emotionally return. They lapse into apathy.

Apathy

Apathy is the most natural and common reaction to prolonged frustration. It is a state of detachment that progressively results in an emotional withdrawal from the job, even though you keep the job.

Where once you voluntarily and enthusiastically put in overtime hours, now you can scarcely stand to put in the minimum required amount of time. Where once you took on new challenges with gusto, now you avoid them. Where once you eagerly looked forward to the chance to meet new clients or patients and the chance to help change their lives, now you look for excuses to avoid them. Where once you believed that all satisfactions stemmed from your job, now you realize that your job provides you with little or no satisfaction. Where once you felt as though you had no personal needs, now your personal needs are so overwhelming that you feel defeated by them.

Apathy is felt as boredom. You become almost numb; you emotionally turn yourself off to other people's needs. You stop caring about others and become preoccupied with preserving your own sanity, health, peace of mind, and very survival.

When you start out in the enthusiasm stage, some detachment is obviously necessary. At some point, you need to move from the condition where you are determined to be all things to all people; you need a healthy detachment to help you become a little more realistic as you settle into the routine. You need a more realistic approach as you determine exactly what you can and cannot do for people—and as you order your priorities to help you be of the greatest service within your capacity.

The apathy stage exaggerates detachment. Apathy isn't characterized by that healthy, necessary kind of detachment; it is characterized by severe detachment that compromises your ability to perform your job at all.

At its most severe, apathy causes you to stay with a job for one reason only: because you need it to survive. You stop caring about the job. You see the problems, but you don't try to change them. You know that by taking a few risks you could regenerate some job satisfaction, but the risks aren't worth it to you. Your major concern is no longer helping other people—it is helping yourself. Your goal, and your priority, is protecting your position. Your principal concern is job security.

You move along, doing as little as you have to to simply maintain your position. The only time you really exert yourself is to keep from endangering that security.

Of all the stages of burnout, apathy is the most difficult to overcome. When you are disillusioned or stagnating or frustrated, it is easier to do things to pull out of it; when you enter the stage of apathy, it is difficult to recover. It took you a long time to arrive at this point, and the feelings that brought you here are by now deepseated and settled. You have simply stopped caring—and, in the face of a major upheaval or concerted efforts at intervention, that feeling can last forever.

Hopelessness

While not a recognized stage of burnout, hopelessness is the end result of burnout. It is the overwhelming desire to give up, to move on. It is the crushing realization that your dreams, hopes, goals, and idealistic notions about helping will not be realized. Hopelessness, which can occur at any stage of the burnout process, convinces you that you are no longer in control. It is the major cause of abandoning your profession.

Intervention

Regardless of the stage during which it occurs, intervention breaks the burnout cycle.

Intervention can take any of countless forms, and it can have a number of results. It might mean leaving the profession and going on to something that is more satisfying. It might mean changing jobs within the profession. It might mean restructuring your own job description to address some of your concerns. It might mean expanding your life outside your job. It might mean taking a vacation so that you can sort out your frustrations and think of ways to solve them. It might mean going back to school to spark your interest or curiosity.

There are two important things to realize about the burnout cycle and the eventual intervention.

First, the various stages of burnout are contagious. When you are enthusiastic, you tend to infect others on the staff with enthusiasm. You bring enthusiasm to your clients, who respond to you with an enthusiasm of their own. When you start to stagnate, others respond with stagnation; a teacher who loses her enthusiasm may discover that her students are no longer motivated, either. When you become frustrated, you often act as a catalyst to frustrate other staff members. And when you become apathetic, those with whom you work—staff and clients alike—tend to respond with apathy.

Second, burnout is not a self-containing or limited cycle that occurs only once during your career. Burnout can repeat itself any number of times during your career. You might progress through the various stages of burnout several times in several different jobs, or you might battle the burnout cycle over and over within the same job. At any point, you can intervene to break out of the cycle—and that intervention should be your focus.

Breaking the Burnout Cycle

Depending on your job, your personal characteristics, and the individual qualities of your burnout, there are a number of ways you can intervene to break the burnout cycle. Depending on your circumstances, try any of the following, singly or in combination:

—Take the necessary steps to brush up on your knowledge or skills. If you find that you are frustrated by your inability to treat victims effectively, get some additional training. Obtain the knowledge you need to act quickly during an emergency; once you have the knowledge and the skill, you will **act** based on your knowledge instead of **react** based on your emotions.

—Learn to concentrate on the victim. When you're embroiled in the burnout cycle, that might be difficult to do; your natural tendency might be to withdrawn emotionally from the victim. You might begin to concentrate on other mechanical aspects of the job, like driving an ambulance in heavy traffic or extricating victims from snarled automobiles. But remember: **everything else you do as an emergency medical worker is secondary to the primary consideration of helping the victim.** The reason you drive the ambulance is to help the victim. The reason you become skilled at extrication is to help the victim. Capitalize on the parts of the job that you enjoy, but make sure that you relate them to the process of helping the victim.

—Keep the stress of your personal emotions under control by making your first priority a simple one: rapid and accurate assessment of the victim's physical condition. When you arrive at the scene of an accident, you have few precious minutes in which to act. Spend those minutes determining what is wrong physically, treating it as much as you can, and transporting the victim to an emergency room. Don't make the mistake of spending your time trying to determine the victim's emotional needs—chances are, you won't have the time to meet them. You can avoid getting emotionally involved in your victim's plight by concentrating on the areas in which you can provide the greatest help in the shortest time.

—Do what you can to remove yourself emotionally from the emergency situation. Use your training and technical knowledge to help the victim and your experience to give yourself mental support in exercising your training—but avoid the temptation to be overcome emotionally by the entire situation.

—The "fight or flight" syndrome is a normal reaction to stress; as you respond to emergency call, you will probably experience rapid pulse and feelings of excitement. If you start feeling stressed, stop what you are doing for a brief instant and take a few deep breaths to calm yourself before returning to your task. If you truly feel that you are going to lose control, ask a partner to take over your task so that you can move to something that is less anxiety-provoking; you might return to the vehicle to get additional equipment, for example, or you might switch to another victim who needs a simple leg splint.

—A critical part of emergency medical care is learning to establish priorities at the scene of an accident; when there are more than a few victims, triage is a necessary exercise for survival. Convert your triage skills into coping with your own situation. Determine what aspects of your job are bringing you the greatest frustration, and which can be changed with some aggressive action on your part. Then start making changes!

—Develop what has been called **altruistic egoism**: the acceptance of the fact that at times you need to be selfish. That doesn't mean that you should be primarily selfish or recklessly selfish. What it means is that you maturely accept the fact that no one else will look after your own needs as well as you will. Take responsibility for meeting your own needs as much as you do for meeting your victims' needs.

—Get some variety in your job. If you have been suffering from stagnation, talk to your superior about the possibility of switching duties or exchanging responsibilities with someone else on the staff. If it would require additional training, take the necessary steps.

—Make sure that you get plenty of exercise or get involved in good physical activity on a regular basis. An excellent way of dissipating the stress that leads to stagnation and frustration is to choose a sport or activity that you truly **enjoy** and to get involved. After a particularly difficult shift, pack a light picnic lunch and bicycle with a friend to the lake!

—Develop outside interests. Find a hobby you would enjoy, take some classes at the community college, or get involved with a political group. Make sure that it is something you can enjoy, something you really look forward to. There's one important distinction: **make sure that it is not similar to your job.**

—Develop some assertiveness skills. Begin by dealing with small personality conflicts with other staff members on a one-to-one basis; once your confidence has increased, you can deal with problems that you're having with superiors. Use confidence and assertiveness to protect your interests when you need to: if filling in for an extra shift would really tax your energy beyond acceptable limits, say so, and offer to do something else that would be of help.

—Learn to appreciate others. You might be so preoccupied with your own frustrations that you fail to see what's going on around you. Start by verbalizing your appreciation; after a difficult run, tell your partner, "Thanks for all your help in administering CPR back there. I don't know what I would have done without you," or, "I'm really glad you're my partner. I always feel confident with you here." Once you start verbalizing, you'll find that feelings naturally follow.

—Learn to say **no**. If someone wants you to stick around the station after hours to socialize with other technicians but you really need to get away, learn that it's okay to say no. Do it with tact, but do it!

—Get away from your work periodically. Take your allowed breaks; take your allowed lunch hour. If possible, physically remove yourself from the reminders of your profession; instead of eating at the hospital cafeteria after transporting a victim to the emergency room, try that new seafood restaurant a few blocks away.

—Take a good look at what is causing you stress on the job. Chances are, you've created part of that stress for yourself; you might have voluntarily offered to clean up the vehicle after each run, for example. If there are stresses you can eliminate, do it! Ask your partner to take turns or alternate with you in cleaning up the vehicle, for example.

—Avoid the temptation to do things for other people that they can do for themselves. You might think that your note taking is more thorough, easier to read, and punctuated with greater detail than your partner's, or you might not like the way he writes. Forget it. Let him take the notes half of the time, and don't worry about the job he does; do the best you can **when it is your turn**, and when it's not your turn, let him take care of it.

—When you take breaks, take your lunch hour, or socialize with your colleagues off-hours, avoid "shop talk." Resist the temptation to hash over all the things that happened on the shift or to flog all your frustrations. Instead, talk about other interesting things—a movie you all saw recently, a political issue involving the local high school, or an upcoming football game.

—As you end each shift, try to concentrate on the positive instead of the negative. As you drive home, remember the good things that happened: the child you resuscitated, the accident victim you calmed.

—Suggest to your superiors that you devote ten minutes of each staff meeting to focusing on the positive: What have we accomplished this week? What have we done that we can justifiably be proud of? What commendations have we received? What did the newspaper say about our daring rescue?

—Avoid the temptation to put off distasteful or unpleasant tasks. At the beginning of each shift, make a short list of the things that **have** to be done; tackle those things first, methodically, while you have energy. The sooner they are finished, the sooner you can relax and do the things you enjoy.

—Delegate as much as you can; let others take on some of the responsibilities.

—Everyone feels helpless sometimes; it's normal, and there's nothing wrong with it. If you arrive at the scene of an accident and don't feel equipped to take care of the victim (regardless of the reason), admit it to your partner. Then offer to do some supportive work—such as fetching equipment, directing traffic, or taking notes—while he works with the victim.

—Schedule time during each day when you can be by yourself. Use the time to do whatever you most want to do: watch a favorite television program, read the editorial section of the newspaper, glance over a sports magazine, or take a nap.

—Get plenty of rest. You might not necessarily **sleep**, but take the time to stretch out under a shady elm tree, swing in a soothing hammock, or snuggle under the quilts on a frosty afternoon.

—If you're not the only one who's suffering from burnout, talk to your supervisor about making some positive changes; you might approach her as a group and suggest shorter shifts, rotating personnel to provide variety in routes, and so on.

—Consider involving volunteers to help reduce workload if your department funds are limited. Volunteers from community agencies could be responsible for many of the mundane tasks that have to be done on each shift, freeing emergency personnel for relaxation or providing more time for more essential tasks that require trained staff.

—Consider volunteering for occasional jobs that take you away from the routine. For example, volunteer to be the one who goes to the grade school on career day to talk about being a paramedic; volunteer to the speaker at a conference on child abuse; volunteer to work with a babysitting class on fire prevention. It will provide a needed break from routine if it is something you would sincerely enjoy.

—When you have time off, make sure that it is truly time off. Make it clear that you will be happy to respond in cases of dire emergency when **it is absolutely necessary** but that you do not otherwise want to be called on business matters during your time off. (If your supervisor has noncritical questions about what happened on a particular call, for instance, he can wait until you come in the next day to get the details.)

—Take an interest in those with whom you work; learn bout their hobbies, their families, their backgrounds. Find topics of conversation other than those concerning work.

—Take a realistic look at your goals. Are they in line? Are they attainable? If you're reaching for the sky and setting unrealistic goals, you will experience little but frustration. Realign your goals so that they are workable.

—If you've been suffering from any physical problems, get a good physical checkup and advice from your doctor. A nagging infection can sap your energy and make you feel defeated.

—If your shift involves a great deal of stress, ask your supervisor to provide a quiet place where employees can rest if possible. It needn't be elaborate; a small room at the back of the fire station with a cot or sofa would do the trick. Then take the time to rest occasionally if the going gets tough.

—Evaluate the station or area where emergency vehicles are parked and talk to your supervisor about any necessary improvements. Then work with others on the crew to improve lighting, clean up clutter, or make other improvements.

—Make sure that you're getting proper nutrition. Avoid the temptation to grab empty calories "on the run;" instead, aim for nutrition-dense snacks and meals.

—Increase the amount of leisure time you enjoy; learn to play hard. Get involved in recreational activities, and learn to do things for the sheer fun of it.

—If you need to consider an option or make a decision, don't narrow yourself to just two alternatives. Use your creativity to come up with at least three from which to choose.

—Strictly avoid drugs unless prescribed by a doctor, and limit your intake of alcohol. Drugs and alcohol merely prolong and intensify your problems.

—Talk to others about your distress; share your concerns and feelings with a spouse, loved one, clergyman, or trusted friend. Don't be afraid to admit that you are in trouble, and never be afraid to ask for help.

—Get involved in a support group; if one does not exist in your area, take the initiative to organize one. Meet on a regular basis to talk over your problems, feelings, and concerns. Use the group as a time to make positive suggestions, not as a time to rehash frustrations and complaints.

—If you feel that you could benefit, consider getting professional help. Your supervisor or the administration at the local hospital could make some valuable suggestions about where to go for help.

—If you try and all else fails, consider switching to a different job within the same profession. If that does not work, evaluate the possibility of changing to a different profession.

REFERENCES

1. Jeffrey T. Mitchell and H.L.P. Resnik, *Emergency Response to Crisis* (Bowie, Md.: Robert J. Brady Company, 1981), p. 188.

2. National Institute on Drug Abuse, Manpower and Training Branch, *Staff Burnout*, U.S. Department of Health and Human Services, Public Health Service, Alcohol, Drug Abuse, and Mental Health Administration, p. 20.

3. Camille Wade Maurice, "Burn Out: How to Prevent It!" *National Safety News*, May 1983, p. 34.

4. Jerry Edelwich and Archie Brodsky, *Burn-Out* (New York, N.Y.: Human Sciences Press, 1980), pp. 15-25, 71-132; Maurice, pp. 34-35; National Institute on Drug Abuse, pp. 189-191.

5. Pamela K.S. Patrick, "Professional Burnout," *Family & Community Health: The Journal of Health Promotion & Maintenance*, Volume 6, Number 4, February 1984, p. 26.

6. Patrick, p. 29.

7. Patrick, p. 27; " 'Burnout' Victims Don't Sizzle—They Just Fade Away," *CESNA*, October/November 1981, p. 57; and National Institute on Drug Abuse, pp. 32-33 and 188-189.

8. " 'Burnout' Victims," pp. 56-57.

9. Edelwich and Brodsky, pp. 27-31; and Donna C. Aguilera and Janice M. Messick, *Crisis Intervention Theory and Methodology* (St. Louis, Mo.: The C.V. Mosby Company, 1982), pp. 179-183.

Understanding and Coping With Stress

Good Stress Versus Bad Stress

STRESS.

You've probably heard that it can be a killer; that it can cause heart attacks, high blood pressure, ulcers, and arthritis; that it can increase your likelihood of developing cancer, asthma, and alcoholism; that it can be responsible for bad breath, offensive body odor, acne, and tooth decay; that it can cause your hair to fall out and your fingernails to break; that it can interfere with your immune system and make it more difficult for you to recover from illness or infection; that it can even drive you crazy.

All that is true.

And if you accept the notion that stress can, in reality, be devastating to your health, can you also accept the notion that stress can be **good** for you?

It seems like a dichotomy, but it is not. The clue lies in the **type** and **amount** of stress.

Dr. Hans Selye, the father of stress theory who first defined the body's reaction to stress in his General Adaptation Syndrome, made an important distinction between two different kinds of stress. The first—the villanous one—he called "dystress." Dystress is, in essence, stress carried beyond rational limits. This is the kind of crushing, oppressing stress that results from unusual life events that pushes us over the threshhold. It is the kind of stress that occurs when you are fired from a job, when you lose a loved one, or when you are about to collapse from financial struggles.

The other kind of stress—"eustress"—is a part of everyday life. It is the force that motivates and excites, that energizes and provides a constant in our lives. Some researchers, including Dr. Selye, believe that it is essential to our well-being and our ability to maintain life itself.

It is only when eustress becomes dystress—or when good stress becomes bad stress—that we get into trouble. Eustress can bring with a feeling of well-being and vigor. It raises performance levels, stimulates alertness, and can result in enthusiasm and enjoyment of living.

But exactly where do we cross the line? The answer is different for each individual. Stress that excites, motivates, and enthuses one person may hurt another. A marathon runner eagerly anticipates his race, and stress is what gives him the final burst of energy that carries him across the finish line ahead of his competitors. But to the average person, the prospect of a grueling twenty-five-mile run is a crippling one. Or consider the professional singer who loves what he does and looks forwad with excitement to a thrilling sellout crowd. To you or me, however, the prospect of facing thousands of people would be paralyzing. One woman on a baseball team may stand at the plate with exuberance, while another—whose batting skills are poor—may face the task with dread.

The difference between dystress and eustress may also be one of degree. The first few days of a challenging job may bring on dystress—you may experience tension and uncertainty as you attempt to determine what is expected and how you can best accomplish it. But the dystress may soon dissolve into eustress as you learn the ropes and eagerly face rewarding challenges.

The difference is also one of individual ability to deal with stress. Some people handle a large amount of stress well, using it to motivate and enthuse. Others handle it poorly.

How Stress Affects the Immune System

George Washington University biochemist Nicholas Hall says that the net effect of stress is to suppress immunity.[1] Scientists believe that there are two paths: one from the brain to the endocrine glands to the white blood cells; the other from the brain to the autonomic nerve terminals to the white blood cells. Either way, the effect is the same—reduced ability to fight infection and disease.

The effect of stress on the body and the immune system has been described as that of a "double-edged sword."[2] The nervous system registers stress. The endocrine glands react to help you respond to the stress—you have greater energy, greater concentration, greater ability to run or fight. The hormones secreted by the endocrine glands in turn suppress the immune system; they kill white blood cells or inhibit their ability to multiply. As a result, your body thinks that it is ready to fight when, in reality, its fighting power against infection and disease has been seriously compromised. Even without hormonal changes, the brain can affect the immune system, suggesting a direct brain-immune system link.[3] Studies have shown that even short-term or lesser stresses such as sleep deprivation, school examinations, or basic military training can suppress the immune system.[4]

Stress produces many physiological effects. First, it causes hormones such as adrenalin and cortisone to be released into the bloodstream. Cortisone stimulates renine in the kidneys, causing blood pressure to skyrocket. It also causes small tears in the walls of arteries; the tears are built up and repaired with cholesterol, which leads to hardening of the arteries and stress on the heart. Cortisone also interferes with the absorption of vitamin D in the body; chronic stress can lead to long-term vitamin D deficiency, with resulting brittle bones and osteoporosis because of the body's inability to use calcium in the absence of vitamin D.

Cortisone stimulates the production of glucose in the liver, which leads to an increased risk of diabetes. Digestion is slowed down by cortisone; long-term stress can result in severe irritation of the gastrointestinal tract, leading to ulceration. And cortisone suppresses the immune system, leading to increased risk of infection and general disease.

Stomach ulcers were one of the first maladies associated with stress; medics during World War II noticed that people with no previous history of stomach disease would develop bleeding ulcers during the course of a single air raid. A long list of other conditions has been developed as a result of studies: heart disease, acne vulgaris, gout, headaches, indigestion, hypoglycemia, cancer, colitis, liver disease, obesity, birth defects, arthritis, and psoriasis.[5]

How People React to Stress

Dr. Robert S. Eliot, director of the new National Center of Preventive and Stress Medicine, spent months studying the effects of stress following his own heart attack. Convinced that stress had been almost fatal for him, he set out to discover how people react to stress.

Eliot found that approximately one in every five people is what he calls a "hot reactor"—a person who reacts so strongly to stress that his body produces large quantities of stress chemicals that lead to significant changes in the cardiovascular system—including a sharp increase in blood pressure. Eliot describes these people as "pressure cookers without safety valves, literally stewing in their own juices."[6] Most of them are not even aware of the price that their bodies are paying for their overreaction to stress.

According to Eliot, hot reactors fall into three categories. The first are young people whose hearts pump extra hard under stress. The second are usually middle-aged people whose hearts pump hard while their small blood vessels constrict, making it difficult for the heart to force the blood through. The third— those at the highest risk—started out in one of the first two categories but have advanced so that the heart pumps harder, the blood vessels constrict increasingly, and the heart finally falters in its attempt to circulate the blood. Most hot reactors have normal blood pressure when they are not under stress, but their blood pressure shoots as high as 160/95 in reaction to mental stress.

Type A Personality

Probably the most significant connection between stress and illness stems from the discovery of the Type A personality. The discovery came during the 1950s when Dr. Ray Rosenman and Dr. Meyer Friedman were studying risk factors that could lead to coronary heart disease. High on their list of factors to study were lack of exercise, obesity, ingestion of fatty foods, cigarette smoking, and high blood pressure.[7] Rosenman and Friedman discovered that many of the heart disease patients were seemingly healthy people who did not suffer from the environmental factors on the list (such as obesity, consumption of fatty foods, or cigarette smoking). Nor did they have a hereditary history of heart disease.

What they did have in common was a striking behavior pattern—most noticeable was a keen sense of competition and a fierce, unrelenting struggle to do more things in less time. Rosenman and Friedman dubbed it the "Type A" and discovered that even healthy Type As developed a series of physiological changes that lead to coronary heart disease.

What kind of changes were involved? Increased levels of the hormone norepinephrine resulted from stress. So did changes in the rate of circulation, increased blood cholesterol levels, increased blood triglyceride levels, and changes in blood sugar levels.

Further studies have borne out a second interesting fact about Type As: they have fewer defensive antibodies in their saliva, which means that they cannot fight off bacteria and viruses as easily and are more prone to developing serious upper respiratory infections. Type As are also least able to cope with psychological stress, impacting immune function.[8]

Type As seek power, prestige, and impact. They are driving, aggressive, high achievers who set almost impossible goals for themselves; they are inflexible in meeting their self-imposed standards. They feel guilty when they sit back and relax. They are aggressively hostile and have a low threshhold for anger and frustration; most are impulsive. Their physical appearance and mannerisms follow suit. They tend to interrupt other people who are speaking, usually in a dramatic way. They are usually poor listeners and often interrupt conversations by signalling their impatience. They often display irregular or unusual breathing patterns. Their gestures are usually exaggerated—they pound their fists, grind their teeth, grimace, and tense their jaw muscles.[9] Most have poor health habits— they avoid regular exercise, eat rich foods, and smoke and drink more than they should.

Type A personalities are at significant risk for heart disease and heart attack. Rosenman and Friedman studied heart attack victims for more than thirty years to form the theory that connected personality traits with heart disease. In one of their studies that involved 3,000 men aged thirty-nine to fifty-nine, the Type A group suffered three times the coronary heart disease than those in the slower, more relaxed Type B group. But when only the younger men were considered—those aged thirty-nine to forty-nine—the difference was even more dramatic. In the younger age group, six times more Type A men suffered coronary heart disease.[10]

Can a Type A personality be changed? Rosenman and Friedman say yes—and that the health benefits go along with the change. In a three-year followup study of 15,000 men who had suffered myocardial infarctions, 600 men underwent extensive behavioral therapy to change their Type A characteristics. In the third year of the study, those who had undergone therapy to change had a recurrence rate of only 2.8 percent. Men who received only medical counseling had a recurrence rate of 5.2 percent, and those who underwent only regular physicals had a recurrence rate of 7 percent.[11]

Even more important, claim Rosenman and Friedman, the men who underwent therapy learned to avoid some of the traps that can set off a fatal chain of cardiac problems: prolonged exposure of the extremities to heat or cold; excessive caffeine or alcohol; excessive altitude; heavy, high-fat meals; emotional exhaustion; impatience; aggravation; anger; and irritation.[12] Rosenman and Friedman estimate that those modifications alone could prevent 5,000 deaths each year and 15,000 recurrent myocardial infarctions.

Relationships with Family and Others

Warm relationships with family members and other people in our lives can impact our health positively; lack of warm relationships leads to susceptibility to infection and disease and shorter lifespan.

Yale University researcher Lisa F. Berkman conducted a number of studies in which social ties were related to health and longevity. In reporting to a symposium of scientists, she remarked that she had found one amazingly consistent factor among healthy people: they were satisfied with their lives in general and had a good social life.[13]

Work and Unemployment

Regardless of your job, whether or not you are happy at it has a profound influence on your physical health. Dr. Erdmore Palmore of Duke University studied a group of older people living in Durham, North Carolina. He was looking specifically for factors contributing to health and longevity. Those who were happy in their work—whether it was paid employment, volunteer work, or work around the house—lived longer and were healthier than those who were not happy with their jobs. Palmore pointed out that work has three critical benefits for health: it keeps people socially active, mentally alert, and physically active.[14]

Just as job satisfaction influences physical health, so does unemployment. Economists keep a sharp eye on the national unemployment figures, but so should any individual concerned with his health. Unemployment has a profound impact on both physical and mental health. For every 1 percent increase in the unemployment figures, health statistics jump, too—mortality rates go up 2 percent, deaths from cardiovascular disease climb 5 to 6 percent, infant mortality jumps 6 percent, prison admissions go up 5 percent, and mental hospital admissions go up 4 percent.[15]

Emotions and How They Relate to Stress

Emotional instability or the inability to express emotion has been implicated in serious—even fatal—disease. For years it was accepted that cigarette smoking caused lung cancer. Scotland's Dr. David Kissen realized that while most of those who developed lung cancer were cigarette smokers, not all smokers developed lung cancer. Where did the difference lie?

To find out, Kissen studied more than 1,000 industrial workers in Glasgow during the 1960s who came to the health clinic complaining of respiratory problems. Each man was given a thorough psychological examination before he was tested physically. Kissen found that men who developed lung cancer had something in common that separated them from those who did not develop lung cancer. The cancer victims, he found, had a striking inability to express emotions.[16]

Drawing on Kissen's study and conclusions, Dr. R.L. Horne of the Cochran and Shreveport (Louisiana) Veterans Administration hospitals and Dr. R.S. Picard of the Washington University School of Medicine conducted their own study and then combined other studies (including Kissen's) to develop a composite scale of lung cancer risks. One of the leading psychosocial risks leading to lung cancer, they determined, was emotional repression—the inability to express emotion freely. With their scale, Horne and Picard were able to predict which men had benign disease and which had cancer 73 percent of the time—a highly significant percentage. According to Horne and Picard, the single most important predictor of cancer was a significant loss experience in the previous five years—and the psychosocial factors that they isolated in their study were almost twice as important as the physical factor of cigarette smoking in predicting lung cancer.[17]

One of the most important studies establishing the link between emotions and physical health was conducted by Dr. George E. Vaillant. In tracking 204 Harvard University graduates over a period of forty years, he discovered that those who were most likely to suffer from early aging, physical illness and disability, and premature death were those who suffered from "emotional maladjustment." In contrast, those graduates who were considered to be emotionally well adjusted were still in excellent health at the age of fifty-three. Vaillant concluded that emotional health and well-being had a far greater impact on physical health than did factors such as obesity or alcohol consumption.

One of the frontrunners in the study of emotions and illness is Norman Cousins, an adjunct professor in the Department of Psychiatry and Biobehavioral Sciences in the School of Medicine at the University of California at Los Angeles. Cousins stunned the medical world by twice using laughter to cure himself of serious, debilitating illness.

According to Cousins, emotions play a profound part in bringing on disease and helping to combat it.[18] During the last five years at the UCLA School of Medicine, he has been struck with an interesting phenomenon. Patients who came to the hospital and learned that they had cancer suddenly experienced a significant worsening of symptoms. Why? Perhaps because they suddenly received an ominous label describing those symptoms. Their emotional well-being was compromised, and their physical symptoms followed.

Cousins has repeatedly related two stories that illustrate the power of emotions over health and well-being. The first concerns a crowd gathered at a stadium in the Los Angeles area to watch a football game. Half a dozen of the spectators became ill with what was diagnosed as food poisoning; the examining physician, after questioning all six, determined that all had consumed drinks from the dispensing machine and ordered that a general announcement be made alerting people to the potential health hazards of the soft drinks. The announcement pointed out that some of the crowd had become ill from the soft drinks.

Within minutes, the stadium became a "sea of retching and fainting people." Two hundred of the spectators had to be hospitalized because of the severity of their symptoms. Finally it was determined that the soft drinks had nothing to do with the illnesses of the original half-dozen people. Immediately upon the announcement of that fact, the symptoms of the other two hundred cleared up. The crowd was suffering from conversion hysteria: their psychological factors became actual illness.

In another case, Cousins was at a California golf course when paramedics arrived and began attending to a man who was suffering from serious heart arrhythmias. Cousins could tell by the monitors attached to the man that he was in serious trouble. Then an interesting thing happened: Cousins began talking to the victim in a calm, soothing voice. "Why, you've probably just gotten dehydrated out there on the golf course. That's quite common—it sort of throws off your body chemistry temporarily. But you're in good hands now, and soon you'll be at one of the best hospitals in the state. You'll be just fine." Within a minute the man's heart started to slow and within a few minutes his pulse was below 100 and his heart rhythms were even.

How Attitudes and Beliefs Affect Reactions to Stress

A positive attitude and a belief that you can overcome illness go a long way in boosting immunity and conquering disease. Many examples have been reported of patients whose positive attitudes helped them conquer their supposedly terminal condition—especially cancer. Most apt to overcome serious illness are those who either exhibit strong faith and positive attitudes or those who become angry and hostile toward the disease.[19]

Theodore Miller, a surgeon emeritus at New York's Memorial Hospital, often operated on seriously ill patients. He made it a practice never to operate on patients who were convinced they would not survive the surgery: almost invariably, he says, those patients who were convinced they would die did.[20]

Researchers who have conducted studies on attitude and beliefs agree with one basic principle: a positive attitude and belief in the body's own healing abilities can certainly supplement medical treatment, but should never replace it. However, the mind definitely has an impact—whether the mindset is a negative or a positive one. In simplified terms, a negative mindset tends to contribute to disease, slow recovery from disease, and even cause premature death. A positive mindset, on the other hand, can help keep us disease-free, can help boost our immunity systems to fight disease, and may even contribute to a longer life.

The Effects of a Negative Mindset

A range of detrimental emotions—such as anger, anxiety, and depression—have been shown in clinical tests to impact health. In the same way, negative life situations—such as the death of a loved one—can negatively affect health.

Anger and Rage

Anger is one of the most complex of human emotions—what happens to your body when you feel angry is probably not like what happens to your neighbor's body when he feels enraged. Anger produces in the body some of the same symptoms and reactions that are caused by other emotions, such as fear, anxiety, jealousy, excitement, and even joy.[21] Psychologist Albert Ax conducted a series of experiments in the early 1950s at Boston Psychiatric Hospital to determine what happens when people feel angry or afraid. He found that anger causes the body to release a mixture of the adrenal hormones adrenalin and noradrenalin; fear caused the release of only adrenalin. Later researchers learned that adrenalin is like an all-purpose fuel in the body—it is secreted in response to a number of emotions and is the emotion that helps the body work with greater energy and prepare for "fight-or-flight." The body, in other words, secretes the same hormones in response to anger, anxiety, and illness.[22]

Because of the kind of life we lead, we rarely experience an isolated emotion, either—our emotions tend to occur in bunches, and it can become difficult to tell the difference between one and another. Anger often occurs in tandem with hostility, frustration, impatience, or sorrow.

As complex as anger is, it is undeniably connected to the development of disease—especially coronary heart disease. Rosenman and Friedman, who discovered the Type A personality, later worked with three other researchers to "break down" the Type A personality into forty-four characteristics.[23] They then tested each separate characteristic to determine which contributed significantly to the development of coronary heart disease. At the conclusion of the study, only seven of the forty-four characteristics could be proved to be related to coronary heart disease:[24]

—The potential for hostility
—Anger that occurs more than once a week
—Anger that is directed toward others rather than toward oneself
—Irritability at having to wait in line
—Competitiveness in games with peers
—Explosive voice characteristics, such as the tendency to speak in loud, punctuated bursts
—A specific kind of mannerism when answering interview questions—vigorous and animated instead of calm and deliberate

A common threat running between all seven characteristics is anger. The researchers concluded that anger is a major component of Type A behavior and that anger itself contributes heavily to the development of coronary heart disease.

Dr. Charles L. Spielberger, coordinator of behavioral medicine at the University of South Florida, and Dr. Perry London, professor of psychology at the University of Southern California, have developed what they call the State-Trait Anger Scale (STAS), a tool to measure anxiety and its effect on health. The scale measures both the **state** (how intense the anger is at a particular moment) and the **trait** (the individual's general tendency toward anger). After using the scale on hundreds of volunteers, Spielberger and London discovered that those who registered high scores on the STAS consistently suffered from high blood pressure—the most important single factor in coronary heart disease.[25]

Other studies confirm that anger has a direct impact on the development of heart disease. Johns Hopkins University internist Caroline Bedell Thomas followed more than 1,000 Johns Hopkins graduates from 1948 to 1964. In her study, Thomas carefully analyzed psychologic characteristics to see how they impacted the development of five major health problems: hypertension, coronary occlusion, cancer, mental illness, and suicide. Her findings were that those most vulnerable to disease were those who were angrier and more anxious under stress.[26]

Hostility

Another deadly tendency of Type A personalities—the tendency toward hostility—has been blamed by various researchers for the development of heart disease and other illnesses. Knowing that Type A personalities were much more prone to heart disease, researchers at Duke University conducted three different studies aimed at determining the levels of hostility and their effects on disease.[27]

In the first study, patients over a seven-year period who were referred for coronary angiography were given the Minnesota Multiphasic Personality Inventory (MMPI) and were rated according to personality type. As expected, Type A personalities were much more prone to have coronary disease than Type B personalities. But regardless of personality type, people who suffered from feelings of hostility were prone to severe coronary disease. The common denominator in the study was hostility, not necessarily personality type.

Distrust

Distrust of other people has been shown to be a significant factor in coronary heart disease. Distrust seems to signal emotional stress—and, as such, may increase the risk factors for coronary heart disease.[28]

Depression

Closely related to grief, bereavement, and loneliness, depression has been shown to affect the immune system. One sudden cardiac death study revealed that forty-one of the fifty-four men studied had experienced depression for weeks or months before their death. And a study of cancer deaths revealed that profound depression had preceded the development of the cancer; the depression had usually persisted for anywhere from six to eighteen months.[29]

The Effects of a Positive Mindset

If all of the above seems bleak, remember: just as a negative mindset can lead to the destruction of health, so can a positive mindset lead to the enhancement of health and the ability of the body to fight off disease and infection.

Hardiness

Recently, Salvatore R. Maddi, professor of behavioral sciences at the University of Chicago, and Suzanne C. Kobasa, associate professor of psychology at the Graduate School of the City University of New York, set out to discover what makes people able to deal with stress. They studied executives at Illinois Bell Telephone. Initially, 259 middle- and upper-level executives agreed to participate in the seven-year study; by the end of the study, 140 participants were still active. Each executive was contacted at least five times during the course of the nearly eight years during which the study took place; each time the executives were tested, Maddi and Kobasa gathered information on stressful life events and symptoms of illness that the subjects had suffered since the last testing.[30]

Maddi and Kobasa found that the personality best equipped to withstand stress and its detrimental effects was what they labeled as **hardy**. What kinds of traits characterize hardiness? Among the executives studied, they had enjoyed healthy interactions with their parents as children; their parents provided them with love, encouragement, approval, interest, support, and recognition of their capabilities. Their parents created situations in which the children could succeed and master even small tasks—the tasks were difficult and challenging, but within reach.

Parents also instilled the environment at home with changes and challenges—and helped children to adopt the attitude that such changes and challenges were rich and rewarding. Children from these homes developed a healthy sense of curiosity and a sound sense of self-esteem that went with them into their adult lives. As a result, they were better able to handle debilitating stress—and were less likely to fall prey to the diseases and premature deaths that accompany such stress in most situations.

What Does It All Mean?

There is a distinct message in all of this: we want and **need** stress—the good kind of stress—in our lives. Eustress brings on commitment; it gives us an unusual degree of commitment and purpose, helps us invest ourselves in good projects, and prevents us from giving up too easily. It gives us a disposition of activity and approach. It helps us to remain open and flexible and give us a feeling of positive control over our lives.[31]

Recent research indicates that positive stress may have a positive impact on disease, too. Research by two associate professors of medicine at the Minneapolis Veterans Administration Medical Center indicates that positive stress may enhance the body's ability to fight off cancer.[32] Dr. Paul J. Rosch, president of the American Institute of Stress, believes that the biochemical effects of good stress may actually reverse the course of various diseases, including cancer. If we can learn to control our stress so that we turn it into a positive force, we can reap benefits instead of suffering from the devastating effects.

Sources of Stress

Personal Circumstances[33]

One of the most common sources of stress is a set of circumstances that influences your expectations from life and your own desire to achieve personal goals. You expect achievements that you don't realize—a promotion at work, a weight loss, a new relationship. You feel great pressure to achieve some standard, and when you fail, you suffer stress.

Ordinary personal circumstances can bring with them a significant amount of stress. A kindergartener who is faced with adjusting to school, a young woman who lands her first job, and mother who adjusts to her first child, and a family who moves to another state all have the potential for stress-related problems.

Then there are personal circumstances that are not so ordinary—losing a parent, getting a divorce, being fired from a job, facing retirement, going through a "midlife crisis," or having an investment fail. All can bring on seemingly overwhelming stress.

Social Change

Sometimes significant segments ot the population are affected by widespread changes in the social, moral, or ethical climate. The so-called women's liberation movement, for example, has resulted in substantial gains for women in many area (such as helping women obtain jobs in formerly all-male fields) but has also resulted in tremendous stress for women who feel "guilty" about staying at home—a role that has suddenly taken backseat.

There are plenty of other examples of social change that result in stress. War is an obvious one; so is a disease epidemic. Some stem from the economy—inflation, high interest rates, and high percentages of unemployment have placed many people and businesses on precarious ground. Still another social change or condition that brings on stress is discrimination— whether it be on religious, racial, or sexual grounds.

Social Pressures

Almost everyone is victim of social pressures. We are all

expected to function in society, to get along with others, and to coexist peacefully. Society has defined how we should act, and we live under the stress of conforming. It is perfectly tolerable for a three-year-old to throw a tantrum on the toy aisle of a department store if her mother refuses to buy her a new doll; it is not acceptable for a thirty-five-year-old woman to throw a tantrum in the parking lot of a car dealership when she learns that her loan was denied.

Depending on where you live, you might also suffer from social pressures that relate to income, employment, education, or housing. If everyone else in the neighborhood has a college education and a well-paying, white-collar position, you might feel stressed with your high school diploma and factory job.

"Covert" Environmental Factors

Many environmental factors can bring on stress, often without your realizing it. A man who lives in an apartment on a busy city avenue may be stressed by the constant noise of traffic. A woman who works in a large factory may be stressed by her constant exposure to artificial light. People who live in large urban areas or in heavily industrialized areas can be stressed by pollutants in the air or water or may be suffering exposure to radiation. People who live in rural areas may come under stress because of pollens in the air that trigger allergic responses.

Even the weather can be a source of stress. A Midwest farmer may find himself anxious, tense, and irritable after months of freezing rain, hail, and drifting snow. A Texas housewife who is enduring a long-term heat wave may find herself drained and exhausted, unable to perform her usual tasks.

Limiting Environmental Factors

As we have learned more how to control the environment, we have become increasingly impatient when we cannot instantly or completely control it. We are irritated when we turn the key in the ignition and the car takes an instant to start. We are tense or angry when we dial a number and hear the irritating crackle of the busy signal. We have grown so accustomed to solid-state television that we bristle with impatience when the sound and picture don't appear instantly on the screen.

We have developed the technology to cover great distances in short amounts of time. We build superhighways to eliminate the irritation of stoplights. When even those are too slow, we board jetliners. Yet, even then we feel impatience and stress at having to sit on the ground in the airport for an extra thirty minutes while the runway is cleared of snow.

Unhealthy Life-Style

Americans have become famous for drastic physical, emotional, and social swings. People go to the extreme, adopting life-styles that place them under stress.

One of the most common is the disregard for sound nutritional principles. An executive who wants to lose weight decides to eat nothing but grapefruit for a few weeks. A student attempting to save on expenses skips breakfast and lunch every day. A young woman away from home for the first time discovers her lack of cooking skills and relies on fast-food outlets for her three meals each day. Other problems include unhealthy habits such as smoking, drinking, caffeine dependency, drug dependency, and overeating. Some put us under physical stress; others create emotional or mental stress.

Disease and Illness

Aside from the physical or mental problems that arise from the actual disease or illness, there is a definite **stress** associated with being ill. That stress can occur whether the illness is terminal or short-lived, serious or relatively mild. It stems from the inability to function up to par, to enjoy a state of full vitality. In the case of terminal illness, it stems from the thought of life ending and the real probability of death.

People who are ill—whether it be physical, mental, or emotional illness—suffer the stress of being removed from the mainstream of life. They are often unable to fulfill what is expected of them (whether it be their own expectations or the expectations of others). There is the actual pain and discomfort with which to deal. And there is the stress associated with painful, uncomfortable, disorienting, or time-consuming treatments.

And sometimes extra stress is placed on a person who is going to get better—he doesn't enjoy the support of others that helps to ease his situation. Family members do everything possible to help the victim of a stroke or the cancer patient, but no one pays much attention to the hay fever victim who is sniffling through breakfast. It just does not seem that serious.

Employment Stresses

Plenty can happen in the workplace to bring on stress. You may be moved to a new area where you are unfamiliar with your new coworkers. You may have the stress of adjusting to a new boss. Your work may be deadline-oriented, bringing stress as deadlines near, or you may have to respond to demands in the industry.

A unique kind of employment-related stress occurs when you are asked to things of which you are not capable. Working on a word processor may be an integral part of your job description, but if you are not capable of the task, stress will result. Stress may also occur when employees are pressured into advancing quickly—you may back yourself up against a wall by moving into positions that you are not competent to fulfill.

Family Stresses

The stress that can arise from the simple fact that you are a member of a family is almost endless. If you are a marriage partner, you have the stress of conforming to your partner's expectations and the stress of living up to your own expectations about what a marriage partner should be. You have the stress of having to adjust your expectations continually as your lives together change.

If you are a parent, you have the additional stress of rearing children. You have expectations about what a parent should be—and your own personal circumstances may prevent you from fulfilling those. You may have always envisioned a father as one who comes home from work, eats an unhurried dinner with his wife and children, then spends the evening pitching a ball to his son or going over homework with his daughter. (That's the way your own father was.) But the fact that your wife has to leave for **her** job an hour before you get home changes your picture drastically—you have to get dinner on the table, clean up afterwards, and rush to accomplish other household chores.

Forty or fifty years ago, roles in the family were well defined: the woman stayed at home to work and the man went away to work. Today, that is no longer taken for granted. Both husband and wife may work, or the wife may work while the husband stays at home. Either or both may be self-employed. In these situations, roles need to be carefully defined—partners may choose to split household duties, or the husband may take sole responsibility. Sometimes, a couple tries this kind of role reversal but finds incredible stress because of misunderstanding or varying expectations: the wife operates on the premise that the husband is going to share in household duties, but that is not what **he** understood was going to happen.

Other stresses—such as problems with inlaws, financial problems, or sexual problems—may also enter into family life.

Financial Stress

At a time when inflation either slowly creeps upward or skyrockets, everyone has the stress of making adjustments to the new cost of living. A person who finds that her income is just enough to make ends meet is under considerable stress because of the lack of "breathing room"—when the car's transmission goes out, there just is not enough to cover repairs. When inflation drives the prices of groceries and gasoline just a little higher, she experiences even more stress.

Families on limited incomes often have to make a decision about where they are going to cut back—often it is groceries. Instead of buying as much meat, they start relying on beans and rice. They are not able to afford cheese or fresh produce. The stress that started out as a financial stress becomes a nutritional one.

One of the worst financial stresses results from impulse buying—the checking account is overdrawn, and there is no income to correct the shortage. A person who cannot wait to buy a new suit until next month, when he will have the money, writes out the check anyway. Once the suit is purchased and the check is on its way to the bank, panic sets in.

Another financial stress occurs when income is not sufficient to pay existing obligations. Every time a telephone rings it is bad news—a collection agency making threats, a bank demanding payment, a credit card company asking for the card back. In this situation, a person lives from day to day, feeling the crushing stress of not being able to get by.

Quality of Life Changes

As a result of a variety of factors, you may find yourself having to adjust your quality of life. You may change jobs, going to one with less income; illness or other conditions may force a second salary-earner in the family to stop working. You may be fired or laid off.

When that happens, changes occur. You may have to sell your home because you can no longer afford the payments; instead, you rent a smaller, more crowded home in a less desirable neighborhood.

Shopping habits almost certainly change. Where you used to buy lots of "extras" at the grocery store, you now stick to the basics. Where you used to dole out allowances freely to the kids, you find that you have to carefully ration them (or stop giving them altogether). You find that you have to stop going on

Sunday drives with the family because you simply cannot afford the gas. In severe situations, you may even find yourself making drastic changes in your use of utilities. All of it is stress, and the stress is compounded by the worry that the situation may even worsen.

Changes in Personal Habit

Any change in personal habit—varying the time you get up or go to bed, changing the amount of leisure time you enjoy, changing your diet significantly—causes stress, even though the changes themselves may be for the better. You may decide to start exercising every morning at six (which necessitates your getting out of bed an hour earlier), or you may decide to cut all sugar out of your diet. Your health will likely improve in the long run as a result, but you will encounter temporary stress as a result of the change.

Setting Personal Goals[34]

Goals in themselves are good: they give us something for which to work, something in which to channel our energies. Goals give our life meaning. But goals also are a major source of stress.

When you set a goal, you set up an expectation: you **expect** that you will be able to meet the goal. If all goes as planned, you are happy and fulfilled; if you fail, you feel disappointed. Even when all is going as planned, and you are working toward fulfillment of the goal, you are under stress—you are striving toward your expectation.

Setting a goal and working toward it can bring order and meaning to life. Unfortunately, some people do not have the ability to set one goal at a time; for them, life becomes a chaotic set of pressures as they struggle to meet an entire group of goals head-on. Others do not set goals with reason and rational planning—they set goals that are either unrealistic or impossible to attain. One woman may set a goal of losing twenty pounds in six months, and she is able to achieve her goal; a second woman may set a goal of losing twenty pounds in a month for her high school reunion—and her goal brings frustration because it is not possible to attain.

Goals that conflict with established circumstances or unrealistic goals bring on stress—but so does a situation in which we have no goals or in which we **want** to set goals but do not know what they should be. A person who drifts aimlessly without any direction feels the stress of being without purpose.

Beliefs and Values

As we mature, each of us develops beliefs and values that govern how we act and determine what we expect out of life. For much of our lives, these beliefs and values stay quietly in the background and act as a guiding force. Eventually, however, each person will experience a situation where her beliefs and/or values are challenged or threatened—and she experiences stress as a result. During such a crisis, she is forced into reassessing her beliefs and values and determining whether she still accepts them. If so, she is under the stress of resolving the crisis that caused her to question her beliefs; if not, she suffers the stress of forming new beliefs and values.

Gaps in Self-Image

Every person has an "image" of himself—his appearance, his abilities, his mental prowess, his physical strength, his acceptance by others. That self-image is either constantly being reinforced **or** threatened by feedback from others. Reinforcement results in satisfaction; threatened perceptions result in stress.

A woman may have a self-image of organization and competence; she may believe that she is doing extremely well in her position as manager over an office staff. But a series of events may threaten that self-image and bring on stress: her boss calls her in for an "evaluation" and points out her weaknesses. Her secretary begins to be critical of her management style. The employees under her start backbiting and gossiping about her inefficiencies. Or a father may think of himself as an excellent disciplinarian whose children are well-behaved and in control. He suffers stress when one of his children is arrested for shoplifting and another is suspended from school for her constantly disruptive behavior in class.

Fear[35]

Fear is one of the greatest sources of stress. There are many kinds of fear. An elderly woman who lives alone has watched the complexion of her neighborhood change over the years from a quiet rural area to a crowded and decaying one. She fears being assaulted as she walks to the grocery store a few blocks away. A teacher in a junior high school fears a threatening student who carries a knife. A Japanese-American man is forced to work in a factory manned almost exclusively by blacks and hispanics, and he is fearful and uncertain about how to deal with them. A woman who was once trapped on an elevator for several hours is stressed every morning as she rides the seventeen floors to her office, and every afternoon as she leaves.

Unique Sources of Stress in the Workplace[36]

Work is essential—to our financial, physical, and emotional well-being. And part of work for at least half the adults in this country involves spending time in a workplace—an office, a factory, a retail establishment, or wherever a person earns a living. Many of the factors that cause stress in general apply to the workplace—but there are also stresses unique to the workplace:

—**Commuting/rush hour traffic.** The pavement is hot, and the air is heavy with the exhaust fumes of hundreds of automobiles jammed into three narrow lanes. You inch along;

someone cuts in front of you, and you lean on the horn. It's a perfect scenario of stress. Your heart starts to pound, your muscles tighten, and you feel like you are ready for a fight. By the time you arrive at work, you are exhausted and tense.

—**Feelings of helplessness.** Any worker—including a top executive—can experience extreme stress as a result of feeling helpless in changing or improving a situation. A worker may have a clear understanding of a problem and know how to solve it but may be prevented from doing so by organizational constraints or company policy. As a result, the worker feels powerless to act.

—**Too much work.** It is a common complaint—too much to do, and not enough time in which to do it. And there are countless variations on the theme: someone calls in sick, so his work has to be divided among those who are left. Someone quits and there is no replacement. A quiet lull is followed by orders to increase production and meet quotas.

—**Personalities of coworkers.** You are forced to work with people you would never choose as friends. Nevertheless, you are together in a working situation for eight or nine hours at a time. Personality quirks that normally may not bother you may become too awesome to handle under the stress and strains of the workplace, and you find it necessary to deal with difficult people. Just walking into the office and seeing that person fills you with a kind of dread that translates into stress.

Robert M. Branson defines three categories of troublesome people in the workplace who are apt to cause stress to their coworkers: "exploders," who fly into a fury at the slightest problem; "snipers," who mask their hostility and fire at you from under cover by making hurtful jokes or comments, said laughingly so that they can get away with it; and "Sherman tanks," who overwhelm you with bulldozing statements and point the accusing finger in your face with vigor.

—**Poor management.** Dr. John H. Howard, associate professor of business administration at the University of

Western Ontario, asked 300 managers of twelve major companies what they found to be the principal source of stress on the job. At the top of the list was poor management—indecisiveness, failure to communicate, lack of direction, and lack of adequate planning. In a situation of poor management, everyone in the structure is affected.

—**Company politics.** Rare is the company that is not affected by politics—and the employee who has to function in a system dictated by those politics feels the stress of it. Who is promoted, who is given a raise, who is chosen to go on business trips, and who is ultimately laid off during cutbacks is often determined primarily—if not solely—by office politics. An employee may feel considerable stress because he is convinced that his efforts and performance take a backseat to the pervasive political system in the company.

—**Unclear organizational structure.** When the organizational structure is not made clear and followed by every manager along the line, stress results. A woman knows that she **should** be answering to her immediate supervisor, but her immediate supervisor has given mixed signals indicating that she should make her reports to others. A manager tries to set up office policies and manage the workers who are under him, but his superior keeps coming in and changing it all without consulting him first—so workers start going over his head, too.

—**Daily work-related conditions.** For any worker, there are daily conditions that create stress. Others annoy you; you are interrupted by phone calls; you have to attend meetings that seem to be an incredible waste of time. You cannot seem to concentrate on any one task long enough to really get into it before someone else comes along with another task. You find that the project in which you have invested so much energy was actually low on the company's list of priorities.

The problem is especially severe for executives: studies reveal that, on the average, an executive has to move on to something new every seven minutes.

Symptoms of Stress [37]

Victims of stress usually start to display certain symptoms or signs. It is a way of the body telling you to slow down, take it easy, and get rid of whatever is causing the tension. The following list is not comprehensive, nor is it an effort to diagnose. It is a list of signs and symptoms that **may** indicate too much stress if they occur continually and over a long period of time.

Grinding your teeth (especially while you are asleep)
Frequent earaches
Dependence on tranquilizers
Sensitivity to certain foods
Frequent headaches, especially those that seem to be tension-induced
Migraine headaches
Problems with eyesight, such as blurring
Problems with speech, such as stuttering or slurring
An increase in drug or alcohol use
Indigestion, heartburn, or a burning sensation in the stomach
Problems with sleep, including inability to fall asleep easily, restless sleeping, insomnia, or nightmares
Frequent colds, flu, or prolonged stuffy nose
Frequent sore throats
Pain in the shoulders, back, or neck
Severe menstrual cramps; painful, irregular, or missed menstrual cycles
Depression, apathy, or a lack of enjoyment of life
Irritability or anxiety
Tendency toward irrational, impulsive behavior
Racing pulse or pounding heart in the absence of physical exertion
Chronic fatigue
Persistent or frequent infections
Dryness of the skin or frequent skin rashes or eruptions
Sexual dysfunction

Overeating or undereating, or a gain or loss in weight that is
   not related to dieting
Inability to concentrate
Forgetfulness
Lack of physical coordination
Tendency to bleed or bruise easily
Vague but persistent pains, especially in the joints and muscles
General feeling of weakness
Gas or cramps in the abdomen
Persistent problems with teeth and gums
Loss of appetite that lasts longer than a day

Wrong Ways to Cope with Stress [38]

Partly because of our culture, Americans have developed a
few common ways of dealing with stress. But they are the
wrong ways to cope with stress for two reasons. First, they do
not get at the root of the problem; instead, they divert our
attention and temporarily soothe the symptoms. And second,
they in themselves pose a considerable hazard to health.

Overeating

When confronted with a stressful situation, many people
actually develop a craving for food. In Britain, a consumer
association asked dieters to make a "food diary" and record the
emotion they experienced when they ate. More than half said
that they ate when they were depressed or worried, and more
than one-third ate in response to loneliness.

Estimates say that about 60 million Americans overeat, and
some think that as many as a third are obese. With that obesity
comes a considerable risk for health problems, including high
blood pressure, coronary heart disease, gallbladder problems,
possible diabetes, and others.

Smoking

Nicotine causes a spurt of adrenalin to be released in the bloodstream—a reaction that is quite different than what the smoker believes to be happening. Smokers typically reach for a cigarette to "relax" or calm themselves, when in reality the cigarette causes the same physical reaction as does stress. A smoker who lights up during a time of stress, then, is actually adding insult to injury. His pulse speeds up, his blood vessels constrict, and he pumps out extra adrenalin.

The dangers of cigarette smoking are widely known. In the United States alone, smoking-related diseases account for more than 300,000 deaths each year from emphysema, lung cancer, cancer of the esophagus, cancer of the pancreas, cancer of the bladder, and heart disease.

Drug Abuse

Rather than providing relief from stress, using drugs actually heightens stress—the user must physically fight off the resulting side effects. Before long, the user becomes dependent on the drug. And if he suffers tolerance as well, then he must search for increasingly stronger drugs to get the same stress relief he got from the mild drug.

Like overeating and smoking, drugs do not really get to the root of the problem. They offer only temporary relief, and that at a terrible cost. And the problem is not restricted to illicit drugs—U.S. doctors write out more than 100 million prescriptions each year for anxiety pills such as Valium and Librium. Valium has become the most commonly prescribed medication in the United States today.

Alcohol

Alcohol actually **does** help people forget their feelings. Tests done at the University of California Medical Center and the National Institute of Drug Abuse Addiction Research Center show that alcohol helps suppress unpleasant memories. As a result, some people feel that having a blank mind is preferable to suffering the agonies that reality can bring. However, that kind of drinking leads to a vicious cycle: the person drinks to avoid unpleasant memories, but his drinking eventually leads to greater problems and feelings of inadequacy.

The health problems from excessive alcohol are as well known as those from cigarettes. Cirrhosis of the liver is a top killer in the United States today, and alcohol-related accidents are the number one highway killer.

Caffeine

Just as some people reach for a cigarette to relieve tension, others reach for a cup of coffee (or for some other drink containing caffeine). However, just as with nicotine, caffeine has just the opposite effect—it stimulates the body instead of relaxing it. The heart rate increases, the blood vessels constrict, and the body puts itself into a fighting mode. Again, as with nicotine, the user is adding insult to injury—placing physical stresses on his body just at a time when he least needs them. Just two cups of coffee will triple the amount of the stimulating agent catechol in the blood.

How to Cope with Stress

There are literally hundreds of ways to cope with stress—just as there are probably hundreds of different causes of stress. A major step involves identifying **what is causing your stress**. Think about the factors listed above. Do you have unreasonable expectations of yourself? Have you set an unrealistic goal that is driving your daily efforts? Do you have financial problems? Is your marriage unhappy? Are you under extreme pressure at work? Are you doubtful of your ability to fulfill your responsibilities as a mother?

Now try to figure out how much of your stress you are causing yourself. Do you get into situations that you know will be stressful when you could avoid them? Do you set unreasonable goals or have unreasonable expectations of yourself? Once you have identified what might be causing your stress, figure out which causes are the greatest or strongest. Work on eliminating or coping with those first.

Following is a list of different coping mechanisms. Check which ones apply to you and your unique causes of stress. Then **realistically** start to eliminate and/or cope with whatever is giving you trouble.

—Do not take on more than you can handle. You know your own limitations; respect them. If you still have two preschoolers at home, look cautiously at what you can take on. Do not volunteer to head up the PTA party in April if you know that you have your daughter's birthday party coming up that month and you have already volunteered to participate in a fund-raising drive for the symphony. Look at your commitments, and weed out what you can. And, above all, do not take on more than you can handle. If you have trouble saying "no," try modifying it: if you are asked to be the chairman of the school Halloween party, say something like, "Oh, I'm sorry. I can't handle that responsibility this month. But I'd be happy to help with refreshments."

—Get enough rest. Most people need seven to eight hours of sleep each night; you might need more or less than that, depending on your own biology. If you are continually waking up feeling exhausted, try getting a little more sleep. You will probably have to cut down on what you are trying to do, but it is essential that you get enough sleep. You cannot cope well with any kind of problem if you are tired.

—Learn to express yourself. Find a sympathetic and understanding person who is interested in you and who is willing to listen. Then start talking about what is bothering you. Try not to hold back; do not let your feelings build up inside you like a pressure cooker. And as you express yourself, learn to listen—your companion will be able to see your problems from a different point of view.

—Learn the difference between a situation you can change and one you can't. You cannot change someone's personality, and if you are forced to work with someone you find unpleasant, you realistically have few options—you can quit your job, or she can quit hers. Obviously, you cannot force her to quit her job—and if everything else about your job is rewarding, you will have to work on changing your attitude toward your coworker.

If you are under terrible stress from financial problems, however, list your options and figure out what you can do about the problem. You might be able to sell a piece of property and use the money to pay your bills, or you might be able to get an extra part-time job until your bills are paid.

If you can change your situation, take the steps to do so; if not, do what you can to adapt.

—Do not set standards of perfection for yourself. Learn the difference between doing a good job and being "perfect." Do the best job you can without causing stress for yourself and others, but do not drive yourself over the edge in an attempt to be perfect at everything.

—Get regular exercise. Exercise has a double benefit: it improves your health, plus it physically helps to release tension and counteract the effects of stress.

—Get proper nutrition. Eating right builds your body's defenses and give you the strength to cope with stressful situations. Good nutrition also helps you resist disease and keeps you on an even keel physically.

—Schedule time for relaxation and leisure activities. Take a break from your daily routine and do something that you genuinely enjoy. Sit back and read a chapter from your favorite novel as you slowly sip a tall glass of cool lemonade, or take a leisurely walk through a meadow and appreciate all the buttercups in bloom.

—Schedule some quiet time. It is important to learn to like yourself and enjoy being in your own company. Lie down in the shade on the grass outside for ten minutes, or go upstairs and sit alone in the bedroom while you just relax. Close your eyes, and imagine a quiet, tranquil scene.

—If you feel like crying, go ahead! There is nothing wrong with crying, and it can be a good way to release tension and frustration. When you have finished crying, take a few good, deep breaths and concentrate on relaxing.

—Realize that you don't **always** have to be right. Your opinions are valid and real to you—but another person's opinions are valid, too. Do not feel threatened because someone does not agree with you. It doesn't mean that you are any less valuable to him, nor does it necessarily mean that he is right and you are wrong. Differences of opinion can be healthy, and a little give and take can lead to cooperation instead of confrontation.

—Try attacking problems one at a time. If you are faced with a number of things to do, do not try to accomplish everything at once. Instead, make a list of what you need to accomplish. Read over the list and realistically eliminate what you can. (Do you **really** need to wash the car today, or could it wait for a few days until you are less busy?) Then decide which are the most important. Work on those items first—one at a time. As you complete each task, check it off and move on to the next. You will gain a sense of relief at being able to take control of the situation.

If you get stuck on one job on the list, put it aside and move on to the next one. After you have had one or two successes and a brief rest, go back to the troublesome task with renewed vigor.

—Learn to realistically judge how long a task will take you. Most people underestimate by about 50 percent, so get into the habit of adding 50 percent to the time you think it will take. If you have allowed yourself plenty of time to get the kitchen cleaned up before you have to leave to pick up your child from nursery school, you won't be frustrated and stressed when a neighbor comes to borrow a few eggs and ends up staying to talk for ten minutes.

Once you learn the fine art of realistically judging how long something will take, learn to avoid crowding your day with too much to handle. Plan on doing the grocery shopping and joining three other men for a doubles game of tennis after work, but leave the three other tasks on your list until tomorrow.

—If you find yourself rushing around, stop dead in your tracks and ask yourself, "Why am I hurrying around? Is it worth it?" Chances are, once you have stopped, you will realize that any benefit you get from rushing around is outweighed by the stress that you are experiencing.

—Avoid making too many life changes at one time. Some things cannot be controlled, but others can—so if you experience an uncontrolled life change, be on the lookout for changes you **can** wait to make. If your spouse dies, for example, resist the urge to move to a different community or home or to start a new job if you do not have to right away. Give yourself time to adjust to the first change before making additional changes that could cause stress.

—If you know that a change is coming up in your life, try to anticipate some of the stresses that it will bring and do what you can ahead of time. If you are moving to a new community, do what you can to familiarize yourself with it. If it is nearby, take several leisurely drives through town; stop at a drive-in for a hamburger, or enjoy a picnic in the park. Learn where shopping centers are and where your church meets. Strike up a conversation with a merchant. Subscribe to the local newspaper ahead of time, and read about your new community.

If the community is too far away to visit ahead of time, get as much material as you can and read about it. The Chamber of Commerce can probably provide you with good information.

—If too many life changes that are beyond your control occur within a short period of time, take control of the parts of your life that you **can** still control. Choose an activity—swimming, reading, or visiting friends—that you can use as a "buffer" to provide a break during hectic times.

—If you are stressed because there is too much going on in your life and you are too rushed, take some time to consider what you could eliminate. Obviously, you cannot eliminate your job—but could you move closer to where you work and eliminate part of the hour-long commute to your office? Or could some of your driving time be used to do other things if you rode the train or took the bus? Many people use the hour on the way to work to do reading that is essential to the job or to organize their day's activities.

You have probably fallen into the trap of thinking that everything you do is essential. It probably isn't. Make a list of the way you spend your time. One woman realized that she was spending valuable weekend time on thorough cleaning that she couldn't accomplish during the week because of the demands of her full-time job. Once she started thinking about it, she realized that if she cut out two restaurant lunches a week for her and her working husband and took fruit and yogurt instead, she could easily afford to have someone come in once a week and do the deep cleaning.

Another woman realized that she was placing herself under a tremendous amount of stress because she had believed since she was a child that all Christmas gifts had to be handmade. With a growing Christmas list each year, she was spending almost half the year worrying about getting all her gifts done. She finally decided to make one handmade gift each year and to rotate her list so that each person on the list eventually received a handmade gift. She decided to purchase a thoughtful gift for each of the others.

Still another couple realized that they were trying to crowd a complicated social life into their evenings and weekends after working all day. They learned to cut down and simplify. Instead of going out with two different couples on two nights, they invited both couples over on a single night for a simple barbecue.

—When you are faced with complex tasks, learn to break

them down and attack one part at a time. If you are having the family over for an anniversary dinner, list the different tasks involved—choosing a menu, shopping, cleaning the house, and preparing the food. Then give yourself plenty of time. Assign some of the jobs to others—you can prepare the shopping list, but your husband can do the shopping. Your husband and children can pitch in on cleaning. And when you select a menu, choose some foods that can be prepared ahead of time. Set the table early that morning instead of waiting until the moment of crisis—you will have time to fold the napkins, arrange the centerpiece, and enjoy it all instead of rushing to get it done.

—If someone demands something of you that you know you won't be able to do, refuse. Saying "no" is extremely difficult for some people, so they accept a responsibility even though they clearly know they won't be able to fulfill it. The result is a crushing stress—wondering how to get out of it, wondering how to somehow magically do it. Muster up your courage instead and say, "No. I can't do that now. I hope you can find someone else to help."

—As part of learning to say "no," get a clear definition of your own values. Make sure that they are **your** values, and not values that you think are expected of you. Two experts on stress management[39] suggest the "six-months-to-live" test. Pretend that you have six months to live. Now make three different lists: the things you **have** to do, the things you **want** to do, and the things you neither have to do nor want to do. Then, for the rest of your life, forget all the things on the third list. You will find that this simple exercise helps focus your values sharply.

—Eliminate chemical contamination of your body and mind. Quit smoking, drink alcohol only in moderation, avoid caffeine, and take only those drugs your doctor prescribes for you.

—Protect yourself against boredom. Set a reasonable, realistic goal that will bring you satisfaction, and work toward it in a rational way. If you are bored with your job, do something about it—talk to your supervisor about the chance to take on a new responsibility, or consider finding a new job.

—Take a little vacation every day. It does not need to be long—maybe as little as ten minutes. Do something you really enjoy: talk with a friend on the phone, soak in a bubblebath, watch your favorite television program, or take a nap. Make sure that it's something you **want** to do—not just something that needs doing or that would be "good for you."

—Take the time and make the effort to develop close friendships. You need a friend who will not threaten you, who will not criticize you, who can relate to you, and who will share time and emotion with you. It takes both time and effort to develop these kinds of friendships. You might have to eliminate some of what you are doing now in order to devote more time to getting to know others.

—Begin to accept yourself. In your process of making friends, you will need to be convinced that you have something of value to offer them. Do not compare yourself to others, and do not make yourself conform to some arbitrary set of impossibly high standards. You are a human being, and you have talents and abilities that are unique to you. Concentrate on your good points, and make friends with yourself.

—You may find it difficult to accept yourself at first because of the feedback you have had from others. Start by making a list of all the people in your life who make you feel negative. Who makes you feel threatened? Defensive? Angry? Sad? Worthless? Who makes you cry? Who makes you feel hopeless? Who strips away your pleasure? Who saps your energy?

Now take a good, long look at that list. There will be people on it with whom you do not **have** to keep associating—a neighbor, perhaps, or a so-called friend. Scratch those names off the list, and in so doing, scratch them out of your life. You cannot afford to spend time with them if they always make you feel like a wreck.

Now—what about the names that you **are** stuck with? A child maybe, or your mother. Decide here and now to take the defensive. What is it your mother does that makes you cry? Why does she do it? Why do you react that way? How can you change the situation so that you are not hurt anymore? How will you react the next time she makes a remark about your job? What will you say? It sounds silly, but rehearse. Rehearse until you feel that you can come out on top, no matter what. You will find that you feel much less stress when you encounter your mother the next time.

Go through the same process for every person on the list.

—Learn to stand up for yourself. When someone puts you down (no matter how subtly), do you fight back? Do you speak up and defend yourself, or do you swallow your anger, smile meekly, and keep everything pent up inside?

Learn to speak up—within acceptable limits, of course. If your boss puts you down, have the courage to say, "I don't think that's fair, Mrs. Reese. I've only had this account for four days, and I should have at least two weeks to get things straightened out before you make that kind of an assessment. I'd be happy to come in and discuss the account with you a week from tomorrow."

Coping with Stress in the Workplace

—Resist the urge to take work home at night or on the weekends. Organize your time while at the office so that you can finish your work there.

—When you encounter stressful situations on the job, talk them over with your coworkers. See if, together, you can arrive at some conclusions for solving the stressful situation.

—Learn to "compartmentalize" your work from your personal life. While you are at work, give it your full attention and effort, but when you get home, learn to blank it out. Just as you should physically leave your work at work, you should also mentally and emotionally leave it there.

—If you are feeling pressure from a particularly stressful

task, take a break for five or ten minutes. Physically leave the area; if your place of employment does not have a lounge, go outside and walk around the block.

—Safeguard your health so that you can function fully at work and have the physical strength to handle stress. Get enough sleep, eat well, and get regular exercise.

—Simplify your job. Take account of you are doing now and how it could be made simpler. Are there bothersome tasks that you could assign to someone else? Are there irritating jobs that you just hate to do, even though they are simple and do not demand much time? Try tackling them first thing in the morning, when you are fresh—then they will be out of the way for the rest of the day.

—Leave some "breathing room" for unexpected stresses on the job. Do not cram your time so full that you do not have the energy or resources left when something unexpected occurs. Make sure that you organize and become effective, but try to maintain some flexibility, too.

—Define your own level. How fast can you go without feeling uncomfortable? How hard can you work without letting other things suffer? How much stress can you endure without getting a pounding headache? Keep those sharply defined, and refuse to exceed your limits.

—If you have to travel to work in heavy traffic or if you have a long commute, figure out some things to do that will be either beneficial or enjoyable during your trip. Get some good cassette tapes and plug them in during your hour's drive. With a battery-powered cassette recorder, you can use the time to dictate letters, record your thoughts and ideas, or organize your day. And don't forget to consider your options. Could you form a carpool? Could you ride a bus or train? If so, you can do plenty of reading (enjoyable or for work), catch up on required magazines or newspapers, or even catch a few extra minutes of sleep.

—As with all other areas of your life, set your priorities. Do the most important things first, when you can give them your full effort. And if you are faced with a myriad of smaller tasks, make a list and tackle one thing at a time instead of letting yourself feel overwhelmed by all of it at once.

—Work on only one job at a time. While you are working on it, put all other jobs out of your mind. When you are finished, put it out of your mind. If you get stuck, put the job aside— physically and mentally—and go on to something else.

—Take breaks during the day. You might be tempted to work through your lunch hour to finish some pressing work, but it isn't worth it. Even if you only take fifteen minutes, you need the time away from your desk (and your body needs the food!). Step outside and enjoy the fresh air, watch people on the sidewalk for a few minutes, or go to a nearby park. You will be much more relaxed and refreshed when you return!

Changing a Type A Personality [40]

You know the Type A personality—achievement-oriented, driving, relentless, and pressured. It is a classical picture of stress, and the Type A personality has been implicated as a high risk for coronary heart disease.

The Type B personality is just the opposite: easygoing, adaptive, patient, and reasonable about expectations. Learning to deal well with stress depends on your ability to modify your Type A characteristics.

To begin making a change, take a realistic assessment. What Type A characteristics do you have? Now decide how you can begin to change each particular characteristic. The following suggestions should help:

—Choose an appropriate role model: someone you know and admire who has a Type B personality. Watch him carefully; observe how he handles stress. Try some of his techniques.

—Determine what in your life causes you to exhibit your

Type A personality traits. If necessary, keep a daily log. Record what is happening when you start to feel hostile, irritated, anxious, impatient, or frustrated. Is there a pattern? What kinds of situations and activities seem to set you off?

Choose **one** situation or event that bring out the worst in you, and contract with yourself to handle it better or to avoid it altogether. Remember—work on **one** thing at a time. When you have successfully changed your reaction to the first situation or event, move on to the next. For example, you may discover that you get irritated and hostile every Tuesday just before board meeting because you feel such an urgency to look prepared and to be impressive. You cannot avoid the board meeting, but you **can** avoid the last-minute panic. Make the first item on your Monday agenda to prepare for the meeting. By noon the day before, you're ready—and you can face Tuesday morning with confidence.

—Simplify your life so that you can learn to relax. Go over your list of activities and figure out which ones you can eliminate, postpone, or consolidate with others.

—If your problem time is morning, with your rush to get ready for work, try setting your alarm clock half an hour earlier. Concentrate on taking it easy—shower slowly, pat dry, sit down with the morning paper for a few minutes, and eat a casual breakfast. Fight the urge to hurry. Leave with a little spare time so that you can drive within the speed limit.

—Learn to relax. Take time out during even the most hectic day to do something truly relaxing. Since you won't be used to doing it, you will have to work at it at first. Begin by listing activities that you would really enjoy and that would relax and calm you; include some items that require only a few minutes, others that take longer, and make sure that you include things that can be done at varying times of day. Here are a few suggestions to get you started:

Sit on the front porch and watch the sunset
Lie on the back lawn and look at the stars
Call an old friend long distance and catch up on what has been

happening in both your lives
Take a nap
Go fishing in the isolated pond at the edge of the woods
Hike to the waterfall and sit on a rock in the sunshine
Saute a pan of mushrooms and eat them slowly
Listen to Handel's water music w th your eyes shut
Feed the pigeons at the park
Go to a movie

—If you are under pressure to complete something by a certain time, take short breaks. Do whatever is necessary to relieve the tension: stop and talk with someone for five minutes, take a short walk, or lie down with a cool cloth over your eyes.

—Carefully assess your work situation. Are you in it for power? Recognition? Money? Or are you in the enviable position of being in it for enjoyment? Ask youself a tough question: "If I wasn't being paid, what line of work would I be in?" If your profession is causing you to drive yourself beyond enjoyment, take a second look. You may not be able to entirely change professions, but you might be able to change to another area that is less stressful and that provides more enjoyment.

—Pay attention to what your own body clock is saying. You have probably noticed that every ninety minutes or so you lose the ability to concentrate, grow a little sleepy, and have a tendency to daydream. Instead of fighting those periods, put down the project you are working on, sit in a comfortable place, and let your mind wander for a few minutes. Use the time to imagine, and let your creativity run wild.

—Learn to treasure unplanned surprises: a friend dropping by unannounced, a hummingbird outside your kitchen window, a child's tightly clutched bouquet of wild flowers.

—Learn to savor your relationships. Think about the people in your life; learn to relax with them and give of yourself to them. Give up trying to control others, and resist the urge to end relationships that don't always go as you'd like them to. Strip yourself of your defensive armor, and really appreciate what others have to teach and give you.

"Hardiness": The Ability to Resist Stress

In studying people under stress and determining what leads to an ability to resist it, researchers coined the term "hardiness" to describe the people who are stress-resistant. Hardy people exhibit three general characteristics: they have commitment (rather than alienation), control (rather than powerlessness), and are challenged (rather than threatened).[41] They are optimistic; they believe in themselves. Even though stress occurs, they view it as a challenge that can be conquered and overcome.

How do people become "hardy?" Researchers have pinpointed a number of influences that combine to result in hardiness:[42]

—Hardy people had good support and positive interactions as children; their parents demonstrated support, encouragement, interest, and approval. Parents who are hostile, neglectful, disapproving, or stifling tend to produce children who view themselves as worthless and incapable of making a meaningful contribution. These children also tend to see the world as an empty place devoid of excitement and challenge.

Hardy people also tended to be encouraged as children to develop their talents and abilities, regardless of preconceived notions or traditional roles. A young boy is encouraged not only in his physical development, but in his unusual ability to demonstrate sensitivity and imagination (traits not usually valued in boys).

—Hardy people had many positive mastery experiences throughout their lives, beginning in their early childhoods. They were encouraged to use their curiosity, creativity, and increasing capabilities to their fullest and were applauded for their accomplishments. These children were given tasks that challenged them—tasks that were not too easy nor too difficult. A parent who continually gives a child difficult tasks that are beyond his reasonable ability to accomplish is guaranteeing failure—and soon the child will begin to feel like a failure. He learns powerlessness instead of control.

Parents who have good self-esteem are able to provide their children with tasks that challenge yet reward. Parents who lack in self-esteem feel an undeniable need to "compete" with their children—and, as a result, they give them tasks that insure failure. The parent always comes out on top—the child never really had a fighting chance.

—Hardy people have been exposed to change, but they learn to view change as a challenge instead of a threat. Parents of these children, in fact, work to produce change (subtle though it may be) to help their children learn adaptability. Throughout the challenge, the parent continues to support and encourage to help the child experience success.

Learning Hardiness[43]

While the foundation for hardiness is established during childhood, it is never too late to learn. An adult can learn to be stress-resistant in one of three ways:

Focusing

Many people who are under even massive stress are not aware of it. They only have the vague feeling that something is wrong. In all probability, they have never given a name to it. Even if they have recognized it as stress, they are unsure about what is really happening.

"Focusing" is a practice that helps a person zero in on what is happening due to stress. A working woman who also has the responsibility of rearing three children may be so used to the tightness across her temples or the knots in her stomach that she doesn't even remember that those are not normal conditions. Focusing helps reverse that.

Once a day, stop what you are doing and focus in on yourself. How are you feeling—physically and emotionally? Is something not quite right? Is there a tension in your temples or throbbing in your head? Now ask yourself why. What is keeping you from feeling your best? What possible sources of stress are you battling? Are you under a deadline at work? Are you fighting with your spouse? Is a child ill? Is your checkbook overdrawn?

Once you have accepted the fact that all is not well and identified the probable culprit, you are in a position of control. Instead of meekly accepting your fate, you can do something about it. Work to ease the stressful source, and you can take control of it instead of letting it control you.

Reconstructing Stressful Situations

You have heard the old adage that "practice makes perfect." It applies here, too. In this technique, you are asked to "practice" being under stress.

Think back over the past few weeks and pinpoint a situation that placed you under stress. On paper, reconstruct it—recall every detail of the situation and how you handled it.

Now make two different lists. In one, list three things that you could have done to handle the situation better. In the other, list three things that you could have done that would have been worse. You'll learn two important concepts from this exercise: that the problem could have been much worse, and—better yet—that you can think of ways to cope better.

Maybe you are a landlord who was faced with the painful chore of evicting tenants who had not been paying the rent. You knew that the husband's paycheck was being garnished for child support payments, and you knew that the wife was not employed, but you could wait no longer for the rent. The couple was, at the time of eviction, three months behind in the rent payments.

You called the tenants on a Monday and asked that they move out by the following weekend. The decision was preceded by a night of sleeplessness and guilt—you felt as though you were turning a helpless family out onto the street, and yet you couldn't let them get any further behind.

Think of some ways you could have handled the situation more poorly. You could have demanded that they be out overnight. You could have taken them to small claims court and sued for the delinquent rent (even though you knew full well that they could not pay it, even under legal harassment). You could have filed a garnishment of your own against the husband's already meager paycheck. You could have had the couple served with papers instead of calling them yourself.

There are also some ways you could have handled the situation better. Since the husband is a professional roofer and the house needs the roof repaired, you could have hired him to do the job and let him trade out for the rent. You could have met with the couple face-to-face and worked out a payment plan. And, as a preventive for the future, you could build into the rental agreement the terms on which eviction occurs so there is a set policy that all parties can use as a guide.

Compensating Through Self-Improvement

Sometimes you will encounter stress that you cannot avoid or control—your child is diagnosed as being diabetic, for example, or your wife files for divorce and leaves no possibility of reconciliation. You may not have control over the specific situation, but you can begin to regain control over your life by taking on a new challenge: learning how to swim, building a new set of kitchen cabinets, taking a class in an unfamiliar but fascinating subject. Taking on a new challenge and succeeding at it reassures you that you still have the ability to cope.

Improving Adaptability

Along with hardiness comes another important trait: adaptability. It means that you are flexible. Try some of the following to improve your adaptability:[44]

—Cultivate your sense of humor—not so much your ability to tell jokes as your ability to laugh at yourself. You will occasionally do things that are amazingly ludicrous—and the best way to deal with them is to later place them in the proper perspective of humor.

—Own up to your emotions, and take responsibility for the way you feel. When you round the corner and see your two-year-old contentedly squeezing the last of the toothpaste into an intricate fingerpainting on the bathroom floor, your first impulse is probably, "You make me so angry when you do that!" But that's not right. No one else can make you angry—only **you** can make you angry. The correct response? "When you do that, I feel angry."

—When you get upset enough to reprimand someone else, keep a few guidelines in mind. Wait until you are calm enough to speak in a normal tone of voice; don't shout or use warlike gestures. Criticize the behavior without criticizing the other person. A colleague can know that you are extremely angry over the way a project was handled but that you still value him as a person.

—Remember that arguments are not won. Agreements are reached instead. Stop concentrating on gaining power and "winning;" concentrate instead on negotiating to a settlement.

—Learn to be flexible. If you plan something and it doesn't go exactly as you had planned, do not scrap the whole idea. Change a few aspects of it, but don't give up the entire project to failure.

—Allow other people to take responsibility for their own behavior; you are **not** responsible for their actions and cannot control them. Learn not to feel guilty if something goes wrong in the life of a friend or family member. Stand by to help, but don't accept blame where it doesn't belong.

The Factor of Faith

Medical and scientific research conducted over the past two decades has demonstrated clearly that what exists is not as important as what man **believes** to exist. Personal belief gives man an unseen power that enables him to do the impossible, to perform miracles—even to heal himself. Patients who exhibit faith become less concerned about their symptoms, suffer less severe symptoms, and suffer symptoms less frequently with longer periods of relief between them than patients who lack faith.

That is not to say that faith should replace modern medicine. Instead, it should be used in conjunction with modern medicine—used to enhance the effects of medicine and strengthen its impact.

Research has shown that people who belong to a church or synagogue tend to live longer than those who do not; the longevity is greatest for members of the Church of Jesus Christ of Latter-day Saints (Mormons) and Seventh-Day Adventists, possibly because of their health and diet codes. Church affiliations, researchers found, usually signify an attitude that encompasses faith—and, with faith, come fewer problems with depression, anxiety, tension, and stress. With faith comes a strong sense of personal worth, a quality that seems to protect health and bolster against stress-induced problems.

Researchers at Harvard University identified hope as one of the primary keys in enabling people to deal with even massive stress, such as the stress of being imprisoned in concentration camps.[45] Hope, in fact, is at the top of the list of attitudes and qualities that enable man to deal with the stresses of life. With hope, there is the promise of a better tomorrow.

The Value of Self-Esteem

You have probably seen people who are self-assured and self-confident: they seem to have what it takes to deal with every problem that comes along. Self-confidence is an outward indication of an inward strength and an inward sense of self-esteem. It can be used to direct your life and to resist being controlled by others.

The opposite condition is one of insecurity—one in which you feel apprehensive and unsure about your abilities. It impacts every aspect of your life.

Building your self-esteem is one of the most important things that you can do for yourself. Try some of the following to boost yours:[46]

—Set your own standards for your behavior, your beliefs, your life-style, your professional activity, and your relationships; do it without comparing yourself to others and without fearing what others may think. Use your standards as a guide as you live from day to day. Establishing standards and sticking to them will give you an important sense of esteem and worth.

—Make a list of the things with which you are blessed. You probably won't be able to do it in one sitting, so start a list and keep it where it is convenient. Add to it throughout the day as different ideas occur to you. Your list will contain such diverse entries as "blonde hair" and "mother who cares about me."

—Start a second list, writing down all the things you have accomplished so far in your life. Write down anything of which you are proud. It does not have to be a major accomplishment—it can be as simple as "conquered my fear enough to give a speech to the Republican women" or "passed by chemistry class." When you start, you might think that the list will be short. You will be surprised to see how many things you have truly accomplished.

—Pinpoint your goals; write them down to remind yourself of them often. List long-term goals as well as short-term goals, and develop a concrete plan for achieving each one. You will discover an important sense of direction.

—Whenever you meet someone, volunteer your own name first: "Hi, I'm Carol Jones. I work on the eighth floor. . ."

—Whenever you are complimented, respond with a simple but courteous "thank you." Learning how to accept compliments graciously is an important skill and an indication of your self-esteem.

—Learn to smile. Have you ever sat in a high-traffic area and watched the expressions of the people who streamed by? Try it sometime. Study the expressions on their faces and imagine what they must be thinking. You will be surprised at how many look angry, depressed, or confused. Chances are, they aren't— but you could never tell by looking at them. A confident smile expresses your positive outlook and sense of esteem.

—When you talk about yourself, talk in positive terms. It is easy to downgrade yourself and find fault, so try the opposite. That doesn't mean you should become a braggart—it means that you should reflect an optimistic outlook and a hopeful attitude.

—Work constantly on improving yourself. You know better than anyone else where you need help. It might be on appearance, or it might be in areas that people cannot see. List your self-improvement goals and then sketch your plan on paper. To avoid discouragement, work on one goal at a time.

—Take a few minutes each day (up to half an hour if you can afford it) to visualize yourself as you would like to become. Try to make your images vivid—experience the emotions you would be feeling as clearly as if it were happening. You might see yourself as a member of a healthy and positive family, being weighed at the spa, or being promoted to vice-president.

—Expand your horizons by reading some of the motivational and self-help literature that is available today.

—If you do experience a failure or shortcoming, resist the temptation to blame it on 'your worthlessness as a human being. If you have a difficult time working on problems that involve accounting at work, don't say, "I'm a failure. I don't know why they hired me for this job. I'll never be able to do it." Instead, pinpoint the source of the problem: you have always had trouble with math. Now set out to do something about it: "I'm going to take some math classes at the technical college so I can brush up on my skills. In the meantime, I'll get Bill to go over the accounting with me. I know I can succeed with this approach, and I'll be more valuable to the company than ever."

—Don't sabotage your self-esteem by trying things that are clearly out of your reach. If you want to learn how to do something, take the steps to learn it—it's a much more rational approach than diving in unprepared.

The Rewards of Self-Discipline

Learning control and discipline is a basic; without it, you lack the skills to handle what will come along in life. As the basis of self-discipline, there are seven fundamental things over which you should gain control:[46]

—**Time.** It is critical to learn to control the clock. Each of us has the same amount of time in a day—and it is up to each of us to decide how to use it. Determining what you will spend your time on involves deciding which things in life are the most important to you. Controlling the clock then becomes a matter of controlling how much time you spend on the less important things so that you have time to spend on the important things. It means putting procrastination behind you—you can't afford it. Robert Frost once summed up everything he had learned about life in three simple words: "It goes on."

—**Thoughts.** Your thoughts can drag you down or they can life you up—it is all up to you. And what you imagine to be can be realized.

—**Relationships.** We cannot choose all of the people who we come in contact with during the course of a day: the man squeezed into the next seat on the bus, the clerk at the grocery store, the crew at the office. But we **can** control which people we spend most of our time with. We choose whether to come home after work and spend time with our families, or we make an alternate choice to stop off at the club and spend the time with friends. The people with whom we associate most closely are those that mold and influence us.

—Communication. No one else can control what you say: you alone decide what escapes your thoughts to be formed into words and heard by others. The message you deliver speaks volumes about you, so you need to control it carefully. You also control, to an extent, how much others can communicate to you: you control how carefully you listen.

—Commitments. We control what we become committed to. At the best, we become committed to family, friends, principles, and things in life that bring genuine happiness. Once we decide where our commitments are, we assign priorities, and we choose our own way of fulfilling our commitments.

—Goals. We have control over where we are headed in life— and our direction is determined in large part by our goals, both short-term and long-term. Each of us develops a game plan for life, and our actions each day (even the seemingly insignificant ones) are a part of that larger plan.

—Reactions. We control the way in which we react to the things we encounter in life. We choose to be concerned about some things (such as attaining happiness) and to be unconcerned about others (such as the social status we achieve).

Having the kind of control to make the most out of life requires discipline. Try to develop your own self-discipline using some of these suggestions as a start:[47]

—Make a list of three unpleasant things that you have been putting off that really need to be done; you might list things such as getting through the mending basket, shopping for shoes, or weeding the vegetable garden. Next to each one, write a date by which you will finish the task. Then do it, and check the tasks off your list. When you have finished, make another list—this time with four items on it. Repeat this experience, disciplining yourself into facing even the unpleasant chores.

—Visualize your goals. Then visualize the steps necessary to achieve each one. Take the time to make your imagery vivid. Then, starting at the beginning, work toward each goal, one at a time. No step is too difficult.

—Increase your self-discipline by getting involved in a sport or activity that involves physically performing; racquetball is a good choice, as is gold or tennis. You will find that the physical activity is a good way to increase discipline and an excellent outlet for stress.

—Practice relaxation techniques so you will have the control to relax when you need to.

—Invest in yourself by learning as much as you can; take classes if they are available. Read books. Study research. The more you know, the more you will be able to master.

—Try setting your alarm clock half an hour earlier in the morning, and then get up when the ring slices through the morning. Use the extra thirty minutes on something worthwhile—accomplishing a goal, studying a new area of interest, or developing your relationships.

Becoming More Aware

All of the traits discussed so far—control, discipline, hope, and a sense of self-worth—depend on an awareness of yourself. Knowing who you are, what you believe, and where you fit in. Knowing what you are capable of and what you are likely to achieve.

How do you find out about yourself? What steps lead to self-awareness? Try some of these to begin:[48]

—Schedule a comprehensive physical examination with your

physician, and ask that she be as thorough as possible. Repeat it every two years. And stop off for a visit to the dentist—have a periodic X-ray and cleaning instead of waiting for a throbbing tooth to drive you into the dentist's chair.

—Try to see the world through the eyes of a child. If you have forgotten what it was like, take one of your own children (or borrow a neighbor's) for an excursion to the park or a nature hike. Note the endless stream of questions and observations: Why are the daisies yellow? What are those little rocks in the street? How do people talk over telephone wires? Why doesn't the swing wrap all the way around the pole at the top? Now mimic that wonderful kind of curiosity about your own world. Study and learn as much as you can.

—Get out of the comfortable rut you are in now. Concentrate on changing your routines for just one month. Instead of taking the kids to the video arcade, take them to a museum or a concert; instead of watching television when you get home from work, read a book. Take a different route to work, and really look at what you pass on the way.

—Figure out what you are doing best in your life and what you could improve on. Divide a sheet of paper in half. On one side, list the things you are good at; on the other side, list the things you could improve. Limit each list to ten items. Now scan the list of your weaknesses and pick the most debilitating one. Forget all the rest of them. Make a plan of how you will specifically make the improvements you would like—and make sure to draw on the strengths listed on the opposite side of the paper.

—Look at yourself carefully and objectively, first through the eyes of others and then through your own eyes. It is a difficult, but extremely revealing, thing to do.

—Take time to be by yourself; remember that you need privacy. Use the time to relax, meditate, and plan. It should be a carefree and solitary time in which you rejuvenate and revitalize.

—Learn to be aware of others; work on developing a deep empathy that will help you understand their needs. A key to good self-awareness is to feel for other people.

Achieving Happiness

Almost everything we do in life revolves around happiness: we set goals that will make us happy. We spend time with people who will make us happy. We get involved in activities that we think will bring us happiness.

Still, happiness is elusive to many. In the Declaration of Independence, Thomas Jefferson promised three things: the right to life, liberty, and the pursuit of happiness. He did not promise happiness itself, because he knew that the government was not capable of delivering it. He did, however, make provisions for each person's right to pursue it.

One reason happiness is elusive is that it has a different meaning for each individual. Think about what happiness means to you. It may mean fun: enjoying yourself at something that brings pleasure. It may mean excitement. It may mean peace of mind. It may mean financial freedom or wealth. It may mean achieving the ultimate career success. It may mean a deep and abiding feeling of contentment. It may mean being surrounded by those you love.

True happiness is a relatively long-term situation. It can temporarily vanish, or it can give way to bursts of depression or disappointment, but it generally returns.

Whatever it means to the individual, it becomes an emotion that is pretty universally understood. Allowing for individual differences and slight variations in emphasis, happiness relies on a number of things—being loved, being recognized, experiencing success, enjoying friends, having good health, and being a part of a family (whether as a parent, a partner, or a child).[49]

Years of research combined with years of experience and generations of the human story have given us some clues about which things lead to happiness. Volumes could be written on it, and even more could be conjectured about it. As a capsule summary, scan this abbreviated list. Think about each of the following in terms of your own life, and consider how you could boost your own level of happiness by taking your clues from these descriptions:[50]

Love and Sexual Relations

No one has ever come up with a simple recipe for producing happiness: the ingredients are different for each person and are blended in different proportions. One ingredient seems to be a universal one, however—love seems to be a vital part of happiness. A second nearly universal ingredient is sex—not the kind of promiscuous sex promoted in popular magazines, but the kind of expressive sex that communicates caring and closeness between two people. According to research, those people who are deeply in love, married, and satisfied with their sex lives are the most likely of all to be happy.

Love seems to be equally important to people from all age groups, all levels of economic classes, all races, all religious creeds, and all occupations. The student and the retired janitor crave love as much as the toddler or the homemaker.

Studies also indicate that people who are in love and who feel that love is returned are the most likely to experience satisfaction in other areas of their lives. They are less likely to suffer from low self-esteem, less likely to experience long-term depression, less likely to suffer the ill effects of stress. They feel like they are in control of their lives, they feel a sense of meaning and direction, and they are more likely to have purpose.

A word about sex: the people who report the highest levels of happiness equate sex with love—they do not value the infamous "one-night stand" or a sexual relation that lacks emotional attachment.

Marriage

During the last twenty years, marriage has taken a bum rap. As divorce rates have climbed, the idealistic view of marriage has taken a nosedive. Society has gradually evolved to allow new arrangements—couples can now live together without the marriage vows, and all sorts of variations have been experimented with.

But marriage has survived—and those who report they are the happiest are those who are happily married. This is not to say that single people cannot be happy—it is simply to say that a strong marriage provides a well-paved road to happiness.

One reason why marriage may lead to happiness lies in one of the results of marriage: parenthood.

Even men and women who are independent and fully capable of living on their own report that they are happiest when they are involved in a marriage relationship. Those who have lost one spouse and gone on to remarry report that the period between marriages was one in which they found it more difficult to be happy—and the second marriage brought back many of the joys they had thought were lost.

Lack of Age Barriers

Research indicates that no particular age group is happier than another. People of all ages report themselves to be happy (even though adolescents reported a greater desire for happiness). Some interesting things should be noted. While older people have the greatest number of health problems, they are **not** the most concerned about their health. Those who are middle-aged tend to let any changes in health or physical condition affect their happiness the most. After about the age of forty-five, it seems that changes in health and physical condition do not affect happiness.

Health

In general, those who have good health are more likely to be happy. But that doesn't mean that people suffering from illness or disease are necessarily unhappy; even people who are dying can experience deep and abiding happiness.

A great deal depends on the person and her individual disposition. A young woman who fell from a trampoline and broke her neck was paralyzed from the neck down from the age of sixteen, yet she is an extremely happy young woman. She fills her time with family members and friends, religious activity, and service to others. It may astound some people that a quadriplegic can serve others—it would be so easy for her to sit in a wheelchair and take service instead. But she has become so heavily involved in the lives of her friends and family members that she is a trusted and relied-on counselor.

People who are in good health do seem to have a greater optimism and a more positive outlook, both of which influence happiness. And while some people are not overwhelmingly influenced by their own health, they do seem to be heavily influenced by the health of loved ones. A father who watches his four-year-old struggle with leukemia is probably less happy than the man who copes with his own gastric ulcer. The poor health of a spouse, child, parent, sibling, or close friend has a direct influence on the tendency toward our own happiness.

Normal Weight

Men do not seem to be as affected, but women who are overweight are less likely to be happy than those who are of normal weight. In all other categories, however, there is a surprising finding—physical attractiveness has very little to do with happiness.

No Income or Education Barriers

It would stand to reason, if happiness were based on the principles of logic, that people with higher incomes and greater education would be the happiest. It just is not so. In fact, the reverse is true. People who get by on very little money can be among the happiest in the world, and those who enjoy opulent wealth can be some of the unhappiest. The same is true of education: those with minimal education often find happiness in the simple things that are not of interest to those with higher educations.

There may be a simple explanation for the phenomenon: when you are highly educated and have a fair amount of money, you tend to expect more out of life. When your expectations—however unreasonable or illogical—are not met, you are disappointed and discouraged. Unhappiness is not far behind.

An important point should be made, though: education in itself does not strip away happiness. It does not turn us into sophisticated people too somber to have fun and experience joy.

Job Satisfaction

The kind of job a person has does not directly influence, but the person's satisfaction with the job **does**. A person who is doing what she loves and who is allowed to express her creativity on the job is generally happy. A hard worker who derives satisfaction from the job he does is likely to be happy.

Where You Live

Interestingly, the region of the country where you live may have some bearing on your happiness—at least survey results show that residents of some regions tend to be more happy than others. The happiest people tend to live in the Southwest, Northwest, and West Coast regions; next are those in the East and South. Those in the North Central and Great Lakes regions tend to be the most unhappy of the group.

Your actual location, however, does not have as much to do with happiness as your personal desires do. If you live in a crowded city but long for the fragrance of hay and the rolling hills in the open country, you will be less likely to be happy than the person who thrives on crowds, excitement, and activity of the city. On the other hand, a person who misses the pounding of the pavement and the waves of people would be less likely to be happy in a country home surrounded by meadows.

Spiritual Values

The happiest people are those who have spiritual values as a guiding force in life. They generally tend to have direction and a sense of purpose, which in turn lead to contentment and happiness. For them, life has meaning—often beyond this mortal existence. They tend to believe that there is a life after death, a belief that takes the horrible sting out of the loss of loved ones and the inevitable frailty of all of us.

REFERENCES

1. Signe Hammer, "The Mind as Healer," *Science Digest*, April 1984, p. 48.

2. Harris Dienstfrey, "Sickening Thoughts," *American Health*, July/August 1983, p. 61.

3. Ibid.

4. "Mind Over Body: Old Theories, New Proof," *Medical World News*, October 10, 1983, p. 60.

5. Ruth Rosauer, "RX for Stress: People, Not Pills," *Total Fitness*, April 1983, p. 25.

6. Robert S. Eliot and Dennis L. Breo, "Are You a Hot Reactor? Is It Worth Dying For?" *Executive Health*, Volume XX, No. 10, July 1984.

7. Joan Borysenko and Myrin Borysenko, "On Psychoneuroimmunology: How the Mind Influences Health and Diseases and How To Make the Influence Beneficial," *Executive Health*, Volume XIX, No. 10, July 1983.

8. "Stress and the Immune System: How Are They Related?" *Data Centrum*, Volume 1, No. 3, March 1984, p. 60.

9. Paul J. Rosch, "Effects of Stress on the Cardiovascular System," *Physician and Patient*, November 1983, p. 31.

10. *The Encyclopedia of Common Diseases* (Emmaus, Penn.: Rodale Press, Inc., 1976).

11. "Mind Over Body," p. 65.

12. Ibid.

13. Reprinted from *10 Ways to Live Longer* by the editors of *Prevention Magazine*, 1982.

14. Ibid.

15. Claudewell S. Thomas, "Health Consequences of Unemployment," *Physician and Patient*, August 1983, p. 42.

16. Borysenko and Borysenko.

17. Ibid.

18. "What You Believe and Feel Can Have an Effect on Your Health," *U.S. News and World Report*, January 23, 1984, p. 61.

19. "Mind Over Body," p. 61.

20. Ibid.

21. Carol Tavris, "The Anatomy of Anger," *American Health*, January /February 1983, p. 76.

22. Tavris, pp. 76-77.

23. Charles Spielberger and Perry London, "Rage Boomerangs," *American Health*, March/April 1982, p. 55.

24. Ibid.

25. Ibid.

26. "Mind Over Body," p. 71.

27. "Hostility: Heart-harming Type-A Trait?" *Medical World News,* February 14, 1983, p. 14.

28. Margaret T. Beard, "Trust, Life Events, and Risk Factors Among Adults," *Advances in Nursing Science,* July 1982, pp. 26-27.

29. Borysenko and Borysenko.

30. Salvatore R. Maddi and Suzanne C. Kobasa, *The Hardy Executive* (Homewood, Ill.: Dow Jones-Irwin, 1984).

31. William F. Fry, "Benefits of Stress," *Healthline,* January 1984, p. 8.

32. "Good Stress—An Antitumor Call to Arms?" *Medical World News,* June 27, 1983, p. 35.

33. This and the next seven references adapted from Barbara B. Brown, *Between Health and Illness* (Boston: Houghton Mifflin Company, 1984), pp. 92-110.

34. This and the next two references from JoAnn Croley, "What Causes Stress?" *Your Life and Health,* n.d., p. 5.

35. Richard C.W. Hall, "Helping Your Patient Deal With Stress," *The Female Patient,* Volume 8, July 1983, p. 53.

36. Hans Selye, "On Executive Stress," *Executive Health,* Volume XVIII, Number 1, October 1981; Hans Selye, "It's Not the Amount of Stress You Have, It's How You Respond To It," *Executive Health,* Volume XIX, Number 5, February 1983; and Bea Quirk, "How Well Do You Handle Stress?" *Total Fitness,* October 1983, pp. 24-25, 61.

37. "A 7-Point Plan to Help You Sidetrack Stress," n.d., n.p.; and Davidson, p. 37.

38. Robert M. Russell, Jr., "The Wrong Road For Managing Stress," *Your Life and Health*, n.d., pp. 17-18.

39. Robert S. Eliot and Dennis L. Breo, "Are You a Hot Reactor? Is It Worth Dying For?" *Executive Health*, Volume XX, Number 10, July 1984.

40. Meyer Friedman, "On Type A Behavior," *Executive Health*, Volume XVIII, Number 8, May 1982; and Sam Keen with Tom Ferguson, "Type A Behavior and the Type B Solution," *Medical Self-Care*, Spring 1983, pp. 36-41.

41. Salvatore R. Maddi and Suzanne C. Kobasa, *The Hardy Executive* (Homewood, Ill.: Dow Jones-Irwin, 1984), p. 31.

42. Maddi and Kobasa, pp. 46-58.

43. Kobasa, p. 68.

44. Denis Waitley, *The Psychology of Winning* (New York: Berkley Books, 1979), pp. 44-46, 102-103; and Denis Waitley, *10 Seeds of Greatness* (Old Tappan, N.J.: Fleming H. Revell Company, 1983), pp. 40-41.

45. "Hope: That Sustainer of Man," *Executive Health*, Section II, Volume XX, Number 3, December 1983.

46. Rochelle Reed, "Insecurity: How to Overcome the Biggest Obstacle of Your Life," n.p., n.d.

47. Waitley, *Psychology of Winning*, pp. 58-60; 131-132.

48. Ibid., pp. 30-32.

49. Jonathan Freedman, *Happy People* (New York: Ballantine Books, 1978), p. 39.

50. Adapted from Freedman.

INDEX

A

abdominal injury, 197-198
abusive men, 241-243
abusive parent, 186-194
accidental addict, 267
acute hallucinosis, 274
adaptability, 397
addiction, 258
addictive personality, 266-268
adrenalin, 362
aggravated assault, 234
alcohol
    dependency stages, 268-269
    emergencies, 268-276, 279-290
        observation and assessment, 284
    intoxication
        effects, 272-273
        signs, 270
        stages, 270-272
    overdose, 287-290
    stress and, 380-381
    stupor, 271
    use, 80
alcoholic, 268
alcoholic withdrawal syndrome, 273-274
    stages, 274-275
altruistic egoism, 344
ambivalence, 88, 298
anemia, 48, 276
anger, 16-17, 44, 363-363
Antabuse (Disulfiram), 291
Antabuse emergencies, 291-292
anxiety, 40, 45, 48, 49
apathy, 340
apnea, 126

appearance, 54
attending, 32
Ax, Albert, 362

B

balance of power, 223
bargaining, 114
battered husbands, 245
battered wives, 240-245
behavior, 14-15, 198
Berkman, Lisa F., 357
blackout, 269
blind person, 66
blood alcohol content, 270-272
body packing, 264
brain tumor, 47
Branson, Robert M., 376
breaking point, 3, 37, 38, 192
bruises, 196
    age of, 197
burn injury, 197
burnout, 311, 322
    intervention, 342
    people at risk, 331-332
    professions at risk, 330-331
    signs and symptoms
        emotional, 334-335
        physical, 333-334
        social/behavioral, 335-336
    stages, 336-341

C

caffeine, 381
cardiovascular disease, 48
case management, 325
catatonic state, 49

characteristics, suicidal, 78-81
child, 62-63, 65
child abuse
   categories, 185-186
   emotional, 200-201
   incidence of, 186, 189, 223
   prevention, 206-210
   reporting, 211-212
   sexual, 193-194, 201-205, 217
   signs, 196-205
   Sudden Infant Death
   Syndrome and, differentia-
   tion, 128, 210
   victim profile, 194-196
chronic illness, 50
chronically suicidal person, 104
cocaine, 263-264
   effects, 263-264
cocaine psychosis, 264
coma, 286
communication, 35
   with handicapped, 66
   skills, 32, 64-66
compulsive drug use, 257
confidentiality, 63
confrontation, 32
confusion, 41, 44
consciousness, impaired, 50-51
conversion, 51-53
conversion hysteria, 360
convulsion, 287
coping, 137-140
coping mechanisms, 4, 232, 382-391
cortisone, 353-354
Cousins, Norman, 359-360
crisis
   characteristics, 6
   definition, 4, 6
   predictable, 6-7
recognition, 11-15

stages, 7-9
unpredictable, 7
cultural suicide, 76-77
Cushing's syndrome, 47

D

danger signs, 19-21
deaf person, 66
death
   child's understanding of, 120-123
   signs of, 112-113
delirium, 46
delirium tremens (DTs), 273, 274-275, 281-282
delusion, 45
denial, 16, 40-41, 114, 130, 135
dependence, 257-258
   physical, 257
   psycholgoical, 257
depersonalization, 151
depression, 40, 45, 48-49, 68, 79, 86-87, 114-115, 126, 224, 314, 364
detachment, 8
developmentally disabled person, 66
diabetes, 47
diaphoresis, 49
disaster
   emotional response, 301-308
      phases, 300-301
   impact, 299
   inventory, 299-300
   phases, 299-301
   psychological care in, 296-299, 314-320
   reaction, 304-305
      abnormal, 308
   recovery, 300

remedy phase, 300
rescue, 300
special risk groups, 309-311
threat, 299
types
    mass-casualty, 295
    multiple-casualty, 296
    multiple-patient incident,
    296
victim assessment, 315-317
warning, 299
disillusionment phase, 301
disorientation, 314
displacement, 41
distrust, 364
Disulfiram (Antabuse), 291
drug abuse, 257
    effects on newborn, 265
    signs and symptoms, 258-261
    stress and, 380
drug emergencies, 279-281,
    282-283, 285-291
    hyperventilation, 285
    observation and assessment,
    284
    overdose, 287-290
drug reaction, 48
drug use, 80
drug use, compulsive, 257
dystress, 351-352

E

elderly, 63-64, 65-66
electrolyte imbalance, 48
Eliot, Robert S.,Dr., 354
emotional injury, 38
emotional reaction, stages of,
    15-17
emotional response, 40-41
emotional shock, 15-16

emotions and stress, 358-360
environmental factors, 368-360
equilibrium, 3, 14
epilepsy, 48
eustress, 352, 366
exploder, 376

F

failure to thrive syndrome, 200-
    201
faith, 399
fear, 40
feedback, 32
fetal alcohol syndrome, 277-279
fight-or-flight response, 8
focusing, 395-396
formication, 264
force, 61
fracture, 198
freebasing, 264
Friedman, Meyer, Dr., 355
fright, 43

G

Gelles, Richard J., Dr., 237
General Adaptation Syndrome,
    351
goals of intervention, 17-18
green tongue syndrome, 270
grief, 17, 129-137
    abnormal, 133-137
    anticipatory, 137
    phases, 130-132
    reactions to, 132-133
    and Sudden Infant Death
    Syndrome, 126-127
    unresolved, 133-137

H

habituation, 257
Hall, Nicholas, 353
hallucination, 44-45, 46, 47
hallucinosis, acute, 274
handicapped, communication with, 66
happiness, 406-411
hara-kiri, 76
hardiness, 365-366, 394-397
head injury, 48
hematoma, subdural, 275
heroic phase, 300
homicidal behavior, 251-252
    signs of, 236-237
homicide, 234. See also murder
honeymoon phase, 300
Horne, R.L., Dr. 358
hospice, 118-120
hostage, 228
hostage situation, 228-233, 250-251
    stages of, 229-233
hostility, 364
hot reactor, 354
Howard, John H., Dr., 376
Huntington's Chorea, 48
Hyperventilation, 285
hypoglycemia, 46
hysteria, conversion, 360
hysterical victim, 316

I

idealization, 131-132
immediacy, 63
immune system, 353-354
incest, 202
infection, 48
insecurity, 400

intelligence, 53
interpretation, 32
intervention
    goals, 17-18
    skills, 27
interview, 216-217
irritation, 30

K

Kobasa, Sizanne C., 365
Korsakoff's disease, 48
Kissen, David, Dr., 358
Kubler-Ross, Elizabeth, 114

L

Lack, Sylvia, Dr., 119
listening, 31
liver disease, 275
lividity, 113
London, Perry, Dr., 363
love, 407
lung cancer, 358-359
lupus erythematosus, 48

M

Maddi, Salvatore R., 365
mania, 49-50
marriage, 408
mass-casualty disaster, 295
memory loss, 43
mental illness, 13-14, 296, 297
Miller, Theodore, Dr., 361
mindset
    negative, 361-364
    positive, 365-366
Minnesota Multiphasic

Personality Inventory (MMPI), 364
mood, 54
motor skills, 54
mourning, 129-137
multiple-casualty disaster, 296
multiple-patient incident, 296
multiple sclerosis, 46
murder 220, 227, 234. *See also* homicide

N

neglect, 205-206
    prevention, 206-210
neutralization, 149, 151
non-English speaker, 66
nonjudgmental attitude, 29-30

O

objectivity, 30
old age, 50
organic brain syndrome, 49
orientation, 54
overdose, 287-290, 292
overeating, 379

P

Palmore, Erdmore, Dr., 357
pancreatitis, 275-276
panic, 49
paranoia, 50, 67-68
paraphrase, 32
Parkinson's disease, 48
patience, 63-64
PCP (phencyclidine), 262
    overdose emergency, 292
personality

addictive, 266-268
    inadequate, 268
phobia, 50
physical dependence, 257
Picard, R.S., Dr., 358
pity, 31, 57
prevention, 21-23
privacy, 41
probe, 32
psychological care, 296-299
psychological dependence, 257-258
psychoneurosis, 50
psychosis, 314
psychosomatic illness, 313-314
psychotic suicide, 77
putrefaction, 113

Q

questions
    closed-ended, 34
    nondirective, 34
    open-ended, 34

R

rage, 362-363
rape
    causes, 155-156
    defense against, 164-168
    false accusations, 173-175
    fantasies, 156-157
    forcible, 143
    myths, 153-154
    prevention, 176-180
    sexual dysfunction and, 152
    silent reaction, 173
    statutory, 143-44
    types, 144-149

unreported, 175-176
victim, 150
    characteristics, 158-164
rape trauma syndrome, 170-173
rapist characteristics, 157-158
reality basis, 28-30
reassurance, 31
reconciliation, 17
reconstruction, 9
reconstruction phase, 301
referred suicide, 75-76
reflection, 31, 32
regression, 40
remorse, 17
resolution, 8-9, 131
resources, internal, 18
response
    emotional, 40-41
    fight-or-flight, 8
restitution, 131
restraint, 61
rigor mortis, 113
Rosch, Paul J., Dr., 366
Rosenman, Ray, Dr., 355

S

schizophrenia, 49
sclerosis, multiple, 46
self-awareness, 402-404
self-disclosure, 32
self-esteem, 399-402
self-protection, 249-250
Selye, Hans, Dr., 351
senility, 49
separation anxiety, 302
seppuku, 76
sexism, 324-325
sex rings, 204-205
sexual dysfunction, 152
sexual relations, 407

"Sherman tank," 376
SIDS. *See* sudden infant death
    syndrome
signs and symptoms, 42-45
signs of death, 112-113
silence, 35
skills
    communication, 32, 64-66
    intervetion, 27
smoking, 380
sniper, 376
social change, 367
social pressures, 367-368
Spielberger, Charles L., Dr., 363
State-Trait Anger Scale
    (STAS), 363
Stockholm Syndrome, 232, 233
stomach ulcer, 354
street resuscitation, 280
stress, 4, 79
    attitudes, beliefs and, 361
    coping with, 381-391
    emotions and, 358-360
    sources, 366-377

symptoms, 378-379
stress response syndrome, 303-
    304
subdued victim, 316-317
subdural hematoma, 275
sudden infant death syndrome
    (SIDS), 123-129
    apnea and, 126
    child abuse and,
        differentiation, 128, 210
    grief and, 126-127, 140-141
    risk factors, 125
    signs and symptoms, 129
suicidal characteristics, 78-81
suicidal person, chronically, 104
suicide, 6, 14, 15, 20, 31, 45, 68

in adolescents, 101-102
causes, 85-87
    in adolescents 101-102
    in children, 98-99
in children, 97-100
    causes, 98-99
    methods, 83-84
    warning signs, 100
cultural, 76-77
elderly, among the, 103-104
incidence, 74-75
methods, 81-84
    of adolescents, 84
    of children, 83-84
misconceptions about, 71-74
notes, 96-97
patterns, 85-87
prevention, 105
psychotic, 77
referred, 75-76
response to, 106-109
risk assessment, 92-96
subintentional, 77-78
surcease, 76
terminal illness and, 73
types of, 75-77
suggestibility, 29
summarizing, 32
support, nonverbal and verbal, 30-31
surcease suicide, 76
suttee, 76

T

talk-down technique, 290-291, 292
terminal illness, 117-120
terminology, 257-258
Thomas, Caroline Bedell, Dr., 363

thought process, 53
thyroid gland, 46-47
tolerance, 258
touching, 30-31
tremulus, 274
triage, 325
tumor, brain, 47
Type A personality, 355-357, 391-393
Type B personality, 391

U

ulcer, stomach, 354
urgency, 23

V

Vaillant, George E., Dr., 359
violence
    candidates for, 224-227
    causes of, 220-224
    domestic, 237-245
        definition, 237
        victims, 238-241
            helping, 252-253
        intervention, 246-253
vitamin D, 353

W

Wernicke-Korsakoff syndrome, 276